Opening
The Schools
Alternative Ways of Learning

Edited by Richard W. Saxe

College of Education
The University of Toledo
Toledo, Ohio

McCutchan Publishing Corporation
2526 Grove Street
Berkeley, California 94704

1/7/80 Beehart Tayler ^ 5. 2^

Preface

In these pages I hope to define a concept of alternatives to in-class teaching as well as to suggest the importance of learning more about alternatives at this time. Because of the reexamination of all phases of education now underway, it is necessary to clarify the particular focus of this volume. In so doing, I will first discuss what the book is *not* about.

A radical reappraisal of the institution of public education is being attempted by individuals and groups dissatisfied with one or many failings of the educational system. One thrust of this force—the pressure to make radical changes in educational institutions, the overall social institution of education—is the creation, and adoption of alternatives to public schools. Along with this creation and adoption would be the diminution and eventual disappearance of public schools. This effort is most certainly an alternative to in-school education. It is not, however, the focus of this book.

The focus of this book is upon efforts to augment, supplement, complement but not necessarily to replace or eliminate the institution of the public schools. It is the editor's position that whenever feasible the agent best able to offer a particular educational experience should be employed. Further, for the present and the forseeable future, we assume that the public schools will perform an essential role of offering or arranging for others to offer these educational experiences. Needless to say, this is not an acceptance of the status quo. It will become clear immediately that the arrangement and implementation of alternatives to in-school education presume important, basic changes in the public schools.

The distinction being made here is not merely semantic. Here we, in effect, focus on the improvement of education through modification of public schools. Others focus upon the improvement of education by abandonment of public schools and the search for alternatives. We shall study alternatives to in-class teaching, not alternatives to schools.

Before defining our conception of an alternative to in-class teaching, it would be well to consider, however briefly, why we must address such an issue at this particular time. To anticipate this argument, it is because once there were a myriad of alternatives which no longer exist.

Background

At one time the lessons learned in school were of little practical immediate use to learners and this was not much of a problem. The subjects were to be a prelude to socially important and privileged professions—e.g.: religion, medicine, law—useful for only a few, favored persons. Practical learning was readily available in the out-of-school life of learners. There were chores to be done, skills to be learned. "Teachers" everywhere. Someone could truthfully remark that: "Experience is the best teacher."

But the world changed. There was an industrial revolution, people moved to cities. The ubiquitous teachers of this, that, and the other disappeared as their lessons became of little utility. Things of this world and of practical value now needed to be learned in the schools. And the schools taught practical things the same ways they had taught esoteric things. It would not have mattered that many children now in schools could not learn practical things presented in the old esoteric style, if the environment had been full of teachers in the old, practical, applied style. But there were no alternative teachers or learning laboratories any more so many children found it difficult to learn. More students and different kinds of students continued to apply to schools at all levels. And as, for many reasons, these new applicants did not perform in or out of school as desired, the problem became ever more acute. Few professional educators—for that matter, few people of any occupation—will dispute the existence of a crisis in education today.

What Are Alternatives?

There are complementary and supplementary institutions (e.g.: church, YMCA) which conduct teaching programs for youth. I do not consider these as alternatives unless they are used in new ways as part of the *formal as well as the informal education program* because they can provide a superior experience to accomplish one or more objectives of the required school program.

There are out-of-class happenings in school which are and have been for some time part of the regularly scheduled school offerings (e.g., sports, dramatics, science club, etc.). I do not consider these as alternatives although I admit they are not precisely "in-class" experiences. Their traditional use as a part of the public school program, even though taught in less formal fashion, makes them as much a part of the usual way of doing things as assemblies and student councils—also not considered alternatives for our purpose.

This is not to say that alternatives to in-class learning cannot be offered in school. It is certain that many highly effective alternatives will be available on site (e.g., tutoring younger pupils, assisting with some school tasks, recording and analyzing data of a pupil conducted survey, etc.).

Alternatives are planned experiences designed as activities to accomplish one or another objective of the curriculum and which do not take place within the regular classroom. It is possible, but not necessary that the teacher—if indeed, there is a designated teacher—be the usual teacher of record.

Investigating pollution in alleys and streets is an alternative to reading about pollution. Making a survey of a community need is an alternative to listening to a teacher lecture about the same need. Watching a merchant—and perhaps making a photograph of the merchant—cheating the poor and the uneducated is an alternative to reading chapters on fair business practices. Tutoring younger children is an alternative to classroom simulated teaching exercises. Planning and executing a series of individual observations in the Toledo Museum of Art (Guggenheim, Art Institute, Planetarium, Museum of Science and Industry) is an alternative to viewing a slide-tape series in the school auditorium. There is a real temptation to fill pages of these types of activities. This arises as a reaction to the apparently serious question, "What are alternatives?" followed usually by "Well give me some examples." ("If you can," is implied.) Obviously, there is no end to the number of alternatives which can be generated. That, however, is not really the point. The point is what alternatives can there be which have possibility of being better means to accomplish a given objective.

Feasibility

Many of the alternatives to be presented in these pages are creative uses of limited resources, not readily available to everyone. Some, (Outward Bound) are expensive. Hence, in one sense, these are not feasible alternatives for the entire population of learners. That is, if *all* secondary school students in Philadelphia replicated the Parkway approach there would be an impossible burden placed upon some of the facilities and personnel now serving adequately and enthusiastically as resources to the Parkway students.

In connection with this point let me share a moderately painful personal experience. In 1950 immediately after the outbreak of hostilities in Korea, I was recalled to active duty with a small group of other World War II veterans.

Our first task was to open a training center which had been closed since 1946. When the small advance party appeared in uniform in the nearby towns we were warmly received. No, we were treated almost like celebrities. When we entered a shop the clerks would summon the manager to greet us personally. We had long friendly chats, they helped us find off-post housing for our families. They really enjoyed having us there.

Then the troops came. Of course, things changed markedly and we former celebrities became so many objects to be processed. Some of our number gave offense to townfolk and all of us in the uniform shared in the earned hostility. I do not castigate the natives for hypocrisy. I believe they sincerely liked us at first. But, clearly, it was an unbearable overload on their emotions and energy to like so many of us, so often. So, the Parkway program cannot be everyone's alternative. (And all teachers and pupils should not take field trips to the zoo in June.)

But, then, who would say that the Parkway package is the best for everyone? If it is viable, and that is a *separate* issue, why cannot the process be utilized with other things, places, and people? Of course there may be one art museum or planetarium or shoe factory or whatever, but these cannot be the only facilities better suited for learning about art or planets or mass production than the classroom or lecture hall. My point here is simply that the obvious limitations of a given set of resources should not be used as a rationale to dismiss the consideration of alternatives.

Our consideration of alternatives to in-class education will be primarily informative rather than hortatory. If readers remain unconvinced that a given alternative is superior to in-class teaching for achieving certain objectives, they will not have completed their assessment. Other alternatives should be evaluated and when no suitable alternative exists, it may be necessary to design one. As with any innovation it is necessary to plan for continuous evaluation. In this connection, note that we reject out of hand the notion that anything done out of the classroom will somehow be superior to what is done in a classroom. Another real concern comes to bear after a potentially superior alternative has been identified or designed. The fact that a physician may be better qualified than a professional teacher to offer certain instruction does not guarantee that he will be willing to offer it or able to offer it within the realistic constraints of resources available. Then, too, serving as an educational agent for nonmedical students may or may not be given a high priority in terms of the physician's estimate of the optimum use of his time and talent. The notion of feasibility includes commitment of the alternative agent as well as competence and cost.

Generating Alternatives

There is always the possibility that there is no superior, feasible alternative to the way we are now operating. However, this possibility certainly does not relieve us from the responsibility of trying promising alternatives and comparing the results with present practices. Inherent in the notion that a search for alternative ways is futile is the notion that there can ever truly be one *best* way. To take this position is difficult in view of the individual differences in *learners,* not to mention teachers and situations.

I don't know how one generates superior alternatives nor how one knows when to stop, for a time, searching for additional options to implement those in hand. The accounts of successful and not-so-successful attempts in this book should help us to answer questions such as these. Certainly the answer will need to be one which permits greater diversity than now exists. And certainly there will be no "best" solutions to be frozen into the educational system.

I know the search for alternatives will be difficult for those of us who are veterans of the system as it is now. To know so well how things are done makes it more difficult to find and try new ways of doing things. We have evidence of this barrier to change in schools everywhere. Today many school districts will report experimenting with an "innovation" such as team teaching. Hopefully not many will report, as did one district, that: "We have ungraded our fourth grade this year."

Despite the difficulty of attempting to be objective in improving an enterprise in which we are active participants, many of us keep trying. We all know of schools which have greatly expanded the offerings to secondary school pupils and varied the length of some offerings. We have asked for and acted on student ideas. Mini-courses are common. Independent study plans abound. Interim-weeks or months for cafeteria-type student selected experiences are not new. Auditing and optional attendance have been introduced in many localities. And, of course, all readers know about the different learning packages made possible by tapes, programmed learning, modular instructional units and the like. I cite all of these examples not to suggest that there has been important progress but as evidence that many educators perceive a very real need to offer alternatives to the tested repertoire of in-class teaching procedures.

Plan

In this first survey of alternatives we shall identify some of those which are currently receiving serious consideration. Persons involved with the alternative will be invited to describe and explain the role of the alternative. If opponents of a particular alternative can be identified, they will be invited to state their objections to the alternative and, perhaps, to indicate additional alternatives.

Purpose

Our purpose is probably implicit in what has been said above. To become more explicit, it is: To provide educational administrators with information about alternatives to in-school education. A second purpose building upon the first is: To influence educational administrators to open the programs of their schools to alternatives to in-school education. An assumption underlying both purposes is that some educational experiences can better be offered out of school. We further assume that the opening of the school to alternatives will have important strategic and political benefits.

It should not be necessary to point out the obvious: that the alternatives considered here are only representative of a population of unknown numbers. There are undoubtedly other alternatives not yet formulated which are superior to these. And, of course, the more closely we identify with those presented, the more difficult it becomes to conceive of other alternatives. I know of no solution to this problem except that the very condition of searching for any alternative opens up the school somewhat and, if more persons are active in the search for alternatives, it should generate a greater variety than if one or only a few participate.

We begin with several considerations of the need for alternatives. These are followed by examples in higher education and then by alternatives at other levels. None are offered as ideals, all are examples of efforts to improve the educational program by a creative use of something other than classroom teaching.

Richard W. Saxe

Contents

Part One
The Need for Alternatives

"Why alternatives?" and "Why now?" are the primary questions that will be answered by the several selections in this section. We begin with Toffler's prophecy of things to come. This is followed by excerpts from the influential Carnegie Report. This controversial document created much interest in higher education. In a recent discussion with a university president I was informed that the Report completely missed the point that we (universities) are now doing things in the best possible way. This may well be so, though—to identify my bias—I think not. However, for our present purposes, the important question is: "How does the president know that this is so?" What alternatives has he, or any of us in higher education, attempted, and with what results? Can we afford to accept status quo without investigating other possibilities? Perhaps a review of the historical development of higher education would reveal how few alternatives were considered over the years.

Because of the characteristics of young adults, there are attempts to develop new ways in higher education despite my complacent informant. Accounts of some of these are presented in Part Two. They are not free from problems. But, then, why should we expect to depart from tradition without some problems?

As we consider secondary education, we find symptoms of the same pressures that seem to have affected colleges and universities. There is, as they say, a lot of it going around. Two selections from different religious faiths serve to establish the nondenominational or ecumenical thrust of pressures for change. The Lenke selection is a brilliant argument for new places to learn.

Readers who do not intend to read all of the selections in Part One should be certain to include Larry Cuban's observations from an urban teacher's perspective. Cuban points out that the poor and black communities demand attention to basic skills. Armed with this information, readers can view the programs described in other parts of the book accordingly. We, too, would not take seriously alternatives designed to enrich the experiences of a small elite corps of middle-class children or selected talented students. Under certain circumstances, such limited arrangements could be worth attempting, but never at the expense of achievement of basic skills for poor kids. This suggests another important question for administrators seeking to explore the utilization of alternatives for in-class teaching. This additional question is: "For whom?" Your editor's bias is that there must exist feasible, superior alternatives to in-class teaching for some objectives for all learners of whatever age or ability level.

Next, we consider a suggested strategy to "breach the educational fortress" and a dispassionate explanation by Sam Yarger of the need to make a beginning. Finally, Russell Doll warns of the danger of alternatives becoming not other options but merely new orthodoxies to be installed and defended by their adherents at the expense of creativity and experimentation.

1

Education in the Future Tense

ALVIN TOFFLER

THE ORGANIZATIONAL ATTACK

Such a movement will have to pursue three objectives—to transform the organizational structure of our educational system, to revolutionize its curriculum, and to encourage a more future-focused orientation. It must begin by asking root questions about the status quo.

We have noted, for example, that the basic organization of the present school system parallels that of the factory. For generations we have simply assumed that the proper place for education to occur is in a school. Yet if the new education is to simulate the society of tomorrow, should it take place in school at all?

As levels of education rise, more and more parents are intellectually equipped to assume some responsibilities now delegated to the schools. Near Santa Monica, California, where the RAND Corporation has its headquarters, in the research belt around Cambridge, Massachusetts, or in such science cities as Oak Ridge, Los Alamos or Huntsville, many parents are clearly more capable of teaching certain subjects to their children than are the teachers in the local schools. With the move toward knowledge-based industry and the increase of leisure, we can anticipate a small but significant

---

Alvin Toffler, "The Organizational Attack," *Future Shock* (New York: Bantam Books, 1971), pp. 405-409. Reprinted by permission.

tendency for highly educated parents to pull their children at least part way out of the public education system, offering them home instruction instead.

This trend will be sharply encouraged by improvements in computer-assisted education, electronic video recording, holography and other technical fields. Parents and students might sign short-term "learning contracts" with the nearby school, committing them to teach-learn certain courses or course modules. Students might continue going to school for social and athletic activities or for subjects they cannot learn on their own or under the tutelage of parents or family friends. Pressures in this direction will mount as the schools grow more anachronistic, and the courts will find themselves deluged with cases attacking the present obsolete compulsory attendance laws. We may witness, in short, a limited dialectical swing back toward education in the home.

At Stanford, learning theorist Frederick J. McDonald has proposed a "mobile education" that takes the student out of the classroom not merely to observe but to participate in significant community activity.

In New York's Bedford-Stuyvesant District, a sprawling tension-ridden black slum, a planned experimental college would disperse its facilities throughout the stores, offices, and homes of a 45-block area, making it difficult to tell where the college ends and the community begins. Students would be taught skills by adults in the community as well as by regular faculty. Curricula would be shaped by students and community groups as well as professional educators. The former United States Commissioner of Education, Harold Howe, II, has also suggested the reverse: bringing the community into the school so that local stores, beauty parlors, printing shops, be given free space in the schools in return for free lessons by the adults who run them. This plan, designed for urban ghetto schools, could be given more bite through a different conception of the nature of the enterprises invited into the school: computer service bureaus, for example, architectural offices, perhaps even medical laboratories, broadcasting stations and advertising agencies.

Elsewhere, discussion centers on the design of secondary and higher education programs that make use of "mentors" drawn from the adult population. Such mentors would not only transmit skills, but would show how the abstractions of the textbook are applied in life. Accountants, doctors, engineers, businessmen, carpenters, builders and planners might all become part of an "outside faculty" in another dialectical swing, this time toward a new kind of apprenticeship.

Many similar changes are in the wind. They point, however tentatively, to a long overdue breakdown of the factory-model school.

This dispersal in geographical and social space must be accompanied by dispersal in time. The rapid obsolescence of knowledge and the extension of life span make it clear that the skills learned in youth are unlikely to remain relevant by the time old age arrives. Super-industrial education must therefore make provision for lifelong education on a plug-in/plug-out basis.

If learning is to be stretched over a lifetime, there is reduced justification for forcing kids to attend school full time. For many young people, part-time schooling and part-time work at low-skill, paid and unpaid community service tasks will prove more satisfying and educational.

Such innovations imply enormous changes in instructional techniques as well. Today lectures still dominate the classroom. This method symbolizes the old top-down, hierarchical structure of industry. While still useful for limited purposes, lectures must inevitably give way to a whole battery of teaching techniques, ranging from role playing and gaming to computer-mediated seminars and the immersion of students in what we might call "contrived experiences." Experiential programming methods, drawn from recreation, entertainment and industry, developed by the psychcorps of tomorrow, will supplant the familiar, frequently brain-draining lecture. Learning may be maximized through the use of controlled nutrition or drugs to raise IQ, to accelerate reading, or to enhance awareness. Such changes and the technologies underlying them will facilitate basic change in the organizational pattern.

The present administrative structures of education, based on industrial bureaucracy, will simply not be able to cope with the complexities and rate of change inherent in the system just described. They will be forced to move toward ad-hocratic forms of organization merely to retain some semblance of control. More important, however, are the organizational implications for the classroom itself.

Industrial Man was machine-tooled by the schools to occupy a comparatively permanent slot in the social and economic order. Super-industrial education must prepare people to function in temporary organizations—the ad-hocracies of tomorrow.

Today children who enter school quickly find themselves part of a standard and basically unvarying organizational structure: a teacher-led class. One adult and a certain number of subordinate young people, usually seated in fixed rows facing front, is the standardized basic unit of the industrial-era school. As they move, grade by grade, to the higher levels, they remain in this same fixed organizational frame. They gain no experience with other forms of organization, or with the problems of shifting from one organizational form to another. They get no training for role versatility.

Nothing is more clearly anti-adaptive. Schools of the future, if they wish to facilitate adaptation later in life, will have to experiment with far more varied arrangements. Classes with several teachers and a single student; classes with several teachers and a group of students; students organized into temporary task forces and project teams; students shifting from group work to individual or independent work and back—all these and their permutations will need to be employed to give the student some advance taste of the experience he will face later on when he begins to move through the impermanent organizational geography of super-industrialism.

Organizational goals for the Councils of the Future thus become clear: dispersal, decentralization, interpenetration with the community, ad-hocratic administration, a breakup of the rigid system of scheduling and grouping. When these objectives are accomplished, any organizational resemblance between education and the industrial-era factory will be purely coincidental.

2

Less Time, More Options

CARNEGIE COMMISSION
ON HIGHER EDUCATION

POSSIBILITIES FOR IMPROVEMENT

We believe that improvements in the approach, content, and structure of higher education can make the post-high school experience more advantageous to many individuals and more useful to society. In a forthcoming Commission report on academic reform we will propose improvements in approach and content. In this report we are proposing modifications in the structure of post-secondary education in these directions:

To shorten the length of time in formal education We are convinced that the time spent on the way to the B.A. can be reduced now by one year for many, and subsequently most, students; time spent on the way to the Ph.D. and to M.D. practice can be reduced by an additional one or two years without sacrificing educational quality.

To provide more options We favor more opportunities in lieu of formal college and more stages at which college-going students can change direction, stop out to obtain a noncollege experience, and drop out with formal recognition for work accomplished.

To make educational opportunities more appropriate to lifetime interests We suggest more chances for reentry by adults into formal higher education, more short-term programs leading to certificates, and, generally, more stress on lifelong learning. We oppose the sharp distinctions now made among full-time students, part-time students, and adult students. Education should become more a part of all of life, not just an isolated part of life. An educational interlude in the middle ranges of life deserves consideration.

To make certain degrees more appropriate to the positions to which they lead We shall make specific suggestions.

To make educational opportunities more available to more people, including women, employed persons, older people, and persons from the lower income levels.

With these goals in mind, we suggest several changes designed to make postsecondary education more forward looking and more adaptable to individual situations than it now is. The proposed changes are not, of course, equally needed or equally desirable in all situations. But the greater range of options proposed should be available somewhere within the system to persons seeking them.

RECOMMENDATIONS

That service and other employment opportunities be created for students between high school and college and at stop-out points in college through national, state, and municipal youth programs, through short-term jobs with private and public employers, and through apprenticeship programs in the student's field of interest; and that students be actively encouraged to participate.

We believe not only that all colleges should encourage prospective and continuing students to obtain service and work experience, but also that some colleges may wish to require it before admission or at some point during matriculation and could, in fact, in appropriate instances, grant credit for it toward completion of degree requirements. The federal, state, and municipal governments can assist in this. We believe that the federal, state, and municipal governments, on a permanent basis, should offer service opportunities to young people. Industry should examine its hiring policies and employment patterns to determine ways in which it can provide short-term jobs for young people who wish work experience before taking further formal education. In a recently published Carnegie Commission study of 1961 college graduates, over three-fifths of those responding felt there should be some stopping out either between high school and college or during college.

That the expansion of postsecondary educational opportunities be encouraged outside the formal college in apprenticeship programs, proprietary schools, in-service training in industry, and in military programs; that appropriate educational credit be given for the training received; and that participants be eligible, where appropriate, for federal and state assistance available to students in formal colleges.

The states would need to accredit such programs and should actively plan for them as part of their provision for postsecondary education.

That employers, both private and public, hire and promote on the basis of talent alone as well as on prior certification.

This will require better tests of talent, more exercise of individual judgment by employers and their representatives, more training opportunities on the job, and more concern for ladders to rise and less with ceilings based on prior certification. The best test is performance on the job. The Educational Testing Service (ETS) and the American College Testing Program (ACT) have had great experience with testing and might turn more of their attention to achievement testing as the basis for certificates that will take the place of degrees. Degrees might also be given as a result of these tests by ETS and ACT independently or with a recognized college or university. But, essentially, employers should do more of their own screening for talent and rely less on the instrumentalities of the college, which are designed primarily for other purposes. Greater reliance by employers on tests developed to screen applicants for positions would be vastly less costly to society than using the B.A. degree to screen. Employers and educational leaders should develop informational programs to make certain that such new policies are generally known and particularly that educational advisers and placement officers are aware of the new practices once adopted.

That professions, wherever possible, create alternate routes of entry other than full-time college attendance, and reduce the number of narrow, one-level professions which do not afford opportunities for advancement.

We believe that more careers should be opened up to demonstrate talent, regardless of formal degrees, that nurses should be able to become medical assistants, that technicians should be able to become engineers. Testing procedures will need to be greatly improved to ensure that advancement on the basis of experience meets all the essential requirements of advancement on the basis of degrees. We are particularly concerned with the growth of horizontal craftlike professions in the health services that impede vertical mobility.

That a degree (or other form of credit) be made available to students at least every two years in their careers (and in some cases every year).

Under this policy, students would be given more points at which to reassess their direction, stop out for work experience, or stop with credit. We now have essentially a two-level structure (B.A. and Ph.D.). We suggest a four-level structure (A.A., B.A., M.Phil., D.A. or Ph.D.). Students would be given two-year planning modules that would give them more flexibility than the basically four-year modules now offered on the way to the B.A. and Ph.D.

Not only should students be encouraged to reassess their plans every two years, but the institution should also reassess each student. We believe, in particular, that students should not be encouraged to proceed past the A.A. degree level (lower division) unless and until there is evidence that they have a clear commitment to academic and/or occupational interest requiring additional college training. The college should not help to prolong indefinitely an aimless search for and experimentation with various life styles and an amateurish sampling of swiftly passing interests; that search seldom benefits either the student or the college. For students who have not made a commitment to college work by the end of the lower division, there are other places where they can explore their potential interests and make up their minds.

We believe, additionally, that there should be the most careful review of a student before allowing him or her to proceed past the M.Phil. level into doctoral study. There is now too seldom a careful check made at this point. The most stringent entrance requirements of all should be set up at this port of entry. Students advanced to candidacy for the Ph.D. should be selected solely on the basis of their research promise.

One way to encourage reassessment of students is to require an affirmative action by the student to apply for the next degree level and an affirmative action by the college to accept him or her. This would reduce the drifting into subsequent stages that now takes place.

That the time to get a degree be shortened by one year to the B.A. and by one or two more years to the Ph.D. and to M.D. practice.

High schools can be accredited by state university systems and by consortia of private colleges to give the equivalent of the first year of work in college. Gradually this could be expanded to cover all, or nearly all, high schools. Fifty thousand high school students are now given credit each year for advanced standing in college. This should quickly be expanded to at least 500,000. Summer-term study can be made available in college for those who do not go to accredited high schools or who have not completed a year of college-level work in accredited high schools. The first year in college can also be made more challenging and useful. Thus the lower division in college could soon become a one-year program except for those needing remedial work. The additional one or two years saved on the way to the Ph.D. and to M.D. practice can be offset by the constant opportunities for additional acquisition of knowledge during careers. The time suggested to be spent in training is quite sufficient to obtain assurance of innate ability and an understanding of basic principles.

That certain new degrees be widely accepted:

The Master of Philosophy Now in effect at the University of Toronto, it calls for two years after the B.A. It is useful for persons intending to teach in high schools, community colleges, and in the lower division in colleges. Generally, we favor more such degrees calling for two years of study after the B.A., as does the M.B.A. For example, we favor an M.H.B. (Master in Human Biology), which would equip a person either to be a physician's assistant, or to teach at an appropriate level, or to go on to an M.D. or Ph.D. The two-year advanced master's degree would serve occupations which require more formal training than the one-year M.A. now provides.

The Doctor of Arts Now in effect at Carnegie-Mellon and the University of Washington, it is being offered, developed, or taken under consideration by at least 75 other institutions. The Ph.D. began as a research degree with the original dissertation at its core. It is a highly respected degree useful for advanced research work and for training students to undertake research. It is less useful for persons who will teach but neither do research nor train research personnel. In fact, for such people it may not only give them a narrower training than their teaching merits but also create pressures both on them to undertake research that does not interest them and on the institutions where they are employed to provide them with reduced teaching loads and facilities for their research.

We favor a Doctor of Arts degree for the nonresearch teacher. It would take the same length of standard time after the B.A. degree (four years) as the Ph.D. Instead of the dissertation required for a Ph.D., there would be a requirement for some independent piece of work showing understanding of the chosen field of study and ability to present lucidly a complex body of knowledge. The Doctor of Arts degree would also call for (a) a broader field of basic knowledge than the more specialized Ph.D. degree and (b) an opportunity to study and practice pedagogic technique. The D.A. program, as we propose it, would not be a Ph.D. program without the dissertation but would be a specially designed course that would lead to the standard degree for college teachers. The Ph.D. should be reserved for those who clearly intend to engage in original research in their lifetime careers. Salary levels and promotional opportunities should be the same for college teachers whether they have the D.A. or the Ph.D.

We consider it of great importance to reduce the impact of specialization and research on the entirety of higher education. The Ph.D. now has a headlock on much of higher education. The greatest rewards are given to those who are highly specialized in their interests and undertake research, sometimes almost regardless of its importance and their own interest in it. The curriculum nearly all along the line is geared to the interests of the specialized instructor and to training the student for specialization. The requirement of the dissertation orients the student toward his research specialization rather than toward the instruction of students; it sometimes results in a "trained incapacity" to relate to students by both the selection process it sets in motion and the standards of performance it imparts. We now select and train a student to do research; then employ him to teach; and then promote him on the basis of his research. This both confuses him and subverts the teaching process.

We believe it will take a degree with a new name and a new program to declare that teaching is also important and will be equally rewarded and that the narrower and narrower specialization of the past century shall not dominate so much of higher education. The Ph.D. has been a most useful degree. It should be continued as the appropriate degree for those who will undertake original research and train others to do so. But it should be a specialized degree for research personnel, for those who plan to pursue lifelong careers in scholarly investigation. The standard liberal arts advanced degree should be the Doctor of Arts. It should be the degree preferred by colleges for those who are engaged to teach at all levels, with the exception of those who teach specialized research methods.

Development of the Doctor of Arts degree will make the preparation of teachers, as teachers, the concern of all departments and not just the school of education. The rapid growth of community colleges and comprehensive colleges will create a ready demand for persons with the degree. But the basic objective of the Doctor of Arts is not to get more teachers but to get teachers who are better prepared and better oriented. The Doctor of Arts degree will also be appropriate for many positions in government, industry, and academic administration.

The Ph.D. should be available subsequently, on application, to holders of a Master of Philosophy or a Doctor of Arts who can show, through minimum course work or through proficiency certificates or examination, the necessary background, and who also publish an important work of original research or who present a satisfactory dissertation. The competitive test of important research published will often be better proof of ability than an internally evaluated dissertation. Published research would become the functional equivalent of a dissertation. The Ph.D. should also be given to current students for a dissertation satisfactorily completed without the necessity of also fulfilling residence requirements. As a research degree, highly competent research should be its primary requirement, whether performed on campus or off, and the additional background requirements, if any, to be met by holders of the M.Phil. or D.A. should be kept to a minimum and should be determined after individual evaluation of each candidate's total educational and professional experience.

In much the same way that the D.A. is designed for those going into college teaching, a greater use should be made of professional doctorates for clinical practice in psychology, social work, and other fields in which the emphasis is less on research and more on practice.

The proposed flow of education beyond high school based on the above recommendations is set forth in Table 1.

That opportunities be created for persons to reenter higher education throughout their active careers in regular daytime classes, nighttime classes, summer courses, and special short-term programs, with degrees and certificates available as appropriate.

Higher education is now prejudiced against older students. They should be welcomed instead. Too often they are looked upon as inferior. Yet older students will help end the *in loco parentis* atmosphere of many campuses, add maturity to discussions, and make a more balanced community out of the college.

That opportunities be expanded for students to alternate employment and study, such as the "sandwich" programs in Great Britain and the programs at some American colleges.

Programs at American colleges that combine work experience and formal study are increasing in number and should be encouraged.

Table 1

Proposed Flow of Education Beyond the
High School (highly simplified)

1. *High school graduation*	Enter employment Stop out for work or service experience Enter college
2. *After A.A. degree*	Enter employment Stop out for work or service experience Continue in college
3. *After B.A. degree*	Enter employment Stop out for work or service experience Continue in college
4. *After M.Phil. degree*	Enter employment Continue in college Receive Ph.D. for published research and completion of any further subject matter requirements deemed necessary for the particular applicant
5. *After D.A. degree*	Enter employment Receive Ph.D. for published research
6. *From employment*	Receive certification of competence without degree Take achievement test for degree Reenter college at any time

That alternative avenues by which students can earn degrees or complete a major portion of their work for a degree be expanded to increase accessibility of higher education for those to whom it is now unavailable because of work schedules, geographic location, or responsibilities in the home.

Recent developments in the United States and in other nations point to increased flexibility in the routes open to persons seeking college degrees:

The College Level Examination Program makes it possible to obtain college credit for independent study.

TV and radio college-level courses are recognized by some institutions.

The mailed syllabus, radio course, local tutorials, and institutional examination form the core of instruction at Britain's new "Open University."

Independent study, sometimes in combination with tutorials, followed by comprehensive examinations, has long been used by the University of London in its external degree program.

The future holds the possibility for even greater flexibility in the routes by which persons may obtain degrees:

Video cassettes and computer-assisted instruction can turn the home into a classroom. In Japan, the Ministry of Education intends to establish an "open university" by 1972 relying heavily on video cassettes that would be available on a rental basis.

Expansion of college-level examination programs and greater use of off-campus instructional programs may eventually make it possible to earn degrees without any college residence.

That all persons, after high school graduation, have two years of postsecondary education placed "in the bank" for them to be withdrawn at any time in their lives when it best suits them.

This would reduce the pressure to enter college directly out of high school or forego the opportunity forever. This can be accomplished by (a) providing no- or low-tuition community colleges within commuting distance of nearly all Americans, as we have recommended elsewhere, or (b) by adding to social security a program for "educational security" to be paid through payroll taxes on employers and employees, with the benefits to be available on application after a period of sustained employment, or (c) by making grants, work-study opportunities, and loans available at any time during life, or (d) by providing through employers and unions the opportunity for educational leaves, or (e) by providing educational grants to persons following military and other service activity; or by some combination or combinations of the above programs.

We plan in subsequent reports to set forth in detail our proposals for national, state, and municipal youth programs, for noncollege postsecondary education, for careers open to talent, for "open universities," and for "two years in the bank."

3

Education Without Schools: Idea and Reality

MICHAEL O'NEILL

The paradox of the current "education without schools" movement is that the idea is growing while the reality is diminishing.

Paul Goodman, still the chief prophet of the movement, may be
as widely read today as John Dewey was in the first flush of
progressivism. Other eloquent voices have taken up the cause,
among them A. S. Neill, Jules Henry, Herbert Thelen, Edward
Friedenberg, John Holt, Fred Newmann and Donald Oliver, Christopher Jencks, James Coleman, and Lawrence Cremin. Reports on
the movement can be found in the sprightly, irreverent *This Magazine Is About Schools* as well as in the sober education sections of
Time, Newsweek, and the *Saturday Review.* Echoes of the movement's basic ideas can be found even in high-level policy statements,
e.g., President Nixon's education message of March 3, 1970.

But all the while the nameless, faceless statisticians in the United
States Office of Education keep demonstrating that schooling increasingly dominates the lives of young Americans.

Historians of education, sociologists, and anthropologists periodi-
cally remind us that although education is a phenomenon found in
all human societies, relatively few societies have developed schools.
Even in European-American societies, for many centuries the greater

"Education Without Schools: Idea and Reality," *Notre Dame Journal of Education,* 1:1, Spring 1970, pp. 49-59. Reprinted by permission. Michael O'Neill is
Superintendent of Schools for the Diocese of Spokane, Washington.

17

part of education took place outside the school. Until recent decades, most young people grew up and were educated with little or no schooling, and even those who spent a good deal of time in school received much of their education from other societal institutions. Twentieth-century America has seen a radical change in this situation. Whereas at the turn of the century the vast majority of American children and youths spent relatively little time in school, now virtually all elementary age children go to school, over three-fourths of American youths complete four years of high school, and half the 18- to 21-year-olds in the country have had some college. The United States is rapidly approaching a situation of universal schooling (*not* necessarily universal education) for all persons from six to 20 years of age. Each year there is an increase in the percentage of children under six and of young adults over 20 who attend school. Further, the hours per year spent in school and in school-controlled activities is rising steadily for all these age groups.

One inevitable consequence of this trend is that nonschool educational experiences are simultaneously decreasing. It is useless to suggest that both school and nonschool education may be increasing; the time demands of schooling make this virtually impossible. After all, a young person needs 10-12 hours a day to sleep, eat, recreate, and relax. For at least 180 days a year, about nine of the remaining 12 hours are spent in getting to and from school, sitting in classes, and doing homework. Weekends and short vacations include many hours given to homework, term papers, science fairs, school play practice, school team practice, school-provided recreation, and R & R characterized by passionate retreat from and rejection of the school culture. There simply isn't time or energy left to get significantly involved in many other educational experiences.

Undeniably, many students still take private music and art lessons, become Boy Scouts, travel, work on community projects, and take jobs after school, on weekends, and during the summer. But anyone who believes that "education without schools" is beginning to carry the day had better look again. However popular the idea may be, the reality is losing fast.

My purpose in the following pages is simply to meditate on this gap between idea and reality from the point of view of a school administrator. It seems to me that one of the great deficiencies of the "education without schools" discussion has been a near total lack of communication between the articulators of the idea and members of the school establishment. One occasionally gets the impression that noninvolvement with school administrators is viewed as necessary to preserving the academic equivalent of ritual purity. There may indeed be considerable justification for this feeling but, given the realities of power in American education, such an estrangement is not likely to promote concrete developments in nonschool education. What is needed now is not estrangement but rather a fusion of prophecy and pragmatism. The progress of "education without schools" faces extremely serious economic and sociological obstacles, which will only grow larger if this healthy intellectual ferment fails to involve itself in the realities of the school world. My specific concern will therefore be some of the practical institutional problems facing implementation of nonschool education in the United States. Finally, rather than detail the rationale for nonschool education, which has been capably done by the writers mentioned earlier,[1] I will simply state three central assumptions, and then proceed to my "administrator's meditations." The assumptions are these: (1) Schooling does not equal education; schooling is only one part of the educational process. (2) It is neither educationally nor socially wise to require all Americans to spend most of their youth in the one type of educational institution which we call school. (3) Education and growing up in America should be characterized by a much greater variety of educational institutions and programs, and by a much greater variety of student and teacher life styles, than is the case at present.

PROBLEMS

One part of the implementation problem lies in the peculiar sociology of educational knowledge. It is readily observable and empirically demonstrable that most educational research and development has strikingly little effect on actual classroom practice. The classic case is that of progressive education, which existed far more in teachers colleges and educational journals than in elementary and secondary schools. The Middletown studies, *Elmtown's Youth*, and other community and school data collected from 1920 to 1950, yield little evidence of the presence of progressivism in average American schools. The economics of educators' salaries, the sex distribution of American teachers, social status systems, and several other prosaic factors had a far more determining influence on American education in the 1920s, 1930s, and 1940s than the whole progressive education movement. More recently, John Goodlad and other leading American educators have expressed deep concern (and some surprise) that the innovations which regularly appear in *Time*, *NEA Journal*, and *Phi Delta Kappan* are somehow not happening in the average classroom. Goodlad, after visiting hundreds of classrooms, many of them in reportedly experimental schools, concluded sadly that the seeds of educational reform are truly being sown in the clouds above, but that little rain ever falls on the parched earth below. Social psychologists like Ronald Lippitt have remarked that the dissemination and implementation of new educational ideas is much slower than the dissemination of new practices in agriculture. The history of experimental demonstration schools has been consistently dismal; these schools not only typically fail to change other schools, but themselves often gradually revert to traditional practices.

Increasing nonschool education necessarily means modifying school operations. Schooling is now such an all-consuming reality in young people's lives that no major growth in nonschool education could take place without an important effect on schooling. Therefore, promotion of "education without schools" will face at least as many obstacles as school reform does, and probably more. It is difficult enough to effect changes which respect the present structures of curriculum and instruction, e.g., improvement of reading and social studies education. Breaking out of these structures, altering the standard school day or week or year, changing the whole concept of the teacher, and dispersing educational activity throughout the community instead of locating it at one site, will present problems that would awe veteran school reformers. For this reason proponents of "education without schools" must not only become thoroughly familiar with the processes of reform through the history of reform movements and with the social psychology of educational change, they must also gain direct or vicarious experience of both successful and unsuccessful attempts at reform. The latter might be achieved best through hiring teachers and school administrators as staff members or consultants in projects designed to implement "education without schools." Nothing can really substitute for the perspective on educational change resulting from several years of experiencing the hundreds of converging pressures which—usually unconsciously—militate against such change. It may seem curious to suggest that members of the school establishment be enlisted to dismantle schools, but, given a careful selection process, few more effective allies could be found. Enlightened teachers and administrators are aware of and even employ forms of nonschool education, e.g., the Parkway project in Philadelphia, summer travel and exchange programs, work-study programs, and "mini-semester" projects outside schools, to name only a few. It would not be difficult to convince some teachers and administrators to take part in aggressive efforts to promote nonschool education; and the extensive experience of these people with students, parents, community groups, and less enlightened teachers and administrators would be an invaluable asset. Close examination of the school establishment will reveal that not all of its members have been corrupted and that some have even had success in fusing vision and tactics. In view of the immense difficulty of significant educational change, this group is a resource that promoters of "education without schools" cannot afford to neglect.

The second point is that American education is very much a political process, and any attempt to change American education must be accompanied by far more political sophistication than is evidenced in most efforts at reform. Public school officials spend considerable time and energy each year soliciting votes for levies and bond issues. Few major administrative actions are taken without some attention to the potential impact on the next levy election. Superintendents and other school administrators are constantly in the public eye and under conflicting pressures on everything from sex education to desegregation; they are and must be not only educators but also politicians. The complexity of the politics within some large school systems is almost legendary. Teacher associations and unions are highly political groups both internally and in their relationships with school boards and state legislatures. State and national educational organizations are engaged in political activity 12 months a year, and are often counted among the most powerful lobbies in the land.

Any attempt to reform American education is in large part a political problem. Failure to realize this has doomed many reform efforts. Groups wishing to change American education significantly —e.g., by the widespread introduction of nonschool education—must determine whether and how this could be made financially attractive to taxpayers, school board members, businessmen, and local politicians, and must analyze the power structure of particular school districts and the motivational system surrounding key persons and groups within the power structure. The same type of analysis should be made in the target communities.

Extensive attention should be given to the structure of incentives within school systems.[2] Failure to understand the operative incentives within schools and school systems has destroyed countless reform efforts in the past.

First of all, public elementary and secondary education is a noncompetitive institution. School enrollment and, therefore, funding level is determined simply by population patterns. A public school system is the only educational agency legally able to receive tax funds and, therefore, the only agency able to offer free elementary and secondary education. Inevitably the great bulk of parents will opt for free education. Faced with dramatic cost differences, parents who see significant advantages in patronizing other schools and have the financial ability to do so predictably constitute a relatively small minority. A public school system, therefore, has little economic or institutional stimulus to gain more students. In fact, most urban and suburban public school systems have strong economic and institutional reasons to fear, e.g., the influx of private school students into public schools. Public school systems are in this respect totally unlike political organizations, which constantly seek more members, or businesses, which constantly seek more customers. In most political and economic organizations, the institutional incentive system is derived from a desire to retain current adherents or customers and attract new ones. This incentive system demands continual attempts either to improve the product or to convince the consumer that the product has improved, or both. This pressing incentive system is simply not present in public education, because the funding of public education does not depend in any significant way on whether parents or students are pleased with the educational "product."

The prime economical-institutional incentives in public education are not to please the consumer or attract new consumers through product improvement and better advertising, but rather to promote the stability and smooth functioning of the organization.[3] As a United States Chamber of Commerce report put it:

> Where market discipline—the knowledge that if the job is not done as well as it can be, someone else who can do it better will get to do it—is absent, both complacency and timidity develop. The complacency comes from the sure knowledge that no institutional substitute is available. The timidity comes from the almost-as-sure knowledge that if glaring mistakes are avoided, job tenure is likely to be prolonged. The businessman in a competitive industry knows that standing still—failing to innovate and improve efficiency—can be a more serious error than minor failure in a bold venture. Failure to innovate and improve creates a market opportunity which a competitor will be quick to exploit. Lack of competition eliminates this ceaseless pressure for progress. And as a result, public schools are less vigorous than they could be.[4]

Title III of the Elementary and Secondary Education Act (ESEA) is an excellent example of what can happen to imaginative proposals which fail to allow for the structure of incentives within the public school bureaucracy. Title III was designed to stimulate "innovative and exemplary" educational projects, and specifically encouraged breaking out of the school establishment. It required that "other cultural and educational resources of the community" be involved in planning Title III projects. Lest this directive be glossed over and forgotten, Congress went on to spell out what it meant: "The term 'cultural and educational resources' includes state educational agencies, institutions of higher education, nonprofit private schools, public and nonprofit private agencies such as libraries, museums, musical and artistic organizations, educational radio and television, and other cultural and educational resources." Thus, one of the main titles in the largest and most important federal education program clearly and strongly recognizes the educational potential of various nonschool agencies, and requires school districts to involve these agencies in Title III funded programs.

Title III seemingly provides an effective way of stimulating nonschool educational efforts. After brainstorming and planning sessions involving such persons as students, teachers, parents, businessmen, journalists, artists, actors, and union officials, projects could be developed which would imaginatively tap the community's non-school educational resources. A school district might free some of its own personnel to initiate "education without schools" or work jointly with nonschool agencies, or simply contract with other agencies to run programs and meet specified objectives. Such "subcontractors" could include an OEO center, a large corporation, a local military unit, a labor union, a private ballet school, a drama teacher, a group of parents, a symphony, a farm, a travel agency, etc. The possibilities are almost limitless. Title III, in other words, is an already-existing, relatively well-funded, widely accepted, seemingly perfect instrument for the development of nonschool educational programs in the United States.

In fact, Title III during the last five years has produced only a bare handful of such projects. There is even reason to believe that the official Title III statistics on the involvement of nonschool agencies overstate the reality. I have personally seen dozens and dozens of Title III and Title I project applications and evaluation reports which presented misleading or simply false information about the involvement of nonschool personnel and agencies, and nonpublic school officials and students, in the planning and implementation of such projects. I have also been told by colleagues in public and private education of similar instances in virtually every section of the country. One problem is that the Office of Education and state offices of education have simply not enforced ESEA regulations strongly and consistently enough to ensure that ESEA programs will fulfill the intent of Congress or even the promises of the project applications. The net effect is that public school districts are given federal funds with few real strings attached. Forms are filled out and evaluation reports are submitted which always show that the project was successful and should be refunded, but there is very little outside, objective, tough-minded appraisal.

The failure of Title III to stimulate more nonschool efforts can be explained by the simple axiom that no organization freely gives away money which it can use itself. Virtually all schools and school districts feel they need more money. Virtually all school systems see themselves as fundamentally capable of any educational task. If a federal grant of $100,000 would enable a district to hire additional personnel and purchase additional equipment and materials for special programs, why should it contract with an outside agency and thus "throw away" the $100,000? The argument that the money might be better spent in the latter way is most unlikely to move the average administrator. The school establishment sees itself as constantly underfinanced but basically capable of meeting every imaginable educational need. No organization with those two convictions is likely to "throw away" education money by contracting with some outside agency. Consequently, nearly all Title III money is spent on programs which school districts plan and operate themselves, programs which will not only help children but also preserve and promote the organization, i.e., the school district. Contracting with outside agencies might disturb or weaken or demoralize the organization, not only by depriving it of additional funds but by giving the impression that some other agency might be able to accomplish some educational task better than the school district.

TACTICS

Efforts to promote "education without schools" must be planned with full attention to at least the basic organizational inertia of school systems, the intensely political nature of school systems, and the major economical-institutional incentives affecting decision making in school systems. Primary attention should be given to such possibilities as redirection of federal, state or local funds; creation of additional funding sources; development of counterlobbies to promote nonschool education; organization of nonpublic schools and nonschool agencies to move in the direction of "education without schools"; and alteration of the professional self-concept of some educators in a way that would motivate them to encourage and stimulate nonschool education. The production of articles and books about "education without schools" will remain an important thrust, but should not be consciously or unconsciously viewed as sufficient to cope with the complex and powerful economic, political, and organizational obstacles to significant educational change. If no book ever seduced a maid, neither did one ever change a school system.

One of the most promising ways of promoting nonschool education, even given the criticism above, is still Title III of ESEA. But further specifications of the law are necessary. Congress could, for instance, amend the law to stipulate that a certain percentage of Title III funds must be subcontracted to nonschool agencies. If a district could not or would not do so, the money would revert to the federal treasury—the ultimate negative incentive. Since county and intermediate district school offices would have less conflict of interest about contracting with nonschool agencies, Congress might direct that the contracting process (including publicizing the availability of funds, soliciting participation, planning, and implementation) be handled by these offices rather than by school districts. Further, Congress might direct that tougher regulations be developed and that there be strict enforcement as well as significant penalties for noncompliance.

With these or similar amendments, Title III might become the most effective way to promote "education without schools." ESEA is five years old, has the support of both public and nonpublic school leaders as well as many other groups, and is funded yearly at a level no other single funding source can match. Perhaps most importantly, Title III already contains the federal government's blessing on efforts to break out of the school establishment.

Other funding sources, such as states and large foundations, should also be explored as possible backers of nonschool educational experiments. Carefully planned, well funded, and highly promoted demonstration projects could certainly assist the development of nonschool education. Promotion or dissemination should be the key element in such projects, and should be a major item in project budgets. As indicated earlier, dissemination of the nonschool idea will face staggering obstacles. Dissemination efforts must be intensive, painstakingly planned, and generously financed.

A more radical way to promote nonschool education would be to change the whole method of funding American education by giving educational grants directly to parents instead of to public school systems. Parents would be given tuition vouchers, perhaps inversely related to parental income, which could be cashed in at any approved educational agency. The state could license various individuals and groups as able to accept and redeem vouchers or parts of vouchers for various educational services. Students and parents could contract with a variety of educational agencies, not only schools but also industrial arts training centers, park departments, and travel bureaus —or any agency which could demonstrate its ability to provide valuable educational experiences.

Tuition voucher plans have been suggested by, among others, James Coleman, Theodore Sizer, Christopher Jencks, Henry Levin, Milton Friedman, and the U.S. Chamber of Commerce's Task Force on Economic Growth and Opportunity. Such a plan would in one stroke eliminate many of the problems involved in changing a school bureaucracy, and certainly would dramatically change the whole structure of economic incentives in American education. Given enlightened licensing by the state, nonschool educational agencies could compete on the same footing with schools for student "consumers." The result might be not only the spread of nonschool education but also vast improvement in the quality of school programs.

The Office of Economic Opportunity recently awarded Christopher Jencks and the Harvard-based Center for the Study of Public Policy a $196,000 grant to study the feasibility of the tuition voucher idea. Also being planned is a five- to eight-year demonstration project. If the latter is funded and succeeds, it might conceivably lead to the adoption by some states of the tuition voucher idea. However, the tuition voucher proposal raises immensely more political problems than even the encouragement of nonschool education within present structures, and one would probably not be well advised to wait for tuition voucher funding to usher in the era of "education without schools."

One potential ally in the promotion of nonschool education might be private school educators. Private schools and school systems do function in bureaucratic patterns similar to those of public school systems, but there are important differences which may merit exploration relative to the nonschool education effort.

There is no absolute demand for the existence of any one private school or group of private schools. Whereas the simple presence of children without a school available creates an absolute legal demand that the state set up and maintain a public school, there is no such intrinsic demand for the existence of private schools. Even when parents, students, taxpayers, city officials, church leaders and businessmen want a certain private school or set of private schools to remain open, the schools may not choose to do so or may not be able to do so. In the past several years, there have been thousands of examples of private schools closing in spite of such outside pressures. It is in one sense irrelevant that private school officials and teachers may be as unhappy as parents about these decisions, and that the decisions are usually forced by lack of funds or personnel rather than by oppositions to the private school idea as such. What is relevant here is that no individual or group can in the last analysis force private schools to exist. The freedom to go out of existence might seem a peculiar type of freedom, but from this basic fact flows the private school's freedom to exist *as* it wants *if* it does remain in existence. In other words, a private school has, by reason of its fundamentally nondemanded status, a certain program autonomy and freedom from community pressure not available to public schools. This autonomy is of course limited by state regulations as well as parental expectations, but it is clear and strong enough to create significant potential for educational innovation.

That such potential has not been amply realized is evident from inspection of American private schools in actual operation. However, it is quite possible if not probable that the failure of private schools to take the leadership in educational innovation is largely a result of their fiscal plight. It is striking enough that these schools, funded solely through tuition and freewill donations, have been able to offer adequate education to nearly 6,000,000 students a year. If other funds were available to private schools, the amount and quality of innovation might be dramatically increased. The availability of even modest additional sums of money is a powerful incentive to most private school educators. This, coupled with the private school's basic program autonomy, suggests important possibilities of cooperation between promoters and funders of nonschool educational projects and private school educators.

One essential element in any such effort should be the redefinition of the educator's role. The basic insight of the "education without schools" movement is that many other societal institutions besides the school can and do educate, and that many other adults (and young people) besides schoolteachers can and do guide others in educational experiences. Private school educators might be especially open to the idea that they should act as planners, consultant-specialists, and evaluators of the educational process rather than the sole imparters of knowledge. No public or private school teacher is likely to be attracted to a plan which implicitly or explicitly rejects the teacher as a significant part of the educational process. But if teachers could be shown that "education without schools" would allow them to use their talents and experience in a more efficient and ultimately more influential way—by acting as planners, diagnosticians, special consultants, and evaluators—teachers might be highly motivated to accept such a scheme. The role of the educator could in this way be made not less but more vital and prestigious: full-time trained educators would in effect be delegating many specific instructional tasks to persons who could handle them equally well or even better, thus leaving the educator free to make major decisions about the community's educational efforts. It could be easily argued and demonstrated that in the long run the educator would thus have far more influence on the education of children.

There are two characteristics of present-day Catholic education, specifically, which might be conducive to teacher acceptance of a newly construed role. First, most Catholic schools exist within broader communities called parishes, and Catholic school educators typically are able to call upon the various manpower resources of this broader community to help meet educational goals. Because of the socioreligious context within which these schools operate, and because of the typically strong relationships of trust and respect that exist between parents and religious teachers, Catholic school educators might find it relatively easy and natural to make more use of the educational resources—professionals, laborers, offices, businesses, etc.—in the broader parish community, and in groups of parishes within the same town or city.

Secondly, the forces unleashed primarily by the Sister Formation Movement (increasing the education and professional training of religious women) and secondarily by the Second Vatican Council have created in many religious communities of educators an impatience with the standard classroom-teacher role. Teaching sisters seem to be working out a tension in their individual and community career decisions between a basic commitment to moral-religious education and a dissatisfaction with the traditional parochial school and classroom teaching. There is too little evidence or analysis of this ferment to offer much more than the above speculations, but it seems at least possible that a creative, newly defined approach to humanistic and religious education, and a reconstrued definition of the educator's role, might have powerful appeal to some of the leaders among Catholic religious educators. "Education without schools" might present just such a challenge.

I should immediately add that there is hardly a group which academic liberals (such as the developers of the nonschool education idea) presently view with more suspicion than Catholic parochial school teachers and administrators. But should the promoters of nonschool education ever wish to examine the present trends and ferment within these religious communities, they might discover with some surprise that a marriage of convenience could turn out to be highly fruitful and not nearly as distasteful as originally imagined.

Some may find it curious that a school administrator did not immediately name parental opposition as an obstacle—perhaps *the* obstacle—to implementation of "education without schools." The reason is simply that I see very little evidence that parents would oppose such a trend. To test this hypothesis, I have one very modest suggestion: give parents—not public school boards or school systems or state legislatures or regional accrediting associations or any of the other groups which decide for parents what is best for their children —the freedom to accept or reject nonschool education, and see what happens. Give parents the genuine freedom, including and perhaps primarily the absence of economic penalties, to choose between a completely school-centered education and an education which used not only schools and teachers but also many other persons and institutions in the community. Give the "education without schools" proponents at least as much money to work with as the school-oriented educators have been given, and let the parents decide. In my experience, parents—both high and low income—give considerable thought to the education of their children, and almost certainly would give more thought to it if they had any real choice among different styles of education, which choice the vast majority of American parents do not presently have. In my experience, parents are not nearly as conservative about education as some would have us believe. They demand to be convinced and they demand proof of success, but hopefully these are not the characteristics of reactionaries. It is reported that there are 10,000 applicants for the 500 student places in Philadelphia's Parkway project. Many parents supplement school education by the use of libraries, museums, travel, camping, Boy Scouts, Junior Achievement, park department programs, private music lessons, and dozens of other educational experiences. One could hardly find more convincing evidence that parents do not consider schools to be the sole locus of education. But again, the most obvious test of the parental opposition hypothesis is simply to give parents the opportunity to accept or reject "education without schools." If very few or no parents chose to enroll in such programs, the idea could be quickly and quietly dropped.

As for student reaction, I personally have very little doubt that most students would opt for a more diversified, active, and reality-centered educational program dispersed throughout the community. At any rate, it should be tried. After all, school has been one of the very few educational institutions in the history of man that has raised serious questions about Aristotle's dictim: "All men by nature desire to know."

The idea of "education without schools" becomes increasingly important as the reality grows increasingly scarce. Human beings laboriously plan and implement minor social changes, and drift unconsciously into major ones, e.g., urbanization, war-centered economy, the shift from kinship groups to nuclear families, ecological disruption, the overpowering presence of television, and universal schooling. It is not at all clear that universal schooling—again, not to be confused with universal education—is socially *or* educationally wise. Thorough rethinking and restructuring of American education, especially through realistic and pragmatic efforts to further non-school education, may be among the most urgent needs in America today.

FOOTNOTES

1. Particularly by Goodman in many books and articles by Newmann and Oliver in "Education and Community," *Harvard Educational Review,* XXXVII (Winter, 1967) pp. 61-106.

2. An excellent analysis of some of these incentives is given in an unpublished paper by James Coleman, "Incentives in Education: Existing and Proposed."

3. I am *not* saying that many *individuals* within public education are not motivated primarily by "product improvement," i.e., improving the quality of educational experiences available to students. I am simply saying that the method of funding public education prevents "product improvement" from being a primary *institutional* or *system* incentive. Actually, my general impression is that public school teachers and administrators typically retain a good deal of "product-improvement" motivation, in spite of the fact that the system as such gives them little if any support in this. But even the accumulation of such individual motivation is powerfully depressed and, in my opinion, largely negated by the structure of incentives created by the system as such.

4. *The Disadvantaged Poor: Education and Employment* (Washington, D.C.: U.S. Chamber of Commerce, 1966), p. 64.

4

An Open Letter: The Public and Its Education

UNITED PRESBYTERIAN CHURCH

This 31-page document was provided as a study guide for "Wide use ... in congregations, presbytery committees, citizen groups, seminaries, schools of education, etc. ..." Although it treats broader issues, the portions selected deal with the exploration of alternatives to in-class teaching.

FOREWORD

Presbyterians have always been concerned about education, both in society and in the church. In the past the church had little difficulty in defining its position on public education. There were operative consensuses in both church and society that tended to reinforce each other, making both issues and positions more clear-cut.

There is still no question about Presbyterians' concern about education. Expressing that concern has become much more difficult. Changes in both society and the church have raised as critical issues matters that used to be quite clear to us. Education is one of the most important, judging from the amount of controversy surrounding it. It is also one of the most complicated.

Special Joint Committee on the Church and Public Education of the Board of Christian Education, excerpts from *An Open Letter: The Public and Its Education*. Philadelphia: United Presbyterian Church, U.S.A., 1969, pp. 9, 10, 27, 28. Reprinted by permission.

In order to help Presbyterians to find authentic, contemporary expressions of their concern, the 181st General Assembly has commended this "Open Letter" to the judicatories, boards and agencies of the church for study. It is not a pronouncement or a statement of official position. It is a call to study an important problem that faces both church and society. It seeks to focus that study by articulating a fresh perspective from which to view the problems of education in the seventies. It asks the questions: "Where do you stand?" "What are you going to do?" "How can we help one another. . . ?"

. . .

Degrees Aren't Enough

A small band of suburban youngsters want something different out of high school. Last summer in an experimental church project, they caught a glimpse of a new world. As one of them said, "No tests, no worry about scores, no teachers up tight, trying to beat it into you—just the chance to read and feel what is going on in this crazy world." Another: "We all know how to read. But will we ever bother with anything worth reading? Man, I want more than a college degree."

Two teachers in the high school understand and want to help. They know that education is often reduced to a process of clearing one "checkout point" after another: grade school, high school, college, and then what? "The nine-to-five life, the mortgage, the ranch house—these kids are running away from that."—"An ulcer, gentlemen, is an unwritten poem." But their high school, these teachers believe, might be different *if* there were some margin of freedom.

Out of their frustration and dreams comes a plan developed jointly by the youngsters and teachers. Their proposal calls for an experimental year for 50 students and two teachers. It involves freedom from the standard curriculum and the fixed "obstacle course" of tests and grades.

The reaction is immediate and mixed. Almost everyone is for "innovation," especially if it enhances the reputation of the school system. But this plan is "controversial." Anxious parents worry lest it jeopardize their children's chance for good colleges. There is talk

about the suggested reading material as being "offbeat," "porno-
graphic," and even "unpatriotic." The town fathers fret about
"kooky kids."

The counterpressures against experimentation grow stronger. The
high school students appeal to adults, more out of desperation than
firm hope. There is plenty of advice and warning on all sides:

> "Don't do anything rash, son; remember the future."
> "These kids need something more than school gives them."
> "What they need is discipline."
> "That Salinger novel is—well, you know—obscene."
> "School is a rat race."
> "What else is there besides a rat race? Be realistic."
> "When I was a boy . . ."

But now that we are adults, what do we have to say in this situation? Anything important?

Beyond Do's and Don'ts

These stories out of current church life reflect a bewildering ac-
celeration in the pace of change in American education. Ten years
ago few social commentators would have anticipated that such problems would face American Protestants in the late 1960s. In fact, it
was just 12 years ago that the Presbyterian Church in the United
States of America issued a General Assembly Report on "The Church
and the Public Schools." That report spoke directly to the anxieties
of postwar America about the health of its schools. Among other
things its authors fought the widespread apprehension that public
education was becoming "godless."

Then in 1957 the Soviet satellite Sputnik spun across the sky. In
its wake came a different kind of worry. The schools are failing, so
the charge went, to produce enough technologists and scientists to
maintain America's place in the "cold war" competition with the
Communist bloc.

Since then the tempo of change has sped up considerably. Just
look at the world around us. Now there are many cold wars—and
some hot ones, too—in American education: the assault of black and
Puerto Rican citizens upon urban schools that treat their children in

literally "godless" ways; militant teachers on strike; the struggle between the generations as symbolized in that ubiquitous phrase,
"student power"; and the charges and countercharges over the meaning of "excellence" or "quality" in education. In each of these
skirmishes the American people are being forced to acknowledge,
however reluctantly, the power of an inbreaking future.

And so it is appropriate once again to take a fresh look at the
topic—"The Church and Public Education." Our intent in this letter
is to speak provocatively of the future and its demands. Our aim is
not so much to give answers as it is to *ask the right questions* about
American education in the coming decades.

EDUCATION IS A PUBLIC AFFAIR

The Public's School

Whom are the schools for?

Not, we would say, for any race. At first reading that appears to
be one of those predictable statements which one would expect to
find in a contemporary church document. We want, however, to go
beyond talk about desegration or integration, important as these
imperatives are. The basic problem is the denial of human solidarity
and a deformation of the public. This is the nub of the matter. If
color becomes the badge of humanity, then a sick society deforms
the public.

Whom are the schools for? Not the school bureaucracy or their
allies in the teachers colleges. When administrators and teachers act
as though they own the schools, they violate the nature of the
public's school. Sometimes this violation is justified in the name of
professionalism. Let us be clear on the point involved here. Our
quarrel is not with professionalism but with paternalism. The professional is often described as one with the requisite knowledge and
skills, recognition by colleagues, etc. But another mark of the professional is that he is *asked* by the laymen to make a decision. Knowledge and skill alone are never enough. No matter what his competence and expertise, the teacher has professional authority only when

he enjoys the respect and trust of the immediate public, the parents and children who invite him to make decisions on their behalf. Otherwise he becomes the unwitting reminder of a paternalism that gives (often generously) without ever being asked, or *never* gives without being pressured. It is that spirit, intended or not, which destroys any sense of mutuality. Those in our society who protest against paternalism are really crying out against a negation of human solidarity and a deformation of the public.

But the schoolman has no monopoly over paternalism. Whom are the schools for? Not only for the local community. The advocates of "community control" can be paternalistic also. They can ignore federal guidelines for desegregating school systems as the work of people who do not have the knowledge and competence to make that decision. Or they "forget" the rights of teachers and destroy their morale, all because of "the community." "The community" is no more acceptable a tyrant than an unfeeling and inept profession. Think back to the story of the high school students and teachers. What protection did they have against the provincialism of the community?

No, the schools do not exist for the profession or the local community. The schools are for the public and its formation. If we keep that affirmation in mind, then we can begin to work in new and fresh ways for the strengthening of the profession and the development of plans for community and student participation in the making of school policy. Because of our fundamental commitment to the public's education, we will be on the search for alternative public school systems to replace the present inadequate structures. There are many possibilities: regional state schools that would be financed by states and could cut across the urban-suburban boundaries; a network of federally financed boarding schools that would allow for genuine diversity in the student body; true "community schools" open to the contributions of those outside the school profession—the block worker who knows the "street," its languages and problems; the mother with a knack for dealing with youngsters; or artists in the community.

These are just a few of the options that deserve exploration. We urge our fellow Presbyterians to join with others in the development.

Now the conversation we have tried to initiate returns to those who are working at these problems in local situations. We encourage them to continue it.

For instance, here are some of the kinds of questions that could launch continuing explorations: (1) Could our denominational boards of education reallocate their support to devote more to the church's experimental work in new ways of public schooling? (2) Can new interdenominational groups tackle together some of these matters at local, regional, and national levels? (3) Why shouldn't the church contribute to the establishment of skill banks to identify existing and needed resources that could be made available upon call by all schools? (4) Can seminaries and church higher education unite with universities and foundations in developing effective resource materials for analysis and study of the relationship of religion to education for the public?

These initial steps mark just a beginning of a new expression of an old commitment: a concern with the public for its education. We offer these suggestions as a way of inviting your response—and, we hope, a continuing conversation about the public and its education.

Where do you stand?

What are you going to do?

How can we help one another, and so participate in the forming of the greater public to come?

5

Intercepting the New Education

HAL LENKE

Education is delusion. We have created unimaginable categories; we have lost our magic; abominations abound and we chatter. What to do about the terrible awkwardness between people? Is it possible that there is someone who believes that what we have done in Vietnam was ever worth it? That is the consummate success of our education so far, each abyss we stretch toward is our latest commencement exercise. We are scholars of nullity. So, we talk of "new education" or of "educational reform" but all our philanthropic nerves are numb. We have moral gangrene.

I have ever less patience with the reformers who devise clever new commercials for the same product, who sell themselves out for $10,000 a year, collapse utterly at $15,000. The price of the contaminated transfusion from "idealist" to "pragmatist." American virtues.

What are the viable alternatives to aspects of the educational system? That's what the editors asked in requesting articles for this issue. The educational system. Viable alternatives.

Well, for one thing, stop what you're doing. Do it differently. Do something else. Outrage a preconception. Promise that you'll answer mail the day you get it. Listen when you speak. Let someone know he is your equal.

Hal Lenke, "Intercepting the New Education," *New Voices in Education*, 1:3, pp. 5 and 6. Reprinted by permission.

We educators are dangerous. We exercise more law, medicine, and psychiatry in a single class than attorneys and doctors exercise in a week of practice. We don't even say that we practice; we are accomplished, finished products. The attorney practices law. The doctor practices medicine. But before our very first day on the job we have already completed our practice teaching; from that moment on it is brazen, unconditional.

We don't consult, the way economists or construction engineers might. We act wholly on our own. We promulgate unilateral treaties and we break them as we like.

We are priests; we have our tacit convenant with our god Norm. We have the sacred texts, the disciples ready-made, our altar, our rituals. We provide our own writing on the wall, our own voices out of the PA. We suffer in our own fiery furnace. We make known our commandments. We take up collections, sell indulgences, hear confessions, assuage sins.

Education is not a system. It is a symptom, of the disease of thinking yourself educated. There are degrees of the affliction; some have raging fevers.

The viable alternative is to let the patient recuperate organically. Nature heals. Love and leave alone. Honor the integrity of all being.

Do these words curl strangely about the educationist tongue? Enough of formulas. Look, we know this: by the end of the first week of class, every teacher knows exactly what final grade he will give every student. Every student knows exactly what to expect (of himself, of the teacher) in any given class. Every teacher in the land is told, perennially, to be strict with the class at the start, and then, when he has it under control, loosen up a bit in late winter, and recover the reins as spring competes with the teacher for its attention.

Surprise is not allowed. There may be no spontaneity. What kills scheduling reform? Why, the administrative insistence (coming from teachers, principals, and guidance counselors), that it be determined ahead of time what each student will be doing, and where he will be, at any point. Remember the canards of the scientific method—prediction, replication, explanation.

Never a creator, always a drone.

Ever notice what the most popular places in school are—the

bathrooms, cafeteria, gym, halls, library. Ever watch kids' bodies change as they go from one of those places into a classroom? Ever hear a librarian complain that the black kids/the greasers socialize too noisily, don't know how to use a library properly? Ever wonder about patrolling the cafeteria, monitoring the bathrooms? The places where bodily functions are at play are the social centers of the school complex; there the bodies accept themselves, exchange occurs, there is some gaiety, some intercourse of the human community. And in the classrooms, where the learning is scheduled? Look at the bodies.

A first reform? Remove the teacher from the focus of the enterprise. Make the teacher indistinguishable from the learning. But that is not enough; an open classroom is a deception in a closed system, it is an open wound in a body of scars. The system is whole, and no student has ever been tricked into believing that one or two or three alluring classes transformed the taut environment.

Still, wherever you are, try. The new education will come into its own when we do not see a separate time, place, and brand on a phenomenon we call education. Education will be, source and consequence, one with our other affairs.

We cannot expect people, young or old, given an open learning enticement, to know what they want to learn. Having no experience with such a choice, none of us can be expected to give any but programmed answers. Great patience must be exercised, in the unlearning process, before a person can believe and actualize his learning freedom.

Democracy reveals pathology. That is, freedom permits variation. We are unaccustomed to democracy; we are also unaccustomed to variety in human expression—everything has been emotionally and politically homogenized before we are exposed to it. When people have the opportunity to violate those boundaries, it is often a confusing, and threatening, experience.

Something learned becomes a reflex. What do our own reflexes tell us? What has our education done to us? What will we be parties to, in inflicting education on others?

Parents don't speak honestly to school officials because they are afraid of retaliation against their children.

A new education is a new sensibility, new convictions, new reflexes.

There are plentiful writings filled with valuable constructions. They seem to have done little good. This is the dilemma I am in: I'm tired of seeing, reading those good words.

The first concept of new education is: try something other than what you're used to, something that feels right.

But perhaps before that, I should say: don't do more harm than is being done already; and if you don't know how much that is, it is you who need some new education.

6

An Urban Teacher Views Alternatives

LARRY CUBAN

Every day is a struggle to decide
whether things are
hopeless or hopeful

Those words, which I think are mine but are probably borrowed, hang above my desk. I've had them with me while I administered two reform programs in the Washington public schools in the 1960s and now while I teach history in a high school there. A note of despair mixed with faint optimism, I feel, is about the most that any participant in urban school reform can muster nowadays. And so it is with me.

The past decade of reform—I confine my observations and judgments to efforts at changing big city school systems—has yielded few returns at the classroom level. Reform seems to have become a series of stale formulas boiled down into almost meaningless catch phrases.

Kids aren't learning? Give 'em new math materials; get some open classrooms working; or install performance contracting. Bad teachers? Staff development will cure that. Inept principals? Improve selection process and give them real authority. Board of education fouling up? Professionalize membership or give them a research staff. Too much red tape? Cut it. Get power into the community. Decentralize administration.

Written especially for this book. Larry Cuban teaches history and trains teachers at Theodore Roosevelt High School in Washington, D.C.

Such exchanges, when they occur, are less of a dialogue and more of a simple-minded game of citing mindlessly the right phrase—a routine not unlike the chatter at cocktail parties. Worse yet the evangelical faddism that has afflicted the nation's schools seems to have fallen into the corporate rhythm of periodic style changes: team teaching in the late 1950s; curriculum reform in the early 1960s; black studies in 1968; community control in 1969; informal education in 1970; accountability in 1971. Clearly none of these shifts is as neat as stated but the shifting around occurs. All of this, of course, is disheartening.

It is disheartening because achievement test results still slide downward; disheartening because so few solid programs with demonstrable results have emerged from the rhetoric of reform; disheartening, finally, because urban school systems gut each new innovation and convert it into pap.

To paint such a dismal picture argues for dismantling the school system. Some would say that revolution not reform is needed. Not so. Revolution would require wiping out public schools. The losers would not be middle-class, leisured whites and blacks who speak from the security of a college degree, a suburban address and private schools for their children; the losers would be black and brown children who have inherited the schools from fleeing whites. The poor have theirs to get; they have fewer choices now. Reform is all they got.

FAILURES OF REFORMS

Why did reform efforts fail in the 1960s? There are at least three major reasons:

Reforms Seldom Addressed Themselves to Repairing Achievement Deficits

Curriculum reform, after all, is just tinkering. The most carefully constructed curriculum materials are not teacher proof. So installing reams of new math, new history, or black history seldom made a difference in student performance. Structural reforms such as decentralization or community control prompted either by school officials' fear of even broader changes or community disgust with prevailing conditions have yet to yield concrete results in reversing low performance.

A nationally known experiment that dealt directly with skill deficits has had a rocky start. Performance contracting, specifically aimed at reading deficits—but recently tainted by reports of rigged testing—offers little hope for long-term, intensive help for students. Business corporations will operate only as long as the profit margin remains substantial. Reversing reading and math retardation is expensive and with budget squeezes predicted for the next few years, the prospect looks dim. Even were this not the case, performance contracting is a confession by the schools that they are indeed bankrupt in dealing with skill deficits among students.

Only one major school system in the country has attacked reading and math retardation through a massive mobilization year in every classroom from kindergarten through the ninth grade in every city school. The Clark Plan, named after Dr. Kenneth Clark, its designer, has suffered from a power struggle between the board of education and a new superintendent; results are fragmentary and discouraging.

Co-Opting Reform by School Systems

Innovation after innovation in the 1960s from team teaching to computer-assisted instruction popped up in school after school. Name an innovation and virtually every big city system had it or was about to initiate one. As with all reforms, getting a program started, usually with federal funds, was the easiest step of all. Were it successful—and evaluation was a dirty word—spreading the program's benefits to other children was either done by diluting the services offered to the point of ineffectuality or mandating its implementation in target schools without providing teachers and administrative support.

Reform by fiat and dilution of effort have been popular tools used by boards, superintendents, and middle-level managers. Superintendents willingly embraced federal projects, Princeton Plans, ungraded primaries, ordering their implementation if it would only give them elbow room from interfering boards of education. And boards to ease the pressure of community activists would enact all sorts of policies ranging from integration to black studies. System bureaucrats in order to preserve stability slowed down, impeded and sabotaged comprehensive reforms—even those demanded by the board of education.

Reforms begun for the wrong reasons (defusing criticism, diverting pressure, co-opting critics, etc.) and forced upon teachers invariably failed.

Absence of Teachers from Conceptualizing and Developing of Reform

Teachers aren't army grunts who can be ordered to take a hill away from the enemy and told not to ask questions. Nor are teachers assembly line workers pushing buttons and raising levers, complying with the foreman's directions. If that is all teachers are—obedient soldiers and laborers—then someone has erred in entrusting the nation's children to semiskilled workers. If they didn't err, and it was purposeful, then few should complain at the results (or the lack of results).

Thus, a basic precept: Those who are expected to change their behavior willingly and without the coercion of a sergeant or foreman, these persons must be involved in planning the change. This, more than any other precept in education, has been ignored repeatedly by would-be school reformers.

Only after years of turning out millions of pages of curriculum materials did national project directors begin to shift their focus to the training of teachers. For whatever the reasons, and there are many, New York teachers fought Ocean-Hill Brownsville and community control experiments. Teachers, seldom consulted by the board of education, invariably opposed performance contracting. Orders to change may work in the military or in corporate organizations but in education directives from the superintendent rarely penetrate closed classroom doors.

Teacher involvement is more than two-day workshops in August when administrators tell teachers about new programs to begin in September; it is more than a professional day when the superintendent, speaking in a cavernous auditorium, exhorts teachers to work harder and love the children; it *is* the weekly skull sessions where teachers, released from classroom duties or paid for evening or weekend work, conceptualize and develop programs with community members, principals and central office administrators.

When integration was ordered in 1954 not every town and city was a Little Rock or Clinton, Tennessee. Individual schools as well as small school districts met throughout those early years with teachers carrying out the necessary planning and implementation activities.

One recent collective bargaining aim of teacher unions has been to guarantee teacher participation in policy making. Few large school systems have yet included meaningful teacher involvement. Until they do, teachers will be a major obstacle to any comprehensive reform focused upon changing what happens in the classroom.

ON ALTERNATIVES

Alternatives to in-class instruction have been around as long as there have been people who have been frustrated by the sterile, pseudofactory efficiency of one teacher drilling twenty-five or more children into a stupor. And that has been a long, long time. The recent surge of interest in schools without walls, street academies and Outward Bound programs mirrors the dissatisfaction of many poor and middle-class families with traditional instruction in the public schools. The recent receptive climate for experimentation produced a spate of such programs sponsored by big city school systems. Chicago's Metro school, Philadelphia's Parkway school and Washington's smaller School Without Walls most readily come to mind.

Such alternatives to in-class teaching often base their programs upon two premises: 1. students must control their own learning and 2. the city itself must become a learning laboratory. Usually enrolling less than 400 students, these programs pride themselves on flexibility, informal teacher-student relationships and confidence in students to do what is right. While an individual teacher can create such a climate in one room for 30 pupils in a large high school, it is most difficult to sustain such a climate, much less tap the available resources. It is no secret that alternative modes of instruction outside the fortress-school attract those of us who spend our days teaching five classes a day, five days a week. Isolated from colleagues, performing as a semiprofessional with groups of kids moving in and out of the classroom, harassed by administrivia—such alternatives come like a breath of fresh air, a burst of hope.

How I would like to work as an advisor, resource person and teacher with students who learn from the community! How I would relish planning with students the intelligent use of learning resources available to us—and not worry if we can get enough bus tokens! Yet my wishes are half-hearted since I know that alternatives to in-class instruction will enroll a tiny fraction of the thousands who attend; I know the enormous obstacles facing such an instructional reform; and, finally, I know that the search for other ways of teaching and learning outside the classroom will miss the vital point about the failures of big city urban schools.

Let me deal first with what I consider to be the political realities that this reform would face. If educational reform in the 60s taught us anything, it is that reform by fiat is disastrous. Ordering principals, for example, to develop alternative modes of instruction would stimulate petty plans and grand mumblings. Initiating pilot projects, as most of the school systems have, runs the risk of ending up a decade later with a ten-year-old pilot project, still serving a few hundred youngsters. In short, to develop a workable scheme for educating people to the benefits of alternatives, administrators and teachers have to be trained, adequate funding must be secured for at least five years, and a broad coalition of board members, superintendent and community must be built. If top administrators tiptoe uncertainly over the reform, if it is restricted in location, if few members of the community know about it, and if the board commitment to change is temporary, then alternatives to in-class instruction will follow the comet-like path of innovations of the 60s: Here one year, gone the next. The politics of reform as well as the funding of reform are crucial to any success. The record is grim for previous reform efforts.

Unless the political dimension is dealt with, the number of students enrolled in out-of-class learning will seldom exceed a small sample of the student population. Perhaps this is best. A safety valve for students who find the conventional program intolerable seems to be the function of many big-city alternative schools. Yet the advocates of out-of-class instruction must know that a small, peripheral operation will have little, if any, impact upon the ongoing program.

But were even the above conditions—funding, consensus of support, and sizeable numbers of youngsters—met, I would still have serious reservations about the concept.

The crisis of public education, especially in the cities, is not whether instruction takes place inside or outside the classroom; the crisis is over who carries it out, in what manner, and toward what ends. Every major instructional reform depends upon answers to these critical questions. Whether the resources of a city are used, whether students meet in nonschool buildings or in the mountains are important but nonetheless secondary questions.

The thrust of most out-of-class alternatives leans—save for the Outward Bound program—toward less structured environments, student choice of what to learn and involvement with social issues. One can infer what the aims are. Personal growth and change, mostly affective, and social reform seem to be the goals. I suspect that such feelings lie beneath much of the thrust for out-of-class alternatives.

Basically, the difference between those that advocate changes within the institution (more in-service training of teachers and administrators, organizational changes in structure of school, etc.) and those who push for alternatives to classroom instruction seems to be over values. Those who argue for affective goals, flexibility, etc. assume (with much evidence) that such values cannot exist in the classroom as presently established. Perhaps they are right. They see the supporters of the public school and academic subjects as people who value cognitive aims, structured surroundings and discipline, both managerial and academic. From each of these clusters of values, the role of the teacher-structurer of lessons, or resource person, flows. From these values, the school is organized in one manner or another. How easy it would be, given the current dialogue on urban schools to characterize the two sets of values as the Black Hats vs. the White Hats. Guess which is which.

Yet no evidence to my knowledge shows a clear-cut edge to either the traditional classrooms or antitraditional out-of-class instruction. By evidence, let me add, I mean achievement, attitudinal differences, and creativity.

Seeing the issues in terms of value differences rather than whether pupils learn more and better in one situation over another may help to clean up what often appears to be the dirty question of where do youngsters learn best. For that isn't the right question. The right ones still seem to be: What are they to learn? How are they to learn? And, have they learned? One's values, not hard evidence, determine the answers.

For big cities, the answers to these questions focus upon basic skills. Stress on the teacher's role in getting children to read, for example, gains increasing support in city after city. Achievement tests, teacher accountability for student performance, and lifting low reading scores sum up the aims more and more of militant and sober community members. Out-of-class alternatives in many poor, black communities have become identified with white liberal parents looking for the school to solve their children's personal hang-ups. Many black educators see the problem for the *race* as "catch-up." No sitting around and rapping about how bad things are. "Read, write, compute, and think—that's the ticket!"

Education has the larger political significance, to many black educators, of equipping a people with the basic tools for success—material, personal or political. Perhaps such views will change. Until they do, out-of-class alternatives will continue to be seen as "frills" suitable for leisured whites but unsuitable for blacks anxious to carve out their slice of the pie.

To sum up, alternative modes of instruction, to date, have not dealt with the political realities of big city school reform. The exercise of power by whom and in whose interest are seldom considered. When advocates do raise the proper questions, debate often misses the point that each side argues from different value positions rather than factual evidence. Values determine the nature of the school and, at the present moment, black leadership seems to emphasize getting the fundamentals. More schooling, more basic instruction, more books are called for—not freedom to choose, freedom to come and go, and freedom to ignore the teacher. For all of these reasons, out-of-class instruction ignoring these values, unaware of urban school politics, will be another passing fad.

What may be closer to big city educators and parents are the Clark Plans and the numerous mini-school experiments such as at Haaren high school in New York. Here and at other places, closer teacher-student relations are fostered through a school within a school idea. But closer relationships are aimed at getting students to learn basic skills in the classroom. These alternatives as well as those aimed at retraining the teachers offer more of a hope to the mass of youngsters who will never come close to a school without walls. I pose these as mutually exclusive choices because limited funds for big-city schools cannot, in my mind, tolerate the luxury of small peripheral experiments that bleed away precious dollars and energy from what has to be the basic task of schools: Get the students to learn basic skills.

7

The School as an Opening System

MELVIN B. MOGULOF

For those of us raised in big cities, and even not-so-big cities, the concept of the school as a "fortress" should be an easy one to imagine. Many of our nation's schools seem to have been deliberately constructed to be out of scale with their environment. If the argument may be carried a step further, this distortion in scale was designed to reflect the great value our society places upon education.

If one can suggest that many communities seek to create physical images of the things they value, then surely we need not be defensive about the relative "grandeur" of our school plants. That which is imposing can also be inviting. Many of our houses of worship, as physically impressive as our schools, have always kept their doors open. Compare this to the perhaps apocryphal situation of the big city school system that locks its doors once its captives (the students) are inside.

Despite scattered, and perhaps increasing, evidence to the contrary, the central argument in this paper is that the American school has carried out its functions to capitalize on its fortress-like physical qualities. The school as a social system has been much more intent on retaining its boundaries than on linking itself to the

Melvin B. Mogulof, "The School As an Opening System: Tactics for Breaching the Educational Fortress," from *Urban Education*, 4:3, October 1969, pp. 231-242. Reprinted by permission.

world around it (Loomis and Loomis, 1961). In pursuing the tasks associated with boundary maintenance, the schools have been no different from other organizations. The schools have simply been more successful in maintaining their organizational integrity than have other groups. They have done this by being able to control their resources, so that their linkages to other social units may be as specific and limited as possible.

All of us can quickly bring to mind activities that point to the school as being intimately involved with other social units: adult education programs, community use of sports facilities, the developing community-schools movement, PTA's, teacher aide programs, publicly elected policy boards, and many more. The argument here is not that schools are unrelated to their environment. It is that they are *minimally* related compared to other organizations. The movement of the schools toward activities that denote linkage, compared to those that are boundary maintaining, is not commensurate with the demands and needs of a rapidly changing society.

Before the argument is carried further, it should be noted that the schools, or any other organization, generally have the option of seeking more contact with their environment, or burrowing in deeper and closing themselves off from their surroundings. Which of these strategies is more conducive to organization survival cannot be predetermined. Organizations with powerful and monopolistic controls over their needed resources can realistically risk a strategy of isolation from their environment as opposed to connection and involvement. Consciously or not, the schools in our society seem to have chosen isolation. Until a short time ago, their choice seemed to have impressive and positive consequences for the survival of the school system.

As long as the school system was aided in its isolationist strategy by its systematic failure with a large group of its students, the school performed one of its primary societal functions. This function was to *differentially* educate the school population and continually to produce a blue-collar and dirty-collar force of people, who were aptly equipped by aspiration and/or skill for life at the bottom.

As long as this task performance by the schools integrated nicely with the needs and values of our other major social institutions, one could predict that the schools would remain relatively undisturbed in their pursuit of organizational isolation. When one combines the inertia that captures all of us with the school's apparent disinterest in connecting to its environment, and the relatively effective performance by the schools of its societal task, one has the prerequisites for maximum system independence. The term "fortress" aptly captures this capacity for independence of the schools.

As with any partial system, of course, the schools are not so independent of their environment as the argument of this paper seems to convey (Loomis and Loomis, 1961). There are certain key resource inputs, which force the school system into relationship with other societal units. Examples of such resources are teachers, students, money, and policy makers. These resources in their more generalized form (personnel, clients, etc.) are hardly unique to the school systems. The schools may simply have been more successful than other institutions in acquiring control over these resources, in a manner permitting them to pursue an isolationist strategy. As previously suggested, the success of the school (until recently) in its relative control over these resources stems from the success of the schools in performing a primary societal function—the delivery of a differential education.

It would appear that, now, the principal threat to the school as an institution (apart from its obvious difficulty in remaining a fortress) stems from two factors in its environment over which the school has little or no control.

In the first place, other societal institutions, primarily economic, seem less able to provide legitimate roles for the failures produced by the school system. Until recently, the capacity of the schools to socialize successfully a large group of students toward membership in the underclass was important in providing a certain kind of labor pool for the economic sector. One must admit that the schools were more than up to the task. Devices such as tracking systems, vocational schools, intelligence and diagnostic tests reflect class rather than capacity and were all part of the professional armamentarium by which the schools legitimated their function of differential education toward sustaining an underclass.

The first chink in the school's armor is the growing obsolescence of a school technology geared to producing people who define themselves as incompetent. The problem is not beyond resolve, but it demands that the schools drop their isolationism, and develop practices that permit more students to negotiate with the school system for a redefinition as a successful product. The consequences of such change are huge and beyond the purview of this paper. However, some of the tactics by which such change can be achieved are already available to educators, and will be reviewed later in this paper.

The second environmental factor that has threatened the school's capacity to survive as a closed system is the redefinition of self and community by the black and brown people of our society. As with all of our other institutions, the schools were absolute in their capacity to recruit black and brown students into the role of school failures. Thus not only did the schools turn out an ample supply of actors for the underclass—they broke every law of probability to insure that black and brown students were over-represented in the supply. The schools, of course, were abetted in their success by all of our other social institutions. An equally great ally was educational technology, which defined failure as personal incapacity rather than social structure.

This simultaneous disenchantment with the schools by the economic sector and by our black and brown minorities has created a crisis for the inhabitants of the educational fortress—a crisis threatening the very integration of our society. The crisis has mounted so rapidly, aided by the grossness of response of the schools, that the schools seem left with little space or time to determine new policy directions. The shock to the schools is further compounded by the dissension in the business sector and in the minority communities. This dissension is most clearly evident regarding the education of the black. While the new rhetoric calls for separatism, every move toward educational separatism finds some (both black and white) who cry racism. In the face of this kind of dissension it is easy to understand why a counsel of caution for school policy makers prevails.

For the schools to wait for consensus in their environment is to invite continued disaster. Precisely because the schools continue to have so much control over their central resources, they are able to take certain actions, *rather than wait constantly to react.* The very factors that contributed to sustaining the school as a fortress (an independent tax base, policy board members elected by the community, a captive clientele in the form of students compelled by law to attend, and personnel produced by training resources that are highly responsive to the needs of the school system), can now contribute to bold decisions by the school to open itself up to its environment.

The remainder of this paper will devote itself to tactics for breaching the educational fortress. *We make the critical assumption that without an opening to more day-to-day impact from its environment, the public school system cannot survive. We also make the assumption that key educational policy makers everywhere understand and are in agreement with this prediction of disaster.* The educational policy makers falter in implementing their understanding on a number of counts: (a) a mistaken search for consensus where none can presently be found, (b) a failure to understand the great strength and relative policy autonomy that continue to reside in the educational system, (c) the romantic hope that somehow the old order could be salvaged through small incremental changes in educational technology, (d) a general paralysis of action born of shock, (e) a trained incapacity to understand how potent a weapon change can be in organizational structure. Like most of us, but perhaps more so, educators are clinically oriented to believing in the sanctity of individually willed behavior without paying equal attention to the social situation defining what behaviors may be chosen.

The central thesis of this paper is that the educational system retains the capacity to act, and that, further, its capacity to act is sanctioned by the larger society. Despite the public educational system's grave failures, we are not yet as a society prepared to dismantle it, and we fully expect that the schools will act to deal with what are their commonly perceived problems. The major solution would seem to lie in efforts *at restructuring the schools so that they are more at one with their environment.* Out of this restructuring will come educational functions appropriate to an institution whose boundaries merge with the minority communities, the business community, and the American family. Gone will be the fortress institution, which so successfully erected boundaries between itself and its institutional environments. While these boundaries may have seemed to "neaten up" educational decision making, it is equally clear that such institutional isolation no longer serves the schools or the larger society very well. Thus we propose a series of tactical steps, all of which are grounded in the same thesis. The thesis is that public education can survive only as the system opens itself up to contact, to influence, and to contract with a variety of social units formally defined as external to the educational system.

This is not to say that all of these tactics can be adopted everywhere, simply because they have been shown to work. However, this paper does suggest that the seven ideas that follow represent the beginnings of a system of action in which each effort reinforces other efforts to connect to the environment. It is suggested that there would be a synergistic effect, whereby each move to open the system would enhance the effectiveness of previously taken actions in this direction. Because this is an exploratory paper, it must be obvious that these seven tactics hardly represent all of the possibilities in opening the educational system.

TEACHER AIDES

The teacher aide is the epitome of a system-opening tactic having resonance. That is, it opens the school to its environment while at the same time enhancing the achievement of other critical goals, such as employment opportunities for poor people.

In middle-class communities the teacher aide program can serve to make parents more knowledgeable about school problems. In poor communities, the parent as teacher aide can be as important an object for the educational process as the aide's children. The teacher aide program has the great advantage of instantly being able to redress the employee color imbalances existing in virtually all schools.

The opportunities for experimentation in what constitutes the most effective pattern of linkage to the community may be made more obvious in the following three patterns of teacher aide deployment: (a) lower-class aides in lower-class dominated schools; middle-class aides in middle-class dominated schools, (b) middle-class aides in lower-class dominated schools; lower-class aides in middle-class dominated schools, (c) only lower-class aides in all schools.

If pattern (c) is chosen, it becomes apparent that the teacher aide program has great utility as an employment program in addition to being a system opening. In that case, it is important that the aide program become a new careers program, with a live opportunity for the aide, by virtue of continuous training, eventually to become a teacher (Pearl and Riessman, 1965; Popper and Riessman, 1968).

From the point of program saleability, the attractiveness of the aide program is that it permits more of the professional's time to be used professionally.

THE SCHOOL-COMMUNITY AGENT

I remember the feeling of shock and delight the first and only time one of my youngsters' teachers came to visit us to discuss school. Lower-class families, particularly those of color, probably never experience that shock except at times of crisis. Some recent efforts in economic opportunity programs to bring teachers into the homes of lower-class families have not been smashing successes. Yet the literature of education places great theoretical emphasis upon the importance of linking school and family. PTA's and open school days are hardly adequate vehicles for accomplishing the task for the lower-class families, much less anybody else.

If the schools need linkage to each family, and particularly to those lower-class homes that may be unsure of the educational experience, why not a school-community agent? (Litwak and Meyer, 1965: 49-98). Schools have a fair number of agents now, most of whom have their contacts with families around points of control and enforcement. Why not agents to link the school effort to each family (particularly to the lower class)? This agent would interpret the school experience, assist the family in helping the child educationally, and help families to deal with schools, individually and *collectively* around the problems that families have with the school system.

Most organizations have some device for reaching the people they consider important clients of their system (e.g., Fuller Brush Men, Welcome Wagon ladies, milkmen). Surely it is not a big conceptual jump to see the family as a prime client of the educational system and, therefore, in need of a school agent who will connect families to the system and by doing so open the system a little further.

Needless to say, the implications for new kinds of educational jobs and career ladders are overwhelming just as they are with the aide program.

YOUTH TRAINING YOUTH

I would venture that most of us who think of the schools as a system are prepared to place the students, in the role of clients, outside the system. In fact, a common problem in organizational analysis is whether to view the client as a part of, or apart from, the organization. Where the client is also a minor, it is even less likely that he will be viewed as part of the system. If our basic strategy is opening the system, there is no group more crucial to open the system to than the student.

We are, and will continue to be, in the midst of revolts on college campuses, with the major purpose of bringing the college student into the governing structure of the system. I have, of course, such sharing of authority with students in mind when I write of opening the system. Once we begin to work within the framework of sharing authority, we may be overwhelmed at how dictatorial we are with the lives of other people under the guise of "the professional and/or the adult knows best."

Apart from changing some of the patterns of governance of the system, an equally significant change in opening the educational system would be the utilization of students as teachers and counselors (Riessman, 1967: 217-228). There is fairly good evidence that we learn best by doing. Further, such a step would formalize a major finding of the Coleman Report that "resources provided by fellow students are more important than those coming from the school board" (Coleman et al., 1966).

As with the deployment of teacher aides, a number of different models might be used, with class position of student-teacher as the key variable. One further benefit would be the possibility of paying low-income youngsters for their performance as educational aides.

It should be apparent that there is nothing revolutionary about this concept. Schools seek to co-opt students in a variety of ways —why not in the central institutional role of teacher, thus blurring the lines between giver and receiver and further opening the system.

COMMUNITY CONTROL

There is nothing in education that makes a school district of a particular size sacred. If minority groups are the overwhelming population of a school or a series of schools, and they appear to desire a separate governing structure, why not? The cost to all of us in *not* reallocating governing authority may grow increasingly great. Certainly, based upon a school's systematic failure with minority youngsters, the minority community interested in separate schooling ought to be able to try it. Decent preplanning can avoid the tragedy of New York's Ocean Hill-Brownsville District, even to including an ability to protect teachers' jobs (Stern, 1968: 17-24; Hoffman, 1968).

To those who fought so hard for school consolidation, decentralization may seem regressive. But, in 1969, it appears that a decentralized school system is more in keeping with our pluralistic society (Jencks, 1966: 17-24).

WORK PROGRAMS

It seems clear that the total separation of students from the world of work for which they are ostensibly being prepared, was never sanctioned by all of the school establishment. A number of colleges have always had block work placements for students, and our better vocational high schools are closely linked to the fields for which their students are being prepared.

There seems to be no reason why all high school students, and even junior high school students, should not be concurrently placed in the business sector. And there is no reason why they should not have a field teacher, employed by the business sector and the schools, who would serve to integrate the expectations and opportunities of both of these worlds.

Without pushing the argument to the extreme, there seems to be no reason why these field placements could not be structured to benefit the public good. We already have a model in the Neighborhood Youth Corps for seeing that such work brings recompense to youngsters. Apart from the fact that neither the schools nor the business sector might want to be bothered, it would even be appropriate to bring the work program into the grade school level. There is nothing so inherently ennobling about school and so degrading about work that the two cannot be mixed at every level.

Again, the central task is to open the school system and perhaps nothing does it so very well as linking the worlds of school and work in the everyday life of the student.

SUBCONTRACTING WITH THE BUSINESS SECTOR

A number of us who observed the Job Corps under the Economic Opportunity Act, suspected that the Corps' capacity to survive had something to do with the fact that a number of Job Corps camps were contracted to private industry possessing a good deal of political muscle.

The schools might be equally advantaged if certain training courses were contracted to private industry. This is not to argue that schools need necessarily have outmoded equipment and outmoded instruction. Apart from the likelihood that industry as the teacher would be more relevant to the work being trained for, subcontracting provides the school with another opportunity for opening itself up to its environment. In so doing, there is the possibility of sharing expectations and problems by both industry and schools, and the likelihood that the youngsters being trained in particular skills will find those skills more saleable.

Some may argue that such skill training, made even more specific when run by a particular industry, has become outmoded. I recognize the argument that, in the course of a work career, many of us will have to be retrained three or four times. The tactic of linking the schools to industry by subcontracting training is meant to give industry a direct stake in the schools, while making whatever training is given more relevant. Of course, there is no reason why training need be done within the school. Clearly the implications of the work program described above, where it was proposed to open the system by subcontracting with the economic sector, lend themselves to an integration of both approaches.

THE SCHOOL AS A UNION OF STUDENTS

The six previously described tactics have aimed at better linkage between the school and three of its potential constituents: the family, the student, and the economic sector. No matter how effective this opening of the school system to its environment, it remains likely that the school will be a central institutional base for youth at every age. The essence of the above tactics is to ensure that, during the years of the school's primacy as an institution for youth, there be better connection between the schools and other crucial environments. For those youth who make the transition successfully the economic institution, at some point, supplants the school as the primary institutional base.

This paper has previously argued that there are two facts concerning the crisis engulfing schools: (1) there is a shrinking market for the underclass prepared by the school, and (2) the school seems systematically to consign a disproportion of minority group youth to this underclass. Despite these apparent failures of the school system, the notion of "student union" to be described in this section is meant to suggest that the school should have a continuing responsibility *to train, to counsel, and to bargain* for all youth until they reach one of the following two stages: (a) They have moved on to another "higher" educational system (b) They have been connected to the economic sector in a manner that yields them a salary above what is defined as a level adequate to support a family unit.

Under this tactic we seek to suggest that the school system must open itself up to assume responsibility for all of those whom it has not successfully prepared to move into other societal institutions. Thus the concept of "dropout" becomes an anachronism—one cannot drop out of the schools until he drops into something else. It seems clear that society cannot afford the current inefficiency by which we move people from an educational institution to other societal bases.

The tactic proposes that the educational institution function as a "union" for all disconnected youth. As a union it would offer protection through work programs (already established as part of the Neighborhood Youth Corps program), and additional training for those whose skills have not proved saleable to the economic sector. Primarily, this tactic would serve to depress the incentive for the school to rid itself of those who do not profit from its current educational technology. The schools would remain the institutional surrogate for all youth until it was clear that such youth were productively connected elsewhere.

Thus, in this last tactic we are suggesting that, not only must the school open itself to other sectors, but it must also open itself to new responsibilities when these other sectors have not productively connected the student. This opening up of system responsibility has imperatives at both ends of the "normal" school age range. It seems clear that the Headstart program already offers important beginnings at one end of the age cycle. The "student union" notion proposed here is meant to establish a continuing role for the schools at the other end of the cycle.

SUMMARY: TACTICS FOR TACTICIANS

We promised the reader nothing new with regard to programs for achieving a more open school system. What is new, perhaps, is the emphasis on the selection of program tactics in order to concentrate a series of efforts, all aimed at restructuring the way in which the school system relates itself to the world around it.

By implication, and now explicitly, we are saying that it seems less important to put limited energies and finances into things like "higher horizons," tutoring, student-teacher ratios, counseling, and other various additive and enrichment devices. All of these are probably blameless efforts, but they do not deal adequately with the need for the school to breach its own walls, to bring parents in, to better protect and connect students, to bring industry in, to share authority with and give authority to students and collectivities from the minority communities. It is the argument of this paper that, when this opening of the system occurs, it will bring with it new actors on the educational scene. At present, "enrichment" programs are most likely to be the slightly stale concoctions of ourselves as middle-class technicians.

Perhaps a closing word about the politics of educational change. No school system is a monolith. There are "bad guys" and "good guys" in various parts of the "fortress." The system-opening tactics suggested in this paper will serve to bring a host of new actors into the system. Many of these new actors will offer great potentials for alliances in moving toward new approaches to education. In addition, the "good guys" in the educational system must not back away from using the sense of crisis surrounding the schools to press for change. Those seeking change must do their homework, particularly in the area of costs. A number of these changes do not necessarily cost additional monies, although they will "cost" in the area of organizational security for those currently part of the system. In other cases, additional monies are available through federal programs, or can be made available by shifting monies from less salient enrichment efforts to new efforts at restructuring the educational system.

As those who have occupied themselves with change know its cost in personal equilibrium can be great. Yet, the school system and the whole of American society are in the position where those who take the leadership for change are functionally the most dedicated of conservationists for the total social system. In 1969, as elsewhere, *not* to change may be a suicidal option.

References

Coleman, J. et al. *Equality of Educational Opportunity.* Washington, D.C.: U.S. Government Printing Office, 1966.

Hoffman, M. "Conflict in a counterfeit community." *New Republic* (November 9, 1968): 17-24.

Jencks, C. "Is the public school obsolete?" *Public Interest* (Winter, 1966): 18-17.

Litwak, E. and H. Meyer. "Administration styles and community linkages of public schools." Pp. 49-98 in Albert Reiss, Jr. (ed.) *School in a Changing Society.* Glencoe: Free Press, 1965.

Loomis, C. and Z. Loomis. *Modern Social Theories.* Princeton: D. Van Camp, 1961.

Pearl, A. and F. Riessman. *New Careers for the Poor.* Glencoe: Free Press, 1965.

Popper, H. and F. Riessman. *Up From Poverty: New Career Ladders for Non-Professionals.* New York: Harper & Row, 1968.

Riessman. F. "The 'helper' therapy principle." Pp. 217-218 in G. A. Brager and F. P. Purcell eds. *Community Change Against Poverty.* New Haven: College and University Press, 1967.

Stern, S. "Scab teachers." *Ramparts* (November 17, 1968): 17-24.

8

Why Alternatives

SAM J. YARGER

That a crisis exists in education is no longer a question. The impoverished child can't read well, has no vocational skills and is becoming increasingly alienated toward a society that he feels is unjust and oppressive, while the affluent suburbanite is reacting to middle-class values by "tuning out and turning on." At the same time, taxpayers are refusing to support education for a variety of reasons, legislative authorities are demanding that educators become "acountable" and romanticists, journalists, civil rights leaders and anyone else who can find a soapbox are diagnosing ills and offering treatments that range from community control to burning the school-house.

Crises are evident, diagnoses must occur, treatments must be implemented and someone will have to be accountable for everything that takes place. Furthermore, if the institution of education is to survive, these endeavors must be performed, to a great extent, by that body of beings known generically as "educators." The question that continually arises in educational forums focuses on what can be done within the constraints of public education that will ensure educational improvement and allow public education to survive. In other words, what are the *alternatives*?

This chapter will not dwell on the diagnostic aspect of American

Written especially for this book. Dr. Yarger is Associate Professor of Education, Syracuse University.

education as there already exists an abundance of diagnoses, but rather on a justification or rationale for attempting something different. Even though the social sciences have not been very active in the problems of education, and perhaps that is wise, there does exist a body of knowledge and principles which can be extrapolated and applied to the educational endeavor in support of alternative plans to in-class instruction. It must be noted that numerous innovative educational programs already exist, or have existed in the past without the benefit of scientific certification. Nothing here is intended to impugn those endeavors, but rather to stimulate and hopefully offer direction to many more programs developed in response to a static, anachronistic educational institution.

LACK OF GOALS

It is a difficult, if not impossible task to provide theoretical support to an endeavor for which the aims, goals and/or objectives remain as vague as those of American education. As early as the eighteenth century, Benjamin Franklin was talking about that which was "useful" and that which was "ornamental," suggesting that everything which is either can be taught (Bruner, 1963). Even then he suggested that we must select that which is most useful and that which is most ornamental. In approximately two hundred years, it appears that we have moved very little in determining and stating precisely what the expectations are of American education. Statements of "philosophy" have been written, books have been formulated and an infinite number of conferences have been convened, yet it appears that the only real change is in the terminology used. Instead of usefulness and ornamental we talk about "skills" and "frills."

This lack of clarity in direction has contributed greatly to the present crisis. Not only has it precluded the development of sound programs, but it has also served to place evaluation in a rather negative position. One is less than enthusiastic about evaluation, when there exists no clear goal that one is attempting to reach. It appears, then, that frequently we don't know where we are going, and we don't know where we have been after we get there. Although this is reminiscent of the punch line in an old joke, it is also accurate in describing the state of American education.

Any instructional program must be defensible, hence it must be evaluated. In turn, evaluation must be related to some set of objectives or goals. In the lack of definitive statements concerning these issues, we shall rely on the statements of Jerome Bruner (1963), that American education has a twofold purpose, first, to help students acquire skills, and secondly to help them develop a general understanding, thus enabling them to "deal with the affairs of life." This dichotomy is in itself artificial, yet it allows one to differentiate between concrete educational goals that are designed to help students acquire *directly applicable* skills, and goals that, if they are to have validity, rely on the application of learned materials to new and novel situations. Generally, the directly applicable skills areas include vocational education, business education, distributive education and the like. The need to develop a basis for alternatives to in-class programs for these endeavors is not great, as their very nature and definition implies experiences that take the student out of the conventional thirty students and one teacher format.

The objective of developing a "general understanding," however, requires a more intensive analysis. Courses of study taught in school which have no direct application generally fall into this category. Social studies, language, mathematics, the humanities and the arts are but a few examples. Elementary school curriculum areas such as reading can also be viewed in this dimension as they represent a process, which, in isolation, has no direct application. That is, reading skills must be applied to a multitude of other endeavors if they are to be useful to a student.

Interestingly, it is these areas of the curriculum that are generally restricted to in-class instruction, and with which we must be most concerned. Incidently, these courses or curriculum areas are the most frequent recipients of student attack, being labled as "irrelevant," "worthless," or worse. One must, therefore, attack the implicit assumption that the content of these areas, if they are to be educationally justifiable, is best dealt with in a conventional classroom setting.

BASIS IN LEARNING THEORY

Frequently when a student encounters a novel situation, he makes a response he had previously learned to make to another situation. This phenomenon, called generalization, is basic to all theories of learning. It also provides the basis for asking such questions as, "Is there a repertoire of responses which, because they are frequently needed, should be part of the curriculum?" And, "How do I teach them?" "How do I know they will be used when needed?" Seeking answers to questions such as these can offer support to a variety of educational endeavors, and at the same time serve as a test of relevance for the student.

Such a strategy would begin with a process of question development that would take both students and teachers not only out of the classroom and the building, but perhaps away from the community. For example, what better way could students anticipate the types of experiences they are likely to encounter on college campuses, in the big cities, in the suburbs, or wherever they are likely to go than by devising a method of systematically visiting these places and sharing their findings with others. One can certainly see that in-class activities could become an integral part of this process, but there is no reason to suggest that such activities would constitute even the cornerstone upon which the program develops.

The results of these experiences could lead to a list, or perhaps even a taxonomy of fundamental behaviors, responses, or skills that are universally acceptable as necessary for a student to possess if he is to "deal with the affairs of life." It would be presumptuous to attempt to delineate these skills, but it doesn't take much imagination to suggest that perhaps such areas as interpersonal relations, problem solving, and group processes buttressed with certain types of knowledge such as mathematics, political science, communication, natural science, and so forth would be essential. Further refinement of these "critical skills" would hopefully lead to the development of specific objectives and instructional alternatives, either in-class or outside of class, designed to help a student enhance his repertoire of response behavior.

Finally, plans could be developed to offer the student opportunity to try out his skills in a variety of situations. This could be accomplished by simulation within the classroom or laboratory, or it could involve other types of experiences that would take the learner from the school and into the world. Even better it could be both, with the latter providing the more sophisticated evaluation of the students' skills. If, then, the acquisition of "general understanding" can be interpreted to mean generalizable skills, then a multitude of activities that occur outside of the classroom are clearly justifiable.

Discrimination is the process whereby an individual makes different responses to two or more stimuli. It is the complementary and less talked about but equally important process to generalization. The importance of developing discriminatory skills can be underscored by looking at the behavior of infants. Soon after a child learns the attributes of "daddy," a process where he discriminates between the essential characteristics of his mother and his father, he is likely to generalize the label to others who share the same attributes. The fact that neither the milkman, the neighbor nor the salesclerk are entitled to that label creates no problems for the child, but is usually a source of embarrassment to his mother. It now becomes necessary for the child to learn the difference between his father and other men. In other words, he must learn to discriminate again. As one can see, the processes of generalization and discrimination are complementary, and must develop in tandem. Generalization of response without discrimination would result in undifferentiated, unintelligible behavior, while the reverse would require the person to learn a new response for each and every stimulus situation.

Applying this concept to educational activities, it becomes clear that the wide range of potential stimulus situations does not exist and cannot be simulated in a classroom. Consequently, even though a simulation technique may prove helpful as a precursor to a more sophisticated field experience, the need to move the educational endeavor away from the classroom is evident. For example, it is not uncommon for first and second grade students to have a mock grocery store in the classroom. Transactions are completed using fake money and ersatz merchandise. The interaction is quite sterile and performed without regard to sales tax, cash registers that calculate, economy of time, or multiple purchases. Consequently, the responses learned by both the "clerk" and "customer," although appropriate for their enterprise, probably wouldn't facilitate shopping in a real market. Certainly a field experience where the children go to the store, make real purchases and interact with the personnel would provide an opportunity for developing a more valid set of generalized and discriminating behaviors. In this case, in-class experiences are perhaps necessary, but surely not sufficient, for learning a set of necessary skills.

Similar examples could be developed around such topics as job interviews, attending social events, preparing for a trip, or simply interacting appropriately with people in a multitude of settings. The simple application of these two well-established concepts provides a clear basis for extending the educational enterprise well beyond the walls of the school.

DEVELOPMENTAL BASIS

An application of the developmental notions of Jean Piaget to the educational endeavor will offer still further support to the case for alternatives to in-class instruction. Piaget's contributions appear more applicable to elementary age children, yet a careful analysis can lead to a justification for the creation of nonclassroom activities for older children as well.

No attempt to summarize Piaget's concepts will be presented. The reader is encouraged to select from the many works available in this area (Baldwin, 1968; Flavell, 1963; Furth, 1970; Ginsburg and Opper, 1969). Instead, two developmental periods will be briefly summarized and then brought to bear on the issues at hand.

During the latter part of the preschool years, the child operates on his environment using what Piaget calls a preoperational mode. Although the child has acquired language skills and the ability to internalize thought, he has not developed the ability to perform operations that require logical thought. Consequently, the child is all too frequently dependent on his perceptions, which frequently mislead him and lead to behavior that a casual observer might classify as unintelligent or stupid.

Somewhere around the sixth, seventh, or perhaps even the eighth year of life, the child begins to develop those characteristics necessary to begin to perform logical operations. Included is the ability to classify, to develop hierarchies, to conserve, and to think in terms of more than a single variable at any given time. These and other skills lead him away from a dependence on his unreliable perceptual skills. In fact, they supplement perceptual skills, thus increasing a child's cognitive powers many times over. The child remains, however, dependent on concrete data as the raw material for logical thought. Consequently, if he is to truly develop an understanding of the world around him, he must interact with things he can see, touch, manipulate and play with. Words in books and diagrams on the chalkboard often force the child, in self-defense, to memorize rather than conceptualize, thus deceiving not only himself, but his teachers as well.

Although educators can and frequently do provide a great many materials and experiences in the classroom to promote a true understanding of that which is being taught, there are an unlimited number of concepts that simply cannot be dealt with in an educationally valid manner in a school room or a school building. The unavailability of concrete data often precludes the development of real understanding for elementary age children.

A third grade teacher once reported that she had developed a unit on the community in which the school and the children resided. As part of the unit she distributed to the class a partially completed map, with some of the landmarks and all of the street names omitted. Her objective was to use a large complex master map of the city as a reference and have the students complete their own, thus developing an understanding of the parameters of what was referred to as the "community." Most of the children were able to complete the task, as they had access to a finished model. Yet when the teacher attempted to assess the students' level of understanding by asking them to find specific locations in the city using their map as a reference, she discovered that most of the students used references that were *not* included in the map. The children frequently gave directions that relied on "Billy's house," "The A & P," and "Smith's Service Station." When the students' maps were checked, it was found that they had included none of these personalized references, and even more importantly, could not locate them on their completed product. In simple words, for many children the map they had completed was unrelated to the community they lived in and understood, at least from their point of view.

This example dramatically illustrates the need for early elementary age children to have concrete experiences from which to develop an understanding of the world they live in. Although the children could copy the map from the master copy, it was neither necessary nor sufficient for them to understand the geographic boundaries of their community. Had the teacher taken the children on a walk through the community, asking them to draw their own map utilizing their own landmarks, the chances for creating an abstract product that was understood by the children would have been greatly enhanced. In addition to this, there probably would have been rather marked differences between maps thus suggesting a divergent approach to dealing with the problem. Finally, the opportunity and data would have been generated for the creation of a "master map" that would have synthesized the children's divergent understanding of the community into a rather complex, but meaningful product. The final experience, by the way, would happen legitimately within the classroom, yet only as a result of the field experience.

Somewhere about the time a youngster goes into the middle school grades, he begins to outgrow the need for concrete data. That is, the child develops the ability to deal with hypothetical constructs. Once a relationship becomes evident, the youngster can begin to systematically consider other possibilities of the same elements. It is at this period, called the stage of formal operations, that one can begin to deal with questions and problems in a scientific, or at least quasi-scientific manner. Piaget has presented a rather formal set of operations that have developed prior to this period and continue to develop during this period. Although the need for concrete data and experiences is no longer crucial, the question of what types of educational experiences are justifiable during the upper school years must be considered.

It would be naive to suggest the optimal ratio between in-class and out-of-class experiences for any group of students. More particularly, it would be a display of colossal rigidity to suggest that such a ratio is even possible for a single student let alone a class or a group of students. Suffice it to note that in the conventional secondary school, students are usually required to be in the building between five and seven hours per day. *Without regard to a defensible ratio, one can take the position that in-class activities 100 percent of the time are not conducive to intellectual development and the growth of understanding that our schools are being called upon to facilitate.*

In light of the fact that high school students do possess the ability to think logically and in the abstract, a certain amount of discussion and other in-class activities are certainly justifiable. However, if the school recognizes that students can develop independent hypotheses, then it must realize that within a group of ten students, ten totally different problems might emerge in any given situation. Once the hypotheses are developed, probably through individual consultation with the teacher, the student must seek ways to ask questions, gather data and relate the data to the original hypothesis. Consequently a good deal of this work can and should be performed independently. In fact, much of it could be done in the local sweet shop as well as in the classroom, though perhaps a library would represent a reasonable compromise.

Assuming that all the data to be gathered are not found in standard reference books, it becomes necessary for the student to have the freedom to seek out information in his own way. It is not at all unreasonable to suggest that this endeavor may well take him away from the school and into the community, or perhaps even further. Perhaps one reason that we find very few students managing their learning in this fashion is the constricted, authoritarian atmosphere in which they must exist. It would be a rather dramatic, though probably superior, break from current practices to have students scheduling appointments with their instructors over a ten-week period while attending, at their discretion, optional seminars.

Once data are gathered and conclusions are drawn, it would seem very reasonable for a student to desire the opportunity to verify his conclusions utilizing some type of applicatory process. Again, this would frequently require that he venture from the school grounds and move into the arena of reality. The students in our secondary schools apparently know better than we that school is frequently a highly artificial world, full of unreality, or even worse, creating a reality that bears little relationship to the world they know exists. It would seem necessary then, that educators not only must allow, but also must create a series of linkages between the four walls of the schoolhouse and the issues that comprise the twentieth century.

CREATIVITY AND DIVERGENT THINKING

David H. Russell (1956, p. 305) once said, "It is trite, but still true, that the progress of civilization depends upon new solutions, upon the creative thinking that people are able to do." If that statement has any validity, and most of us would agree that it does, then we must be concerned about the extent to which the educational system stimulates creative thought.

Creative thinking involves the production of new ideas. The source of these ideas and the process by which they are generated is still an issue to which we have very few answers. Yet most would agree that a group of thirty students and a teacher holding class each day, discussing the same readings, dealing with the same questions and usually producing the same answers would not be considered facilitating. In fact, most teachers in most classes expect and frequently demand that all students produce the same "right" answer to questions. This practice must certainly retard the development of divergent thinking.

There are many strategies that can be employed within the classroom that will lead to greater divergence and more creative problem solving, and these should be encouraged. Yet the fact that thirty students receive the same input, listen to the same teacher's opinions and discuss the issues among themselves must certainly produce a normative or averaging effect.

When a trigonometry teacher stands before the class and describes a ravine forty feet deep and twenty-two feet across, suggesting that the class is going to design a bridge for the ravine, it is automatically assumed that there is one correct structure that should be designed to traverse the gap. No one dares think that a pretty bridge should be developed, because this is a trigonometry class, not an art class. A student who suggested that the ravine be filled in would probably flunk, because his solution would not require the appropriate computations. The suggestion that the road be built so that it avoids the ravine would also be scoffed at. Finally, a dam, followed by flooding and a pontoon bridge would be unacceptable. The final answers would, in all likelihood, be very similar to each other and very similar to what the teacher wanted right from the beginning. In other words, creative thought is not only not promoted, it is inhibited. Those students who attempt to create new and novel solutions usually pay such a price that they "learn" to respond appropriately, or they leave the situation they find so intellectually debilitating.

Carrying the issue one step further, imagine, if you can, the reception a student would receive if he suggested that the problem was dull and uninteresting and didn't deserve his time or effort. Educational romanticists such as Holt (1964) contend that is exactly what students do, but not openly. Instead they study the teacher carefully and develop a survival strategy grounded in the belief that school is designed so that students can tell teachers that which teachers want to hear. Whether or not such an analysis is not only meaningful but also correct is not the issue. The issue is that schools inhibit rather that stimulate creative thinking both in the delineation and solution of problems. The hypotheses that students are capable of generating are not allowed unless they happen to be the same as those of the teacher or the curriculum guide.

It would be inappropriate to blame teachers for this condition, as they are frequently constrained. In light of the examinations a student must take, the demand to produce students who can get into college, and a school system with a very rigid set of rules and regulations, they often become victims, much as their students do. It seems, then, if we are to turn the situation around and develop an environment where creative and divergent thought are encouraged, alternative strategies must develop.

One can think of many ways that might stimulate and encourage creativity, yet three conditions must be considered necessary:

> 1. *Acessibility to a Multitude of Stimulus Situations:* Students who are going to define problems and conceive solutions in new and different ways must have access to a multitude of information, ideas, and objects. There should be no attempt, at least initially, to structure, categorize or

limit the accessibility of stimuli, as it can only serve to inhibit creativity. Obviously, the teacher cannot be the sole source of these stimuli as any products would then be as much a product of the teacher's creativity as that of the students. It should also be noted that the availability of stimuli should not be restricted to a classroom or a building, as these are both very sheltered environments. Freedom to encounter stimuli and stimulus situations becomes, then, a paramount issue.

2. *Reinforcement of Novel Responses:* Students are generally unaccustomed to thinking divergently, as historically it has not been reinforced. In fact, inhibition has frequently been learned, making it very difficult to be creative when the opportunity exists. Therefore, the school must be very sensitive to the creative efforts of students and use whatever influence it has to help a student feel a sense of accomplishment for a creative effort. This might mean displaying enthusiam and interest for an idea that the teacher either doesn't understand, or doesn't appreciate.

3. *Provision for Independent Study:* It has been shown that creative children prefer to work on their own (Torrance, 1964, p. 114). This does not mean that in order to be creative a child *must* study on his own, but only that whenever a child wants to pursue his or her efforts independently, it should not only be allowed, but encouraged. This may seem like a minor and rather simple point, but when one looks at the structure of our schools, the problem can become almost insurmountable. Independent study does not mean being allowed to go to the library, although that might be a place where a student wants to visit. It means being free to go wherever his interests take him whenever the urge is present for as long as necessary. In other words, it means being free to approach a problem in a unique, hopefully divergent manner. It means providing an alternative for in-class instruction.

Allowing for and encouraging creativity in children also can present problems, particularly in a norm-referenced milieu such as the public school. Creative behavior may alienate peers, as the process of creating frequently requires a person to adhere to divergent values or deviate from age and sex norms. The role of the teacher and the school is to help all parties accommodate to these differences rather than to react to them. Independence and autonomy are frequently required for a true creative effort! In some cases, this is likely to require that a teacher radically personalize each student's program, perhaps meeting as a total group rarely or not at all. There can be no doubt that the promotion of creative and divergent behavior will require major revisions in the concept of a typical school program. In fact, one could conceive of a component of the school program that never meets in the usual sense of the word. Creative behavior and alternative educational strategies seem to be made for each other.

THE TWENTIETH CENTURIES

Postman and Weingartner (1969, p. 10) in their popular *Teaching as a Subversive Activity* make use of a dramatic illustration of the "Change Revolution" by visualizing events on a clock face representing 3,000 years and a minute equalling about 50 years. In this frame of reference, they tell us, the automobile appeared ten minutes ago and antibiotics about a minute ago. Television is ten seconds old.

What they did not include in this exciting metaphor was the chronology of significant changes in the way societies educate their children, and perhaps it's just as well. In spite of the fantastic growth in technology and the concurrent multiplicity of "things to be known," we adhere to the techniques initiated at least two or three minutes ago according to the "change" clock, while an analysis of the situation suggests we ought to be changing on a second-by-second basis.

Other factors intensify this situation also. People, particularly young people, are far more mobile than were their parents (and in many cases, teachers). Even in the day-to-day activities of high school students, it is not unusual for them to travel many miles into many different communities, face many different decisions and respond in a manner so flexible that, if their parents were aware, would cause a great deal of anxiety. Students have attempted to articulate this inconsistency between their reality and the reality of their teachers and their parents. They have created the concept of the "generation gap." They have talked about the lack of credibility in the older generation. They have held demonstrations, protest meetings, and strikes. The signals have been strong and the message has been clear to those who chose to listen and to try and understand. The problem is that too few people associated with schools have listened—have responded. This can probably be understood within the context of a frightened generation attempting to maintain and transmit their information and their values to those who will soon be leaders. The problem that educators have refused to face is that many of our children see our values, and our information as either irrelevant or, even worse, unworthy of them. Schools have not faced the fact that this rapidly changing world demands new strategies, a new curriculum, a restructuring of conventional values and a general revamping so great that it is probably incomprehensible to many of us.

Marshall McLuhan (1964) coined the term and developed the concept of the "global village." Most of us have probably admired the ingenuity of the concept, thought a minute or two of its application to the world we live in and then dismissed it. We haven't yet understood that *our* conception of the world has to be very different from that of our children. Consider the impact of the civil rights movement of the 1960s. The fact that white America had been performing atrocities on black Americans has never been a secret. Prior to 1960 most of us were aware of Jim Crow. We knew that dual school systems existed. Separate living and dining accomodations were hardly skeletons in America's closet. Yet, it wasn't until one could watch this treatment on television that people were mobilized to action. These were, for the most part, young people. However, the activity of a twenty-one-year old college student in the early 1960s of marching in Selma or helping to register black voters in Mississippi is seen by the twenty-one-year old college student of the early 1970s as a dark moment in American history. How many history teachers can view this movement in a historical perspective rather than as a current event?

The modern day college student was somewhere between seven and ten years old when he saw black Americans fire-hosed into submission, when he saw dogs used to attack nonwhite demonstrators, when he saw electric cattle prods used to inflict pain on human beings. The callousness of the acts is not the point, but an analysis of the influence and impact on seven-to ten-year-old children who watched it on television should help us understand why the subjects and values being promoted in schools today frequently seem unimportant to our students.

Youth today fully understand the concept of the global village. They do not, for example, see the war in Southeast Asia, or the

Near East for that matter, as a conflict that is so far removed from them as to be unimportant. Politicians are in for a big surprise when they find that the removal of fighting troops from Viet Nam has little or no effect on the youthful opposition to that war. While those of us associated with the "older generation" clearly desire an end to this war as well as future wars, America's children see any war any place in the world, with or without our involvement, as a threat to the peace and security of all people. They view this planet as a unitary "village," not as an unrelated conglomeration of countries, each with its own autonomy and its own problems.

Growing up with television has, to a great extent, been responsible for this phenomenon. Those of us who grew up with the radio find it very difficult to understand the point of view expressed so frequently, in so many different ways by American youth. Yet, the inability to understand, particularly on the part of educators, intensifies the crisis which we find ourselves currently facing.

The point of all these examples is that the frightening speed with which technology has changed the world has created a dangerous vacuum in the adaptability of established institutions. Education is just one of those institutions like government and the church, but it is probably the institution where the greatest possibility for change exists. It is also the institution that comes in contact with nearly every child born in America. What is required is that those charged with the responsibility of educating America's children recognize the crisis and open themselves to the possibility and the necessity for change. In other words, once again we face the issue that if the institution of education is to survive, alternatives must be found.

What form shall these alternatives take? Given the confusion that exists and the lack of understanding that educators have exhibited toward their charges, it would seem that the question must remain open. The only principle to which we should adhere is that education has in the past and should in the future remain a public institution designed to offer equal educational opportunity to all children. After that, it would appear logical to look toward the student, confused as he is, for some direction. We must strive for an understanding and acceptance of reality as defined by the student if we are to help that student profit from twelve to fifteen years of interaction with the system. It simply makes no sense to proliferate a series of experiences which have been instrumental in creating the problems we now face.

The last few paragraphs do not argue for any specific approach or suggest that particular programs must be developed. Instead, the intent has been to develop a rationale based on the rapid rate of growth in many different areas in the twentieth century which simply underscores the need for an educational system that listens to its clients and is open to whatever changes prove helpful. The problems are too grave to suggest that such changes must be structured within the framework of the six hour, fifty-minute period with which we are so familiar. Programs of change based on some rationale must be attempted, with a feedback system sensitive, not only to those who administer the programs, but also to those who are the program recipients. It is neither possible nor wise to suggest what those programs will be, but it seems likely that they will include a massive retreat from the classroom with which we are so familiar.

Titling this section the twentieth "centuries" was not a typographical error. The rapid pace of development has crammed the historical equivalent of many centuries into about three-quarters of the twentieth. Not only have the technological aspects of civilization "growed" like Topsy, but so have art, music, and literature—those elements so frequently viewed as timeless.

The challenge facing us is immense. Whether or not we can assimilate sufficient understanding of the world to accommodate it is a crucial and frightening question. The role of education must be to facilitate this understanding by allowing previously unheard of flexibility for both its students and its teachers. We must explore together the multitude of possible ways that learning and understanding can occur. To make a plea for alternatives to in-class instruction is a tremendous understatement of the need—the real need is for survival.

SUMMARY

The concepts presented in this chapter were neither new nor startling; they weren't intended to be. Instead, well-established principles in the areas of learning, cognitive development and creativity were selected for the purpose of building a rationale and basis supporting many types of educational strategies. The only commonality was the need to leave the classroom, the school building, and sometimes the community. No argument was presented for specific alternatives, and this, too, was intended. The purpose has been to stimulate educational practioners to attempt new and varied techniques.

The source of the potential activities for schools of the future will have to come not only from those charged with the responsibility for teaching, but also from their students, from parents, from the communities that are affected by education, and finally from any other source willing to address itself to the current crisis.

The need exists, the resources are all around us, the skills to evaluate are abundant, the impetus to begin is all we have been waiting for. The contention of the last part of this selection was to build an argument for such a catalyst. History, if we have one, will have to judge our willingness to adapt. If it's true that necessity is, in fact, the mother of invention, then perhaps there is hope.

References

Bruner, Jerome S. *The Process of Education*. New York: Vintage Books, 1963.

Baldwin, Alfred L. *Theories of Child Development*. New York: John Wiley and Sons, Inc., 1967.

Flavell, John H. *The Developmental Psychology of Jean Piaget*. Princeton: D. Van Nostrand Company, Inc., 1963.

Furth, Hans G. *Piaget for Teachers*. Englewood Cliffs: Prentice-Hall, Inc., 1970.

Ginsburg, Herbert and Opper, Sylvia. *Piaget's Theory of Intellectual Development: An Introduction*. Englewood Cliffs: Prentice-Hall, Inc., 1969.

Holt, John. *How Children Fail*. New York: Delta Publishing Co., Inc., 1964.

McLuhan, Marshall. *Understanding Media: The Extensions of Man*. New York: McGraw-Hill Book Company, 1964.

Postman, Neil and Weingartner, Charles. *Teaching as a Subversive Activity.* New York: Delacorte Press, 1969.

Russell, Charles. *Children's Thinking.* Boston: Ginn and Company, 1956.

Torrence, E. Paul. *Guiding Creative Talent.* Englewood Cliffs: Prentice-Hall, Inc., 1962.

9

The True Alternative or
Convert 'Em or Kill 'Em

RUSSELL C. DOLL

> We ordain that the name of Catholic Christians shall apply to all those who obey this present law. All others we judge to be mad and demented; we declare them guilty of the infamy of holding heretical doctrine; their assemblies shall not receive the name of churches. They shall first suffer the wrath of God, then the punishment which in accordance with divine judgment we shall inflict.
>
> "Codex Theodosianus, 438 A.D."
> *History of the Byzantine State*

> But it is no wonder that you deny the Mahdiship, for you did not believe in the apostleship of Mohammed; but the wonder is that the learned men of wickedness, who are raised to prominent position, and whom God has left to go astray, and whose hearts he has closed, whose ears he has sealed, and over whose eyes he has put a veil . . . and have taken you as a teacher, have waged war against Believers. . . . If you are content to remain as you are, then prepare for what shall come; but if you knock at the door of repentance, peradventure it may be opened unto you.
>
> Letter to General Gordon from
> Abdullah Mohammed during the
> siege of Khartum, 7th or 8th
> December, 1884

This volume is intended to provide the reader with alternatives to in-class teaching. One of the problems in offering alternatives to

---

Written especially for this book. Dr. Doll is an Associate Professor in the School of Education, University of Missouri-Kansas City.

anything, whether they be alternatives in religion or in education, is that, over time, the alternatives become the doctrine. Those who happen to see the alternatives as good things flock to the feet of the founding prophets and become the converts and disciples, bent on proselytizing and gaining other converts. In the early stages the proselytizers are often seen as being mad and demented. The proselytizers tend to see those outside of the teachings of the alternative as having a veil over their eyes, closed hearts and sealed ears. If the alternative gains official recognition it must then be followed by all or they suffer the consequences. The followers of the former Truths have now become the heretics.

Little wonder that we end up, again, with no alternatives, unless some new prophets want to offer their alternatives. And so to their feet would come new disciples as intent as the former in making everyone else see the truth of their word and to follow the teachings. Thus, another alternative would be well on its way to the elimination of other alternatives—except the one proposed.

Obviously, then, a major problem in offering and implementing alternatives is to remember that they must remain alternatives. There is no *one* educational approach that should be followed by everyone. Unfortunately, however, we find an alternative which works in one situation and with one group and tend to implement it in all situations, for all groups, and especially for every person working with the same situations in which the alternative has been proven.

It is this kind of thinking which leads to the general paranoia found among teachers. It leads to teachers being forced into "subversion" in their classrooms. And I am speaking here as well, of the good traditional teachers who get results in their *own* way and cannot follow the doctrinaire alternative. They are the heretics under the Codex Illivichianus or Codex Goodmanus.

This kind of thinking also forces the nontraditional teacher into an "underground" classroom situation as she is besieged by her principal who wants more order and quiet, less frills and more drills.

But if the alternatives work why should there not be a policy to implement them across the board? If we know open classrooms, storefront schools, schools without walls, and schools relating to communities seem to produce better results, certainly teachers should be encouraged to follow them. They should see what the prophets have done and in seeing, *believe.*

It is not as simple as that. There are a number of compelling reasons (in Codex Doll) why most approaches to educational training, organization, etc., should remain as alternatives. The first reason relates to the prophets; the second to the disciples and the great unwashed; and the third to the teachers and pupils.

THE PROPHETS

Quite often those proposing alternatives are exceptional people in the highest sense. They can not only provide good reasons for the alternatives and construct models upon which actions are to be based, but they are usually successful in implementation. The problems arise later when the not-too-exceptional people have to deal with the exceptional ideals and ideas. The problem of both the prophet and education becomes that which was faced by a missionary in a cartoon in an issue of *Saturday Review.* A rotund missionary with habit and clerical collar is pictured running from a hut with a pained expression on his face. He is waving a Bible and running towards a group of African natives dancing in homage around a gigantic statue of the selfsame missionary. The missionary is shouting, "No! No! That's not what I mean."

An example of the dangers inherent in the latter point may be seen in the almost unqualified acceptance of the position of two prophets who have expressed their ideas in the books *36 Children* and *Death at an Early Age.* [1] The positions have led to the development and acceptance of an educational model which is considered to be an outstanding alternative and one which is urged on many teachers. [2]

Both men have written books outstanding in their sensitive portrayal of children caught in the web of low-income life and the meat grinder of large urban school systems. They deal with the successes of understanding teachers. Unfortunately, some ideas are advanced which, though not necessarily the primary message, have been the key points frequently emphasized by the media, by lay people, college professors, and those engaged in teacher education. The messages are:

1. If teachers would only have more empathy, dedication, and higher expectations for their children, as have these authors, the children would learn.

2. Children will learn if teachers were as creative and energetic in their instructional approaches and construction of materials as were these authors.

3. Teachers, like the authors, can triumph over great odds if they only want to do so (the "teacher-up-by-the-bootstraps" idea).

4. The "system" is screwed up and stultifies creative teachers.

It is hard to disagree with the last point. The first three are almost truisms and rather innocuous. Yet, an uncritical acceptance of the first three points has taken place and these points are often included as critical parts of teacher training models and, in some instances, they receive the main emphasis. This would raise problems for teachers going into high problem oriented schools in a big city.[3]

The problem lies in the emphasis on the simplistic "empathy" approach. To suggest that love, understanding, and dedication will carry the day over the multitude of socio-psychological dynamics with which the average teacher is faced is irresponsible. This is not to deny that love, understanding, and dedication are needed. But a model of teacher behavior based solely on the experiences of the authors of books of this type overlooks many important differences between the men writing these books and the average teacher. The major differences are as follows:

1. Offering these experiences as a model is unrealistic. For one thing, the average teacher is just that—average. He is an average person who, as often as not, happens to be bright, likes children, and wants to assist them in learning. He is somewhat like his college professor. The authors of the books are not average. They are exceptionally talented and creative in regard to teaching. In fact, they are probably more talented and creative than are those critics and reformers offering them as models.

2. Studies have shown that a teacher's sense of demoralization, threat, and lowered self-esteem are related to behavioral problems

and negative student attitudes. The problems and negative attitudes increase in frequency and intensify around the sixth grade. In highly problem oriented, and to a lesser degree, in partially problem oriented schools, the teacher's main concerns are control of student behavior and coping with "hostility." After the sixth grade the teachers must cope with both a deprivation of skills and a growing pattern of behavioral disruption, overt, and covert hostility. In the lower grades the teacher's concern seems to be a skills or academic concern. Behavioral problems, while present in the lower grades, are not as upsetting to the teacher as in the upper grades.

The authors advocating the "affective" techniques have taught in the beginning middle grades. One of the most influential of these authors taught not only in the early middle grades but he also taught the brightest of the groupings. The authors' potential for success was certainly enhanced by the type of teaching situations in which they worked. Their potential for the development of positive relations was enhanced. To extrapolate these instructional successes and positive "emotional" experiences to all grades, as has been done, is to ignore some basic socio-psychological dynamics which the teacher might face in grades beyond the fifth or sixth.

3. The most potent demoralizing factor teachers in highly problem oriented schools face is the cumulative effect of years of responding to the needs and problems of many students and parents; the cumulative effect of daily and yearly physical and emotional drain; the cumulative effect of having to, year after year, day after day, give one's *all* in motivation, technique, and preparation, and receive only a modicum of return. In regard to this point, consider a similar situation at Fort Benning, Georgia. A young soldier, newly returned from Korea, was stating proudly to a group of grizzled old World War II and Korean veterans, "I was in the line for ten months." "Shucks, sonny," one veteran replied, "that's not enough time to know if you're scared or not."

The authors of these books have never faced the situation of having to maintain *yearly* the teaching pace and emotional involvement reported in the books. They went in, did their thing, gave it their all, gathered their impressions and data and then they got out. They wrote a book and became instant experts. It is questionable whether, over the long run, these professional writers could have kept up the pace and continued their great emotional investments at the level suggested as models for teachers. Indeed, it is questionable whether those in university courses presenting Kohl and Kozol as models could keep it up for very long. These points are not meant to denigrate the fine work reported in the books mentioned and in similar works. They are meant to point out the differences between the ongoing teaching situation the average teacher must face as opposed to the short exposure these brilliant and creative men have had to a teaching situation. People not having had extensive contact with problems of urban education might see, as have much of the media, university professors and lay public, the affective model as an answer to urban school problems.

But the affective model has its basis in an artificial situation. It is a popular kind of model because in its simplicity it is easy to grasp and in its abundance of feeling it is nice to contemplate.

But utilizing this model alone has already taken its toll in some instances. The writer has been deeply involved in a number of special urban teacher training programs, including a two-year Teacher Corps program. The world of reality was shattering to even those deeply committed, sensitive and socially aware youngsters. Much of the fault for their initial disillusionment can be traced to their unqualified adaptation of the "love-'em-and-all's-OK" school of thought reflected in these books. Youngsters in these programs (and other teachers as well) possessing creative energies and empathy rivaling those of the authors, began to slow down, stall, and give up after about three years. For primary grades the decline was not so severe nor so soon.

It is simply unfair to teachers to allow them to think that the success of the author-teachers can be duplicated year after year simply with understanding, love and creativity. It is unfair to expect and demand that all teachers follow this particular model. To think this particular alternative can or should be used by all everywhere is to court disaster. To enforce it by the district, university, etc., is to play the role of grand inquisitor to the heretics.

THE DISCIPLES AND THE GREAT UNWASHED

It has usually been the case with disciples, before the appearance of the prophet, that they have an idea something is wrong. The problem is they are not bright or creative enough to make an accurate analysis, nor do they have the natural talent, or a skill with words, or the charisma to start the movement. It is also the case that disciples tend to be more rigid in their interpretations and teachings than the prophets. At the same time disciples are, or seem to be, maybe by virtue of their proximity to ideas central to certain tenets, brighter and more creative than the Great Unwashed whom they are to instruct.

So it is with those in the universities, in our case professors of education, who provide the greatest number of active disciples and proselytizers for certain alternatives. There is a tendency to consider the college as the temple; to consider the pilgrim-students as the great unwashed; to frown on deviation from the teaching of The Word, especially if The Word is an "alternative" they are offering.

Frowns deepen as pilgrims may argue alternatives based on their experiences during their pilgrimage through the real world. Too often the frowns are indications that the disciples have lost contact with worlds beyond The Word and are presenting "alternatives" as dogma applicable to all situations. The College based disciples can come to view those not embracing the pure dogma as well-nigh doomed sinners. Unfortunately, viewing others in this fashion is not conducive to rapport and heightened creativity.

Because of doctrinal rigidity, alternatives are often forced upon preservice teachers and teachers in in-service training which cause more harm than offer help. Many of these alternatives are adopted only on the surface while the teachers continue the academic equivalent of the Black Mass in their classrooms, using methods which, while not the alternatives given them in college, are the alternatives more appropriate to the classroom in the real world.

TEACHERS AND PUPILS

Much is said of the Procrustean Bed to which pupils are made to conform. Little is said of the Procrustean Bed of alternatives into which teachers are all too often forced. There is a certain irony in the fact that many of the alternatives to in-class teaching are offered to help meet students' individual differences. *Yet the teacher's individual styles of teaching are totally ignored in many of these approaches.*

If we are serious in providing alternatives then we must seriously consider the differences in personality, ways of relating to students, perceptions, etc., among classroom teachers. The differences cannot be pushed into one teaching style or alternative to make an effective teacher. If it is a marvel that God works in mysterious ways, then Lord, the mystery of what makes an effective teacher is also a marvel. If in His house are many mansions, then there certainly ought to be room in many classrooms for different kinds of teaching styles and different alternatives. Those who argue for open classrooms over more traditional; who argue departmental over self-contained; who argue John Holt over Miss Dove, who argue free self-expression over structured progression, are not arguing alternatives but arguing doctrine. Of course, the same may be said of those who argue the opposite. The real question is: Do we provide alternatives to allow the teacher to be most effective in his own right, or do we provide alternatives which best suit our concept of The Right?

If teachers have individual teaching styles which might be enhanced or hampered by particular alternatives, children have particular learning styles, personality characteristics, backgrounds, cultural characteristics, etc., which might be enhanced or hampered by particular alternatives. Further, certain children have particular learning needs, related to kinds of learning models and environments, which cannot be met within the frameworks of some alternatives. The styles and needs might even violate every basic tenet of proposed enlightened alternatives.

In one of the most significant, albeit overlooked, books to come out in many moons, David Hunt reports on his research relating to the development of a model which helps to match student and teacher; student need and teacher style; student need and teacher style and learning environment. Hunt states in his preface:[4]

> ... The relation between a student and the educational environment may be viewed in terms of how well they are matched for certain purposes ... For example, a structured lecture may be well matched to

students who are compulsive and authoritarian, but poorly matched for independent students. In this example, matching refers to the likelihood of a certain outcome—an acquisition of information, for example—resulting from a certain person-environment combination. Well matched combinations are more likely to produce the desired results . . . than are poorly matched, or mismatched combinations.

He continues in the text:

There is a lack . . . knowledge (regarding 'match' because of) the failure to take seriously the implications of an interactive model that coordinates the effects of educational environments upon particular types of students to produce specific objectives. Individual differences are given much lip service, and even more drawer space in the form of filed test results, yet educational planners and decision makers continue to work from models for the student in general. To ignore the importance of differential student characteristics leads to questions about the general effectiveness of educational procedures, such as whether a discovery approach is more effective than a structured approach. No account is taken of the differential effectiveness of such approaches on different kinds of students.

In a bit of conceptual, theoretical and research virtuosity, Hunt makes a case for environmental variation in teaching and the offering of alternatives. Some students do need high degrees of structure. A teacher would be guilty of academic, social and personal murder to apply the ideas of Goodman, Kohl and Illich to them. In other cases, teachers would be guilty if they didn't provide alternatives proposed by Goodman, et al. It should also be kept in mind I am speaking, too, only of teachers whose style and effectiveness fits into the alternatives offered by the above mentioned prophets.

In no way should teachers be told The Word must be given to all children in one fashion. In no way must an enlightened alternative (storefront school, open classroom, British Primary, discovery method, etc.) be accepted as an alternative for students. Students and teachers work best under different alternatives. The task is to find out which alternative is best for whom.

Perhaps a personal experience makes this point. The author grew up in the Back of the Yards area in Chicago. Most of us ate teachers alive and used their bones to sharpen our teeth. Well meaning teachers attempted to "love" us (we wanted only respect) and to "let us learn by doing" (we needed definite and structured help) and "discover ourselves" (we interpreted this as not giving a damn) and we became so frustrated, so lost—and so cruel. When we got to the tough teachers (structured, good discipline, take-no-crap) we straightened up and flew right. We achieved academically and behaviorally and found pride in ourselves by so doing.

There *were* kids in our school, however, who *responded* to "love" and did their "discovery of themselves" and related to "those" teachers. They liked "those" teachers and died under the "tough" ones. Both groups needed different "alternatives."

BENEDICTION

Thus, alternatives are doomed to failure in an across-the-board implementation simply because too many people of differing ideas, temperaments and skills will be involved. It will be impossible to implement the alternative as presented by the prophet because too often small bands of dedicated people are the best ones to implement the alternatives.

Once an across-the-board implementation is attempted, the real world demands too many compromises to the spirit of the idea. The Grand Inquisitor in Dostoyevsky's *The Brothers Karamazov* sentenced Christ to die at the stake upon His second coming. He did not want Christ to mess up the adaptations made in the teachings in order that the teachings might fit the needs and realities of the world and the weaknesses of men. The Inquisitor knew that if the teachings were to be viable not only among the elect, wholesale change was needed. The Grand Inquisitor knew the world could not take the word as given. He knew the commandment to preach to the nations was unrealistic if it was expected that no major changes had to be made to implement a small part of the teachings.

If alternatives are going to work as planned and proposed, then careful selection of disciples and cathedrals, synagogues, mosques, etc. must precede implementation, as well as an understanding that adhering to the Faith is not enough. What is needed is an assurance that a systems approach will be considered in the implementation.

For example, in Louisville, Kentucky the faculties were changed in fourteen schools and replaced with volunteers expressing the aim of the program of the schools and teachers who were selected as those most likely to be able to implement the programs. Further, there was special training given and a concentration of aid. In Kansas City, a school was staffed with teachers specially trained for a particular kind of educational approach as well as volunteers who agreed with the program goals.[5] To have implemented the programs without selection and help would have been disastrous, although even with the help and selection things are still a bit sticky.

Even in these situations, in which a match of teacher-idea-system is attempted, there are those who will change their minds. There must be other alternatives for them. And so, if eternal vigilance is the price of political liberty, then eternal awareness of differences and the providing of many alternatives is the price of truly believing in the liberty offered by educational alternatives.

FOOTNOTES

1. See Herbert Kohl, *Thirty-Six Children* (New York: American Library, 1968) and Jonathan Kozol, *Death at an Early Age* (New York: Bantam Books, Inc., 1968).

2. Assisting in this acceptance of one of the Prophets was his public "crucifixion" by the Boston School District. As Peter Weiss said in Marat/Sade, "Crucifixion is the most sympathetic way to go, and Lord knows, every movement does need its martyrs, self-made or no."

3. The most difficult school of a four school typology based on the functioning of the school's social system. The typology, school characteristics and implications for urban educational improvement are reported in: Russell C. Doll, *Variations Among Inner City Elementary Schools: An Investigation into the Nature and Causes of Their Differences.* Center for the Study of Metropolitan Problems in Education, Kansas City, Missouri, June, 1969. Russell C. Doll, *Types of Elementary Schools in a Big City,* unpublished Ph.D. dissertation, University of Chicago, December, 1969.

4. David D. Hunt, *Matching Models in Education: Coordination of Teaching Methods with Student Characteristics.* Ontario, Canada: Ontario Institute for Studies in Education, 1971, pp. v, 1.

5. In another school in Kansas City an attempt is being made to provide alternatives without selection but with special help and inservice training. It is meeting with some resistance, but progress is being made.

Part Two
Alternatives in Higher Education

We have seen the development of many alternative programs in higher education. Some of these—Peace Corps and Vista—offer experiences of another type than the university curricula; they have different objectives. Teacher Corps, however, includes alternatives designed to meet many of the usual objectives of the professional education component of a teacher education program. The alternatives in Teacher Corps programs were mainly secured by an unusual emphasis on field centered—public school—experiences. Other aspects of Teacher Corps—community service—required alternatives to meet essentially new objectives.

To begin this section of the book, Richard Graham, the former director of Teacher Corps, discusses that program as well as the entire gamut of alternatives aided by federal project funds. It still remains to be seen if the strategy of funding areas of strength and excellence in the hope that other institutions will observe and adapt the new practices will prove successful. Unless there is firm commitment to the alternative way of learning by important elements of the funded institution, the alternative can vanish with the expiration of the federal grant. This point, made by Graham, needs to be applied to alternatives of any type. Institutional commitment is necessary for success beyond the experimental stage. Additional funds are helpful, but they are certainly not sufficient influence to make a lasting difference.

Graham writes from a new perspective in the Washington office of a new full-scale alternative to in-class teaching—The University Year for Action. Readers will need to keep in mind the difficulty of this accomplishment—persuading universities to award credit for experience primarily earned in a service role external to the university. The difficulties of this activist role as well as the opportunities are highlighted again by the experiences of Antioch East. Because of the importance of this move to off-campus college experience, it is represented by another selection as well.

Outward Bound is something else. The rather complete account of one such program is included in the hope that administrators will see parallels in the radically different environments surrounding their institutions. Whether one accepts the notion of challenge to the extent involved in Outward Bound or not, the concept of group and independent exploring and self-testing is worthy of consideration.

Needless to say, these are but a hint of the alternative arrangements in higher education. Some involve learning in the usual fashion but in unusual surroundngs—prisons, barges, sailing vessels. Adelphi University has recently arranged with the Long Island Railroad to offer four courses on commuter trains. Other than the unique classroom, however, this need not differ from the same instruction on campus. These are not, then, really alternatives to in-class teaching any more than the familiar extension courses. Even some of the "nonestablishment" student arranged experiences resemble the usual classroom approach to learning.

The awarding of credit by testing is not really an alternative since no attention is given to the way in which the ability is acquired, merely to the evaluation. Many institutions award credit to veterans for minor areas conceivably mastered during the service experience. These are usually not evaluated and are in some respects similar to the five point head start given veterans on civil service or job placement tests. They are not really alternatives.

Higher education provides both a great potential for improving on the usual classroom mode of teaching as well as a rich tradition firmly opposed to liberalizing sacred elements of the university culture. The experiences of colleagues attempting alternatives are highly visible to the profession. Failures as well as successes will be widely reported. Perhaps added impetus for increasing the options will be created by the influx of new students, themselves graduates of innovative secondary schools.

In this volume we can deal with only a token representation of alternatives in higher education. Those selected should, however, suggest improved tactics to educators at any level. They will certainly point up the problems of articulation.

10

Federal Support for Alternatives

RICHARD GRAHAM

The federal government has in the past few years done much to support the development of alternatives to in-class learning—in higher education and in secondary education—and it will provide greater support in the future. But, the kind of support it should give is open to question as a glance at the number and variety of the programs which receive support from agencies of the federal government will illustrate. An examination of a few of these programs and the recommendations now being made to the Congress should provide a sense of things to come.

The Office of Education has provided support for the development of the University Without Walls. Title III of the Elementary and Secondary Education Act has made possible experiential learning in secondary school; Washington, D.C.'s School Without Walls and the Cherry Creek Colorado Educational Participation in Communities (EPIC) programs, for example, are mostly supported by Title III. The Job Corps, College Work Study, the Neighborhood Youth Corps, Peace Corps, VISTA, federally assisted on-the-job training, apprenticeship programs and cooperative education, the Career Opportunity and New Careers programs, the Teacher Corps and the University Year for ACTION, all provide other examples of federal support for alternatives to conventional in-class schooling.

Written especially for this book. Richard Graham is Special Assistant for Education Programs with ACTION.

Federal support is apt to become more pervasive. Seven of the ten task forces at the recent White House Conference on Youth recommended federal support for off-campus learning, usually in combination with programs of national or community service. Legislation for the support of service-learning programs is now being drafted. Some form of support seems certain, at least for the developmental stages of these programs.

SERVICE-LEARNING

Service-learning is a form of experiential education in which a student works, full-time or part-time, at a job in a day-care center, a drug clinic, an internship as assistant to an alderman, in juvenile offender rehabilitation, as a tutor or in some other public service capacity. A program of learning, with precisely established educational objectives, is developed and agreed to by the student, his instructor and his job supervisor. The job description and the entry-level requirements are prepared by the employer. Job entry level preparation of student candidates is provided by the schools or colleges. Supervision is provided jointly according to an agreement entered into by the school and the public service employer. Where funds are available from Neighborhood Youth Corps, the University Year for ACTION, or a similar program—local, state or federal—the service-learning student will at least be compensated for out-of-pocket expenses for transportation and the like and may receive a stipend.

It is in *service-learning*, rather than in work-study or cooperative education, that the greatest growth can be expected. For, while the number of full-time and part-time jobs in the private sector is limited for young people, the work opportunities in many areas of the public sector is limited only by the resources available for project development, administration, supervision, and for the preparation of students and supervisors for their responsibilities. The total number of available jobs—both public and private—can only be estimated, but we know enough to undertake rapid expansion of program designs which have already proved successful. In the meantime, the National Committee on Secondary Education, with the support of the National Association of Secondary School Principals, is undertaking a study of job availability and, based upon this study, will make recommendations for educational alternatives which would be made available to all young people between the ages of 15 and 21.

It thus seems likely that there will be federal support for rapid expansion of educational alternatives which involve experiential learning. In view of this probability, it seems advisable to examine recent experience with federal programs to consider their problems and their potentials as well. This examination will center on the experience of programs which I know well—on the Teacher Corps and on the newly created University Year for ACTION, both of which provide support for unconventional, field-centered programs of learning.

EXPERIENCE WITH FEDERAL PROGRAMS

To review, the purpose of this book is to provide examples of out-of class learning and to tell how they have fared so that a prospective adoptor/adapter may avoid the pitfalls and exploit the advantages. The Teacher Corps and the University Year for ACTION program will, therefore, be examined as federally supported programs which possess certain advantages and disadvantages in common.

The principal advantages of federal programs, other than of outside support for a locally-designed project, are in a commonality of project design. This provides an ability, because of the experience of others, to state purposes with some clarity, to be exposed through guidelines, seminars and technical assistance programs to the thoughts of people who are running similar projects elsewhere. It gives access to the products of their work—to the learning protocols they have produced, to agreements for learning which they have developed, to their research designs and to their techniques for long-term planning and plan management.

The outside resources which a federal program brings may be enough to tip the scales within a college or school system, to provide support sufficient to enable a group of faculty and administrators to undertake a program that would not otherwise have been possible. The resources may give them the power within their own organization to make the changes they see as needed. When federal programs are undertaken for this purpose, they are treated seriously and they offer some promise for change. But where a Teacher Corps or University Year for ACTION project has been taken on as a "federal program" to be run by the school or college, as a program apart from the major interests of the school or college, then it is not likely, therefore, that there will be clarity of purpose, that there will be clearly understood criteria for project success in achieving those purposes, or that there will be an effective program of evaluation to determine whether the project has met these criteria. Moreover, even if the project is successful according to the criteria, the reforms probably will not be adopted.

The purposes of federal programs generally are to provide support for needed services which could not otherwise be provided or to provide support for educational reform according to national priorities but also, within guidelines, according to local design and management. The federal programs to be examined here fall in the second category—national priorities—and, hence, should be judged not only on how well local project designs work out, but, in addition, they should be judged on the degree to which successful designs are adopted and continued with funding from local sources.

TEACHER CORPS

The Teacher Corps, because of substantial size and six years of experience, probably provides one of the best examples of a federally-supported program of out-of-classroom learning. It has implications not just for teacher education but for experiential education everywhere, for secondary and higher education alike.

Teacher Corps projects are developed jointly by school systems and nearby universities which, together, call upon community groups, teacher organizations, student representatives and state departments of education for help in the project design. Typically, a Teacher Corps project calls for the service and training of twenty to fifty teacher interns who serve with experienced teachers and other school personnel in teams having responsibility for the learning of a group of children. The interns are generally young college graduates many of whom have majored in a field other than education or they may be upper division undergraduates in teacher education.

With increasing frequency, the schools view the projects as a means of developing a complex of "portal schools" which are used by a school system as a means to train new teachers, to retrain present personnel and to introduce new curricula, new teaching methods and new staffing patterns. These portal school projects are viewed also as a means to establish new links with the outside community; with parents and with agencies which can assist with outside-of-school learning. In all projects, the universities use the program to help introduce and test a program of competency-based teacher education. One of the purposes of the Teacher Corps is to "encourage colleges and universities to broaden their programs of teacher preparation" and, by this means, to help achieve the major purpose, the improvement of educational opportunities for children from low-income families. The way that the Teacher Corps was to help colleges broaden programs was through internships—experiential, out-of-class learning. Though student teaching has long been a feature of most programs of teacher education, it has generally been viewed as an exposure to teaching and to schooling the way it is. A reexamination of the effects of traditional student teaching exposed it as mostly a form of apprenticeship to existing practice and, frequently, a modeling by student teachers after the worst of practices.[1]

Clearly, these methods of out-of-classroom learning in teacher education were in need of improvement, and it became the purpose of the Teacher Corps to support that improvement. Fortunately, a design for doing so became available in late 1968. The first reports were then being released on the "models of elementary teacher education," the design of which had been supported at nine universities by grants from the Bureau of Research of the Office of Education. In contrast with traditional student teaching, which is characterized by ill-defined learning objectives, the models called for internships through which precisely defined learning objectives would be achieved. All of these designs were "performance based," that is, as described by Stanley Elam,

> In performance-based programs, performance goals are specified and agreed to in rigorous detail in advance of instruction. The student preparing to become a teacher must either be able to demonstrate his ability to promote desirable learning or exhibit behaviors known to promote it. He is held accountable, not for passing grades but for attaining a given level of competence in performing the essential tasks of teaching; the training institution is itself held accountable for producing able teachers. The emphasis is on demonstrated product or output.[2]

Unlike traditional student teaching, academic credit was not to be given for experience but for the attainment of learning objectives which would be realized by virtue of experience backed up by study which would give context to the experience. The "models," and the Teacher Corps programs on which they were based, represented a highly significant departure from commonly accepted practices in out-of-classroom learning.

There are, of course, a number of other designs for out-of-classroom learning. Cooperative education programs in which students alternate between periods of conventional university study and work experience in related fields probably has the longest, modern day, experience with out-of-classroom learning in higher education.[3] Cooperative education jobs are intended to complement classroom study and to give it relevance. But the learning to be achieved while on the job is seldom precisely defined; indeed, a spokesman for cooperative education says that it is better to leave learning objectives loosely defined. He says the important thing is to find a job which presents unquestioned opportunities to learn, for the interests of the student will change as new situations appear; to establish in advance precisely defined learning objectives is as apt to inhibit learning as it is to enhance it.

NEED FOR BEHAVIORAL OBJECTIVES

Both the "models" of teacher education and the Teacher Corps programs are based on views contrary to these. The models and the Teacher Corps programs hold that more will be achieved when precisely defined objectives are agreed upon by the student, his instructor or counselor, and by his employer. Generally they hold that an understanding of what it is to be learned should be formally agreed to in writing and that, in light of experience or changing goals or conditions, the understandings should be changed by amendments which are adopted in the same way as the original agreement. And, because these agreements are directed to the achievement of precise learning objectives, success should be judged by the degree of attainment of the objectives as measured by previously agreed upon criteria, not the amount of time spent on the job or in college classrooms. It is educational output rather than input by which learning should be measured.

The Teacher Corps in 1969 decided to limit its support to institutions which wanted to try out programs of learning which were performance based, programs which would enable a student to pursue his objectives by a variety of means of his own choosing, and within limits, at his own rate. Concurrently with that decision, we decided to examine the long and rather dreary history of nontraditional programs of higher education in the United States, this in an effort to see why so many previous efforts had failed and whether similar failure could be avoided.

It was not hard to find a common reason for the past failure of these programs: Neither students nor faculty liked them. The reason for that appeared to be that faculty and students alike were neither prepared for what they were to do nor to find satisfaction in doing it. Even in the best of these programs some students felt exposed; some professors felt harassed. In programs where the student first determines what he wants to learn, how, how fast, and how his learning is to be measured and then agrees to learn according to his own terms, the burden is personal. If he is uncertain about his purposes or his commitment, it is far more difficult to escape detection than when he can be swept along with others, hide away in classes and get by, provided only that he turn in his papers and take his exams.

The professor, too, is exposed. It is unlikely that he will know all routes to a given end. He must learn with his students, he must continually reevaluate both purposes and means. He becomes less a pontiff, more a guide for fellow explorers. His lecture notes are devalued. In experiential education, he takes on a number of new responsibilities; he must find new sources of satisfaction and prestige. Some of the differences are listed by Albert Wight in his article "Participative Education and the Inevitable Resolution:"[4]

Participative	Traditional
1. Students and instructor define and redefine objectives, using provisional objectives, which are established by instructional staff as a base.	1. Instructor decides on objectives. These may be more implicit than explicit and may or may not be communicated to the students.
2. Students and instructors identify significant problems and questions.	2. Instructor lectures to students or assigns readings on things he thinks they should know.
3. Students identify and make use of available resources to obtain information they need to solve problems.	3. Instructor conducts demonstrations; students observe.
4. Students explore alternative solutions to problems.	4. Instructor assigns practical exercises or problems. Students complete the assignment.
5. Students and instructors examine, compare, and evaluate the various solutions.	5. Instructor prepares tests for knowledge and understanding. Students take the tests.
6. Students and instructors evaluate individual performance and learning needs, and redefine objectives.	6. Instructor evaluates the student's performance and assigns grade.

Because the professor's role is different, and because past history has indicated that the success of experiential programs depends on faculty who are prepared for the job, the Teacher Corps commissioned the development of a series of self-instructional materials for college faculty. Most of these materials are available both in printed and in audio-visual formats.

The experience of Teacher Corps programs seems to lend support to the high expectations for experiential learning. *When adequately prepared,* students and faculty are convinced that these programs provide better education—education which is at least equal in content and is superior in process. Experiential education is superior in the sense that it has helped students to develop habits of self-directed learning.

But, experience to date has confirmed also that it is far easier to start something new than to revise something old. New colleges, which could adopt these programs from scratch and could hire faculty who were committed to the idea, have found that their experiential programs could become operational in a year or two. But well-established colleges and universities found it difficult to carry on their traditional programs and, at the same time, introduce totally new programs of learning. Almost without exception, well-established institutions have either begun piecemeal or have given their go ahead to a small group of faculty who have enrolled a group of students in a special, self-contained program, in effect, a school within a school.

UNIVERSITY YEAR FOR ACTION

Much of the experience of Teacher Corps projects is mirrored in the University Year for ACTION projects which, after only a few weeks of preparation, first got underway in July of 1971. Typically, these ACTION projects consist of thirty to fifty students who serve a year in a poverty community and earn a full year's academic credit. Their work serves a dual purpose: it provides needed services to the poor and it provides an opportunity to learn —from experience and related study—at least as much as would be learned in a conventional college year. As noted in an article which appeared in the February issue of *Change* Magazine:

> The proposals generally call for thirty to fifty students to serve a year in a poverty community. Here is how some of the programs are being carried out:
>
> The participating university takes full responsibility for recruitment and selection of volunteers, for finding work assignments and for the learning and accrediting of the students. But job descriptions and job supervision are furnished by the community organization or the public service agencies which co-sponsor the project. University faculty members plan guided off-campus study which complements the jobs to be performed. ACTION generally covers students' off-campus living expenses of about $200 per month, transportation included, for one year.

The agency also pays the university for student supervision, figured on the basis of one full-time supervisor for ten to fifteen students, plus faculty per diem and travel to and from student work sites. University support from ACTION, not including the stipends paid directly to the students, comes to about $2,500 per calendar year. The student continues to pay his own tuition just as he would for conventional, on-campus study.

The techniques for guiding and measuring academic achievement vary considerably. Some follow the traditional practices of cooperative education or independent study. Others make an effort to correlate on-the-job learning with the content covered in conventional courses. Still others assume that if public service jobs are well matched to a student's interests in sociology, psychology, political science and similar subjects, learning at least equivalent to that achieved in college courses is almost certain to occur and can be shown in logs, reports, case studies and comprehensive examinations. And some institutions require that the content of standard courses be learned by lectures, faculty-led seminars, independent study of course texts and supplementary reading, or a combination of these approaches.

Some institutions also require a formal written agreement between the student and his counselor or professor, in which specific learning objectives are identified along with the criteria for measuring achievement. The professor may suggest a variety of ways for reaching objectives; the student selects from these and agrees with his professor on the approximate rate at which he expects to meet his objectives.

SURVEY OF ACTION PROGRAMS

The University Year for ACTION, although after only a six month period of operation, appears to have provided just the support some institutions needed to initiate or expand their programs of experiential learning. However, a recent survey of the first ten programs indicates that not all the lessons learned elsewhere are being applied. Findings of the survey are reported below.

1. Seven of the ten project directors make reference to agreements for learning; only three institutions indicate that they are now using such agreements. Of those that use agreements, only one submitted a sample form, two said their forms were being revised.

2. The agreements for learning apparently are more precise about what a student is to do than they are about what he is to

learn. The agreements do not appear to apply the techniques developed in the past few years for writing behavioral or performance-based objectives and for specifying criteria for measuring achievement of these objectives. For example, the requirements for three of the six courses for which one volunteer received academic credit were:

Speech 130—3 units: Volunteer will keep record of all speaking engagements. These will be furnished at the end of the trimester for evaluation.

English 360—3 units: Volunteer will keep copies of all business correspondence, schedules, agendas, etc. related to Project (Named). He will also be required to read *The Elements of Style* by William Strunk and E. B. White.

P.E. 128—Bowling—1 unit: Volunteer will keep record of 15 bowling games and turn these in at the end of the trimester.

3. There is little evidence of a well developed research design for determining how well the programs are proceeding with their plans nor how well they are achieving success in establishing alternative means to higher education. Nowhere was there evidence of intent to determine program success on the basis of cost effectiveness in comparison with conventional programs of instruction.

4. Only two of the ten programs require, as a condition of admittance to the program, some evidence of ability on the part of the student to undertake programs of independent study.

5. Five of the programs provide no training for their faculty in the development and administration of experiential learning though this is not surprising in light of the quick start which was necessary. The institutions which do provide faculty training, typically do so by means of seminars or a 'three-day workshop.'

Each of these ten universities indicated that, in addition to their ACTION program, they are awarding academic credit for other programs of independent study or experiential learning. This would suggest that the techniques that have been found to be important to the success of experiential learning have not yet been widely adopted, either in ACTION programs or in comparable university programs elsewhere.

Finally, the ACTION survey indicated that University Year for ACTION, like the early Teacher Corps program, is viewed by most of the universities as a government program with its own purposes and regulations. In only a few universities does it appear that ACTION is seen as a means of support for new designs for learning which the university would like to investigate and, if successful, adopt.

The Teacher Corps and the University Year for ACTION thus point up both the advantages and disadvantages of federal support. The outside support may make it possible to launch a program wanted by a group of administrators or faculty seeking reform, but these outside resources may also act to set the program apart from the regular affairs of the university; they may, as Matthew Miles suggests in his analysis of "temporary systems,"[5] create alienation between the group involved in the federally-supported program and regular faculty or administrators.[6] There may be failure to establish a linkage between systems. As Miles says, "the decisions reached on the cultural island may be unworkable, inappropriate or very difficult to communicate to those on the mainland." Still the expansion of federal support for programs of this kind in higher education seems assured. And federal subsidy for the development of comparable programs at the secondary school level seems equally predictable, though such development is apt to lag by two or three years behind higher education. The arguments for subsidy at the secondary level are even more compelling since secondary education is an acknowledged public responsibility. And, though subsidy from federal, state or local services is probably needed, it is much more apt to be provided if a rationale and general design for service-learning can be agreed upon. I'd suggest the following for a starter.

PROPOSALS FOR SERVICE LEARNING

1. *Subsidies.* Subsidy for the development and administration of a program of experiential learning, for the training of faculty and staff, and for the per pupil costs of instruction, guidance and accreditation, will be approximately the same as the costs to the public for comparable academic achievement through conventional schooling. These subsidies may be divided between school systems and employer to cover, on the one hand, the school system costs

of program development and accreditation and, on the other hand, the employer's costs of administration, supervision and instruction.

2. *Eligibility.* Eligibility for experiential learning will be the same as for conventional schooling except that, as rapidly as possible, all age limitations will be removed for both kinds of learning and participants will be entitled, at any age, to the same amount of municipal, state or federal support for programs of education at the secondary or post-secondary level as he would be if he were to pursue a comparable program by conventional means at a conventional age.

3. *Cost-Analysis.* "Net per-pupil costs" in experiential education will usually be less than in conventional schooling since they will be calculated as the sum or pro rata costs of program development, administration, personnel training and retraining plus the individual costs of instruction, guidance and accreditation, less the value of services rendered by the person in the experiential learning program.

4. *Stipend and Subsidy Determination.* Where the "net per-pupil costs" of the experiential program are, by virtue of the value of the compensatable services rendered, less than the costs of a comparable program of learning to which the participant is entitled through conventional schooling, the participant is paid a stipend roughly equal to the difference between conventional costs and the "net per-pupil costs." By this means, participants who could not otherwise afford to continue with their education, will be able to do so at any convenient time. The effect will be to offer greater equality of educational opportunity.

"Compensatable services rendered" refers to work which is normally paid for by a private firm or public service agency and for which there are funds available. In private firms, funds become available when the benefits of the program exceed the costs by at least normal profit margins, taking into account all benefits and all costs, direct and indirect. In public service agencies, funds become available when the benefits/costs ratio of the service learning program exceeds normal operating benefits/costs ratios, taking into account all benefits and costs, direct and indirect, and when no bargaining agreement, agency regulation or legislative limitation prohibits.

If a company attributes value to the recruitment and training of potential employees, it in effect increases the benefits and hence the benefit costs ratio. If a company or public service agency, by virtue of its participation in the experiential learning program, becomes eligible for a "public interest" grant from a foundation or government agency, the net costs of participation are reduced and the benefits/costs ratio increases.

"Public interest grants" refer to subsidies designed to serve the public interest by (a) influencing career decisions to relieve perceived or anticipated national shortages in such fields as education, health, foreign languages or military service; (b) introducing reforms or sustaining programs which are perceived to be in the national interest, e.g.: programs in support of cooperative education, bilingual education, the right to read, drug education, sex education, the Neighborhood Youth Corps, college work study and other programs for persons in need of financial assistance.

The excess of public sector funds available for education over the *net per pupil costs* must provide stipends large enough to permit many persons to continue their education who would not otherwise be able to do so. And, programs of this kind, with or without stipend, should offer more educational options as to means, content and rate of progress to all Americans at all times in their lives.

Subsidy, as required, will be provided for continuous in-service training of instructional personnel who will be certified, or in some other manner judged to be qualified, on the basis of demonstrated teaching or guidance competencies. These costs will be considered a regular part of program administration.

In private sector jobs, the aggregate value of the subsidy from educational institutions in the public sector, the public relations value, and the benefits of training new employees and retraining present employees must exceed—by normal profit margins—the direct and indirect costs of administration to the employer. (By indirect administrative costs, I refer to complication of bargaining agreements, insurance policies, and the like.)

5. *Essential Conditions.* Programs of experiential learning will be designed and developed by representatives of employers, labor and employee organizations, business associations, local government,

school boards, administration and teacher organizations. In general, the conditions will be that:

a. the employer's subsidy is sufficient to provide incentive for a public agency or business firm to become a participant in the program.

b. the program does not have the effect of taking the job of someone who is or would otherwise be employed and does not adversely affect the promotion, pay increases, working conditions or other rights of regular employees.

c. the programs are open equally to all regardless of race, sex, age or religion.

6. *Agreements.* Educational agencies—secondary schools, technical schools, community colleges, colleges and other post-secondary institutions which provide instructional programs at public expense—will enter into agreements with employers in business firms and public services agencies whereby the employer will:

establish the job descriptions and entry-level job qualifications for participants.

provide on-the-job supervision and administration both for the participant's work and for the job-connected program of study. The supervisor will be a party to this agreement, entered into between the student-participant and a professor or guidance counselor at the educational institution, for what is to be learned by the participant in the experiential program, how he is to learn, and the criteria by which achievement of learning objectives is to be determined.

join with the educational institution in preparing proposals for funding by the College Work-Study Program, the Neighborhood Youth Corps, ACTION, the Teacher Corps, the Community Action Programs, programs of the Environmental Protection Agency, the Law Enforcement Assistance Agency, the High School Dropout program, the Model Cities program, Juvenile Delinquency programs, on-the-job training programs and similar federal, state and local programs.

join with the educational institution, labor and employer organizations to develop program designs which do not adversely affect the job and promotion opportunities of employees who are presently or who would otherwise be employed.

give particular consideration, when job openings permit, to the employment of participants who successfully complete the program and show promise as potential employees.

As its part of the agreement, the educational institution will:

select and prepare students to meet the required entrance level job qualifications.

provide financial support equal to the cost of conventional programs of study which have comparable learning objectives.

establish, with the student, criteria for measuring achievement of learning objectives.

award academic credit and appropriate certificates, diplomas or degrees for the completion of programs of learning.

7. *Liberalize Academic Policies.* Educational agencies will reexamine their policies with respect to experiential learning with a view to liberalizing their regulations with regard to:

awarding academic credit for *prearranged* programs of learning in connection with work or independent study during periods of deferred admission, "stop out" or part-time or full-time employment.

awarding academic credit *retroactively* for demonstrable learning which took place as a result of work or independent study during periods of deferred admission, "stop out" or part-time or full-time employment.

8. *Objectives.* Educational objectives and criteria for measure of achievement will be at least as well defined as in conventional schooling.

Students will be offered an opportunity to achieve at least entry level job qualifications in a field of their interest and one in which employment opportunities are good.

9. *Jobs Available.* The number of part-time jobs available in some areas of the public sector is limited now only by the costs of work program development, by the cost of training, supervision and transportation of participants and by the cost of development

of programs of study which complement the work experience. Tutoring, day care, removal of lead-based paint hazards, monitoring of air and water pollution, preventive health care, and juvenile offender programs provide examples. The number of jobs becomes virtually unlimited when normal per public costs of education are available to supplement the operating budgets of the agencies which administer these programs.

CONCLUSION

Arrangements of this sort will permit rapid growth of out-of-classroom programs. This is true even though the record to date would indicate that experiential learning could either represent a major advance in American education or it could become an educational hoax.

Experiential learning which identifies in advance precise learning objectives and defines precise criteria for achievement—how, where and when achievement is to be demonstrated and to what degree—can help students acquire the habits of self-direction. There is no anomaly in agreeing in advance on precise performance standards for self-directed learning. Much of what we do throughout our lives must measure up to standards, though we may go about it as we will. But if experiential learning is no more precisely defined than to write a report on what you did on the job or on your hitchhike across America, or on your experiences in a drug clinic, or turn in your bowling scores, then it may be a form of learning to be sure, but it will be accidental if the experience provides context and ordering for ideas, a quickening of interests, a stimulus for study, and a responsibility for performance which together will lead to self-directed growth. There would be little reason to consider this kind of learning a proper concern for universities and secondary schools.

Earlier, I suggested that federal programs which are created to promote educational reforms should be judged by the extent that they encourage development of improved designs for education and by the extent that successful designs are adopted and continued with funding from local sources. By these criteria, what measure of success has been achieved by the Teacher Corps or by the University Year for ACTION?

It is clearly too early to attempt evaluation of ACTION's program. And in the presence of many factors favoring the development of experiential learning, it will be almost impossible to determine to what extent ACTION has been responsible for the development of these programs. There is comparable difficulty in assessing the Teacher Corps though it was clearly the first government program to direct its resources exclusively to the support of programs of competency-based teacher education and to the design for experiential learning on which they are, in part, based. Similarly, the Teacher Corps was the first to promise its support exclusively to school systems which would adopt portal schools as a means of school renewal and thus provide a setting for experiential learning which served as a "center of inquiry."[7]

If these designs take hold—as it now appears they will—the Teacher Corps can be counted a success in its past few years of operation. And if so, it would suggest that categorical federal support can provide comparable impetus to the development of programs of experiential learning at the level of secondary schooling as well.

FOOTNOTES

1. B. Othanel Smith, *Teachers for the Real World,* Washington, D.C.: The American Association of Colleges for Teacher Education, 1969, p. 102.

2. American Association of Colleges for Teacher Education. *Bulletin,* Washington, D.C., 24:9, December 1971.

3. For a comprehensive survey of such programs at the secondary school level please see James Buffer's article in Part Three.

4. Albert R. Wight, "Participative Education and the Inevitable Resolution," *The Journal of Creative Behavior,* 1970, pp. 244-282.

5. Matthew B. Miles, "On Temporary Systems," Chapter 19 of *Innovation in Education,* New York: Bureau of Publication, Teachers College, Columbia University, 1964.

6. See also Nathaniel Blackman's analysis of this same phenomenon in his analysis of Metro High in Part Three.

7. The term used by Robert Schaefer in *The School As A Center of Inquiry* to describe a school which has many of the features of a "portal school."

11

The Trials of Antioch East

ELLEN HOFFMAN

> Try to put out of your mind any preconceptions that college education
> necessarily involves a campus with students doing such things as taking
> courses, earning credits, meeting pre-set requirements, getting grades, tak-
> ing tests, doing assignments, or majoring in a subject defined by an
> academic department.
>
> Antioch-Columbia brochure

With these and other brave words six faculty members and about
75 students set out in the fall of 1969 to build the college of the
future in the city of the future.

Most of the faculty members came from Antioch College in
Yellow Springs, Ohio—one of the reform fountainheads of American
higher education—where the idea for the new college originated. The
students came from 29 colleges including Antioch. The "city" where
they chose to build their campus was Columbia, Md., a planned "new
town" billed by its developers as "The Next America." At that time
Columbia's population was around 5,000.

Today Columbia has 12,000 residents, and what started out as
Antioch-Columbia College has become Antioch-Baltimore-Columbia-
Washington College. There are more than 300 students and 14
full-time and about 30 part-time faculty members working out of
three "campuses" as far as 35 miles apart.

Ellen Hoffman, "The Trials of Antioch East," from *Change*, 3:3, May/June
1971, pp. 23-25. Reprinted by permission.

In the beginning the founders were not sure what they wanted, but knew what they did not. "We came in with a negative concept of education ... We had a very down view, pessimistic about American higher education, saying we've been brainwashed, we need to get unprogrammed," recalls Dean Stephen Plumer. In line with this view, Plumer says, the campus became an experiment*ing* one, not experi-men*tal*.

Thus—in what appears to the casual visitor and traditional educator as a chaotic, amorphous educational environment—Antioch-Columbia is pushing for new types of college students, different roles for faculty members, a new curriculum, a flexible physical setting for learning, and new administrative procedures.

Briefly, here is how it approaches each component:

Students: "We will deliberately seek some students who, for financial reasons or because of their social background, would not be likely to attend a liberal arts college," declared the first Antioch-Columbia brochure.

The board of trustees in Yellow Springs is on record in support of "educational diversity and cultural pluralism," and the new campus' avowed aim is to seek students from ethnic minorities, older age groups and varied educational and occupational backgrounds. They are also committed to taking some students considered to be "academic risks."

From a primarily white, middle-class student body in fall 1969, the enrollment has changed to encompass about 30 black and poor-white, inner-city Baltimore residents who hope to use their education for professional advancement and community organization work; some young black students; a number of "dropouts" or "push-outs" from other colleges; and a floating population of largely professional, near or over-30 residents of the new city of Columbia.

Faculty: In addition to faculty trained and experienced in traditional ways, Antioch-Columbia has taken on a variety of adjunct teachers who teach and work on projects with students on a part-time basis. An example is Denis Hayes, national coordinator for "Earth Day" last year, who teaches political ecology. Among the more traditionally trained faculty members are a Ph.D. marine biologist who heads the Human Ecology Center and a theater instructor with experience at other colleges who heads the wide-ranging arts program. In some cases, students themselves teach classes.

Administration: The roles of student, faculty and administrator are intentionally blurred. In addition to teaching classes, students to a large degree hire faculty; the "administrators" of the academic centers are students; and Antioch-Columbia's governing councils are made up of representatives of all three groups. Antioch-Columbia receives no money from Yellow Springs. The budget, which ran about $875,000 in 1970-71 and will be $1.1 million next year, comes from tuition and grants that the school is able to solicit from foundations and government. With one exception, the campus operates on the principle of renting, rather than building, facilities, so there are no long-range construction costs.

The relationship between Antioch-Columbia and the home campus has been a stormy one. After a number of attempts to define the relationship between the two campuses, a study of governance of the whole Antioch community got underway, (Antioch-Columbia is not the only geographically separated Antioch campus), and recommendations on future ties are due to be made public soon. Similarly, the ties connecting the three "geo-centers" of Baltimore, Washington and Columbia, remain in flux. Each is run by a council of faculty and students, with varying methods of selection and responsibility.

In Baltimore and Washington the Antioch programs operate out of faded but substantial rowhouses on the fringes of the inner city. They include classrooms and offices which provide a base for projects in poor communities and for interaction with the establishment in courts, school board offices, etc. A jitney bus that ferries students between the campuses has not proved very successful, and new ways of bringing the physically separated programs together are being sought.

Antioch rents some dormitory space near the Washington center and has been serving as landlord for students living in apartments and townhouses at Columbia. The result has been a lot of outstanding rent. A recent issue of the campus newspaper featured a list of some 60 students owing more than $9,000 in back rent.

The Antioch-Columbia of tomorrow will be housed in an inflatable, vinyl bubble, the first of its kind to be used for an educational institution. Under the guidance of a University of Maryland architecture professor and a student, Antioch students have been experimenting with construction of small "bubbles" in anticipation of constructing one that will span a whole acre and hold up to 200 persons in classes, study halls and seminars.

The bubble will look "like a big barn . . . with nine valleys separated by a system of hills you can't see over," explains architect Rick Ekstrom. Once the materials have been delivered, the $200,000 structure should go up in about two weeks. The bubble will be easily collapsible, so it can quickly be put on a truck and moved to another site, Ekstrom says. In a typically optimistic fashion, the Antioch community is planning to use the bubble starting next fall although the source of the $200,000 has not yet been determined.

Each geo-center shelters certain programs, most of them interdisciplinary and some of them overlapping. There is no such thing as freshman English or an introductory course in biology. The Human Ecology Center at Columbia has taken the new city's environment as its focus. Students and faculty are working on such projects as attempting to get phosphates banned by the community, and to establish a municipal procedure to review and monitor developments in Columbia. The arts program has spawned a cooperative campus-community theater; faculty and students are taking a leading role in organizing and recruiting for the Baltimore arts festival in May.

The Baltimore Center for Social Research and Action offers courses in social theory and problems and encourages students to undertake projects and jobs that bring them into contact with social questions. In Washington, where the program was founded by black students who felt that the Columbia environment was not relevant to their studies, the meat of the curriculum is minority group problems, cultural studies and strategies for giving groups formerly excluded from the political process (urban blacks, Appalachian white, American Indians) a chance to exert influence.

Unlike the traditional Antioch work-study program, in which students alternate between jobs and classes, students at Antioch-Columbia work and study concurrently. Some kind of academic credit is given for the work. The ideal is for each student to work at a job that contributes not only to his income but also to his education. For example, a student chose to work in a psychiatric halfway house. He was then given materials to read on psychology, education and related subjects as a kind of academic tutorial. Plumer believes that even "if a student is a Xerox operator at a government agency . . . he can get an academic experience out of it . . . learn about organizational roles and the sociology of organization" but he admits that such an experience would require strong guidance. He also admits that Columbia's work-study program has not lived up to the hopes for it, and his feeling seems to be shared throughout the institution.

From these brief descriptions of academic programs a few underlying principles emerge:

Strong involvement in the "real world," including the new town, and the urban ghetto.

Individualized courses of study including formal classes, work experience, projects for academic credit and any other needs identified by the student or faculty.

An emphasis on interdisciplinary and intercultural themes.

An emphasis on teaching students how to continue to learn throughout their lives.

The components described in the above sections add up to an institution emanating constant feelings of tension and challenge for both faculty and students.

A faculty member, receiving a call from a student that is termed "a matter of life and death," rushes out to meet him at 10:30 p.m. Faculty members are working 60 to 70 hours a week, according to a committee undertaking a self-study of the campus. "Either we will continue to burn them up at a fantastic rate, or a less demanding method of organizing the campus must be found," says self-study committee chairman Michael Metty.

"This campus talks a lot about cultural pluralism, but hasn't come to grips with what implications the phrase holds . . . Until recently almost all the important decisions were made primarily by white males," says a student. Blacks and whites, poor and middle class, share classes but more of the blacks are concentrated in one or two curriculum areas.

"The files of those planning to graduate in June are in miserable shape," says a self-study committee report. In the frenzy of starting a college from scratch, routine documentation has been overlooked in many cases. It's hard to tell exactly how many students are enrolled where at any time, how many have left formally or just disappeared for a few weeks or months.

"I was going to get my degree in political history. It sounds like what I've been studying. But there might be a problem getting a job teaching in a high school. What would "political history" mean to a superintendent when you're applying for a job? Maybe I'll change it to American history," says a student. Antioch students generally want to make it in the outside world even if they didn't want to make it in a conventional college. They know that they will need a degree if they are to become professionals. The whole question of degrees and accreditation figures prominently in the current self-study. The most specific graduation requirement at the moment is a two-year residency.

Self-study chairman Metty, who heads the Baltimore center as well as the committee, believes that through the study the campus is beginning to pull itself together. And as the prospect of seeking accreditation impinges on the campus (it is seeking approval both as a center of Antioch and as a separate campus), more problems have been unearthed than resolved.

How fast should the campus grow? How can the new sliding scale tuition (from $200 to $3200, depending on ability to pay) provide enough money to operate a campus of the diversity required by such varied student population? Should new students be expected to fit into existing programs or can new programs be undertaken now?

The immediate answers to such questions are being thrashed out on the campus now. The long-range answers can come only through a continuing process of study and evaluation. The concomitant of a continually experimenting college must be continuous evaluation. "Can we learn anything that's worth repeating? If not, why do it?" asks Metty. Yet he acknowledges that "I have to impose a discipline on myself to spend one day a week in self-study" because he has other commitments—particularly to fostering urban social change. He suggests that colleges would have an incentive to experiment if they could postpone accreditation worries until after their early, formative period. A person or group of persons in an experimenting college should take on evaluation as their job, Metty proposes. In return for the guarantee of this systematic research and evaluation, accrediting agencies should waive traditional requirements for, say, five or ten years. At the end of the trial period there would be a body of material to use in extending or withholding accreditation.

The frantic pace of daily life at Antioch-Columbia may be unappealing to many students and faculty who like to feel confident of their role in an institution. Plumer quickly admits that his campus is not an "all-things-to-all-people college." It is a place where persons alienated from the predominating higher education system can come with their ideas about how that system can be made more flexible and responsible without its being destroyed.

12

The Big Move to Noncampus Colleges

ERNEST L. BOYER

In this financially alarming but comparatively strife-free year for American colleges and universities, perhaps the single most dramatic development has been the announcement of several plans to enable students to earn academic credits and even college degrees without having to live on a campus, or even attend classes there.

The new plans have propellants within them that could trigger one of the most significant shifts in the structure of American higher education since the introduction of large-scale, federally financed research during World War II. Phrased in the muffling jargon of educational prose the new proposals may not appear radical, but they do share certain broad assumptions about what higher education really is all about.

For years, the word "college" has to most Americans meant four uninterrupted years in one institution, in a place removed from the diversions of ordinary life. It conjures up nostalgic memories of classroom lectures, fraternity and sorority parties, glee clubs, football weekends, hectic final exams, term papers, trips home for the holidays, beery bull sessions, and romance beside the Virginia creeper. More recently it has also meant protest marches, extracurricular volunteer work, and rock concerts with Joe Cocker or Sly and the

"The Big Move to Non-Campus Colleges," July 17, 1971, *Saturday Review*, by Ernest L. Boyer and George C. Keller. Copyright 1971, Saturday Review, Inc. Ernest L. Boyer is chancellor of the State University of New York. George C. Keller is assistant to the chancellor.

Family Stone. In short, it has been the physical and social aspects of campus life that have traditionally defined "going to college."

Central to most of the new noncampus programs, however, is the assumption that the fundamental process of acquiring a college education need not be dependent upon the familiar campus setting. Not where or for how long a student goes to college, but what actually happens to him intellectually during his collegiate years is what counts. Many innovators believe that the preoccupation with the physical and social context of higher education has obscured the more crucial questions, which concern what is happening inside the student's head.

A second, and closely related, assumption is that the parietal element in higher education has been far too heavily emphasized. Too many colleges still implicitly operate on the premise that they are dealing with reluctant, lazy children who must be continually prodded and threatened if they are to learn anything. The process of higher education too often has borne disturbing similarities to the force feeding of geese destined to contribute to the world's supply of *pate de foie gras*. While explicit parietal rules and social regulations have been liberalized or abolished, the fundamental structure of college education has remained implicitly coercive.

The new assumption is that the individual's own motivation, his desire to learn and to grow, should play a more central role in the formulation of educational policy. Ideally, the acquisition of a college education should represent a positive act of individual volition rather than passive acquiescence in an institution's routines and requirements. A closer approximation of this ideal is what the innovators are striving for.

In the conversation and writings of those responsible for the new proposals, one finds the conviction that genuine intellectual competence, and not some magic number of "years in residence" or "credit hours," should be the single most important criterion for the baccalaureate degree. What a person knows, not how many courses he has taken, should be the fundamental concern toward which all academic planning is directed.

The various off-campus and noncampus schemes that spring from these shared assumptions and concerns generally fall into four broad categories.

The first, and least radical, represents the continued development and extension of efforts that have long been made by many American colleges and universities to increase the opportunity for off-campus learning experiences within the broad framework of the traditional pattern of campus residency. For decades, undergraduates have enjoyed a "junior year abroad" or participated in various types of work-study interludes. The newer programs add such possibilities as a hitch in VISTA or a semester in a ghetto, a museum, or a specialized school, such as a dance studio. The programs may be quite highly structured, such as Chapman College's "World Campus Afloat," which offers undergraduates courses on a ship that travels around the globe with field trips ashore; or fairly loose, as at those institutions where gifted students are allowed as much as a year off to write a novel, study French literature, or pursue other special interests—all for academic credit.

These off-campus extensions of the curriculum are not without problems. For example, how many academic credits should a student receive for forty hours of tutoring migrant workers? And how does one maintain "quality control" and prevent a genuine, if unconventional, learning experience from degenerating into a merely frivolous and self-indulgent frittering away of time?

But far outweighing such practical difficulties is the fact that all such efforts represent a movement toward a concept of higher learning that is far more in tune with the conditions and opportunities of contemporary life—a concept which recognizes that we have erected too high a barrier between the campus and the real world "out there." For the proponents of such off-campus programs, the individual college campus remains an essential intellectual base, but it is also seen as only one element in a far broader educational environment—an environment that includes the ghetto, the threatened wilderness, the polluted lake, the industrial laboratory, the social service agency, the city halfway around the world.

A second category of off-campus plan, the largest and most familiar, is to permit conventional academic work to be done off-campus, often over a time period longer than the usual four years and often through programs designed chiefly for adults.

The prototype is the famous external-degree program of London University, which has for decades enabled students from Nigeria,

Australia, the Bahamas, or India to work toward their degree in any manner they wish, and in any part of the world, so long as they passed the required examinations set by the university.

Since 1961 working adults from all over America, unable to take the time to live or attend classes on a campus, have been studying in the University of Oklahoma's pioneering B.A. program in liberal studies, which combines independent home study, correspondence work, and annual three-week residential seminars at the university. Recently Syracuse University, the University of South Florida, and the State University of New York at Brockport have established similar programs, sometimes supplemented by television and on-campus laboratory work in the sciences.

Two interesting new versions of these adult programs are Britain's "Open University" and the U.S. Navy's smaller program for "Afloat College Education." The Open University is Britain's attempt to democratize its traditionally elitist university programs quickly, with limited resources. The hope is to allow vast numbers of housewives and other adults with jobs to earn academic degrees in three to six years at a total cost to the student of less than $1,000. Last January, coal miners and clerks, salesmen and schoolteachers began enrolling in the Open University. There are six degree programs: humanities, science, social studies, technology, education, and mathematics. Thousands are listening to radio lectures, going through correspondence course packets, watching television courses, and reading in local libraries in preparation for examinations they will take at one of the 250 local study centers, where they also meet with some of the 2,500 tutors and counselors who are acting as study assistants and advisers. They will also attend a week of summer school at one of the 12 regional centers or at one of England's established colleges.

In the U.S. Navy's program, ship crewmen can earn up to two years of college credit at one of five colleges (Harvard is among them) by passing examinations based on heavy on-board reading, mastery of filmed courses, and attendance at lectures and seminars conducted by professors who visit their ship while it is in port. Under this program, the Navy has even flown professors to remote bases in the antarctic.

The most unusual program in this category is the recently initiated "University Without Walls," whose founding father is Samuel Baskin, an imaginative professor of psychology at Antioch College in Ohio. Professor Baskin had been seeking support for his plan several years before recently obtaining a U.S. Office of Education planning grant of $415,000 and a Ford Foundation grant of $400,000. What he envisions is an innovative educational program confined mainly to the campuses of 19 cooperating institutions, including such diverse schools as the large University of Minnesota, the small Staten Island Community College, the University of South Carolina, the predominantly black Howard University, the Quaker Friends World College, and the Catholic Loretto Heights College.

Within each of these institutions, 40 to 100 interested students will pursue a distinct academic program with guidelines established by the University Without Walls, a kind of academic holding company with little in the way of formal staff or administrative bureaucracy. Part of the time these students may take conventional courses at their own colleges, but they may also move about to one or more of the cooperating colleges or universities; serve supervised internships in businesses, hospitals, or museums; or study independently with the aid of reading lists, televised lectures, records, and tapes. Professor Baskin's program clearly rejects the traditional concept of college education with its exclusive stress on single-campus residency, classroom lectures, and narrow departmental majors. It also widens our conventional notion of "the faculty" to include experts and talented individuals from the "outside world"—artists, businessmen, musicians, or government officials.

The third off-campus "category" is in reality a single program: the New York State Education Department's unique new external-degree program, through which the associate in arts and bachelor of business administration degrees will be awarded to anyone who passes a set of comprehensive examinations. (Unlike the "Open University" program, this will involve no actual instruction, simply the administering of examinations and the awarding of degrees.) This program, with the aid of a joint planning grant from the Carnegie Corporation and the Ford Foundation, will permit persons who have studied on their own, in whatever fashion, to receive a sheepskin without ever enrolling at a college, setting foot on a campus, or paying a penny in tuition.

This category may expand, though. At a recent meeting of the

American Association for Higher Education in Chicago, Jack N. Arbolino, executive director of the Council on College-Level Examinations of the College Entrance Examination Board, proposed a "national university" that would, like the New York State Education Department, grant degrees to anyone in the nation who passed its degree examinations. The program that Mr. Arbolino heads already has made a small start in this direction by administering tests in two dozen different subjects, from American government to data processing, for which the student, upon passing one or more of them, may request academic credit from his college.

The fourth and last of these varied approaches to off-campus education is the State University of New York's new Empire State College, which is in the active planning stage. This experimental "college without a campus" (supported by a $1-million joint grant from the Carnegie Corporation and the Ford Foundation) will be similar in some respects to other programs we have described. It certainly owes much of its inspiration to innovations at other colleges, in other countries, and within the State University itself. But it also will have certain distinctive characteristics of its own. Unlike most external degree programs, for example, it will retain the opportunity for occasional on-campus study. It will encourage a close student-teacher relationship and will offer a wide variety of educational options to the student.

Because New York has placed all its public institutions of higher education under a central leadership, the State University is particularly well suited to undertake such an experimental venture. SUNY is actually a single entity made up of 70 separate institutions, including liberal arts colleges, specialized schools (in agriculture, forestry, engineering, etc.), community colleges, and four major universities. This means that New York already has in its State University a kind of multi-faceted consortium of institutions with widely varied characteristics and resources.

The central idea of Empire State College is to create an academic program that will free the student of the restraints of residence on a single campus and make available to him the resources of the entire university system. A combination of home study, off-campus work-study experiences, educational films, cassettes, correspondence courses, and periods of study elsewhere in America or abroad will enlarge enormously the options open to each student. While some may elect to do half or two-thirds of their work in residence at one or more of the State University's institutions, others will spend most of their time studying off-campus. Time limits, too, will be freer. A college degree may be attained in two, three, four, or eight years, depending on the individual student's specific circumstances and individual capacity for academic work.

But Empire State College is not conceived as a "do-your-own-thing" institution. A small core faculty at a central headquarters, with resident tutors at 20 regional study centers to be set up around the state, will design and direct the programs, prepare the correspondence courses, approve each student's plan of study, and counsel with students by telephone, mail, and in periodic personal meetings. In short, the educational experience of the student will be guided and evaluated at every stage by trained and committed scholars. While the student will complete assigned papers, reports, and examinations, he will be largely freed of grade pressures (grading probably will be on a pass/fail basis) and of specific credit-hour requirements. He will be able to concentrate more on his own education and less on the requirements of a specific institution.

Implicit in the design of Empire State College are several notions —rooted in the more general educational assumptions mentioned earlier—that seem alarmingly simple to some and simply alarming to others:

Formal classroom instruction, while still important, is no longer the sole or even the principal means of acquiring information and ideas at the college level.

Given the present wide variety of students, the continuing explosion of knowledge, and the emergence of new fields of academic concern, the curriculum no longer should be the exclusive concern of the faculty. Responsibility for its design and content should be shared by faculty members and students.

Residency on a single college campus is no longer a requisite for quality education. (One-fifth of America's college students already study at more than one institution during their undergraduate careers.)

Four years, and certainly four consecutive years, are not an inviolate block of time essential to an undergraduate degree. Longer or shorter periods of study, possibly interrupted by other activities, do not damage—and may actually improve—the net effectiveness of collegiate study.

While frequent and intimate contact with mature scholars is vital to a good college education, no faculty member can any longer be regarded as simply a purveyor of factual knowledge, even in his field of specialization. Increasingly, professors must act not only as sources of information but as sensitive intellectual guides, as concerned questioners of personal and social actions and values, and as provocative stimulants urging students to discover their own capacity for critical and creative thought.

None of these assumptions, taken singly, is entirely new. But taken together, and taken seriously, they add up to a new vision of what the college experience can, and should, entail.

To some skeptics, all these new schemes for off-campus learning are chiefly the brainchildren of presidents, faculty committees, and foundation officials who, desperate about the present financial crisis in higher education, are blindly stabbing at ways to process more students for less money.

Undeniably, a search for economy is a factor in the development of the new programs. A resident college education next fall will cost parents about $4,500 a year at most of the nation's leading private colleges and universities, and close to $3,000 at many public colleges and universities. By 1980, the charges could be $8,000 and $5,000 respectively. To anyone seriously concerned about providing some form of higher education to every American who desires it and can benefit by it, the economic situation is patently serious. It is neither shameful nor contemptible to be searching for new modes of providing high-quality education at a lower cost.

But there are, we think, more fundamental and long-range reasons for the current interest in the radical restructuring of American higher education. These derive from quantitative and qualitative changes in American youth, in the character of American society, and in present trends within higher education itself.

Disgruntled souls who shake their heads and mutter that young people aren't what they used to be are, as a matter of fact, absolutely correct. Young people *have* changed appreciably, and not just in the more publicized and superficial ways.

Physically, young people are larger and healthier than they were 50 years ago. Girls and boys are about three inches taller and ten pounds heavier than they were in 1920, principally because of advances in nutrition and medicine. Childhood diseases that used to stunt and maim, and even fill the cemeteries, have almost been wiped out. (The chief cause of death for persons under 21 is now accidents, primarily automobile accidents.) These same advances in nutrition and medicine have also caused adolescents to mature physiologically much earlier than in the past. In the United States the onset of puberty for girls has dropped from an average age of 14 in 1920 to 12.4 today, and, for boys, from 15 to 13.5.

Today's young people differ intellectually as well as physically. Kenneth Keniston of Yale, among others, has noted that the average American 16-year-old today has had five years more schooling than his counterpart in 1920. A recent U.S. Census Bureau study revealed that the number of young adults with high school diplomas has doubled since 1940, while the number with college degrees has tripled.

The average student today scores approximately one standard deviation above the student of a generation ago on standardized tests of intellectual achievement. A level of performance that places a student in the middle of his graduating class today would probably have placed him in the top 15 per cent 30 years ago. Or, to put it another way, in achievement, a teenager today is approximately one grade ahead of his parents when they were his age.

In the more amorphous psychological realm, numerous observers have noted the new mood among contemporary youth, the sense of generational uniqueness, the imagination and audacity, the impatience, the social concern, the disdain for history and authority. One can only speculate as to causes. Television, which began commercially in 1948, entered most homes 15-20 years ago. Thus, as has been widely noted, this is the first college generation raised on television practically from infancy. According to surveys, many young people in college today watched television about 20 hours a week when they were children, for an annual total greater than the number of hours they spent in school.

In addition to the ubiquitous tube, such factors as greater mobility, affluence, and longevity have also contributed to a different psychological state. For instance, because of the low life expectancy of former times—47.3 years in 1900—it was not unusual for a young person to lose one or both of his parents before reaching college age. Today, with the average life expectancy almost 70 years, orphanage has virtually been wiped out. Now, ironically, it is the continuing lively presence and pressure of both parents that many young persons perceive as a serious problem.

Yet, while young persons now are significantly different from those of 50 or even 20 years ago, American higher education is structurally much the same. Our colleges and universities (not to mention our grade and high schools) urgently need to recognize these important facts, and to redesign their programs accordingly. To keep nearly one-third of our young people occupied in an institutional setting that effectively segregates them from the world of "grown-ups" for seven to 10 years beyond the onset of puberty appears a more untenable arrangement with each passing year.

Another major force affecting the colleges has been the knowledge explosion itself. New technologies and sciences have burgeoned—from cybernetics to marine botany; new social problems—the urban crisis, the population explosion, pollution—have generated new study areas. Campus faculties have multiplied, splintered, and regrouped under the impact. Advances in photography, sound engineering, optics, communications, and transportation have revolutionized the movement of information, ideas, and people themselves. They make possible such things as a telephone seminar in astrophysics among scientists from several countries, a short intersession of anthropological study in West Africa or Peru, or the study of Eskimo culture through films.

In the face of all these changes, the old yardsticks of higher education—faculty-student ratios, years in residence, credit-hours for courses, and grading—become increasingly difficult to apply. The notions that there is a fixed "body of knowledge" to be delivered to the young, that college faculties necessarily know what is best for students, and that the departmental major is the only desirable method of organizing intellectual inquiry, are seriously challenged.

Moreover, we are at the beginning of a second admissions boom—that of older persons reentering college. Until the end of World War II, colleges catered chiefly to the privileged and the gifted. College admissions was the art of keeping people out. Since 1945, however, admissions policies have expanded until currently half of all high school graduates—two out of five of all young Americans—go on to college. Now, with technological change, increased leisure, new conceptions of womanhood, and greater affluence encouraging and requiring changes in career and lifestyle, continuing education is emerging as a new frontier of higher education. Most colleges and universities, especially public ones, are trying to help people *in* rather than screen them *out*. And as colleges admit greater numbers of students from more varied socioeconomic backgrounds, their curriculums have altered in order to serve effectively the expanded new clientele with its broader range of preparation and aspirations.

To shift one variable, such as the kind of students served, while attempting to hold constant all the rest of the components of the university structure is to court disaster, as too many institutions have learned. Likewise, to try to accommodate the knowledge explosion on the campus, with the increased research, field work, and specialization that it demands, without reexamining the traditional "liberal education" requirements is irresponsible.

As the recent Carnegie Commission report *Less Time, More Options* suggested, today's college and university clearly must offer many tracks, many options, and many different programs to serve the new variety of students and to assist in the exploration of new areas of intellectual inquiry. Large universities may have to break up into several colleges. Smaller colleges may have to establish links with other colleges and other kinds of learning institutions in society. And all will have to allow increased opportunities for independent and off-campus study.

It is these profound transformations—in our young people, in our society, and in higher education, as well as the grave financial condition of the colleges—that compel radical changes in the venerable but outmoded patterns of American collegiate study. The many proposals for off-campus or noncampus study contain many details to be worked out and objections to be overcome. But they represent serious efforts to experiment with fresh patterns of undergraduate education. The alternative is a continuing and ever louder dirge about the poverty, disruption, and "irrelevance" of our campuses.

It would be tragic if the social institution that has contributed so much to our civilization should fail to respond vigorously to the challenges that confront it at this crucial moment. The present crisis is assuredly one of dollars. But even more, it is one of will, of creative energy, of new ideas. Higher education is in a period of painful transition. The greatest need is to act boldly, with fresh vision, in the face of new conditions. The training of the mind and sharpening of the sensibilities are still the best hope of mankind.

13

Challenge to Grow:
The Outward Bound Approach

RICHARD KATZ
DAVID KOLB

Education of the whole man has been an enduring concern, and still seems a relevant response to contemporary crises such as the crises in race relations, urban areas and emerging nations. Such an educational process involves an integration of emotional, physical and moral or spiritual learning with intellectual learning. Allport (1954) and Alschuler (1968) have discussed some educational methods which attempt to impart more than intellectual knowledge, including sensitivity training and creativity training. In this paper we will describe Outward Bound, a program which is unusual in that it works directly on the individual's emotional, physical, spiritual and intellectual functioning. This comprehensive approach to education makes Outward Bound an excellent case study in the area of education for personal growth.

Outward Bound is a school offering a 26-day residential course in an isolated, wilderness setting. Typically, the course is for males aged

Richard Katz and David Kolb, "Outward Bound as Education for Personal Growth." Research supported by Office of Juvenile Delinquency; Health, Education and Welfare Administration, Grant No. 66013. The authors wish to acknowledge the assistance of the directors, staff and students at the Colorado, Hurricane Island, and Minnesota Outward Bound Schools in the summer of 1967, in particular Jerome Pieh and John Williamson; also Thomas D'Andrea, Haverford College; Francis J. Kelly, Massachusetts Youth Service Board; Joshua Miner III, Outward Bound, Inc.; and Mrs. Mary Maxwell Katz.

16-23 from a variety of racial, religious, educational, and socio-economic backgrounds.[1] An attempt is made to limit the proportion of full-paying students to about half of any course. The curriculum contains a variety of primarily physical activities such as wilderness travel and camping, mountain climbing, canoeing and seamanship. Activities are meant to become increasingly difficult for students, both physically and psychologically.[2] The school tries to challenge its students to go beyond what they considered their psychological and physical limits in order to increase students' knowledge and appreciation of themselves and others.

Outward Bound was founded originally as a survival training school for British merchant seamen during World War II. Shipowners found that young seamen were the first to give up and die when in exposed lifeboats; whereas the older men, officers and petty officers, though less fit physically, were more likely to live and to save others.

The shipowners turned to Dr. Kurt Hahn, headmaster of the Gordonstown School in Scotland, who had already incorporated concepts of service, rescue training, physical challenge, and adventure into his educational practices. Hahn worked out a program that was highly successful in preparing young men to cope with defeatism and to prevail amidst hardships. Hahn believed that success in meeting a severe challenge often depends more upon attitude than physical prowess. The literature on individuals' reaction to disaster and crisis supports this assumption (e.g., Burns, Chambers and Hendler, 1963).

The success of Outward Bound during the war suggested such schools could serve a useful function during peacetime. There are at present six Outward Bound schools in England, four in Europe, four in Africa, five in the United States, and one each in Malaysia, Australia, and New Zealand.

Outward Bound is now involved in another phase—developing its applications to a variety of educational settings. Outward Bound has been an input in Job Corps and Peace Corps training, high school and college programs, and the treatment of juvenile delinquents (Outward Bound, *Into the Mainstream*). This process of applying Outward Bound to other settings has had mixed success. One of the key problems is the failure to clarify the Outward Bound educational methods or principles. This paper attempts to meet this problem.

The primary source of data for this paper is the research reports of three participant-observers.[3] Before this, information about Outward Bound had been limited to public relations material or descriptive articles. We were professionally trained as participant-observers in the social sciences, particularly social and clinical psychology, which was thought to increase the likelihood of our gathering impartial information about Outward Bound. Our professional training, however, is affected by its own ideology. We tried to avoid using certain components of our social science ideology to *misinterpret* the Outward Bound experience.

Our goal as participant-observers was to understand Outward Bound as a culture, as a system of education for personal growth. Personal growth deals with growth in the individual's understanding of self and environment. To do this, we tried to isolate Outward Bound's key educational principles and methods. We also tried to examine how the school functioned and how students were motivated and affected by the Outward Bound experience.

On our arrival at the Outward Bound schools, our role as participant-observers came suddenly clear. Without extensive participation, we could not really understand Outward Bound. And so participate we did. We were introduced as educators trying to learn more about Outward Bound. Since the Outward Bound schools are by now accustomed to visitors and observers, our entree was not difficult. Generally, we participated along with one of the regular groups of students as they went through the course.

There were at least three reasons for extensive participation. First, so much of Outward Bound operates from the inside, from within the culture. To appreciate the culture's impact, one has to be immersed in it. And the experiential impact of Outward Bound was something we perhaps could not have prepared for. Moreover, only by extensive participation could we acquire enough skills to observe in critical situations. We were not willing to observe students on a climb or expedition unless we felt reasonably confident about our own wilderness abilities.

And finally, there was an unwritten law that respect and camaraderie were based on a person's willingness to at least try those Outward Bound activities which befitted his age and condition. Since we were apparently young and physically fit, few activities were seen as inappropriate for us. Once we began to participate, it was not easy to abstain from parts of the program because we were "Ph.Ds" or "not really part of the program." Much of the success we had in observing Outward Bound depended on the respect and camaraderie generated by our participation.

This immersion in the Outward Bound culture had important implications. The need to categorize—seemingly universal, but particularly rampant among social scientists—had to be abated. The Outward Bound experience too often demanded so much that there was little energy or interest left for categorizing. If you were really scared on the rock-climbing exercise, your categorizing had to wait until the exercise was over. The observer part of our role was most often performed at night, in the tent, where one could reflect on the day's experiences. The daily journal kept by participant-observers became quite important because feelings and observations would change from day to day, often dramatically. After completing an Outward Bound course, as one's perspective gradually developed, these journals became an invaluable source of data.

We also found extremely useful those many categories which laymen use to describe human experience, but which social scientists avoid. Words like "courage," "hard work," "life-death situation," and "boredom," seemed important for describing Outward Bound.

OUTWARD BOUND: AN EXPERIENTIAL VIEWPOINT

Now that we were spending more time in the field, we felt like we were shifting into high gear. Only the staff knew exactly where we were going in the morning, which sort of left you wanting to know more about what was planned. We rode for a while in the truck, going over bumpy mountain roads, sharing in an early morning adventure, joy-ride.

We reached our destination and looked up. It did look big. "It," was a rock face, something which later we would respect much more than we did that morning. Hiking up the gully we arrived at the base of the rock face. It looked even more awesome and magnificent than from the road below. There were some other patrols there, close to 40 students and five or six instructors milling around.

Soon the demonstration began. With apparent ease, confident at least so it seemed, several of the instructors demonstrated rock-climbing. We looked up the rock face as they gracefully worked their way up, looking for the proper hand holds and foot holds. After a few more climbs by the instructors, the task was ready, the challenge set forth. And then began the slow process of each student confronting the task each in his own manner.

Who should go first? There was much jockeying around for that "privilege," and, as usual, the guy who "always wants to go first" went first. Watching one of your peers negotiate the same climb that only the instructor had done previously made the task seem within your own reach, made it seem possible, perhaps easy. Soon, however, there were students who began to encounter difficulty. Their climbs were not effortless, not graceful. They were struggling up the rock, fighting against the rock rather than working with it, searching frantically for holds rather than carefully finding them. Then, the task again appeared difficult. You started to make judgments about how you would do based on how others were doing. But once your peers started climbing, the task was one you had to confront.

Ever so slowly each student had his chance to walk up the base, check his knot, and begin his climb. But the progress was slow. Three routes were going, but there were nearly 40 boys, and they did not climb fast. And each climb was spotlighted. Observed by various peers to get pointers for their own climbs or to make judgments about the climber. Observed by the instructors, for their job was safety, to keep people out of trouble. So there was lots of waiting, lots of idle chatter, some concern for the fact that you would be climbing soon.

After several students had completed their climbs, they took over the other part of the task for the day, that of belaying. Those who were belaying had the responsibility for insuring that the climbers did not have a serious fall. The rope attached to the climber's belt was held by the belayer at the top of the rock face. The belayer had to continually "feel" the climber at the end of the rope, giving him just enough slack so that he could climb freely, not so much slack that if he slipped he would fall too far. This ultimate responsibility, this balancing of another's life was easy to talk about, harder to really feel. When the climb was not going smoothly, when the climber perhaps slipped, then innocence would vanish. The belayer felt the climber's life in his hands.

Lunch came, a break in activity. A time to exchange some of the fear, some of the exhilaration that went into the rock climbing activity. But a time for most of the boys just to eat peanut butter and jelly sandwiches, talk about the weather, kid each other, and generally act as they did on all other lunches in the field. A time to relax, except for those whose climbs were yet to come; they felt some tension, at the very least a sense of expectancy. The lunch was short. It had to be. There were many who still had to climb. Back up the gully, along the loose rock, back to the base of the rock face.

My turn. It was not that I was holding back; it's just that I wasn't one of the most eager ones. I went to the base, with confidence. The ones who had climbed the route that I was going to take looked like they were having a relatively smooth run. Roped-in. Check my knot out with the instructor, a couple of times. And then I began to climb.

The first several moves were easy, and I developed overconfidence. I climbed without really thinking ahead and looking for my next moves, and soon I was in a terrifying position. I could see nowhere to go. Up, down, left, right, there seemed no route open to me. I got really frightened, scared, and forgot that I was roped in. It became an ultimate situation for me, my life was at stake. I tried to move to the left. I reached high, too high, and that was it. My grip couldn't hold any longer, and I slipped. The feeling inside was a sinking, *a real sinking*. I knew that was the end. Split-seconds later I was on the ground. I hadn't fallen more than eight or nine feet, possibly ten. Inside, however, I had passed through death, and there I was on the ground again. I was shaky but my next thought was to start up again. There just didn't seem to be any other reasonable alternative.

I began to climb again, this time with a little less confidence than was appropriate, and the climb was not easy. There were several spots where I was there for what seemed a long time, looking for the right path, seeing none, then taking a chance, coming up with a hand-hold which seemed to work, scrambling more than climbing. Above me another student was having real problems, and he froze. He froze for quite a time, and beneath him I had to stay flat against the rock waiting for him to move, in any direction. He tried several ways but couldn't get going again. Eventually the instructor came out and assisted the boy above me off the rock face.

Arriving at the top of the rock face after my climb was not exhilarating, not exciting; it was just good to be there. Once at the top I joined a special league created just on that day, a league whose admission was climbing from the bottom of that rock face to the top. It was not a hard league to join. Everybody but one or two of the 40 boys made it, but still, it was a league, and being a member of it brought you that much closer to the people around you. Closer, not because you knew them any better, but because you and they had gone through an unusual experience together.

Today was a long one. By the time all the students had a chance to climb the rock face, it was late in the afternoon. As we walked down from the face, again down the gully, tired this time, I realized that the situation had provided me with an ultimate moment. Undoubtedly, I had been prepared for such a thing, but the situation encouraged and stimulated such a moment. Down on the road again, walking back to camp I felt much more humble, still a little shaky. I really felt that my Outward Bound experience would not be easy. There would be moments like that one on the rock face, where I had died in my own mind. It was in hope of just such moments that I had come to Outward Bound.

The hike back to camp was very "professional." We knew where we were going, we decided what pace to set. We all felt much more involved in our mountain environment. And we had done something which professional climbers do, they with much less effort and much more skillfully. But we had done it, we could talk about it, and it made us feel more "professional."

At night, the fall was still with me. I relived it several times, the sinking feeling was real. I thought—it seemed almost a vow—that in the future I would not "give up" when the consequences were so dire. I felt more aware of that moment when "it's all over," and wanted to maintain that awareness. There were no lights on in the other tents. Most boys were probably already asleep. Had many reflected much on the day? They were instinctively storing up energy for the next day, which seemed a good idea.

THE OUTWARD BOUND IDEOLOGY

The Outward Bound ideology is both powerful and pervasive. It presents Outward Bound as a dramatic, important, potentially life-changing experience. It portrays Outward Bound as a way of actualizing one's potential, particularly in the area of character development. The ideology markedly affects what happens at Outward Bound. It both facilitates and obstructs the schools' educational effectiveness.

Outward Bound is portrayed as an effective, tradition-tested way of self-discovery. There are numerous references to the Outward Bound movement, and the people who through the years have taken the Outward Bound path. The assumption is that the program is intrinsically educational, and, moreover, that Outward Bound can be successful with all types of boys, each boy benefitting in his own way.

Through primarily physical activities which are increasingly stressful and demanding, a student is supposedly forced to confront himself. Plato's statement is quoted: "Let us build physical fitness for the sake of the soul." Another favorite quote is: "Outward Bound trains *through* the mountains and not for them." The student supposedly discovers aspects of his essential nature and thereby begins to develop character. Important ingredients of character are: self-reliance, the desire to serve others, courage, self-discipline, realistic self-image, resourcefulness, will power, and appreciation of nature and man's place in it.

Moreover, Outward Bound claims to develop what is essential to human functioning but particularly lacking and difficult to attain in modern youth. Kurt Hahn, the founder of Outward Bound, says:

> The purpose of Outward Bound is to protect youth against a diseased civilization. Three decays surround the modern youth: The decay of care and skill; the decay of enterprise and adventure; and the decay of compassion." (Outward Bound Schools, brochure)

Many who work with Outward Bound see it as a response to William James' call for a moral equivalent to war.

A variety of public relations materials are employed in communicating the ideology. Most of these materials emphasize a dramatic (almost heroic) and existential quality to the Outward Bound experience. The lead quotation from the Outward Bound course catalogue is a student's analysis of Outward Bound:

> Only under the pressure of stress does a person get the chance to know himself. Outward Bound is not easy; it is not meant to be. It is something very good. (Outward Bound Schools brochure)

It is hard for a prospective Outward Bound student not to feel that something significant will happen at Outward Bound after he reads such a statement.

The more formal public relations materials are continually supplemented by the talk and action of the Outward Bound staff. Staff members often seem to personify the Outward Bound ideology. There is a core value system shared by most of the staff, stressing the Outward Bound experience as a path of self-discovery and service to others. But there are as many modifications on how this core is presented and elaborated as there are staff members.

The ideology can enhance the experience at Outward Bound and facilitate its educational effectiveness. It can serve as a powerful motivating factor. Staff members have a special sense of pride. They feel that they are involved in a special job, an extraordinary educational experience. This feeling seems to derive not only from the realization that students' lives depend on their instruction, but also from their feeling that they are a part of the Outward Bound movement. The Outward Bound ideology also generates in students a feeling that they are involved in an important educational experience.

Ideologies often can have a self-fulfilling property. According to its ideology, Outward Bound is an *effective* way of discovering one's self. Students, and especially staff, hold this belief. Having the belief can help, in fact, to make the Outward Bound experience meaningful and effective. Most students come to Outward Bound to change or be changed. This would include the high school student who feels he will become (physically) tougher and the college junior who feels he will develop leadership ability; the boy sent by his parents to "become a man" and the boy sent by the correctional institution to be "reformed."

But the ideology, by its very power and pervasiveness, can also obstruct the educational effectiveness of Outward Bound. Expectations based on the ideology are often unfulfilled. The Outward Bound ideology does not focus on gradual, undramatic change, the kind of change whose cumulative effect is so often the key to personal growth. Instead, the ideology considers change in a broad and dramatic manner, for example, "learning to deal with fear" after experiencing a particular crisis. Students therefore find it more difficult to be satisfied with and build upon minor experiences of change.

Students' experiences at Outward Bound usually do not seem so dramatic as the ideology leads them to expect. It takes a certain kind of courage to accept one's own experience as valid when the drama is not apparent or the experience is not clearly "something very good." The student finds it difficult to describe his experience in his own words. He often uses the language of the public relations material, which is unfortunate. It is even more serious, however, when ideology is substituted for experience.

The ideology can even lead some students to take a passive approach toward Outward Bound. Since the Outward Bound experience is portrayed as so powerful, students can feel that it will happen *to* them. This passive attitude is continually discouraged, but even staff members can be overwhelmed. They can feel that the Outward Bound program "automatically" works. Thus, their efforts at "making it work," so critical to success at Outward Bound, are lessened.

The ideology assumes that Outward Bound can be successful with all types of boys. This assumption results in extremely varied student bodies at the schools. But with some types of boys, Outward Bound can be an educationally unrewarding experience.

For some students, Outward Bound has a diminished impact. The more mature college students tend to be less motivated than the usual student who is still very much at the high school stage. The mature student has perspective and does not become as thoroughly immersed in the Outward Bound culture. Also, students who are experienced woodsmen, sailors or climbers do not generally get as much from these activities at Outward Bound as do other students. Much of the challenge and excitement due to the novelty of the task are absent.

Other types of students may be adversely affected. Outward Bound is not at present capable of educating more than a few boys with psychological problems in any one course. If, for example, a boy has intense fears, it presents particular problems. Having him confront fear can lead to increased fear unless the confrontation is handled with extreme sensitivity and competence. Few of the staff had experience or time enough to work with psychological problems. Moreover, some staff members felt that specialized attention was beyond their responsibility.

The Outward Bound approach values treating all students in essentially the same way. In part they assume that if you treat a "problem" student like the other students, as if he were "normal," he will begin acting "normal." There is some evidence to suggest this can be an effective approach *if* handled with great interpersonal sensitivity and understanding. However, this same approach can lead to ignoring a student's intense problems, and perhaps increasing their severity. At Outward Bound, since few of the staff had the necessary sensitivity and understanding, such problems were often ignored. At present Outward Bound seems particularly suited to educate "normals."

OUTWARD BOUND'S EDUCATIONAL METHOD

Outward Bound relies primarily on an experience-based, action-oriented method of education. Learning occurs in a "total culture" which generates commitment and excitement. Many of the students' experiences and actions have an intense, ultimate quality, which increases the educational potential of the method. A key technique in the method is self-confrontation. Self-confrontation encourages the individual to surpass what he thought were his limits. Staff are the critical factor in Outward Bound's method of education. The staff members must guide a student's experiences and actions if education is to be maximized. But Outward Bound schools do not emphasize preparing a student psychologically for an experience; nor do they emphasize dealing with his psychological reactions to the experience. This approach may reduce the educational impact of the student's experience.

Total Culture

As Goffman (1961) has described, "total institutions" exert a comprehensive and compelling influence on their members' values and standards. Outward Bound can be considered such a total institution. The schools are physically isolated, indeed remote; the mass media are not available to students; and for the entire 26 days students are involved in Outward Bound work. Visitors to the school are looked upon as outsiders. Students feel that they are in a retreat, in a "special place" to do "special work." If one accepts Outward Bound, then one's entire life can revolve around the school and its program. Most of the students have such a relationship to the school.

Students become immersed in the Outward Bound culture. Things they never would have attempted become standard practice. Students slide over the gorge, feeling "kids back home should see me now." Old values and standards for behavior are replaced by the Outward Bound values. The immersion is both sudden and gradual. Almost immediately after you emerge from the bus which takes you to the school, you are doing something you would never have attempted before, e.g., running headlong down slippery rocks through the bog. Also, as the course progresses, your values become Outward Bound values: "Of course I'll run and do the dip, what else do you do when you get up in the morning."

Indeed it is hard to be anything but completely involved in the program. As we described in the beginning, we really had to participate in order to be participant-observers. Students who were only marginally involved in the program could not stay very long at the schools.

The Outward Bound ideology is a key influence in shaping the culture. There is a prevalent value that only the "strong," the "men" are able to finish the course. Persistence is a virtue. Students feel that what they have to do at Outward Bound is what *should* be done. It becomes very difficult for a boy to "walk away" from a challenge.

Challenges, particularly when they are felt as dangerous, when one's life is at stake, seem irresistible. The excitement of the challenge, the sense of adventure, is contagious. Exciting events intensively involve the students in Outward Bound. Many students feel they have come to Outward Bound specifically to meet these challenges to their lives. More remember such challenges as the highlights of their Outward Bound experience.

The opportunity to really test one's limits is very important. The adolescent's search for clarity about his identity is particularly keen (see e.g., Erikson, 1959). Challenges, particularly those felt as dangerous, are often approached as opportunities for defining oneself. Many students look upon Outward Bound as an "initiation rite," a not particularly pleasant but "real" way of finding out who they are, what their limits are. Many approach Outward Bound as if it were the initiation rite which will effect their transition from boyhood to manhood. In contemporary America, such a clear transition is absent, though the adolescent need for it may still exist. Some of the compelling quality of Outward Bound certainly derives from its role in making this particular transition. But Outward Bound is also compelling because it seems to be a contemporary representative of a group of institutions (e.g. initiation rites, secret societies) which historically have effected major transformations in individuals (see e.g., Van Gennep, 1960 or Campbell, 1956).

The development of competence and confidence in meeting the Outward Bound tasks becomes important. As White (1959) has discussed, competence (mastery) generates a sense of personal worth and a feeling of accomplishment. Competence is a particularly relevant issue for the adolescent. Students develop pride in their competence, an almost professional feeling about their sailing, climbing or canoeing abilities. There is also a strong desire to be able to deal with danger confidently. It becomes important to be able to face one's fear and still complete the task. Students are not comfortable with the feeling that "I'd never do that again, it was too scary."

There is a strong desire among students to be seen as "men" not "boys." They do not want to be considered soft or cowardly. Hard work becomes intrinsically rewarding and a source of pride and the sense of accomplishment. The students talk about the weight of the pack they carried or the number of hours they rowed. Students who take short cuts, or have a lazy attitude, rarely occupy positions of influence or respect. Outward Bound is "hard work," not "fun." Rarely does a student enjoy Outward Bound. Rather, it is something he *should* go through. To be considered "chicken" is a supreme insult at Outward Bound.

Peer, staff, and family expectations exert great pressure toward conforming to the Outward Bound culture. As on the climb up the rock face, when everyone is doing it, the individual student finds it hard not to join in. Each boy is associated with a group of 12 throughout the course. This smaller unit also exerts strong pressure toward completing tasks and the course. Intergroup competition is based on individuals' performances on tasks, particularly on completing tasks.

Staff members have completed tasks similar to or more demanding than the Outward Bound program. They expect that their students will also complete the Outward Bound course. In fact, part of their reputation as instructors depends on how all their group completes a task or finishes the course.

Parents add a final pressure toward completing the course. Many boys are "sent to Outward Bound to become a man." Also, the parents expect that when one goes to a school, one finishes the course and gets his diploma, or in this case, certificate.

Experience-Based Confrontation

Critical self-discoveries are brought about by placing the student in experiences where he must confront himself and his limitations, rather than avoiding or "smoothing over" what he sees. The situations *demand actions* which challenge his self-definition and encourage him to explore and surpass what he thought were his limits. The self-confronting situations range from the mundane to the dramatic where a life might be at stake. The confrontation could take place in a student's private world or in a very public arena.

The climb up the rock face was one example of a limit-stretching experience. Another example was when a student faced a jump on the "ropes course"[4] which psychologically was very difficult, i.e., it *seemed* that he was very high up. He was there a long time, and a number of his peers gathered to watch. He constantly and continually described how he was going to make this critical jump, how he wasn't afraid, how he just needed a little time. He made the issue of his courage very explicit. After some time, he had to give up and climb down. He also had to deal with a modified image of his courage. There was also the boy for whom the mountains evoked self-discovery. He confided his private fear: "You're not going to get me up there—I'm scared of those mountains, I might get lost or I might fall down. I didn't realize I'd be so scared." Many of the situations which presented the most substantial challenge to students were situations they all had to go through, situations which were "part of the course."

The technique of self-confrontation seems critical to personal growth. The research on T-groups, which employ self-confrontation as a primary technique, supports this assumption (Schein, Bennis, 1965). Outward Bound adds an intensity and ultimate quality to self-confrontation (not usually found in T-groups) because the confrontation often demands that the student act, not merely talk, and because the student's physical life can be at stake.

The Outward Bound experience, and certainly those aspects which are especially self-confronting could be described by Maslow's (1962) concept of a "peak experience." They have an ego-transcending quality of significance for the student. As both Maslow and James (1929) have suggested, such peak experiences *can* lead to (dramatic) personal growth. But such experiences do not invariably lead to personal growth. For example, the individual's expectations about experience and the setting within which the experience occurs, affect the nature and degree of his subsequent growth (see e.g., Ungar, 1963).

Self-confrontation at Outward Bound does not *automatically* engender personal growth. Self-confrontation is often an intense and volatile experience which requires sensitive attention. If experiences are to be self-confronting, the "limits" of a student must be sensitively assessed. It is not easy to know how much someone can stretch himself or what is the right time for him to try. These judgments rested with both students and staff. More often than not the decisions that were made at Outward Bound seemed wise.

There is an emphasis on making information (or content-learning) experiential. The feeling is that a student should grow into knowledge, learning through his own trial and error. Indeed there is a certain unwritten rule that a wilderness expert does not pass on to others all of his knowledge, all of the lessons he's learned from his own experience. Lectures, when given, are usually followed by exercises or actions which employ the principles of the lecture. Sometimes the action was not too difficult as when, for example, you tried out one of the drown-proofing swimming strokes. Sometimes the action represented a major challenge, as when, for example, you checked the way you had just been shown to rope yourself in, because in the next moment you were going down the side of the cliff for the "big rappell."[5] Those days when lectures predominated, were felt to be "slow days."

This emphasis on experiential learning had certain limits, of course. When there was insufficient time or when there was a life and death issue, the staff became quite didactic. If one met a section of coast which was particularly difficult to navigate, the staff took command. Instructions were given clearly and forcefully when a life was at stake. Then, one could not "afford" experiential learning. This did not seem to detract too seriously from the power of the Outward Bound experience.

Action is constantly required. In an important sense, things don't happen at Outward Bound until people "do" something. Performance is the true measure of the man. Bravado, bragging, and boasting are quickly exposed by peers and staff. Of course, *not* acting is equally important. Much of the Outward Bound experience occurs during those times the student faces a particular task, for example, the next move up the rock face, and stops, hesitates, or becomes immobilized for a very long time.

Action-Oriented

Actions are valued more and more publicly than thoughts and feelings. Physical prowess and conditioning become a source of pride and interest among the students. Feelings like fear or loneliness are touched upon mainly in private or in small groups, if at all; and then they are discussed in a joking manner, minimizing their importance. The student whose contribution is mainly intellectual, for example, the one who has ideas about solving an initiative test,[6] is often more tolerated than admired.

Finally, two things about physical conditioning contribute to this higher valuation of actions and the physical realm: students rather quickly "get into shape"; and "being in shape" is a concrete measurable arena of accomplishment.

We have already mentioned that being in the field put the program "in high gear." There is a general feeling among both students and staff that canoeing (or climbing or hiking or sailing) is "what we are here for"—not spending time at the school's home base. A logical extension of this emphasis, courses which are held entirely in the field (mobile courses), get closer to the core of Outward Bound. Being in the field also provides a more total exposure to the Outward Bound culture. Students have fewer of their own strategies for coping with the wilderness as compared to the school compound. They are therefore more receptive to the Outward Bound approach when in the field.

Course Requirements

There is a strong pressure at Outward Bound for everyone to receive the standard treatment, for everyone to take the same course. This is a particularly significant pressure considering the variety of boys attending an Outward Bound school. There are actually, however, many different courses at any one Outward Bound school session. In terms of his actions, and more importantly in terms of his reactions and attitudes, each boy has essentially his own course.

The requirements for a particular Outward Bound task or for an entire Outward Bound course are often modified for an individual student. The decision about how and when to make such modification is not an easy one. But the judgments about helping a student explore his limits are not easy. Staff had the authority to make such modifications. They consider the physical and when possible psychological capacities of a student. For example, they can give a lighter pack to a boy who is somewhat weaker than others; or assign a normal expedition route to a boy who can push himself in spite of a bruised ankle; or give a different solo site to one of the more resourceful boys. Staff members try to avoid insulting a student by saying in effect that he cannot complete the standard course. Often, however, staff and student do not mutually recognize the need for particular modification.

Sometimes the decision to modify the requirements of the task or the Outward Bound course depends on the student's judgment and/ or actions. In the climb up the rock face we described, certain students purposely took more difficult climbing routes. Students vary in the degree to which they push themselves on final expedition. Finally, student bravado is often taken literally. Students who boast about their ability to do certain things are usually challenged to put their words into action.

The fact that each student takes essentially his own course increases the educational *potential* of Outward Bound. Certain problems, however, prevent this potential from being realized to any large extent. Outward Bound is not really prepared for such individualized instruction and treatment. Often, for example there is insufficient psychological preparation to facilitate a student's *individual* educational experience in one of the "standard" tasks. Moreover, there are no easy guide lines for the decision about when a modification in the course is necessary, when appropriate, or when a "cop-out." This creates some confusion in both students and staff. And since the general expectation among students is that everyone should do the same course, you often hear complaints about modifications: "some guys aren't really doing their job," "some guys are getting off easy."

Psychological Preparation and Follow-up

As social scientists, we must be especially careful at this point. We will not try to misinterpret Outward Bound so as to confirm our professional bias toward emphasizing psychological functioning. It does seem, however, that adequate psychological preparation for and follow-up after an experience is lacking.

First let us make clear what we mean by psychological preparation for and follow-up after an experience. We do *not* mean intellectualizing about an experience. We do *not* necessarily mean talking about or conceptualizing an experience, though one might. As demonstrated by "basic encounter" groups talking about things can be an intense experience (see e.g., Rogers, 1967). "Psychological" also includes emotional and nonverbal preparation and follow-up. By "psychological" preparation we mean being psychologically ready to learn from an experience, *not* being told what to experience. By "psychological" follow-up we mean being psychologically able to sustain the educational impact of the experience, *not* being told what you experienced.

At Outward Bound, preparation for and follow-up after an experience is handled effectively on the physical dimension. For example, students are adequately clothed, and receive adequate medical attention. They gradually build up their physical climbing skills before going to the mountains. Debriefing sessions were most often skill-oriented.

Some attention is paid to psychological factors at Outward Bound. Work on the ropes course also prepares students psychologically for their climbing, e.g., it develops confidence. But there are two particularly important areas in which psychological preparation and follow-up seem inadequate, thereby decreasing the educational effectiveness of experiences. First, the intense, volatile emotions (e.g., fear) generated by some experiences seem inadequately handled. Second, the variety and range of particular experiences seem inadequately explored. Though some staff worked effectively in these areas, there are few formal structures supporting them in this effort.

Many of the experiences at Outward Bound involve intensely felt and volatile emotions such as fear. When a student confronts himself, such emotions usually arise. Psychological preparation and follow-up become particularly acute at those times. Fear, for example, is often engendered without an appreciation of the effects it might have on an individual. Follow-up is often too minimal to direct the fear into productive directions. In such cases the student becomes less able to deal with or understand the fear. An emotion experienced in such a way is too often gladly forgotten or avoided. The potential learning that could have occurred, which was great, is severely limited.

The solo exemplifies an experience whose range of possibilities seems inadequately explored (Katz, 1968). Preparation and follow-up for the solo was primarily on the physical dimension. Many students spent their solo "caught" in one or two routines (e.g., getting wood for the fire, thinking about food). They were unprepared to learn more by examining alternative behaviors. Others found themselves unable to do even the simplest things. They became disappointed in themselves. There was little post-solo examination of such "limited" behavior, though examination could have turned that behavior into an educational experience. Instead of merely being disappointed in himself, a student could learn how this behavior explained something about himself.

There are students who "come prepared" to enhance the educational impact of experiences. They naturally consider the meaning of their behavior or the implications of an action. The vast majority of students, however, need guidance in order to turn Outward Bound experiences into educational experiences. These students might benefit from more psychological preparation and follow-up both at critical points in the course program (e.g., before and after the solo) and at critical points in their own course (e.g., when they must exercise leadership for the first time). Perhaps discussions might be helpful, e.g., describing how the fear felt, and sharing this description with others who also give their reactions to fear. Being able to clarify or conceptualize an experience, even in a very rudimentary form, is often helpful in understanding the experience. The danger, of course, is overpsychologizing. Then the concept becomes substituted for the experience; introspection leads to immobility. But Outward Bound seems far from this danger.

Staff

Without the proper guidance from staff, the Outward Bound program would work only fortuitously. The physical locale, the tasks to be performed, the schedule—all seem ancillary to the Outward Bound experience. They are "equipment" which must be used. Depending on the quality of the staff, they are used in a way which produces more or less of an educational experience. A student can be pushed to constructively explore his limits or pushed too far or too fast. The difference often lies with the instructor in charge of the activity. Staff members are often not aware of the extent of their influence on Outward Bound. We have already mentioned the feelings many staff had that the mountains, the forests, the Outward Bound program itself are automatically educative.

Staff is in constant and immediate contact with the students. The key unit in the Outward Bound experience consists of two staff members and twelve students (the "patrol," "brigade" or "watch"). The patrol spends most of its time working separately from other patrols, which leads to a great decentralization. The low staff-student ratio and the decentralization gives the instructor a great deal of influence. This influence is further enhanced by the immediacy of the contact between staff and students. A closeness develops on the various field expeditions.

Not only is the contact between staff and students constant and immediate, but the staff has great authority in the program. Staff in effect runs the program. Outward Bound is not a "participatory democracy." Students are only rarely consulted in planning the route and length of expeditions. The 26-day schedule is largely preplanned, and number of open periods at a minimum.[7] Staff knows what to do and how to do it—they have the skills. Being in control of the program and having the skills to carry it out heighten the degree of staff influence on the Outward Bound experience.

Outward Bound requires an exceptionally talented staff; generally it is able to recruit qualified people. An instructor's job is extremely difficult. It is hard to judge when to let the student learn by trial and error and when to offer guidance and in what amounts. Staff must be more sensitive to the individual qualities of a student than his peers usually are. The value of meeting challenges must be carried out more sensitively and flexibly by staff than it is by most students. Added to these (more subtle) difficulties is the enormous responsibility Outward Bound instructors have—their students' lives often depend on the quality of their instruction. One final element is the expectation that students will change in important ways. This puts additional pressure on the staff.

There seem to be at least three important aspects to a good staff member: technical proficiency, skill as an educator, and dedication to the Outward Bound idea.

Most of the Outward Bound staff are exceptionally qualified in the technical realm. Outward Bound's "classroom" is the sea, the mountains, the lakes and streams. *Before* one can teach effectively there, one must have enough technical competence to instinctively make the "right move." An instructor who had to worry about his own performance too much would be at a disadvantage. He couldn't devote enough attention to his students. Moreover, his relative lack of skill or confidence would be noticed by the students, diminishing their respect for him. Also, technical competence is essential to effectively encourage students to test their limits. Instructors have to know about the actual physical and technical difficulty of the various tasks in which limits are tested.

Certain staff members seemed "too competent" or "too professional" for Outward Bound. At times they seemed to demand too much perfection in the way an act was performed. And other staff members did not seem sufficiently aware of how difficult the beginning stages of a climb or portage were for a student.

Throughout, however, their high degree of technical competence was essential for safety. Their standards of safety, often based on an experience with a tragic accident, were an essential aspect of the Outward Bound experience. And they spoke out when they felt these standards were being compromised either in the area of equipment or supervision.

Fewer on the Outward Bound staff are effective educators. It takes great skill as an educator to know when a person is stretching his limits. The effective educators usually were not among the most technically proficient. Having some instructors who were not physical "supermen" helped students communicate with staff and learn from them. An instructor who became winded in the morning run seemed more accessible to the student who had a similar experience. The primary teaching mode is an example.

Staff members are generally quite dedicated to their job. It is hard to imagine how they could accept the considerable demands on their energy, patience and understanding without this dedication.

As important as it is to have good instructors, it is even more important to avoid "bad" ones. Unqualified instructors are rare, but in the one instance that we observed the effect was near disastrous. This instructor at times severely compromised safety standards, at other times perverted education into militaristic regimentation and seemed a "cheerleader" for a cause he neither understood nor participated in.

Staff selection, therefore, is critical. Staff training programs are employed at Outward Bound schools both to understand staff better, selecting out the unqualified, and to orient staff toward the Outward Bound approach. Another good staff selection and training procedure is the extensive in-service program at Outward Bound schools for staff-trainees, many of whom have recently completed an Outward Bound course. These staff-trainees assist instructors and there is ample opportunity to judge their potential as regular staff.

OUTWARD BOUND'S EDUCATIONAL GOALS

Outward Bound functions more in terms of experiences, actions, and activities than explicit educational goals. Its theory of education and personal growth is implicit and unarticulated. There are, however, educational goals which guide the selection and development of these experiences and activities. The basic goal is to encourage personal growth. Other goals, which are in a sense vehicles for encouraging personal growth, focus on developing courage, will power, a style of functioning which stresses pacing oneself, living efficiently and relying on one's natural resources; interpersonal competence to improve task performance, a desire and ability to serve others; and a religious attitude.

In discussing these goals, we will comment on two aspects: the discrepancy between the goal which actually operates at the schools and the educational goals stated in the Outward Bound ideology; and the degree of success in attaining the former goals.

Personal Growth

Encouraging personal growth is perhaps the basic and overriding educational goal at Outward Bound. One very important aspect of this goal is that personal growth be sustained *and* generalized after Outward Bound. The Outward Bound idea is to educate *through* mountain-climbing, canoeing, or navigating on the open sea. For example, overcoming a physical obstacle is a teaching analogy for overcoming a psychological obstacle. There are serious obstacles to making this idea operational. The problem is that educational implications of the physical activities are not always *automatically* perceived or experienced.

Generally, students do not intuitively or immediately see the relationship between, for example, climbing a mountain and the issues which concern them back home. An obvious case is the city-dweller who remarks that there are no mountains or lakes on his block. This concrete approach is most prevalent and takes time to overcome. The staff at times unwittingly reinforce this dilemma in students. There is a strong feeling that all a student has to do is climb one of the taller peaks and an important educational experience will occur for him.

Moreover, students often want to become competent in the activity at hand, to the point where the activity can easily become an end in itself. For example, as students develop skill and competence in navigation, they often become captivated by an image of themselves as professional sailors.

Other features of the Outward Bound experience make it seem unrelated to the situations most students face after the course. For example, the schools are located in retreat-like wilderness settings quite unlike the urban, industrialized environments most boys are in contact with. This difference between the Outward Bound environment and the home environment can serve as a stimulus to change while at Outward Bound. In a new environment individuals often try out new behaviors. This difference also, however, makes integrating the Outward Bound experience into daily functioning after the course more difficult.

Post-course conditions are not conducive to supporting personal growth changes in students. Students have few procedures available for integrating the important and special Outward Bound experience into their daily functioning. Some Outward Bound students can talk with others who have been to Outward Bound. Other students try to bring small parts of Outward Bound into their daily functioning on their own. For example, they may run every morning. But this is not easy to keep up. A few of the Outward Bound students continue actively in the Outward Bound organization as staff-trainees and then as staff.

Without such integration into a student's daily functioning, the Outward Bound experience can elicit feelings not conducive to long-term change. Students can easily become nostalgic, looking back on the Outward Bound course as a major life experience which is a "past" event, something which could never be duplicated. They may even wonder how they were able to do what they did at Outward Bound. This can happen when, after getting distance from the Outward Bound experience, one feels more completely the fears which accompanied particular challenges. Changes in self-image felt during the course may begin to seem alien to a person. The tendency to exaggerate the dramatic and dangerous aspects of the course to the exclusion of the frequent experiences of *gradual* change increases the difficulty of sustained personal growth.

Courage

There are many kinds of danger at Outward Bound, and many fears are evoked. Outward Bound tries to develop students' courage, their ability to deal with danger. Physical dangers, at times involving a student's life, are emphasized both in the public relations media and during the course. But there are other dangers which seem potentially to have a great impact on students. There is, for example, the danger of not succeeding, and the accompanying fear of failure. On the long hikes, one can never be sure all the time one will make it. Confrontation with what is *subjectively* felt as dangerous is a crucial part of a student's Outward Bound experience. Were it not for this, Outward Bound would become just another summer camp.

In examining the element of danger and its accompanying fear we will focus on physical danger. Of all the dangers present at Outward Bound, physical danger seems the best understood, the most carefully worked on, and the most emphasized, particularly by students.

An educationally-effective amount of danger, involving a balance of "objective" danger and what is "subjectively" felt as dangerous, is not easily attained at Outward Bound. Tasks which are objectively dangerous are not always synonymous with tasks which are subjectively felt as dangerous. Climbing up loose rock is in fact (objectively) quite dangerous, but students do not instinctively feel it as particularly dangerous. The rappell, on the other hand, is usually felt as being quite dangerous, though it is, in fact, fairly safe.

Most often tasks which are subjectively felt as dangerous depend on the students' inexperience with the task requirements. The first time one climbs a rock face, or "shoots the rapids" or is on the sea at night in an open boat is entirely different from the second or any succeeding time. The unknown is critical to generating a feeling of danger. Often, as a student gains experience with such tasks they feel less dangerous and *can* become objectively less dangerous. But students can also make the tasks objectively *more* dangerous through overconfidence.

Some tasks seem designed to provide the students with a "new thrill," a new danger experience. Some of the more professional staff objected to this, particularly when the task did not seem to prepare students for functioning in their wilderness environment.

Yet if objective physical dangers were eliminated, the Outward Bound experience might be much less intense than it now is. It seems likely that many of the instructors would no longer operate as effectively. Since they know there are objective dangers, they retain a very intense and active participation.

The approach of the more professional staff members to physical danger is that they believe in exploring limits, but with continued knowledgeable and careful assessment of the dangers involved and the probabilities of surviving those dangers. Their approach is safe and reasonable, while they continue to extend themselves and confront danger. The importance of technical competence *and* judgment again becomes clear.

Tasks which involve physical danger are clearly defined. Rules for meeting these tasks are specified and adherence is demanded. The dangers inherent in the task are explained and methods for dealing with them are outlined. It is made very clear that "one wrong step" really can mean the difference between life and death.

Students are instructed against doing "reckless" things. They are told to appraise the situation, and determine the probability of success, the degree of danger. Once a particular action is deemed appropriate, the student is told to complete the action successfully. He literally cannot afford to think about how frightening that moment is until he has performed the action. Too much introspection could lead to dangerous self-consciousness, even physical immobilization. That is probably what happened to the boy who froze on the rock face. It is not easy for students to focus on the next hand-hold and ignore the fact that they have never been more frightened in their lives.

The fact that certain procedures and rules are necessary to meeting dangerous tasks has important implications. A student cannot participate in certain parts of the course if he has not mastered the rules.

Having a boy on a climb who has not mastered the safety rules is quite different from having a student in a class who does not understand the math problem. A boy on the mountain who is not aware of the safety precautions can endanger his own life and the lives of others. Because of the cumulative nature of the learning at Outward Bound and because techniques are taught rapidly it becomes essential that a student participate continually and from the start of the course. Special instruction to develop a skill is not always available since the staff is already overworked.

Moments of danger are embedded in the "daily" requirements of persistence. The times when a student has to confront danger often come unexpectedly. A climber might approach a crevasse, and a moment of danger is unexpectedly at hand. Or a dangerous task could be expected; one could work toward mastering it. For example, students were aware of the "big rappell" even before they began the course. But throughout, there was need for persistence. Tasks which require persistence take up more actual time in the Outward Bound course than tasks requiring other capacities. Tasks involving danger, however, are often emphasized more and considered more significant by students.

Will Power

Outward Bound tries to develop the capacity for persistence or will power. The persistence needed is both physical and psychological. The need for physical persistence is quite clear. The long hikes, the long rows, the long portages, all require substantial persistence. Well after fatigue has set in, when physical pain has already come and gone, students must continue. In the conditioning exercises, for example, though a student is completely exhausted, he is asked to "do one more" pull-up, etc. The need for persistence often leads to a fatigue which lowers psychological resistance.

Psychological persistence is equally important. We talked of the waiting at the rock face, the long waits before it was your turn to climb and face danger. Students also must stay with a task even though the rewards are few or scattered far apart. The long expedition often involved sleepless nights. The three-day solo experience is primarily a test of persistence. It becomes a single dramatic event in *post hoc* descriptions, rather than so many minutes, hours or days facing boredom and loneliness.

The need for persistence imparts a sense of continuity to the Outward Bound experience. Were they not set within the context of persistence, the moments of danger would more likely become merely discrete "spectaculars." Set within the context of persistence, these moments are more likely to have an effect on personal growth.

Style of Functioning

The individual must develop a particular style of functioning. A steady, regular pace is needed to master many of the tasks and to meet the demands made upon one's energy. As we saw on the climb up the rock face, steady, regular movements are required. "Scrambling" makes the task extremely difficult and dangerous. The hikes, expeditions, canoe trips—all demand energy expenditure spread over long periods of time. Especially in the early part of the course, students do not have a regular rhythm to their canoe paddling and will put forth spurts of hard paddling amid generally lackadaisical paddling. It is only in time that students realize how important it is to have a regular rhythm. Not all students learn this, and for those who do not, a long day of canoeing, hiking, or rowing is extraordinarily difficult. The urge to "work hard and get there faster" has to be subdued, and regular breaks are essential.

There is an important difference between pacing which is externally imposed and pacing which evolves from within, based on the student's own characteristics. The former is very mechanical, the latter is more of a rhythm. Most students do not develop this ideal rhythmic pacing.

Within this steady, regular pace, the individual must also be flexible, ready for unusual demands on his energy and able to adapt to a changing environment. On white water, one must be able to make "just the right stroke" at a specific time. One has to be able to react quickly, and one's instincts must be right more often than wrong. Students must learn to regulate their body temperature by making adjustments in their clothing; one must also keep dry in changing weather conditions. If one's pacing is merely mechanical, this flexibility is more difficult to attain.

The individual must learn to live simply, efficiently, and economically. On expedition, the students can take only the essentials, because the weight of the packs must be kept down. Gear must be organized and packed efficiently. Space, too, is at a premium. The solo experience for many students epitomizes this need to live simply, efficiently, and economically. The idea of the body as a "machine" becomes important. For example, one takes on expedition small amounts of higher energy food and feeds the body as you would stoke a furnace. Food is fuel, to provide energy. Simplicity, efficiency, and economy are much more characteristic of behavior in the field than at the school's home base. Still there are very few frills at school, for example, no TVs or radios, and students live in tents.

The individual must continually exert his own effort without employing shortcuts. There is a conscious emphasis on the use of the most basic (often archaic) modes for student training. You hike at Outward Bound whenever possible. Rides are available only if walking would take too much time. Whaleboats equipped with oars, at times using sails, are used instead of power boats.

Technological aids are used primarily by staff, particularly to insure safety. Various communication devices and power boats are available for rescue operations. Staff members also sometimes "treat" themselves to the "luxury" of modern conveniences, such as the latest in alpine stoves.

The tasks which require efficiency, economy, and use of one's own resources are considered "lessons" in getting close to one's "natural conditions." These lessons, however, seem short-lived. Perhaps the best example of this is the solo experience. The student alone must deal with his basic needs for food, warmth, shelter and companionship at a very primitive level. He must also meet his more subtle needs associated with time itself. Four days and three nights alone in the woods is a long time, and boredom is one of the major elements in the solo. During the solo he comes to understand his basic needs more intimately for he often has difficulty in meeting them, let alone fulfilling them. Unfortunately, much of this understanding seems tied to the particular task of completing the solo. After solo, students very quickly forget many of the things they learned.

There seems to be insufficient amounts of fun, play, release, and exploration. These seem necessary counterpoints to the pacing, efficiency, and economy. There is a tremendous pressure to take a longer route, to push on further before making camp. This pressure means that recreation must be sacrificed, for example, an evening dip in the lake, or exploring an island. When recreation is sacrificed too often, things seem to get stale. Fatigue builds to an unproductive level.

Interpersonal Relations

Outward Bound seeks to develop interpersonal competence and sensitivity, primarily *toward* improving task performance. Extensive or intensive interpersonal relationships are not encouraged, nor are they frequent. This presents a problem, for often such relationships seem necessary to the Outward Bound experience. We talked, for example, of how the educational impact of a fear experience might be increased if the student could share this experience with others. But sharing feelings of fear in a constructive way usually requires a good deal of understanding and trust among people. A relationship of such depth is not frequent at Outward Bound.

The fact that interpersonal relations are oriented toward task performance also influences the concept of Outward Bound as a "melting pot." Although there is great opportunity for Outward Bound to be a melting pot experience, what in fact happens is that a heterogeneous group of students learns to function as a team but the individuals do not come to understand each other in any depth. The initiative tests are a good illustration of how students develop teamwork. The teamwork develops on the basis of an appraisal of the particular strengths and weaknesses of the individual members. For example, someone who is quite strong fulfills one part of the task, someone who is light and can jump high fills another. But the variety which makes up any one person is not explored. The part of him which is functionally important, that is, which will lead to the solution of a task, is emphasized. Students easily acquire labels, and these labels are misleading. They can make empty and facile the Outward Bound idea that "each boy has a contribution to make." Too often a student's contribution becomes a not too subtle smokescreen for a failure to accept him as a person. Also, the teamwork which develops does not seem particularly durable.

Impressive learning could occur if interpersonal exploration were encouraged. Since the group composition is heterogeneous and there are a number of intense, shared experiences, groups could communicate about important things. This kind of interchange does happen spontaneously, on occasion, and the results seem fruitful.

The helping relationship provides a further example of the task-oriented nature of interpersonal relations. "To help" and "to be helped" are important aspects of Outward Bound. Students depend on each other in an ultimate but circumscribed way. As we described in the climb up the rock face, the climber depends in an ultimate way on the belayer. But the belayer is more a role than a person. Any student could belay for any other. The exigencies of the task seem to bring out the helping response, which in other less demanding situations is conspicuously absent.

Competition with standards of excellence and concern with effective performance are rather fully explored. Intergroup competition is an explicit issue at Outward Bound. There are days set aside for group competition and daily scores are often kept. Competition with oneself is also stressed. Students are encouraged to improve upon their past performances. On the rock face, the need to immediately climb a second time and this time not fall, was in complete harmony with the Outward Bound idea. Tasks like the conditioning exercises encourage the individual to gradually improve his skills and better his prior performance. Inter-individual competition, though not encouraged, is allowed. The marathon race, for example, is often an opportunity for individuals to compete against each other, in spite of the fact that group scores are kept. Much of the impetus for competition comes from the staff. The staff are continually trying to do a task more efficiently, or present themselves with a harder task to complete. The staff members also compete with each other, often using their groups in this competition.

There is little support for expressing what are traditionally considered more feminine concerns, such as, tenderness, caring about others, sensitivity to others' needs. Overprotective concern for others is often ridiculed. There is a tendency to polarize these expressions of tenderness and sympathy into a concept of femininity (and weakness) as contrasted with masculinity. Feelings and appreciation of beauty also tend to be pushed into a concept of femininity.

The deemphasis on exploring interpersonal issues seems to result from both characteristics of the Outward Bound program and staff preferences. It is thought that exploration of interpersonal issues can make task performance ineffective, at least in the early stages. Again, because of constraints of time, as well as the fact that real dangers exist with many tasks, tasks must be performed effectively quite soon. Finally, few structures encourage exploration of interpersonal issues. There are, for example, few times devoted to group discussions.

Most of the Outward Bound staff do not see their jobs as encouraging interpersonal exploration. They feel that task performance is the essential aspect of Outward Bound. Interpersonal understanding, if it occurs, is seen as an outgrowth of task performance.

Service

Outward Bound works in three areas to develop the desire to serve: it develops confidence in being able to help others; students are taught certain service skills, e.g., fire-fighting, first-aid; and it encourages a service attitude or orientation. The schools serve as official search and rescue centers for their areas, and many members of the staff have participated in a number of rescues.

"Real" perhaps dramatic service opportunities seem important to developing in students the desire to serve. There are a number of simulated rescue operations. But rarely does a faked injury convince many of the students. When the rescue is real, it is completely different. Involvement is higher because the stakes are higher. Students go beyond themselves on the real rescues, whereas on the simulated ones, they do not. The rarity of real rescues is fortunate, but it does somewhat detract from the intensity of the service opportunity for the students involved.

Real and dramatic service opportunities (for example, a rescue) engage students more than do real but mundane opportunities. This encourages a limited, immature concept of service. Too often it seems that, in the minds of the students, service becomes equivalent with rescue operations. Keeping the woods clean on a canoe trip to prevent fire hazard does not engage students' interest or energy. But such more mundane service opportunities are frequent. They also seem central to serving others, relating to a more *general* desire to serve, a *general* concern and feeling of responsibility for the welfare of others. This general desire to serve does not necessarily spring from a student's involvement in a rescue operation.

Religious Attitude

Daily morning readings, followed by a period of silence, are the formal religious vehicle. The readings deal with themes such as man's insignificance in relation to nature, the beauty of nature, the importance of persistence. Often, however, students do not listen attentively. In the field, religious moments are less frequent but usually more powerful. When a student is called upon to give grace for the meal which follows a long hard day of canoeing, the grace can be quite inspiring. The impact of a magnificent view on a climb can be quite powerful.

Much of the religious attitude at Outward Bound focuses on men's relationship with nature. At the start of the course, students usually struggle with or fight against nature. As the course progresses, they learn more how to cooperate with nature and, on occasion, to appreciate it. The first climb of a mountain is usually a conquering of the peak. As students learn more to pace themselves, they move more towards a cooperation with nature. They begin to understand the significance of the solo preparation for the island off Maine: "When the tide is low, your dinner table is set."

Staff generally cooperates with and appreciates nature, and values a "return to nature." They have a somewhat neutral attitude toward nature. They feel that they have a job to do and that nature has her own ways. They try to maximize the congruence between their needs and nature's ways. Staff highly value the more natural, uncomplicated, primitive way in which they can live in the field.

Rules of conduct are pervasive, and are ethical as well as functional. The rules against smoking and drinking make sense in terms of physical conditioning. But they are also presented to the students as having a moral implication. The "rules of the wilderness" likewise have both the functional and moralistic quality. One keeps the campsite clean of litter so as to prevent fires, but also out of courtesy to the next user and adherence to a "woodsmen's code." The pledge students make at the beginning of the course to abide by Outward Bound rules is both given and taken seriously and with strong moral overtones. Boys often turn themselves in when they violate parts of the pledge. The violations are conceived of primarily as moral violations.

EVALUATION AT OUTWARD BOUND

"Success" at Outward Bound is determined less by what the student does than by his attitude. The criteria of success are, moreover, ambiguous and individualistic. This gives added validity to the remark often made to students: "Only *you* know how you've done in this course, whether you stretched your limits." The formal evaluation process, culminating in the award of a certificate, is, however, controlled by staff.

Most students complete all of the Outward Bound program. Completing tasks is particularly important in the mind of the students. It is an easy way for them to measure how they are doing and how they compare with fellow students. There are many modifications in the tasks to be performed. But some of the most demanding and dangerous parts of the program are considered essential to complete (e.g., the solo, the marathon).

Perhaps the most important quality a student must show is the desire to confront himself and go beyond what he thought were his limits. Frequently, a student will confront himself, yet not be able to explore or stretch his limits extensively. A student may overcome his bravado but still not acquire new ways of dealing with his fear. Certain other student attitudes are valued at Outward Bound and serve as important criteria of success. It is important, for example, to do things because one wants to, or because one is willing, rather than because one is forced. It is important that students continually try. Though one does not have to be joyful or cheerful while going through an Outward Bound course, one should not be a thorough-going complainer. It is also important to work toward more than a minimum performance. The student is expected, for example, to be constructive during his solo rather than just lie all the time in his sleeping bag (if he has one). The ideal is to have the student desire excellence in his performance.

Though it may be easy to judge if a student has physically completed a particular task, it is not easy to decide what the specific task for that student should be. Students' reactions and attitudes, the more important criteria of success, are even more difficult to judge. Moreover, instructors have differing ideas about the appropriate attitude or approach to the Outward Bound course.

The problem of "malingering" highlights the dilemma of determining success at Outward Bound. Who is to say whether the sprained ankle or aching back is enough to put one out of commission? What will lead one boy to give up may be taken by another as a challenge. In the final analysis, each student knows how he did, whether he pushed himself or eased through. This seems valid, for the Outward Bound experience is in essence an internal one. Yet when it comes to deciding who passes the course, the responsibility shifts to the staff.

The criteria of success are ambiguous. Staff occupies a powerful position at the schools. A student will naturally look to the staff for some indication as to whether he is doing well. And staff freely gives feedback to a student about his performance and attitude. Staff, however, decides whether a student formally passes the course.

Giving staff this decision-making power seriously undercuts the idea that the student himself must be the ultimate judge of how he did in the course. Instructors, of course, try to find out a student's self-evaluation. There are interviews set aside for this purpose. Often, however, the instructor spends most of the time giving the student his (the instructor's) frank evaluation of him, leaving little time for the student's own evaluation of himself. Self-evaluation can be a valid assessment technique as well as an educational process (Kolb, Winter, Berlew, 1968; Katz, ditto). Considering also the particular importance of self-evaluation at Outward Bound, it would appear useful to include students in a more meaningful way in the evaluation process.

Being awarded the Outward Bound certificate is the formal sign of passing the course. The certificates are awarded in a serious ceremony which is viewed by staff and students as the culmination of the course. Certificates are accepted with pride. Even the boy who played the role of the court jester becomes quite serious when he walks up to accept his certificate.

There are, however, no easy formulas for deciding who gets the certificate. With many students the decision about a certificate becomes a question of balancing his strength and weaknesses, or balancing Outward Bound standards with a student's own personal growth. If a student has fulfilled all the task requirements, it is hard not to give him a certificate, unless his attitude has been poor. On the other hand, if a student has an excellent attitude, he can be awarded the certificate despite the fact that he has not finished all parts of the course.[8]

There is a general belief that certificates are awarded to those who deserve them. The assumption is made that certificates are an accurate external sign of students' internal judgment of their own success at Outward Bound. In some of these cases, certificates are awarded to encourage the student to act *so as* to deserve it. Rarely can a student maintain belief in his own judgment about the certificate when it conflicts with the staffs' judgment. Decisions about certificates thus have a compelling and final quality.

In addition to certificates, a report is written on each student by his instructor. This report attempts a more extensive and intensive description and evaluation of the student's behavior and attitude during the course. The report is sent to the student's parents or sponsors. With these reports, evaluation becomes more of a learning experience because instructors usually discuss with a student the content of his report during an interview at the end of the course.

SUMMARY

We have tried to present the data about Outward Bound as social scientists. Careful, objective descriptions and evaluations have been our aim. Such an approach does not allow for enthusiasm. In our summary statement about Outward Bound, we wish to express enthusiasm. We feel enthusiastic about Outward Bound's potential and capacity to educate for personal growth. We feel, however, that this enthusiasm should be coupled with several recommendations. Foremost is that Outward Bound continue to engage in critical self-examination, expressing the results of this examination in modifications of its approach and program. The mobile courses and courses for adults are exciting modifications.

As the demand for new types of Outward Bound programs continues there must be some guidelines for developing these programs. What educational principles of Outward Bound must be retained in any modification of the standard program? In what sense must Outward Bound move from the wilderness retreat to the urban environment? What does it mean to have self-confrontation in the classroom? What kinds of persons may not find Outward Bound a particularly educating experience? A second important area involves what a student does *after* his Outward Bound course. Procedures are needed for maintaining and developing some of the changes begun during the course. Finally, there is the problem of maintaining staff quality. With the increasing popularity of Outward Bound and Outward Bound type programs, the need for accurate staff selection and thorough staff training becomes acute. How can staff be recruited in large numbers when the requirements for the job are so demanding? Outward Bound's effectiveness and future development depend on how it deals with such issues.

FOOTNOTES

1. Courses for females aged 16-23 and for male and female adults are conducted, e.g., at Minnesota Outward Bound.

2. Generally, the first 10 days are spent in developing wilderness skills and going on a two to three day wilderness expedition. This is in preparation for a long expedition, approximately 10-15 days, towards the end of which is the "solo-experience." Students spend approximately four days and three nights alone in the wilderness with minimal resources for food, warmth and shelter. At the end of the course students have increased responsibility in planning and conducting expeditions.

3. Thomas D'Andres attended the full course at Minnesota Outward Bound; Richard Katz, the full course at Colorado, and Minnesota and three days at Maine; David Kolb, two weeks at Maine.

4. The ropes course consists of a series of physical tasks demanding balance, agility and some strength; they are often performed at considerable heights.

5. The rappell is a method for descending a rock face in which the person at times "walks down" perpendicular to the rock face.

6. Initiative tests demand that students collaborate with each other and put together physical resources to solve an apparently unsolvable problem within a time limit.

7. A recent Outward Bound innovation—"the mobile course"—has a more flexible schedule. Mobile courses occur entirely in the field. Because they must respond to exigencies of the field situation their scheduling is more open.

8. Certificates are sometimes awarded contingent on what the student does for a period of time after the course formally ends. Violation of Outward Bound rules, such as smoking and drinking, disqualifies a student from receiving a certificate. If this student, however, has done well enough in the rest of the course, he is given what amounts to another chance. For example, if he smoked during the course, but does not smoke for a specified period of time after the course, he may be awarded the certificate.

References

Allport, Gordon. "The Historical Background of Modern Social Psychology." In G. Lindsey, ed., *Handbook of Social Psychology*. Vol. I. Reading, Massachusetts: Addison-Wesley, 1954.

Alschuler, Alfred. "Psychological Education." *Harvard Graduate School of Education Alumni Bulletin.* In press, Winter 1968.

Burns, Neal M.; Chambers, Randall M.; and Hendler, Edwin, eds. *Unusual Environments and Human Behavior.* Glencoe, Illinois: Free Press, 1963.

Campbell, Joseph, *The Hero with a Thousand Faces.* New York: Meridian Books, 1956.

Erikson, Erik. "Identity and the life cycle." *Psychological Issues. I,* no. 1. New York: International Universities Press, 1959.

Goffman, Erving. *Asylums.* New York: Doubleday and Co., 1961.

James, William. *The Varieties of Religious Experience.* New York: Random House, 1929.

Katz, Richard. *Self-assessment Workshop,* Human Development Foundation, Cambridge, Mass., 1970.

Katz, Richard. "Solo-survival: An Experience for Personal Growth," *Educational Opportunities Forum,* New York State Department of Education, August 1969. Reprinted in Purpel and Belanger, eds., *Curriculum and the Cultural Revolution,* Berkeley: McCutchan, 1972.

Katz, Richard. *Preludes to Growth: An Experiential Approach,* New York: Free Press, 1973.

Kolb, David; Winter, Sara; and Berlew, David; "Self-Directed Change: Two Studies," *Journal of Applied Behavioral Science,* 1968.

Maslow, Abraham. *Toward a Psychology of Being.* Princeton, New Jersey: D. Van Nostrand (Insight Series), 1962.

Maslow, Abraham. *The Further Reaches of Men.* New York: Viking Press, 1972.

Outward Bound. *Into the Mainstream.* Outward Bound, Inc., Andover, Massachusetts: Brochure.

Outward Bound Schools. Outward Bound, Inc., Andover, Massachusetts: Course brochure.

Rogers, Carl. "The Process of the Basic Encounter Group." In J. Bugental, ed., *Challenges of Humanistic Psychology.* New York: McGraw-Hill Book Co., 1967.

Schein, Edgar and Bennis, Warren. *Personal and Organizational Change Through Group Methods.* New York: John Wiley & Sons, Inc., 1965.

Ungar, Sanford. "Mescaline, LSD, Psilocybin and Personality Change." *Psychiatry.* 26 (1963): 111-125.

Van Gennep, Arnold. *The Rites of Passage.* Chicago: University of Chicago Press (Phoenix Books), 1960.

White, Robert. "Motivation Reconsidered: The Concept of Competence." *Psychological Review,* 66 (1959): 297-333.

Part Three
Public School Alternatives

In this section we begin by sharing the experiences of alternative arrangements that have endured and become institutionalized: business-industry cooperative programs and community schools. Both areas are rich in their potential resources for all students and for particular students. These are followed by a consideration of some possible legal issues involved in out-of-class experiences. This is offered not as a barrier to opening the schools but as a guide to how to go about it with the least chance of inviting sanctions from the courts.

Accounts by administrators in St. Louis and Toledo will make the point that those cities are even now significantly involved in the use of alternatives. These accounts are followed by a pair of articles on each of two cities, Philadelphia and New York. In each of these sets we begin with an article by the superintendent, followed by another describing alternatives in the city. We begin with Philadelphia and Parkway School. The superintendent-author has since resigned. There is no suggestion that pressures which led to this had anything to do with the Parkway Program. However, the overall situation suggests the nature of the administrator's dilemma. There are powerful forces seeking to bring about changes in the educational institution. This is easily recognized. What is sometimes not so evident is the strength and determination of forces seeking to prevent the very changes sought so vigorously by others. The lesson for our present purpose—to consider alternatives to in-class teaching—is that it does require some risk taking. But isn't that something that now comes with the school administrator's territory?

Two articles which suggest specific tactics are presented by Bailey and Cunningham. These are followed by the only selection from the group of writer-teacher critics of education—Kohl's piece on "Options." Principals and teachers will find the remainder of articles in this section of particular interest. They deal with the specifics of alternatives. One in particular on the role of parents should be read by everyone involved in the planning and implementation of alternatives.

No models are provided in these selections. However, there is much to be learned by the experiences described and even more to be suggested by the process itself—seeking to provide superior alternatives. This process is represented in ways varying from almost an innovative system within a system—Parkway—to merely providing additional options to in-class teaching—independent study, optional class attendance. As educators consider alternatives, it seems important that they not take the role of succumbing to pressures—however fierce—to change so much as they determine alternatives which would be potentially superior methods of in-class teaching. Then, it follows that there is a burden of proof to be accomplished by a plan for evaluation.

14

Tested Alternatives:
Industry and Education

JAMES J. BUFFER

INTRODUCTION

The concept of formulating alternatives to in-class teaching is not entirely new to teachers of industrial arts, trade and industrial education, business, agriculture, and home economics. Historically, these practical arts and vocational educators have recognized the need to develop cooperative working relations with business and industry to plan, operate, and evaluate occupational-career education programs that are appropriate reflections of existing techno-logical-cultural developments and social needs. A variety of programs designed to provide learners with first-hand experiences in industry as an integral part of their formal secondary education have been in existence for several decades. They are probably the only alternate forms of educational strategies and practices to the traditional in-school concept that educational practitioners can assess as a means of evaluating the efficacy of this form of educa-tion. They have been around for awhile so we do know something about them.

This report contains a review of information that should provide educational administrators with a basic understanding of coopera-tive activities between industry and industrial education. It includes

Written especially for this book. James J. Buffer is an associate professor at Ohio State University.

a descriptive analysis of selected programs that are representative examples of education-industry cooperative arrangements that have existed in the past and those that are currently being practiced. We leave it to the school administrators to decide what elements of these arrangements have important implications to help them in their search for alternative ways to learning in other areas of the curriculum.

The term "industry," as used in this selection, will refer to the broad spectrum of industry, including construction, manufacturing, business (merchandising), agriculture, and various hybrids, such as agribusiness and servicing. Practical arts and vocational courses which draw their body of knowledge from industry as defined above, will be referred to as "industrial education."

Clarification of Terminology and Purpose of Industrial Education

Unfortunately, there is confusion among educators and industrialists regarding the meanings assigned to the terms used in vocational and practical arts education and their role in public secondary education curriculum. *Vocational education* refers to that part of the school program which is designed to provide information and skill that would enable students to obtain employment in a specific area immediately upon their successful completion of study. Training is provided in four industrial areas—trade and industry, business and office occupations, homemaking, agriculture, and service occupations (barbering, etc.). Courses traditionally found in conventional secondary school vocational programs include machine shop, automotives, welding, business and office machines, care of swine or dairy herds, clothing, horticulture, and cosmetology. Students typically spend from two to four hours a day in these laboratory based courses for a two year period in the eleventh and twelfth grades in preparation for specific careers, or occupational skill is developed on the job as part of cooperative work experience courses. School systems receive financial reimbursement through federal legislation for operating these programs. Their other secondary school subjects might include vocational or trade related courses such as shop math or drafting, as well as general education subjects needed for graduation.

Courses classified as practical arts include industrial arts, home economics, and business education and have as their major thrusts the preparation of all youth for active involvement as socially responsible and productive citizens. Such courses include crafts, personal typing, sewing, child care and development, cooking, woodworking, power mechanics, and graphic arts. Industrial arts for boys and home economics for girls are generally required for one year during grades 7-9, and are elective in grades 10-12. Secondary school practical arts have been fully financed by local boards of education since vocational education funds have not been traditionally available. Also, students only spend an average of 40 minutes a day, 3-5 days a week in these courses and supplement their remaining educational program with courses from the total curriculum depending on individual educational and career aspirations. These educational experiences are considered to benefit all regardless of their occupational and educational goals.

An important aspect of the formal school is to provide technological literacy for all people who are attempting to function as socially competent, resourceful, and productive citizens. This information and skill may be applied to leisure, social, political, and occupational activities depending on one's abilities and interests. Obviously, technologies have changed societal conditions to include new occupational and sociocultural behavior patterns and life styles. Now the conventional industrial arts courses of woodworking, metalworking, and mechanical drawing which dominate the junior high school curriculum are no longer appropriate to provide youth with an orientation to their industrial, man-made culture. Many of the vocational-technical practices studied in the upper levels of secondary schools are either outdated or not expected to be in existence during the next decade. The equipment, tools, and materials used in many of these programs have long been discarded by industry. Unfortunately, industrial educators have been forced to scrounge for resources since their entry into public education and, as a result, antiquated equipment is being used to educate young men and women for nonexistent jobs. Then, too, many vocational industrial teachers could not improve their instructional programs because of their limited personal training in one trade specialty. Numerous technical innovations may have occurred since they were practicing craftsmen. Clearly, industrial teachers need continual in-service education to provide relevant technical information and skill.

In fairness to vocational-technical education, courses are available which provide excellent pre-employment preparation. However, the vocational classes available have been limited to a very small number of the construction and manufacturing crafts such as machine shop, auto servicing, carpentry, radio and television servicing, and the like. Few programs relate to the health occupations, for example. We need to expand the breadth of occupational offerings as well as to weed out the vocational deadwood and update career education.

Unfortunately, there is friction between vocational and practical arts educators. For example, some vocational educators have perceived industrial arts as strictly a prevocational course where boys gain an understanding of industrial tools and materials to help select a specialized trade to study in a vocational education program. Industrial arts teachers are thought to have a "bird house" mentality, undoubtedly a leftover from the time when thousands of industrial arts teachers accepted the challenge of the Audubon Society to provide shelter for our cherished wildlife. Vocational trade and industrial education has been perceived as providing highly specialized skill training too early in one's lifetime and often the technical practices were not current or applicable only to job preparation. Teachers were considered craftsmen but not professional educators. Fortunately, articulation between both professional groups is improving and attempts are being made for continued cooperative efforts (Linson, et al., 1971). Recent curricular developments, such as the Industrial Arts Curriculum Project (IACP) at Ohio State University and American Industries Project at Stout State University, are representative of cooperative efforts of educators and industrialists to provide more relevant industrial programs for American youth.

Recent Social Factors Affecting Industrial Education

The last two decades have been rather exciting periods of time in American public education. We have witnessed almost mass revolution by educators, lay people, politicians, and various vested interest groups to modify the existing school curricula.

The launching of Sputnik in 1957, and the concurrent criticism of such educational critics as Professor Arthur Bestor and Admiral Hyman Rickover, who saw the public schools responsible for the scientific and technical superiority of the USSR, provided the stimulus for the passage of the National Defense Education Act (NDEA) of 1958. Now, through bandaid approaches in good old-fashioned American tradition, it was thought that the problem would be solved by placing a stress on science, mathematics, foreign languages, and technical education. Also, guidance counselors would be trained and employed in greater numbers to identify mentally superior students who could be channeled into college preparatory sequences to help fulfill this urgent national need. The "other" children were left to find appropriate experiences for themselves. This usually meant occupationally oriented curricula—shop for the boys, and sewing and cooking for the girls.

By and large, this was not very different from the program selection procedures traditionally followed in the past. However, there were now thousands of dollars of federal money available for the in-service preparation of specialized teachers, work experience coordinators, and counselors and, also, for the purchase of specialized instructional hardware such as tape recorders, overhead projectors, and language recorders to supplement the instructional program. So, many bright young secondary students continued to enroll in college preparatory courses and the remaining were left to shift for themselves in such nebulously labeled courses as "general," or "commercial," or "vocational." Those who could not find satisfaction and adjust to these programs became "dropouts," often unemployed or unemployable, thus becoming social dependents.

Educators were very concerned about the dropouts, especially in our larger urban centers where the figures often reached 60-65 percent in inner city schools. Although numerous studies were done to identify potential dropouts, only a few successful modifications were made in the school program to provide educational treatment for this group. One of the earliest recommendations was the work-study program that allowed students to attend school on a part time basis and also be employed on a part time basis. The administrative structure and nature of these programs varied, but, basically, they attempted to involve cooperative activities between the school, industry, and the student.

Unemployment, illiteracy, delinquency, and crime have been increasing, particularly in our crowded inner urban centers. There is little doubt that much of the recent federal legislation affecting education was drafted as a means of modifying educational programs to help combat social illiteracy as well as to develop educational skills in order to prevent the social disruptions that were so evident in major cities during 1967.

The impact of these problems upon industry—construction, manufacturing, agriculture, and business—was severe. It became apparent that recent technological developments were providing new and more complex industrial techniques and practices to produce material goods and services. The need for skilled operators, installers, servicemen, and technical specialists has probably made industry more concerned with education. Complex automated machinery was being designed and manufactured, but who would operate and service the equipment? Could the journeyman machinist, for example, be retrained to use the new complicated equipment or would it be necessary to recruit and train new personnel? Who would be responsible for developing and operating occupational training programs—public schools, industry, government? Also, would society continue to function and improve itself or would social strife continue along with social disintegration?

A Need for Articulation

It was becoming apparent that industry wanted schools to provide the fundamental information and skills (social and technical) that would provide at least entry level employment in industry. Industry could no longer afford to be taxed twice for the basic education of the labor force by supporting public education through the payment of corporate taxes and again by conducting their own industrial based educational programs. Students, parents, and taxpayers were also demanding that curricula be modified to provide relevant educational experiences to enable entrance in careers and occupations other than those traditionally available to the typical high school graduate. Thus, improved articulation and cooperative activity between industry and public education has become a necessity rather than a public relations venture.

A concerted effort of practical arts and vocational educators can provide leadership to modify existing narrow skill and task oriented programs by broadening the occupational education base to provide experiences which foster total career development for our technological society. Cooperative arrangements between industrial representatives and public school educators are necessary, if relevant education programs are to be structured for *all* boys and girls to produce citizens who are *technologically literate* as well as for those who wish to gain occupational information and skill which may be applied to some future *career* or *occupational choice.*

COOPERATIVE EDUCATION-INDUSTRY ACTIVITIES

One might argue that the vocational-technical public school industrial courses would not exist in the public schools if economic and political support had not been provided by private industry in the early 1900s. The increasing demand for skilled workers by industry and their inability to recruit sufficient numbers from the traditional apprentice training programs and European markets probably caused them to support federal legislation, which resulted in the passage of the Smith-Hughes Act in 1917. Smith-Hughes was the first piece of federal legislation to provide for direct financial support for training secondary school youth for industrial occupations.

Throughout the several decades during the evolution of federally reimbursed industrial education, additional federal legislation was created and made into law to supplement and improve vocational and technical education. Of particular importance is the Vocational Education Act of 1963, and its 1968 Amendments. It had become apparent that vocational programs had to be modified to meet the changing needs of youth, industry, and society. Too often, secondary school vocational programs were not preparing youth for existing occupations. Also, administrative functions as structured by former legislation restricted broader curriculum development, thus providing for few creative and dynamic educational programs. The new legislation was designed to eliminate these problems and provide impetus for change and real career education.

There is little doubt that the jobs created by industry have provided the impetus for expanding vocational education for youth and adults with an impact on education, possibly second only to the financial contributions industry has made through the payment of property taxes. Fortunately, industry has now begun to assume a social responsibility and is attempting to ameliorate social problems including unemployment, rioting, delinquency, and inferior education. Industry has become involved in the war on poverty and social crisis in America. Witness the partnership programs where industry has literally "adopted" a school or school system to help improve the education of children. Also, numerous job opportunities have been made available to unemployed and often unemployable men and women from disadvantaged (economically, educationally, and socially) groups. Many of these opportunities include in-plant training programs or cooperation with schools or other institutional agencies for educational training.

Numerous examples of cooperative arrangements between industry and education can be cited. Several examples of these practices and programs are reviewed, and some techniques that teachers and administrators could use to solicit assistance from industry are discussed in the remaining part of this selection.

Education-Industry Advisory Committees

A long-standing assumption among policy makers is that representatives from industry as well as business, labor, management, politics, and the community be involved in formulating policy in vocational and technical education. At the local levels, industrialists have functioned as members of *advisory committees* providing professional advice and guidance to educators in the planning and operating of vocational education activities. It has been estimated "... that some 20,000 advisory committees are functioning in schools offering vocational and technical education, and that approximately 100,000 industry people are involved. Nevertheless, the value of many such committees could well be questioned, especially those that meet only once a year for several hours" (Burt, 1967, p. 4).

Advisory committees could provide expertise that relates to the development of educational specifications, selection of equipment, facilities, tools, materials, and the development and selection of instructional materials. In some cases, the advisory board would help with the selection of teachers and/or adjunct professional staff from industry and education including consultants, supervisors, laboratory assistants, and the like. Generally, the group serves in an advisory capacity and does not accept any responsibility for the direct administration or control of the program, but merely provides suggestions and helps to formulate policy. Often, the committee can assist with the obtaining of financial and material resources, such as equipment, from private enterprise as well as local, state, and federal agencies.

It is not desirable to limit one's attempts for improved education-industry articulation through a formal advisory board, although this strategy seems to be one that can function very effectively. Members of advisory committees can provide much guidance and direction as well as obtaining human and material resources from other industrialists and representatives of management labor, and goverment. Educators can go directly to professional industrial groups to obtain support and/or economic and manpower resources rather than use a formal advisory group or in addition to using an organized group. For example, professional, management, and labor groups are looking for innovative programs and creative educators who are willing to change to improve the vocational education.

The writer has had an opportunity to work cooperatively with an organized advisory board which included representatives of management and labor, as well as interacting directly with several international and local labor unions, management associations, professional groups and societies, and business representatives during the past several years. This was an effort to improve education-industry articulation and gain professional support and financial assistance for the development and field testing of an innovative industrial arts program to improve the technological literacy of junior high school youth (Buffer, et al., 1971). The support was phenomenal, including numerous dissemination articles in trade and professional magazines; financial grants for research, development, and scholarships; motion picture films; photographs; and written instructional materials. Additional professional assistance was received by having industrial representatives from top positions in management and labor contact school board members, superintendents, and supervisors. In effect, many industrial representatives soon became intermediaries of our project and actively promoted the development, dissemination, and adoption of the innovative instructional program. This support from industry not only helps ensure future productive work forces; it may assure industry of support for such future issues as construction bonds for schools, sewage systems, and highways; and will reap consumer education benefits as well.

Basically, the assistance provided by the committee can be *advisory*, by providing guidance, direction, and help to formulate policy for programs. Secondly, the committee's task can be *operationally* oriented and could be concerned primarily with the accomplishment of some predetermined tasks as specified by the educational director.

The 1968 Amendments to the Vocational Education Act of 1963 require industry involvement in public school vocational educational programs. Educators are charged with the responsibility of initiating strategy for involving representatives from industry, business, and labor, to serve as advisory committee members. School systems may elect to appoint a full time vocational coordinator to serve as a liaison between education and industry and to provide planning and coordination for continual education-industry cooperation. Also, the Vocational Education Act of 1963 provides 50 percent reimbursement for the salary of such personnel.

Unfortunately, many school systems have neglected to formulate advisory boards of industrial personnel for purposes other than providing of "advice" for fear of too much "outside interference." Not only can active advisory committees provide professional assistance in improving local school programs, but they can also assist in improving the economic development of the state. For example, new plant site development relies on current and future manpower available in the community. Labor supply and vocational-technical education influence industrial development. Local and state economic developers are aware of this, and evaluate local vocational education facilities and programs accordingly, in order to attract industry; they assist educators in developing an appropriate vocational-technical system and advise legislators of the need for funds. Burt (1971) reports that South Carolina is a good example of where this practice has worked and where technical schools have attracted industry. Arkansas is similar, but there evaluation is done by industrial personnel rather than economists, and professional educators consult and advise.

Some school systems use advisory boards as evaluation agencies to do cost and result analyses, which means that educators have to keep financial and other records accordingly, probably in a new and different way. Because of these specific records and having to justify the various types of occupational education programs, and having to demonstrate advantageous utilization, some educators mistakenly hesitate to invite industry to cooperate with school systems.

A review of cooperative industry-education activities suggests that they may be grouped primarily under the following topics: (1) planning of occupational programs (manpower needs and skill development); (2) acquisition of tools, equipment, and materials; (3) selection and preparation (orientation) of instructional staff, students, and instructional materials; (4) promotion (public relations) and dissemination of program activities; (5) solicitation of professional and financial resources; (6) evaluation of instructional programs. It becomes apparent that these advisory committee functions could easily be operational and/or advisory, depending upon the leadership provided by the educators who are coordinating the committee and the initiative and professional commitment of the members. Needless to say, an advisory committee composed of industry (management and labor), educators, public or private social agencies, and representatives of the community (interested lay people) who are vitally concerned with the improvement of educational opportunities in vocational education, can be a viable technique to improving or providing *articulation* between educators and industrialists. Also, the effective use of advisory committees can result in more meaningful occupational educational experiences for youth who are concerned with career exploration and development.

Cooperative School-Industry Programs

Industry can provide support for education in numerous ways. Probably the basic reason one would seek cooperative assistance is to acquire the benefit of human and/or economic resources that would help to improve the educational process. For example, industry personnel can assist local school systems (and state systems) in planning educational specifications for vocational education in general or by designing specific programs to prepare youth for selected occupations. In addition, industry can provide employment opportunities for youth who desire occupational training and education along with wage earning while completing their secondary school education.

One of the oldest forms of cooperation has been achieved through *work-study* programs where students have released time from their in-school studies to "earn and learn" while employed in industry. The benefits of these arrangements include providing learners with an opportunity to explore their occupational interests and career aspirations in a realistic setting that usually involves the use of current industrial equipment, materials, and processes. This arrangement would be most beneficial if school counselors were able to provide adequate guidance before the job placement. Unfortunately, many children who are involved in such programs are working where jobs just happen to be available regardless of their future educational or career aspirations.

The concept of supervised work-study programs in secondary education is relatively new. Formal cooperative programs originated in the secondary schools of the South, where systems were faced with perenially low school budgets although programs existed at the college level decades before. Enrollments in work-study programs grew from none in 1930, to 190,000 in 1967-68, with a phenomenal growth of approximately 67,000 occurring between 1966 and 1968. Although accurate figures of current enrollments are not available, it is estimated that an additional 20 percent are now participating in work-study programs, primarily in grades eleven and twelve. The increased interest in cooperative education can be attributed, in part, to recently enacted federal legislation and to the fact that cooperative education has the best record of job placement after training of all vocational programs (Evans, 1971, p. 194).

The primary purpose of cooperative work experience (CWE) programs is to provide occupational education for students who are preparing for immediate employment upon graduation from high school. This is a highly coordinated program involving a full time teacher-coordinator who manages the students' activities in school and on the job. The coordinator works in partnership with the employer to plan and evaluate the students' total educational experiences. While the CWE programs of part time school and part time supervised work experience in an area of the student's occupational interest are less expensive and more successful than other traditional vocational programs, as judged by student placement in areas for which they were trained, only about 15 percent of the nation's 27,000 public secondary schools had CWE programs in 1966 (Evans, 1971, p. 195).

Many cooperative work education programs are functioning without benefit of federal funding because their educational-work experiences may not appropriately "fit" the guidelines specified in state vocational education plans. Nevertheless, most school administrators are, by necessity, interested in obtaining additional financial resources to operate exemplary educational programs. Many creative professionals have found alternate ways to finance and support exciting and relevant career education programs for youth. Such examples would include work-experience programs for socially disadvantaged youth, mentally retarded children, and many of the health occupations. It should be mentioned, however, that innovative educators working with liberal state boards of vocational education are finding support for new cooperative, industry-education programs which show promise of providing opportunities for youth that will aid in their education, career aspirations, and subsequent employment.

A number of cooperative programs exist under various titles.

The most common are in the areas of business and office occupations, home economics, off-farm agricultural occupations, trade and industrial occupations, and distributive education. Other programs also exist that include a combination of the above cooperative activities and special purpose cooperative programs. The largest number of students are currently enrolled in distributive education (DE) and diversified occupation (DO) programs, the latter being an example of a combination of interrelated cooperative activities. While each program is concerned with developing different career goals, each involves a similar teaching-learning strategy—that of providing actual work experience and related in-school education coordinated by an experienced teacher and cooperating industrial representative who assists the student in developing occupational competency.

There are two basic classifications of cooperative education programs—cooperative work-study (CWS) and cooperative work experience (CWE), as defined by the Vocational Education Acts of 1963 and 1968. The CWS programs are designed for students who have a financial need to remain in school. The employer may be the school or some other local community or social agency. Generally, no attempt is made to coordinate work experience, career counseling, and class studies. Students are often employed in school lunch rooms as attendants, ticket collectors at athletic events, or to provide low level maintenance skills (housekeeping) in the physical plant and on the school grounds.

Cooperative work experience (CWE) provides supervised on-the-job training coordinated by a teacher-coordinator and an industrial representative, along with related classroom studies designed around the student trainee's occupational aspirations. The program is limited to 16- to 18-year-old students in the junior and senior high school who anticipate entering a selected occupation upon completion of their secondary school education.

Industrial representatives assist with the training and education of students. This cooperative experience provides the employer with the opportunity to assess student workers and recruit superior students as full time employees after graduation. The employer is responsible for managing the student's work experience and providing him with opportunities for developing knowledge, skill, attitudes, and values relative to the world of work. The school will provide a range of educational experiences to insure that the student will become socially and culturally literate. Guidance experiences to help students assess their vocational and educational aspirations are essential to help the student-worker with his complete educational-career development and adjustment.

Advantages. Several shared benefits and advantages of cooperative education programs can be listed (Evans, 1969 and 1971; University of Minnesota, 1969; Huffman, 1969, and Swenson, 1969). Financially, cooperative programs mean lower capital costs for the school and lower individual costs for students who are earning scale wages. School-community relations are strengthened because student attitudes toward the dignity of work are improved, they are introduced to local employment opportunities, and they can develop into productive citizens who stabilize the work force by taking advantage of employment opportunities which will retain them in the community upon completion of their education.

In a successful program students, educators, and industry all may benefit greatly. Students gain early work experience which helps them relate education to occupational interests. Educators see some alleviation of dropout problems, and are aided not only in instruction, but with finances, facilities, and curriculum construction. Industry gains recognition in the community, stabilizes its work force, and acquires useful information to help improve its training programs.

Limitations. Cooperative programs are not guaranteed to be always as successful as outlined above. They can have serious limitations. Restrictions may be imposed by parents, school boards, labor unions—just to name a few problems. Some limitations have been noted by Cushman (1967), Evans (1969), McCracken (1969), Griessman and Densley (1969), Huffman (1967), and Wallace (1970). Chief among these are union and apprenticeship requirements, which may limit the types and number of jobs available. Unions may also view vocational education programs as competition; including labor leaders in planning sessions for cooperative programs might eliminate such hard feelings.

Qualified teacher coordinators may also present a problem in terms of shortage of such personnel. Another shortage, that of available jobs, may cause layoffs which will interrupt an otherwise successfully begun program.

Traditionalists may balk at the exclusion of traditional training; industry may balk at expected exclusion of training which has not been a part of traditional vocational education. Employers may have productivity expectations which differ greatly from those of students, parents, and educators, whose expectations run first to educational accomplishments and, secondly, to job skill acquisition. The U.S. Department of Labor also has expectations and these are that child labor laws be observed. Deviation from such laws must be based on local, state, and federal specifications; hence, the teacher-coordinator has the job of ascertaining the legality of time elements involved in the program.

To insure some measure of success regarding career-cluster mobility, programs must not be too narrow; rather, students must be provided with a planned sequence of skill development which will allow progression and a wide career choice.

Geography is a concern in large cities where the job training location is not always convenient for the teacher-coordinator who visits several programs. On the other hand, smaller communities may have a narrow range of training facilities and limited opportunities.

Finally, the student trying to meet local or state course requirements may not "have room" for elective vocational subjects in his schedule; thus he may sacrifice a useful vocational education program for required courses which may or may not prepare him for a career.

Contractual Arrangements. Written contractual agreements between the school, employer, students, and parents help to identify and structure the work-study experiences that the students can expect. This technique also provides for objective accountability of the role and specific responsibilities on the part of each participant. Some schools utilize another printed form which details the specific responsibilities that the student-worker agrees to perform. Those procedures help reduce the possibility of the student-worker from being exploited or that his school-work experiences will not be relevant to his career development program. Also, the printed documents may be perceived as dictating the educational tasks for which each participant is obligated and legally responsible.

School-Industry Partnerships

It became quite apparent that, after the summer riots of 1967, industries decided to enter the world of education as active participants. The thought was that problem-solving methods which were found successful in the management of industry and business would alleviate problems of public education.

Over thirty companies "adopted" secondary schools in twenty cities during the period of 1967-1970. Avco, Ford, Proctor & Gamble and General Electric, for example, adopted the entire school system of Lincoln Heights, Ohio, a predominantly black suburb located in the Cincinnati metropolitan area (Carlson, 1970).

Generally, the partnerships involve the exchange of commitments between school and industry. The companies provide human and material resources and assist with the operational organization of educational training projects to benefit financially hard-pressed school systems and those with large numbers of students who are neither satisfied with nor successful in the conventional educational experiences available in their local schools.

Businessmen, especially in large urban centers, see a need to provide something more than just jobs for students in order to develop the skilled work force necessary to meet the demands of our complex technological world. As a result, management personnel from industry have begun to take a more active role in cooperating with school officials to structure school-industrial arrangements.

It is generally recognized that top school administrators should assume a leadership role in the city power structure and assist with the shaping of community attitudes regarding education. Improved power and support can be obtained from the community and elected officials when the school administrator enjoys the backing of industry and business. Such cooperative arrangements could help improve not only articulation between schools and industry, but also provide the necessary support which school administrators often need to obtain funding for research and development projects from governmental agencies, grants from industry and philanthropic foundations, support of local bond issues, and encouragement for the development and passage of legislation relative to the management of schools.

A study conducted by the Institute for Educational Development (IED) in 1969 identified 76 educational partnership projects involving 33 companies with 32 schools in 23 cities. Twenty-five of the programs were specifically related to occupational education, career counseling, and job placement. Other major topics included health services and drug abuse, remedial education, literacy skill training, curriculum development, material and financial resources, and school-business relationships (Burt and Lessinger, 1970).

While there is evidence of partnership programs operating since 1967, which include occupational education programs for secondary school students, Burt and Lessinger (1970) report that they had not heard of any vocational or technical schools which had yet been "adopted." However, in Newark, New Jersey, the Western Electric Kearny Works adopted the Department of Practical Arts of the Newark Public Schools. The primary goals of the partnership program were to assist with the installation and evaluation of the IACP developed programs, *The World of Construction* and *The World of Manufacturing,* in the junior high schools. In addition to assigning a full time company representative to the Newark Director of Practical Arts for the school year 1970-71, Western Electric also provided financial assistance for the purchase of the IACP instructional software and hardware. After the decision was made to expand the program, the team representing Newark and Western Electric helped to evaluate the effects of the program upon reading, behavior problems, and school achievement. Techniques were developed for systematizing the ordering and inventory of tools, hardware, and materials needed to teach these courses. Western Electric also provided audio-visual materials, prepared news releases and articles to help publicize the program, and provided the stimulus for having the program video taped for television exposure. Needless to say, an innovative program like the IACP, which required the expenditure of funds not immediately available to a large school system like Newark, probably would not be available to the total junior high school student body if not for a successful partnership between industry and education.

A Review of Selected Programs. Several other education-industry partnerships that relate directly to occupational education, career guidance, and cooperative work study will be described briefly to provide a general understanding of the cooperative arrangements. Additional information regarding the actual programs may be found in the references listed at the end of this chapter.

Michigan Bell Telephone Company and Chrysler Corporation are involved in a dozen programs in two Detroit secondary schools. Activities include the provision of part time jobs for students enrolled in cooperative work experience programs, instruction for special education students, remedial tutoring and professional counseling to assist with educational and psychological adjustment problems. Some specific aspects of the programs include a cash bonus paid to student-employees by Chrysler if the student places 10 percent of it in a savings account. Michigan Bell underwrote the development of a card game used to teach mathematics as a part of a remedial education program. Thirty-two programs were developed cooperatively by Michigan Bell and Northern High School in Detroit. Five of the programs are listed to suggest the kinds of activities (Logan, 1969).

1. A pre-employment guidance class was taught once a week to graduating seniors.

2. A ten-week training class was held on Saturdays for boys. Those enrolled received $2.05 per hour and a job offer from the phone company at the end of the session.

3. Seventy-six graduates who undertook cooperative education programs at Northern High now work full time at the phone company.

4. Northern High counselors benefit from the advising services of Bell business consultants and aides.

5. The English Department was given a teletrainer to improve students' oral communication skills.

Additional examples of school-industry partnership programs in Detroit include a cooperative work experience program by

Michigan Consolidated Gas for 100 secondary school boys and the Campbell-Ewald Advertising Agency summer work program to recruit employment for blacks.

The Aetna Life & Casualty Company adopted Weaver High School in Hartford Connecticut, and provided the following services: (1) counseled on the operation of a school newspaper; (2) developed and operated an office machine training program on weekends; (3) provided assistance with photography to a class working on a special project; and (4) made Aetna employees available as resource personnel to assist with extracurricular activities in the school.

The Hawthorne Works of the Western Electric Company in Cicero, Illinois (Chicago metropolitan area) is operating a Big Brother Program. Essentially, this involves the pairing of a high school student with a Western Electric employee who works in an industrial area of common interest.

Another program in Chicago involved the Ford Motor Company and the Chicago Board of Education. Ford provided specialized equipment, tools, teaching aides, and on-the-job training for secondary school juniors and seniors.

In Cleveland, Ohio commerce and industry established an inner city youth training program directed toward eliminating the poverty-welfare cycle. For example, the General Electric Company, Corning Lamp Division, donated a four-story warehouse in a ghetto area to the Cleveland Public Schools so that education and job training could function in the same building.

Employees of the Prudential Life Insurance Company spent company time in public schools teaching a wide range of subjects including art, math, creative writing, and tutoring in a variety of subjects.

A final cooperative venture reported by Holzman (1969) involves over 100 firms in New York City representing banking, retailing, insurance, manufacturing, and merchandising that employed nearly 5,000 students in cooperative work programs.

Additional cooperative school-industry programs are operated that received funds from federal sources other than the Vocational Education Act of 1963 and its 1968 Amendments. For example, a work-adjustment program in Detroit designed for potential and actual dropouts provides in-school remedial education, counseling, and on-the-job training under careful supervision. One-third to one-half of the trainees are employed as nurse's aides, pharmacy helpers, kitchen helpers, orderlies, and stock boys in hospitals and convalescent homes. Of the approximately 9,000 student-trainees, ages 16-21, who participated in the program, about one-third were employed, one-third returned to school on a full time basis, and the remainder were lost through pregnancy, transiency, or lack of interest (Rasof, 1971). Financial support for the program was obtained under Title I ESEA.

Financial assistance is also available to conduct work-study programs for economically disadvantaged students who completed junior high school. Students eligible under federal poverty guidelines have participated in the In-School Neighborhood Youth Corps (NYC) in major urban centers including Chicago and Detroit. Participants in these programs are paid to work in the school and community as an incentive to remain in school and complete their formal education. Student-workers receive additional counseling to help with personal adjustment problems and also receive guidance from their employers. These programs have been financed under the Federal Economic Opportunity Act of 1964 and provide an excellent example of school-government partnership since it is often difficult to find a substantial number of businesses and industries to employ youngsters 14-16 years of age.

Problems and Benefits. Many of these programs have experienced some problems, namely difficulty in developing procedural and operational practices. In some cases, industry and education have failed to reach cooperative agreements. Many of these programs have been labeled as "public relations gambits" and "white paternalism" by various members of the community (Carlson, 1970). Studies reviewed by Burt (1970) tend to support these notions. Industry is often treated with suspicion when assistance is offered. It seems that some feel that industry is using the schools as a market for their products. On the other hand, when industry is accepted, public education is able to tap a wealth of human and material resources to enrich programs. Also, industry feels that good schools are essential before other ills of our urban society may be solved. Thus, the stage is set for improved articulation between industry and education.

Curriculum Development and Dissemination

The previous review may give the impression that cooperative arrangements between education and industry are limited to providing work stations for students enrolled in work-study programs. Industry is also interested in the invention of new educational programs which will improve the preparation of people for the work force and social participation. As mentioned earlier, industrialists, several labor groups, professional societies, and management associations "adopted" numerous schools and school systems to achieve these goals. Industry also adopted the Industrial Arts Curriculum Project (IACP), a curriculum research and development project at The Ohio State University funded by USOE. Generous contributions of both human and material resources were provided to supplement governmental funding and to allow the project staff to function more efficiently and effectively in developing and testing school-based industrial education programs.

Related to this adoption has been the experience of such groups as chapters of the Associated General Contractors of America (AGC) who provided construction materials and specialized tools and equipment to many local school system to help initiate *The World of Construction* (IACP, 1970). Financial grants were also made by local AGC chapters directly to industrial arts teachers, school systems, and colleges to support inservice teacher preparation workshops in various parts of the country. Other industrial groups provided similar assistance for manufacturing education. For example, The Society of Manufacturing Engineers (SME) provided a grant to supplement the printing cost of one of the early developmental editions of *The World of Manufacturing,* so that it could be field tested, evaluated, and revised before developing a commercial edition for public distribution (IACP, 1971). The field testing of the materials would have ended without SME contribution because of a cutback of USOE funds.

Examples of additional support from industrial, professional organizations and governmental agencies included the following:

1. The Ohio Joint Industry Council of Contractors and Building Trades Unions contributed funds to provide the professional services of an audio-visual consultant.

2. The International Brotherhood of Electrical Workers contributed funds for the development of audio-visual materials.

3. The American Society of Civil Engineers provided, at their expense, a resident consultant for six weeks to assist in the substantive review of *The World of Construction.*

4. The Associated General Contractors of America and the American Institute of Architects appointed educational committees specifically to contribute time to the substantive review of materials.

5. The officers and staff of the Society of Manufacturing Engineers, the Ohio Manufacturer's Association, and the National Association of Manufacturers contributed time for identifying consultants, for writing materials, and for substantive reviews.

6. Each of the AFL-CIO Building Trades International Unions of the Bricklayers, Carpenters, Electrical Workers, and Sheet Metal Workers sponsored and funded thirty-minute colored motion picture films to project specifications.

7. The Ohio Bureau of Employment Services contributed, at no cost, four writers and reviewers who contributed substantially to the authenticity of the occupational information in the courses.

8. The International Brotherhood of Electrical Workers and the National Electrical Contractors Association jointly provided scholarships to support the preparation of secondary school teachers of construction technology.

The purpose for listing the above groups was to identify examples of the growing volunteer, private support from various industrial and governmental publics for a single educational endeavor, and not to suggest that those identified would be interested in providing assistance to other groups. Nevertheless, school systems should attempt to solicit industrial support and resources for curriculum development and evaluation as a means of cooperatively fostering innovation.

Industrial Teacher Preparation

In the past, it has been difficult for school administrators to recruit excellent craftsmen from industry to become vocational-technical teachers. Usually, a good craftsman earns more in the trades than by teaching. Advisory committee members were often asked to recommend potential vocational teachers. Often, these requests were directed to trade unions, trade associations, and local construction and manufacturing employers asking for recommendations.

Industry has been cooperative not only in identifying and selecting prospective vocational teachers, but has often supplemented their salaries to keep them in line with what a union craftsman would be earning on the job in industry. In addition, industry has sponsored workshops, conventions, seminars, and correspondence education to help maintain and improve those technical skills necessary to be successful vocational teachers. Industry will often waive the fees for vocational teachers as a means of encouraging them to improve their technical skills and teaching potential.

School administrators can also encourage their industrial teachers to take advantage of these educational opportunities. For example, some school systems provide released time for industrial education teachers to attend short-term workshops and recognize the successful participation in these endeavors as professional study credit applicable to salary schedules. Another option is for school administrators to request that industry provide special workshops for a group of industrial teachers in a large school system to provide innovative technical and related information relative to the teaching of occupational education.

Three programs provide examples of technical education available to in-service teachers by industry. General Motors Corporation organizes training programs for automotive teachers. Specialized subjects that deal with such topics as automatic transmissions, automotive electricity, carburetion, and power train systems are taught in GM Training Centers throughout the country. Courses are generally short-term, concentrated workshops offered on weekends or during the summer.

The Flick-Ready Corporation in Bensenville, Illinois, is a progressively managed manufacturing plant. In addition to its modern technological production practices and its liberal social approach to employer-employee relations (a swimming pool, gymnasium, tennis courts, fishing pond, motel, training center, and other attractions are located in the plant or on the company grounds for employees and their families), it conducts one week workshops for industrial teachers on air power, air hydraulics, and fluid power. Motel and recreational facilities are maintained within the plant for the students' convenience.

The Sun Electric Corporation also has training centers located throughout the country which provide short-term workshops related to the servicing of automobile electrical systems and engine testing for automotive teachers.

The above three programs are available to industrial teachers in the Chicago metropolitan area. College credit could often be earned through cooperating local universities which prepare industrial education teachers. Administrators and teachers can learn of other educational opportunities in their communities by contacting local industrial personnel and their advisory committees.

There are well over two hundred colleges and universities that prepare secondary school teachers of industrial education. In addition to campus programs, many institutions provide evening classes off-campus in order to serve better the professional needs of industrial teachers, especially those without a bachelor's degree. Often industry will lend personnel and space to assist with off-campus instruction. Also, several industrial groups, such as the AGC, SME, and NECA-IBEW, have provided direct financial assistance to pre- and in-service industrial teachers preparing to teach construction and manufacturing practices.

Additional support of this nature can be expected in the future. However, local school administrators must provide more leadership in supporting the in-service preparation of teachers to become familiar with new curriculum innovations. Such enticements as released time with salary, payment of tuition, sponsoring local workshops, and providing summer employment for study and development are examples of practices which school systems can undertake. Industry will generally supplement such activities with human and material resources to provide "seed" money for educational change.

Cooperative Arrangements of Educational Associations and Industry

One of the earliest forms of cooperative efforts in industrial education between educators and industrialists was through their creation and active participation in the National Society for the Promotion of Industrial Education. This organization provided the leadership for encouraging congressional representatives to sponsor and pass federal legislation providing financial resources for the expansion and support of vocational education in public schools. Professional and financial support for this group came from industrial and business management personnel and representatives from organized labor (Barlow, 1970).

An example of a more recent cooperative arrangement between industry and educational associations is the Man/Society/Technology Forums sponsored by the American Industrial Arts Association in cooperation with the Bureau of Educational Personnel Development, USOE. Regional forums are designed in a three-phase effort to bring more segments of society together to deal critically with social problems that might be alleviated through industrial arts education. Leaders representing organizations of industry, education, labor, and government are attempting to identify relationships, roles, responsibilities, and resources of the participating groups through which social, cultural, economic, and environmental problems caused by technology can be converted to new benefits for mankind. The forums are being held at NASA centers, college campuses, industrial facilities, or military installations in various regions.

This example of education-industry-government partnership illustrates one technique that educators can use to improve articulation between schools, industry, and government and to attack social problems cooperatively.

FUTURE EDUCATION-INDUSTRY PROGRAMS

The professional staff at the United States Office of Education (USOE) is apparently convinced of the success of industry-education cooperative programs as a viable form of vocational and career education (Evans, 1971). This, coupled with the charge that career education will be one of the very few programs emphasized by the USOE in the 1970s, has stimulated the development of a Comprehensive Career Education Model for grades K-12. In order to achieve this goal, four different career education models are being developed: (1) School-Based, (2) Employer-Based, (3) Home/Community-Based, and (4) Residential-Based (Burkett, 1971 and CDRI, 1971).

The creation of these *career education* models is being undertaken to investigate alternate forms of providing all secondary school students with information and skills that will enable them to find suitable employment and to switch jobs if the need arises. The terminology has also changed from vocational to career education since the emphasis will be on all of man's occupations and not limited to selected production or service oriented skills.

Models are being structured to conceptualize, develop, evaluate, and disseminate educational programs to enable all students in kindergarten through grade twelve to become more aware of their career potentials and to integrate their regular academic experiences with occupational choice and education. Therefore, upon graduation from high school, students should be able to enter the labor market in career occupations or pursue postsecondary school education in areas of their choice.

The Center for Vocational and Technical Education at The Ohio State University has been named project manager and prime contractor to provide central management for the School-Based Comprehensive Career Education Model (CCEM), and to provide assistance to local school administrators who are cooperating in the development, field testing, and implementation of this project. Six local educational agencies (LEA) have been identified to serve as model development and demonstration sites: Mesa, Arizona; Los Angeles, California; Jefferson County, Colorado; Atlanta, Georgia; Pontiac, Michigan; and Hackensack, New Jersey. The project staff plans to have the CCEM developed for dissemination and adoption by other systems at the end of the 1972-73 school year.

Employer-Based Model

The *Employer-Based Model* was proposed to provide an alternative vocational education program for secondary school students, ages 13-18, in an employer based setting. The program will be operated by a consortium of employers as a means of extending the base of community participants, particularly by involving organized labor, industrialists, Chamber of Commerce, and parent-teacher associations to help improve the relevance of the world of work and the world of education. The program will be designed to provide students with a broad base of on-the-job work experiences, relevant occupational information, appropriate work attitudes and habits conducive to occupational responsibility, understanding of the changing technological society and its affect on work, and a knowledge of the diverse range of occupational opportunities, requirements, and personal factors related to employment.

The employer will manage and develop the total educational program including reading, mathematics, social studies, and even physical education, in addition to providing occupational guidance, information, and skill development through a variety of employment experiences. If this program is found to be feasible, it is quite probable that it could become an alternative to the conventional secondary school program especially for occupationally oriented youth. Also, it will involve new relations between public school educators and industrialists, and will have marked implications for public school organization and administration of occupational education.

Home/Community-Based Model

The *Home/Community-Based Model* involves the utilization of television, radio, and other audio-visuals in the home to provide career education for adults with an emphasis on the special needs of women.

Residential-Based Model

The *Residential-Based Model* is currently being tested on a former Air Force base in Montana. Complete families of disadvantaged backgrounds from neighboring states live and study together preparing for future work. After the adults complete their career education programs, the families return to their home state where employment is provided. Unfortunately, very little information is yet available for this program.

The first three models reviewed could have direct implications for school administrators. Their success could provide viable alternatives to conventional secondary school programs. These models are now in the developmental stages and it is too early to predict their effect. However, it is reasonable to suggest that secondary school administrators keep informed of dissemination materials regarding the Career Education Models to determine whether their schools could participate, either as a local educational agency in the School-Based Model, or as a feeder school to an Employer-Based Career Education program.

The results of the Home/Community-Based Model may also be of interest to school adminsters since it is quite apparent that educational hardware and media are developing rapidly and we may soon find learning laboratories being installed in homes as common as television entertainment centers. High speed computerized consoles are a reality and it is apparent that educational technologists will soon be experimenting with their usefulness as an alternative to in-school education.

SUMMARY

Conventional practical arts and vocational education courses have been criticized as not being representative of the current technological practices in society. Recent cooperative efforts of education and industrialists have provided examples of how industrial education could be made more relevant and contribute to the total career education of youth.

Industrialists are actively seeking ways to work cooperatively with educators to improve the education of our youth. In the past, cooperative efforts have been limited to donating material resources and hiring a few students who were not having much success in the normal school program. Industry was generally cautioned not to "interfere" with the management of the school program.

The success of education-industry advisory committees in providing leadership for initiating and coordinating occupational education programs, curriculum development, and teacher improvement should make the utilization of this technique a must. Representatives of business, industry, and organized labor can serve as intermediaries between the local school system and community, governmental, and philanthropic groups to obtain support for legislation, program development, and financial assistance.

Industry is fast entering the world of education not only as producers of instructional software and hardware, but also as formal schools providing instruction in all subjects. Singer/Graflex Corporation and Westinghouse Learning Corporation are two examples of large corporations that have acquired performance contracts with the Office of Economic Opportunity (OEO) at a rate of over 6.5 million dollars in 1970, for educational service in 21 school districts (Schwartz, 1970). Although the instruction has been limited primarily to remedial reading and mathematics, it is apparent that with the development of the new Comprehensive Career Education Models sponsored by USOE, industry might also be competing for federal funds to support occupational education programs. RCA, Dictaphone, Columbia Broadcasting System, and Bell and Howell are examples of private companies that are already active in the preparation of technicians, secretaries, and paramedical specialists (*Business Week,* July 31, 1971).

School administrators must assume a leadership role to provide relevant career education information skills to learners or other groups—private and public—will find it necessary (and profitable) to take over the school's historical mandate of educating youth. Only through effective communication and planned strategy between education and industry can educational programs be modified and technological illiteracy eradicated.

Improved articulation between education and industry could result in up-to-date curriculum based on current technological practices; the utilization of modern tools, materials, and processes; and the incorporation of industrial hardware that is truly representative of that used in the world of work. It becomes apparent that educators must seek not only advice from industry, but also assistance in the planning, organizing, mediating, and controlling of the total occupational education program. The results of these management practices could provide additional input to the educational administrator enabling him to manage effectively and efficiently the educational strategy and instructional technology necessary for a comprehensive occupational education program.

References

Barlow, Melvin L. *History of Industrial Education in the United States*. Peoria, Illinois: Charles A. Bennett Company, Inc., 1967.

Business Week. "Blue Collar Training Gets a White Collar Look," July 31, 1971, pp. 76-77.

Buffer, James J., Donald G. Lux, and Willis E. Ray. *A Junior High School Industrial Technology Curriculum Project: A Final Evaluation of the Industrial Arts Curriculum Project (IACP), 1965-1971*. Columbus, Ohio: The Ohio State University Research Foundation, 1971.

Burkett, Lowell A. "Career Education Pushed at USOE," *American Vocational Journal*. 46, October 1971, p. 10.

Burt, Samuel M. "Changing Relationships Between Schools and Industry," *Vocational Education: Today and Tomorrow*. (Somers and Little, eds.) Madison: University of Wisconsin Center for Studies in Vocational and Technical Education, 1971.

————. *Industry and Vocational-Technical Education*. New York: McGraw-Hill Book Company, 1967.

————, and Leon M. Lessinger. *Volunteer Industry Involvement in Public Education*. Lexington, Massachusetts: D.C. Heath and Company, 1970.

Carlson, Elliott. "Education and Industry: The Troubled Partnership," *Saturday Review*, August 15, 1970, pp. 45-47.

Council for Development and Research (CDRI). *Development and Research Report*. Denver, Colorado: Council for Development and Research, Inc., 1:4, 1971.

Cushman, Harold R. et al, *The Concerns and Expectations of Prospective Participants in Directed Work Experience Programs*. Ithaca, New York: State University of New York, 1967. (ED 019 494).

Evans, Rupert N. "Cooperative Programs Advantages, Disadvantages and Factors in Development," *American Vocational Journal.* 5, May 1969, pp. 19-22.

_____. *Foundations of Vocational Education.* Columbus, Ohio: Charles E. Merrill Publishing Company, 1971.

Griessman, Eugene B., and Kenneth G. Densley. *Review and Synthesis of Research on Vocational Education in Rural Areas.* Las Cruces, New Mexico: ERIC Clearinghouse on Rural Education and Small Schools, New Mexico State University, and Columbus, Ohio: ERIC Clearinghouse on Vocational and Technical Education, The Center for Vocational and Technical Education, The Ohio State University, December, 1969. (ED 034 632).

Holzman, Seymour. "Industry—New Partner in Education," *Senior Scholastic.* 94, March 21, 1969.

Huffman, Harry. "Cooperative Vocational Education Unique Among Learn and Work Programs," *American Vocational Journal,* 5, May 1969, pp. 16-18.

_____. *Guidelines for Cooperative Education and Selected Materials From the National Seminar Held August 1966, A Manual for the Further Development of Cooperative Education.* Columbus, Ohio: The Center for Vocational and Technical Education, 1967. (ED 011 044)

Industrial Arts Curriculum Project. *The World of Construction.* Bloomington, Illinois: McKnight and McKnight Publishing Company, 1970.

_____. *The World of Manufacturing.* Bloomington, Illinois: McKnight and McKnight Publishing Company, 1971.

Logan, Edgar. "Schools and Corporations—Partners in Detroit," *Senior Scholastic,* March 21, 1969, p. 14.

McCracken, David. *Work Experience for Broadening Occupational Offerings: A Selected Bibliography for Use in Program Development.* Columbus, Ohio: ERIC Clearinghouse on Vocational and Technical Education, The Center for Vocational and Technical Education, The Ohio State University, November, 1969. (ED 034 062).

Rasof, Elvin. "Detroit Combines Students' Worlds," *American Education,* 7, June 1971, pp. 25-27.

Schwartz, Ronald. "Performance Contracts Catch On," *Nation's Schools,* 86, August 1970, pp. 31-33.

Swenson, Leroy H. "Are Co-Op Programs Possible in Small High Schools?" *American Vocational Journal,* 5, May 1969, pp. 22-23.

University of Minnesota. *Guide for Cooperative Vocational Education.* Minneapolis, Minnesota: Division of Vocational and Technical Education, September, 1969. (ED 037 564).

Wallace, Harold R. *Review and Synthesis of Research on Cooperative Vocational Education.* Columbus, Ohio: ERIC Clearinghouse on Vocational and Technical Education, The Ohio State University, March, 1970. (ED 040 274).

15

The Community Education
Approach to Learning

W. FRED TOTTEN

The ultimate goal of this statement is to help people understand why Community Education is succeeding as an emerging force to help solve human problems. Community education as a process gives greater emphasis to the third dimension of learning than any other method presently in use. Since social problems are created in the hearts and minds of men, they must be solved in the hearts and minds of men. Hence, what a man holds in his heart—his attitude toward, appraisal of, and love for his fellow man—has greater impact on the redirection of societal trends than all of the knowledge he has and all of the skills he possesses.

Community education has great meaning for the school administrator because of the shared responsibility for learning. People in all walks of life become involved in the learning process and assume some responsibility for their own learning. Community organizations, agencies, and groups join hands with school personnel to make learning a multipurpose process. The school administrator becomes a coordinator for learning experiences for all. The chief school executive is no longer "Superintendent of Schools," he is, "Superintendent of Community Education." People support what they understand. By being involved and taking some responsibility for their own learning, people improve their understanding of the

---

Written especially for this book. Dr. Totten is a consultant in Community Education.

real purposes of the educative process. They know why they must support their schools in order to make a better world. In some communities, there is a division between the authority for the public schools and the people in the community. The superintendent of schools and his staff along with members of the board of education may proceed autocratically and without consideration for the fact that the citizens as a whole are the real stockholders in the enterprise of organized learning. The school authorities may overlook the fact that the owners wish to have a voice in how their investment shall be used.

On the other hand, because of lack of understanding and lack of involvement, individuals or groups in the community may virtually wage war on the school authority for not doing the things they wish to have done. When the community education approach to learning reaches a high degree of maturity in a community, any power figure or structure working against the learning establishment is usually short lived. The people who are involved in the learning program can soon build a positive power structure capable of detonating the negative forces.

Thinking people know that an individual learns from his total environment. Traditionally, the educational establishment has given attention primarily to the learning which takes place in the organized school setting—in the schoolhouse. Most of this learning has been formal in nature. Except by the community education approach to learning, there is little effort to bring the informal experiences in learning gained in the home and in the community into relationship with the formal learning experiences in the schoolhouse. In fact, in many respects and in many places, learning experiences in the "public school" are in conflict with learning experiences in the "school of the public." The school of the public out-teaches the public school in many areas of learning.

In order for total growth and development of citizens to reach the greatest height, there must be an amalgam between formal and informal learning. Some planning and organization is necessary to accomplish a gestalt-like learning pattern. Efforts of the public school and the school of the public can be synchronized. Strong home, school, and community relations can be established. Much of the informal learning experience which takes place haphazardly in the community can be integrated with the formal experience and directed by school personnel.

Just as much valuable informal learning experience can come into the schoolhouse program and be directed by professional educators, so can some of the formal learning experience be shifted into the community and strengthened by utilizing the knowledge and skills of nonprofessional educators. The school-without-walls-school in the community has succeeded for some groups of superior high-school students. The formal learning experience for these students is scheduled in the community outside the schoolhouse. There is good reason to move toward school in the community for high school youngsters who cannot cope with the regimented practices of the traditional day school. Where student riots have occurred, it has been estimated that not more than ten percent of the student body has been involved. While traditional school curriculums are not adequate for all of the other ninety percent, it has been observed that about ninety percent will live with the curriculum as it is and with circumstances as they are. It is the other ten percent who will not "take it" nor let things run smoothly for the rest. While state laws require that young people of prescribed ages go to school, the laws do not say that they must attend school in a schoolhouse, nor do the laws require that all learning effort be made between 8:30 a.m. and 4:00 p.m. each day, Monday through Friday, for 36 to 40 weeks each year. Hence, students who cannot or will not tolerate the routine of the schoolhouse-school, and/or who do not find the course offerings to be in accord with their abilities, interests, and needs, can and should be assigned to school in the community.

This arrangement permits the student to engage in learning experience on his own terms to a very high degree. Effort on any one task may continue indefinitely in most cases. No bell rings requiring the effort to be discontinued when the task is only partially completed. If he would rather go to school in the late afternoon and evening than from 8:30 a.m. to 4:00 p.m., it can be arranged. He may also have some of his formal learning experience on Saturday and/or during summer weeks. If he can't "take it" for more than three weeks, six weeks, or nine weeks at a time, it can be arranged. All required courses can be developed in three-week units if desired. The completion of six such units is a semester's work.

School in the community relates learning to life in a very real way. People with know-how in various fields of work become a part of the teaching staff. Factories, lodge halls, libraries, churches, government buildings, stores, offices, business buildings, and homes become the composite schoolhouse. The curriculum is a continuum of all of the student's learning experiences.

THE COMMUNITY IS THE SCHOOL

While no attempt is made in this writing to outline the details, it can be said with professional accuracy that learning at its best can become a reality by combined effort of the public school and the school of the public. By using facilities on a continuous basis and by using the resources of agencies, organizations, and individuals in the community, much important, informal learning can be integrated with the formal learning which takes place in the schoolhouse. Likewise, the community outside of the schoolhouse can absorb much of the formal learning experience for some students and therefore bring about a balance between the formal and the informal learning programs. The utopia is for the entire community to become the school. All persons become learners and all people become self-teachers and many assist in the instructional program of others.

Most of the readers of this statement are familiar with the quatrain:

> I had six honest serving men;
> They taught me all I knew;
> Their names were What and Where and When
> and How and Why and Who.

Community education is the what, where, when, how, why and who method of learning. The learner has a part in determining *what* is important for him to learn. *Where* he learns what he needs to know is not important. It may be in a schoolhouse or somewhere else in the community. Only the learner can determine *when* learning experience can be most meaningful to him. For example, the second shift factory worker who needs to improve his skill in blueprint reading, either to hold his job or to qualify for another, must be able to have this learning experience after eleven o'clock at night. Such an adult education course normally scheduled for early evening is of no use to him because he is at work at that time. The method of learning—the *how*—is most important.

Unlike the traditional "use of words" process, the community education concept depends upon the laboratory process for much of the learning program. People explore, investigate, analyze and experiment. Rather than being told, the learner is challenged to discover. Community education encourages self-examination. It challenges all learners to know *why* they should engage in a particular learning activity. It has often been said that a child will learn to read when he discovers that he needs to be able to read in order to obtain some self-fulfillment.

The sixth of the honest service men is *who*. Community education puts self at the head of the list of those who contribute to one's learning. Again self-discovery is high in the realm of method. In addition to self and the formally designated directors of learning (called teachers) one's peers, relatives, and neighbors form a part of the who. If a young man wishes to become an insurance salesman, certainly there is no one better able to help him learn this field of work than a successful insurance salesman.

SCOPE OF COMMUNITY EDUCATION

At this point it seems appropriate to outline the scope of community education, designate the learners, and identify some of the goals. There should be no misunderstanding about the scope of community education. In the truest sense, it is the total learning program for all people in the community. It includes the formal, required program for children and youth in the daytime school as well as the optional program for these and other citizens in the community which may be conducted either during daylight hours or at some other time.

In many respects community education is a way of life—a movement toward the establishment of the good society. The major realms of learning experience, indicating the general scope of community education, are listed below.

The conventionally required subjects and experiences for children and youth of legal school age.

The learning program for adults which grants conventional credit toward completion of the elementary school certificate, the high school diploma, and/or the college degree.

The enrichment program for children and teenagers, related to the required program of studies.

Activities selected by children and youth in areas that are not specifically designed to enrich their required work—activities that are recreational, social, cultural, vocational, and economic in nature, and in the field of health.

Well-baby clinics for infants.

Tot-lot programs for young children.

Big brother and big sister programs.

Programs designed to foster gracious living.

Farm experience.

Camping experience.

Olympic-type game programs.

Informal, noncredit programs, for out-of-school youth and adults in areas that are recreational, social, vocational, cultural, spiritual, of homemaking nature, travel, and activities involving language study.

Health and safety learning programs for all: swimming and survival swimming, hiking, jogging, cycling, sports, health clinics, innoculation programs, health-guarded programs for children, safety first, and others.

Community development and community service projects relating to housing, parks, sanitation, safety measures, law enforcement projects, and other government related programs.

Service to nonschool agencies and use of nonschool agencies in the community education program.

Assistance to shut-ins and the ill.

Learning programs for persons in jail and in other penal institutions.

Rehabilitation programs for persons released from prison.

Programs of learning and assistance for persons of all ages with emotional and physical difficulties.

Programs of support and assistance to business and industry.

Sheltered workshops for adults.

Skill centers for persons from upper elementary grades to senior citizens.

Programs relating to improved transportation.

All types of family learning projects.

Programs of learning for all social deviates—alcoholics, drug addicts, and others.

GOALS OF COMMUNITY EDUCATION

The goals of community education are comprehensive but change according to the changes in the requirements of man to meet social conditions which may exist at any one time. During a single life span, the goals of community education will change along with the changes which occur in society. Hence, it is not possible to list all of the goals for all time, nor is it possible to list all of the goals for all of the people. The following list should be considered as only some of the goals which are readily identified at the time of this writing.

Community education is a process designed to:

Help people realize their own potential for solving their own problems and the problems of the various communities in which each individual lives.

Help people establish self-confidence. For many, this means replacing resignation with hope.

Raise the literacy level of people in the community.

Improve the mental and physical well being of all citizens.

Help people prepare to cope with the impact of societal change in a new kind of world.

Enable people to "retool" and qualify for new jobs or for upgrading the jobs they hold.

Help those in unfavorable circumstances gain upward social mobility.

Help frustrated people of great affluence experience the job of sharing their talents, human service, and, as they wish, their means with those in need.

Help people improve their leadership skills, their communication techniques, and their human relations practices.

Encourage retired people and other older citizens to continue service in their communities—reclaim those who have resigned from life.

Enable adults to meet (on their own time schedules) the requirements for certificates, diplomas, and degrees at elementary, secondary, and college and university levels.

Create a home-school-community relationship and program which will enable each individual to have the best possible chance to develop an adequate self-image, establish appropriate life goals, and build his personal traits and abilities to the highest possible degree.

Harmonize the contributions to learning of all individuals, agencies, and organizations in the community for total community education.

Eliminate such barriers to social progress as selfishness, bigotry, prejudice, intolerence, and indifference.

Improve the economy of the community.

Help people find methods which will bring greater returns from the expenditure of public funds for service to humanity.

Bring about understanding among men and make each community a better place in which to live.

LEARNERS IN COMMUNITY SCHOOLS

Just as for the goals of community education, there should be no misunderstanding about the scope of the student body. It has been indicated in earlier paragraphs that in the community education approach to learning, no learning need goes unattended nor does any facility which can be utilized as a learning space go unused. It can be stated, also, that no individual is left out. Community education can contribute to the well being of:

the unborn as well as the aged.

the healthy as well as the ill.

the affluent as well as the poverty burdened.

the able-bodied as well as the crippled.

the learned as well as the illiterate.

the emotionally secure as well as the emotionally disturbed.

the free as well as the incarcerated.

the employed as well as the unemployed.

executives as well as laborers.

urban residents as well as rural residents.

homeowners as well as renters.

the religious as well as the irreligious.

the happy as well as the sad and/or bitter people.

the socially secure as well as the dependent.

natives as well as the foreign born.

the liberal thinker as well as the conservative.

those of the power structure as well as others.

housewives as well as employed women.

those working in the fields of public service as well as those engaged in free enterprise.

leaders as well as followers.

parents as well as children.

HUMANISTIC EMPHASIS

From the above lists, of the scope, goals, and learners, it is clear that community education is basically humanistic. This characteristic adds much to its significance when we recognize that the total learning program during preceding years has become seriously unbalanced with respect to progress in the scientific and humanistic aspects of learning. When our society became predominantly urban, the change in environment contributed much to the progress in the realm of the scientific. Urban society provides better laboratories, better facilities for research, and better tools with which to explore and make discoveries.

With respect to progress in humanistic learning, the new environment of urban society had a reverse effect. Youngsters no longer were economically important to their parents. There were no chores to do to help the family business. The young were denied the opportunity to participate with their parents in their work and the opportunity to learn on an apprenticeship basis. While in rural life, the barnlots, the open fields, gardens, orchards, and streams formed a haven for youngsters to explore, to recreate, to fish and to hunt, and to learn from the animals, any facsimile of similar experience in urban life has to be scheduled and is a poor substitute, at the best. Learning in the humanistic realm is quite different in an environment of crowded buildings, narrow streets, dark alleys, taverns, brothels, and pool halls than it is in the open space conditions in the country.

In order to reclaim some of our losses in society, we must find ways to move toward a better balance between the scientific and humanistic phases of learning. In an effort to make progress toward the fulfillment of this challenge, community education recognizes two fronts. The most obvious is the immediate front—that which deals with the circumstances of the lives of people here and now. The second has to do with the removal of the causes of social ills. This front is long range and requires faith that an educative process which will help to make a better world can be developed and implemented. Progress on this front cannot be hurried. It should not be expected that positive results will be immediately obvious. Just as in the scientific realm of learning it has taken man more than 100 years to learn how to explore the universe, it may take man 100 years or more to learn how to live in peace and harmony. The important thing is to begin.

To work toward the elimination of the causes of social problems, we must first identify the causes. When identified, we can begin to form plans for their removal. A review of the cycle of rise and fall of world empires reveals that serious decline began in each case when the people reached a generally high degree of affluence. Hence, in order to try to secure the "good life" for generations yet unborn, we must find ways to cause people to eliminate the misuse of material wealth. The most effective approach to the curtailment of waste in talent, effort, and substance is to involve those who have more of the world's goods than they can use for their own personal enjoyment. Many people of affluence have become frustrated and miserable because they have discontinued sharing of themselves with others. The community education plan needs and uses everyone.

Efficient Use of Resources

There are many recorded examples of individuals who have gained a new lease on life because they have been called upon for service to someone else or to their community. In a great city of the southwestern portion of the United States, there are many wealthy people—many of them retired. A visitor to this city can readily detect a high degree of waste. For example, merely for convenience to the wealthy and not because of need, there are 176 banks in the city. A bank president indicated that 10 to 20 banks would be enough. In the same city, there are thirteen school superintendents receiving a combined annual salary of over $300,000. This is public money. Officials in the nearby state university believe that there should be one superintendent of education and that four associate superintendents are needed to assist with school administration in the four quarters of the city. The combined salary of these five administrators would not be more than $120,000 per year.

Within thirteen miles of this fabulously wealthy city is an Indian village where people live in poverty and deprivation. The people in this village need to learn how to live like people. If the $180,000 of public money, not needed in the big city, could be used for a learning program for the Indian village, it would do much good. Also, the people in the Indian village could gain a great deal from the knowledge, talents, and skills which lie dormant within the retirees who compose a large portion of the population of the large city. It is exciting to know that under the guidance of the neighboring university, a community education program has been implemented in the total area. People of affluence and people with time on their hands are responding and are giving service to the people in the Indian village. Within a span of only two years, much improvement can be observed in the circumstances of the citizens of this village.

Humanizing the Power Motive

A second cause of social problems has to do with the motives of persons in power positions. A primary element in the rebellion of youth against our various establishments is the misuse of power by persons in charge. Many have used their power selfishly rather than for the good of humanity. They have used people as their private commodities rather than as people. Persons in power have "hammered down" those with talent and with ability to rise to higher levels of productivity, because they have feared competition. One of the great challenges to education and to all other establishments is to *humanize* the motive of power. This means change—change in motive, change in the hearts of those in power positions. In order to effect the kind of change needed, some legislation is needed to open doors. Also, money is needed to establish new approaches to the solution of problems. This does not necessarily mean new or additional public money. It means redirecting the use of money already available and putting it to use for positive ends. It means better use of money now being squandered and wasted. Even though legislation and money are needed, we know that we can neither legislate nor buy change in people's hearts. People have to learn how to change. Through involvement, experience, and service, they will learn that motives which are humanistic are far more satisfying than motives which are predominantly self-centered.

In order to humanize the motive of power, the barriers to social progress must be removed. It is only through association and sharing that people learn to respect and enjoy other people. Community education is succeeding in the removal of barriers to social problems for a number of reasons. People of different races, religions, levels of schooling, and socioeconomic circumstances become involved on an equal basis. People learn to know one another best and respect one another to the greatest degree when they share experiences. It is not unusual for a person of great power in the community to serve on a community school council on an equal basis with a person of low socioeconomic circumstance.

The community education program reaches out for those whose talents and skills are needed—especially for retired people. A most effective way to change an arrogant person or a bigoted person, or a selfish or prejudiced person is to involve him on an equal basis with persons who are humble, compassionate and even of a different racial, ethnic, or socioeconomic background. This sort of humanizing experience occurs in elementary ways when all of the people in a community have an opportunity to become involved in learning experiences of their own choice.

It is not unusual to see in a square dance set a laborer and an industrial executive enjoying one another as equals. It is highly possible for two adults to enter a building on a college campus, walking side by side, one going in to learn how to read and the other to work on his doctoral dissertation. It might be difficult to detect which is which. Human worth and human dignity must be respected at all levels of society.

A further effort to humanize the motive of power is to bring into concert all of the learning forces and factors in the community. All institutions, agencies, organizations, and individuals have a contribution to make to the learning program for people. Traditionally, the various units operate as separate entities. There is little coordination of effort and there is waste due to overlapping and unnecessary duplication of services. The community education approach to learning sets as a high priority goal the unification of effort of the different groups and individuals.

This does not mean that anything is taken away from any group or person; it merely means a harmonization of efforts to help people learn how to take care of their needs and solve their problems. A council of representatives of the various institutions, agencies, and groups can do much to strengthen the service of each group and to eliminate unnecessary duplication. Since certain groups are more able to give particular services than others, there can be a high degree of unification through diversity. The important thing is that the diverse services do not stand alone and unattached. They should be coordinated parts of one whole pattern of learning.

A campaign to encourage each individual to do something every day for someone else can have great positive effect on humanizing the motive of power. A person who grows up in this spirit will certainly not misuse his authority when he is placed in a power position. The consistent practice of sending notes to thank people for things they have done for you, to congratulate those who have accomplished something significant to them, to express sympathy, or merely to extend greetings and good wishes is not an unreasonable expectation for everyone.

Schools as a Focal Point

For the community education plan to be implemented, there must be one agent to take leadership for bringing into concert the learning forces and factors of all other agents. The school system is the logical agent to take such leadership. Schools are commonly owned by all property owners in the community. The school is probably the most neutral and unbiased agency in the community toward persons of all faiths, races, and backgrounds. Thirdly, learning is the business of the educational establishment.

While the entire community becomes the school, the schoolhouse in each district becomes the organization headquarters. The school in its totality becomes a human development laboratory. Some laboratory learning can best be acquired outside of the schoolhouse, from nonprofessional teachers, but under the authority of the school's administrative staff. Ideally, in order to establish the community education program to its fullest extent, the school-house should be available for service to citizens 24 hours a day, every day.

It is not the purpose of this writing to detail the organization and function of the community school. It will suffice to say that the school is devoted to the concept of being a center of service to help all people in the community fulfill their unmet learning needs.

Before concluding, it is appropriate to summarize the progress community education has made at the time of this writing toward becoming the universal learning system. The general developments are outlined in the following pages.

GENERAL DEVELOPMENTS

Support of U.S. Office of Education Personnel. Strong indication is given that top level administrators in OE support the concept and that they will encourage universal consideration.

Support by Individual States. Six states have enacted legislation to provide funds to be allocated to individual school districts to help pay salaries of community education coordinators. These states are, Maryland, Michigan, Utah, Florida, Washington, and Minnesota. It is known that other states are giving favorable consideration to such legislation. The Minnesota Department of Education has established the position, "State Coordinator of Community Education Service."

Support of the North Central Association of Colleges and Secondary Schools. NCA officials have activated a Committee on Community Education. Members of this committee offer service to schools and communities wishing to explore the community education approach to learning—throughout the nineteen North Central states. A total of 17,000 copies of a special newsletter describing the structure and function of the committee have been distributed.

Regional Centers for the Development of Community Education Programs. Fourteen strategically located colleges and universities have been designated as centers for the advancement of the community education concept. The establishment of other centers is contemplated. Each center has a director of community education services and a supporting staff. Personnel of elementary and secondary school districts and of higher education institutions in each of the fifty states can obtain service from one of the fourteen regional centers. Money from a subsidy provided by the Mott Foundation can be allocated by a regional center director to an individual school district to help with the implementation of a community school program. Regional Center personnel offer credit courses, seminars, and workshops in community education; conduct conferences and make other presentations to community groups; disseminate descriptive materials; give consulting service to school board members and school administrators; and give other service in the field of community education as requested.

Prominence in Model Cities Programs. The community education approach to learning is in perfect accord with the development process in the Model Cities areas. It is being implemented in several of these areas and is being considered by most of the others.

Development in Countries Other Than the U.S. It is known that the community education approach to learning is being studied and implemented in several places in Canada, Mexico, Portugal, Spain, Japan, Korea, the Philippines, Italy, Ethiopia, and South Africa. In all probability, it is making headway in other countries.

Leadership Training Programs. Several preservice and in-service programs have been established to prepare leaders for service in the field of community education.

Graduate Study Program. This program, centered in Flint, Michigan, was the first leadership training program to be established. Since its inception in 1955, over 4,000 persons have completed one or more courses in community education—327 have completed the masters degree in community education and 19 have completed the education specialist degrees. Course work is accredited and degrees are granted by Eastern Michigan University and by Michigan State University. The program has been financed by the Mott division of the Flint Board of Education and by Eastern Michigan University.

Inter-Institutional Clinical Preparation Program. The seven graduate schools in Michigan have united in the offering of an advanced degree program for persons preparing for leadership responsibility in the field of community education. Some 72 administrative interns come to Flint each year for a full year of graduate study either at masters level or at the doctoral level. Each student is awarded a very attractive fellowship stipend. About 400 graduates from this program are now serving throughout the U.S. and in some other countries.

Short Term Intern Program. Three or four groups of from 15 to 20 come to Flint each year for an intensive training program, usually of six weeks duration. Most of these persons are serving or will serve as community education coordinators. About 250 persons with this experience are serving in leadership positions in community education.

Colleges and University Workshops. Upwards of 40 workshops in community education of from one week to four weeks duration have been offered in various parts of the U.S. At least 1,000 students have earned credit through these workshops. A majority of them are serving in the field of community education.

Florida Training Program. The Florida Department of Education allocated funds for the development of a training program design, for preparing leaders in the field of community education. During the school year 1970-71, all persons known to be active in the field of community education in Florida were invited to offer suggestions as to what should be included in such a training program. A team of four representatives (one each) from Florida Atlantic University, the University of Florida, the University of South Florida, and Florida State University reviewed the suggestions, provided other ideas and materials and developed a comprehensive guide for conducting training programs for community education personnel. A series of workshops using this material was conducted during the summer of 1971.

The National Community School Education Association. This is a professional organization of over 1,000 members designed to serve the cause of community education universally. A monthly newsletter keeps members and others acquainted with developments and innovations in the field. The executive secretary and other officers keep abreast of the developments in education and in society, compile useful reports, conduct research, prepare descriptive materials, represent the community education interest in state, regional, and national meetings, and in other organizations, and assist with the development of conferences, symposiums, and workshops at local, state, regional, and national levels.

Individual State Associations. There is interest and some action being taken to develop state branches of the National Community School Education Association—NCSEA. Michigan has activated the MCSEA and other states are moving in this direction.

Supporting Journals and Newsletters and Descriptive Materials.

The Graduate Study Program has developed 153 different pamphlets, booklets, brochures and papers for free distribution. About 150,000 copies of these have been distributed.

Regional University Centers have produced a number of items for distribution.

The special publication of TODAY of the North Central Association of Colleges and Secondary Schools distributed 17,000 copies of a two-page brochure.

The Community Education Journal of from 50 to 100 pages appears four times a year.

A four page paper entitled, *The Community School and Its Administration* is issued each month from the Clinical Preparation Center.

NCSEA prepares and distributes a Newsletter several times each year.

New Books Are Being Published. In the last four years, the Pendell Press has published five books in the field of community education and Allied Education Council has produced two.

Titles of Pendell Press books are:

Toward Perfection in Learning

The Role of the School in Community Education

The Power of Community Education

The Community School Director

Education II Social Imperative

Titles of Allied Education Council books are:

The Community School

The Community Education Concept and Nature and Function of the Community School (a 54 page booklet)

SOME SIGNIFICANT FACTS

It is known that 400 or more school districts in the U.S. have implemented the community education approach to learning in one or more schools.

At least 200 colleges and universities have conducted one or more conferences and/or symposiums on community education during the past five years.

It is known that at least 100 colleges and universities offer one or more courses or workshops in community education.

It is known that over 1,500 persons have had special training at collegiate level for leadership service in community education and that most of them are serving in this field.

Research indicates that for an additional annual cost of from $9,000 to $12,000, an elementary school of medium size (400-800) which operates on a seven to eight hour day, with an occasional use in the evening, five days a week for 39 to 40 weeks in the year, can be converted into a human development laboratory serving people of all ages and backgrounds, and can be in service 14 to 16 hours each day, six-plus days each week, and for 52 weeks in the year.

1. At least 14 different federal acts provide funds for the support of various phases of the community education program.

2. It is known that people in some communities have given voluntarily enough money to make possible the implementation of at least one multipurpose school.

3. Several foundations make contributions for the support of community education programs.

4. Six states provide state funds for the employment of community education coordinators.

5. The people of some local school districts have voted extra millage to provide funds necessary to convert their schools into multipurpose institutions.

SUMMARY

The community education approach to learning is no longer an experiment. With its methods, many social problems are being solved in many communities. The process is well on its way toward becoming the universal approach to learning. The learning target is basically *humanistic*. Community education is *our best hope for society*.

Finally, the community education design for learning is succeeding because it brings people together around great ideas. People work, study, and play together on an equal basis. The grassroots learning wants and needs of people of all ages, circumstances, and backgrounds are being served. The social orientation is forward. Community education is an effective, emerging force for the eradication of moral indifference of an affluent nation and for humanizing the motive of power.

16

Alternatives and the Law

DAVID S. ROSENBERGER

Any commentary on the legal aspects of seeking out-of-class alternatives may seem like looking for reasons why a given alternative cannot be carried out. In no sense is this discussion intended to slow the process of brainstorming or stifle creative plans for making learning have meaning to young people.

The administrator needs to look for reasons why things can be done. Too often he is perceived as an obstacle. In many settings, the originator of an idea finds it necessary to convince his associates that there are no insurmountable financial, legal, or logistical barriers. The decision-making process does require that the possible risks and consequences of a plan of action be explored prior to making the choice. Here the emphasis should be upon minimizing or overcoming the risks so that the new practice can be used.

Somewhere between the free-wheeling idea session which produced the alternative and its actual implementation it would be wise to consider legal implications. The following paragraphs discuss some of the topics which may arise when alternatives to in-class activities are sought.

Virtually hundreds of legal topics impinge upon school operation. It is not possible to predict with complete accuracy which of

Written especially for this Book. Dr. Rosenberger is Professor of Administration and Supervision at the University of Toledo.

them might come into play with the move toward alternatives. One can conjecture which ones are likely to produce activity.

It is conceivable, for example, that a question would arise in some states as to whether a supplemental teacher's contract were necessary to cover out-of-school activities. It is possible that the teacher's position regarding pupil control and discipline could come into question as students find themselves in an environment less restricted than that of the traditional classroom. Perhaps transportation would provide some additional problems for school-owned or public carriers beyond those encountered in carrying students to and from one building. In all of these topics, it is difficult to see the potential for a great amount of litigation or any major challenge to the position which the courts have taken in the past.

This discussion is directed at the posture of statutes and the courts with regard to legal topics which this writer believes are likely to arise. These topics cluster around the matter of tort liability. The term "tort" is applied to a group of civil wrongs, other than breach of contract, for which a court will afford a remedy in the form of an action for damages. Most tort liability results from the failure of one party, who owed a duty to another, to avoid acts or omissions which the party could reasonably foresee would have likely produced the injury to the one to whom the duty was owed. This failure to forsee is called negligence.[1] The most common source of litigation is for student injuries.

There are three major classifications of parties against whom such action charging negligence could be taken by students; the school district, a private party upon whose property students were having the learning experience, and the staff personnel of the school.

SCHOOL DISTRICT LIABILITY

In the majority of states the doctrine of governmental immunity still prevails. This point of view, handed down in common law through the years, holds that government entities are immune from tort liability for injuries suffered by pupils. This immunity applies to their own negligent acts, as well as to the negligent acts of their officers, agents, or employees; or for injuries arising from dangerous or improper care and maintenance of school buildings and grounds, defective appliances, or unsafe operation of the school transportation system.[2] The assumption here is that the school district is engaged in a nonproprietary or governmental function. Such functions spring from purposes for which schools were legally established and tend to be those which promote the cause of education.[3]

It would seem that school district liability in states holding the rule of governmental immunity would not be influenced by programs using a broader geographical area as the arena of learning. This rule may also apply to such facilities as swimming pools and art galleries when operated as a governmental function, not a proprietary one. There is a more divided opinion among courts regarding zoos and parks making it difficult to generalize.[4]

In those states in which governmental immunity has been abrogated, school districts can be held liable and public funds used to pay judgments against them. In some states, there are legal limits as to the amount of the liability and school districts are empowered or required to carry liability insurance. Generally, such cases arise from injury on school property. Such conditions as defective or unlighted stairs and broken playground or gymnasium equipment are commonly alleged to have constituted negligence. The operation of school buses constitutes another major source of such claims against districts.

One question which the use of places away from school property will foster is the liability of school districts for torts which involve neither school real estate nor property such as buses. Whether an injury occurring off school property but at a place chosen by the district as the locus of learning would constitute district liability is a matter yet to be decided. The question could be phrased something like this: "Could a school district be held liable in a case involving defective equipment not owned or rented by the school and on property not owned by the school, but where the district has regularly sponsored or sanctioned learning activities?" Sufficient precedent does not exist to answer this question.

Another area of potential litigation aimed at school districts would have to do with claims of inadequate supervision of young people. Such cases are comparatively frequent now but deal with events which occur on school property. There is little reason to believe that the location of the alleged tort would make a great deal of difference in the decision of a court as long as the injury occurred at the locus of a school district sponsored or sanctioned learning activity. The topic of supervision of young people will be discussed later as it relates to the liability of staff personnel.

LIABILITY OF OWNERS OF PRIVATE PROPERTY

As alternatives to in-class learning are found, it is quite certain that a variety of student activities will be occurring on private property. The liability of the owner depends upon whether the student is on the property as an invitee or licensee or trespasser. An invitee is one who visits at the express or implied invitation of the owner for the benefit of the owner or for the benefit of both owner and visitor. For example, a company widely advertising an invitation to visit its manufacturing plant as a means of selling its product, is visited by invitees. The owner owes the visitor the duty of having his premises in reasonably safe condition.[5]

A licensee is one who visits the premises for his own purposes. The owner's only duty to the licensee is to point out hidden dangers which are not likely to be seen by a visitor himself. An invitee may become a licensee by entering a part of the premises to which he was not invited or by using the premises for purposes not included in his invitation.[6] It is also possible that by remaining on the premises beyond a reasonable time after his invitation has expired, an individual's status would change to that of a licensee.

Generally, no duty of care is owed a trespasser except to refrain from wilful or wanton wrongdoing. An owner, being aware of the presence of a trespasser, is required to use ordinary care to avoid injury to the trespasser. It should be noted that younger children have been held not to be conscious trespassers.[7]

The most likely prevailing condition would be that students and teachers will use private property as licensees. Owners may possibly

refuse to grant permission to use property due to incurring liability. However, any use of the property by others probably requires the owner to secure insurance coverage. That coverage could
be checked to be sure that the use by students would be covered.
It would seem that the major problem presented by the legal
position of the owner is one of convincing him to grant permission
for use of his property. This should not be insurmountable except
with the most recalcitrant individual. There may be wisdom in
apprizing the owner of his position and urging insurance coverage
partly for his benefit, but also for the possible benefit to an
injured student.

LIABILITY OF STAFF PERSONNEL

The whole topic of staff member liability is too complex to be
discussed fully here. The major conclusions reached from the study
of existing statutes and cases will be pointed out and the implications for out-of-class activities will be examined.

Basically, if any school employee is negligent in the performance
of his duties toward pupils, he is legally responsible for the injuries
that follow. He will have to compensate the pupil out of his own
funds unless the loss is covered by insurance.

The test of negligence is the conduct of a reasonably prudent
person in like circumstances. It may result from acts of omission
or commission. The degree of care expected will be measured in
the light of the danger involved and the age of the child. Greater
care will be expected when pupils are exposed to dangers beyond
the normal classroom situation.[8]

Any review of the general picture regarding negligence should
make it clear that certain factors reduce the likelihood of the
courts imposing liability upon the employee. Contributory negligence on the part of the student is the first of these. Whether the
student is so chargeable must be determined by the court in
individual cases. The age of the child is important in judging what
degree of care he should be expected to use.

The second factor has to do with whether the employee could
have anticipated the danger as opposed to the accident being

unavoidable or nonforseeable. The nature of the warning to the student or the precautions taken are important here. The third factor is the determination of the proximate cause of the injury. If there were an intervening act or event, often resulting from the conduct of a third party, the employee may not be held liable, even though he has been negligent.

The last factor is a determination by the court whether the injured student assumed the risk. Unlike contributory negligence which is based on carelessness, assumption or risk can be charged when it is shown that the student accepted a danger that he clearly understood, and that he had a foresight of the consequences and a readiness to accept them.[9] Naturally, the age and maturity of the student have a great deal to do with making this determination.

There are a variety of situations in which these factors come into play. For some of these the location of the learning activity makes little difference. Liability in matters of pupil control would be similar as would liability stemming from the type of care given a student after an injury. The question of the amount and quality of the supervision given students arises as a major consideration. One can hypothesize that there will be closer supervision of students in traditional classroom settings and on school property than when alternatives to in-class learning are sought.

A recent District of Columbia case is exemplary of prevailing court opinion regarding supervision.[10] A junior high pupil was struck in the eye by a piece of metal thrown by a student as he entered the print shop classroom to which he was assigned for instruction. The teacher was out of the room and did not return until five to ten minutes after the class was scheduled to start. His absence was due to the principal's assignment to him to supervise halls and cafeteria during that time. In making this assignment, the principal had given the fourteen students in the printing class specific rules they were to follow if the teacher were absent at the start of class. In holding the teacher not to be negligent, the court stated:

Thus faced with the knowledge that children, and especially thirteen-year-old boys, will throw at, kick, hit or push a fellow pupil if a teacher is not immediately present, and using the available supervisory personnel, the authorities balanced the need for a teacher to supervise several hundred students milling about the corridors and cafeteria against the need to supervise fourteen students in a certain classroom for a short period of time.

It is worthwhile to note that the teacher was absent for a short period of time, for an important reason, and in line with a reasonable general plan of supervision. In addition, students had been given instruction as to their conduct during such periods. The case indicates that courts do respond to the principle that against the likelihood and gravity of harm there must be weighed the utility of the conduct.

The conditions surrounding the supervision of students must receive strict attention by those planning student activities. The best plan would seem to include having continuous supervision by a responsible adult. Failing this, the general conditions outlined above need to be provided as a minimum. Again, the younger the students, the greater the expectation of adequate supervision.

In addition, students need to be given specific information regarding possible hazards on property with which they are not familiar. A duty of care is owed to students as they engage in learning activities.

Another occurrence is likely when students are not confined to a building. Use of private automobiles to transport them to various locations becomes a possibility. Most automobile liability policies which protect the owner or driver against damage suits do not protect him if the car is used for transporting persons for hire. If a person is paid for the use of his car to transport students, special coverage should be added to his auto insurance policy.

Still another likelihood of a more open approach to learning is the possibility that students be sent on errands. A rationale may well be built to prove the educational benefits of an errand. Yet it is also necessary to show reasonable prudence in case the runner of the errand might be injured and negligence charged. Beyond this, the pupil becomes the agent of the adult who sends him and, under *respondeat superior,* such adult is responsible for any negligent act of the pupil that may cause injury to a third party.[11] The age and disposition of the student, the conditions under which he was sent and the place to which he was sent (including the territory traversed) may influence the judgment of a court. Adequate instructions to the student and insurance coverage for the adult are essential elements in dealing with this type of risk.

This discussion may give the impression that the major reason for taking steps to protect students against their own acts, the acts of others, and property hazards is to escape tort liability. While this is one of the reasons, it is hoped that the major motivation is a desire to provide the best learning experiences under conditions which maintain the health, safety, and welfare of students.

Having said this, it is worthwhile to point out that all adults— administrators, teachers, paraprofessionals and student teachers— should order their affairs in a manner calculated to keep themselves out of the hands of juries. Beyond this it is also worthwhile to suggest that adults seek to arrange financial protection for possible claims brought against them. Illustrative of these is the following statute which states, in part, that it shall be the duty of a board of education:

> ... to save harmless and protect all teachers, practice or cadet teachers, and members of supervisory and administrative staff or employees from financial loss arising out of any claim, demand, suit, or judgment by reason of alleged negligence or other act resulting in accidental bodily injury to any person within or without the school building, provided such teacher, practice or cadet teacher, or member of the supervisory or administrative staff or employee, at the time of the accident was acting in the discharge of his duties within the scope of his employment. . . .[12]

The statute provides specific authority for a board of education to arrange for and maintain appropriate insurance. In states where such statutes do not exist, insurance arrangements must be made by the individual. Some staff members receive liability insurance coverage as a part of membership in professional organizations. An individual can purchase a liability policy with limits of $50,000 for a yearly premium of approximately $25.00. Group insurance or endorsements on home owner's policies could reduce the cost.

While the position regarding liability of the student teacher or teacher aide may not be exactly the same as that of the certificated teacher, there is sufficient evidence to indicate the desirability of their having insurance protection. Statutes and court decisions vary as to the status of these individuals.

It is possible that the teacher in charge might assign students to be supervised by such persons. There is possible vulnerability to liability in this act. However, in the case of student teachers, it would seem that courts could be convinced that it is necessary to give them experience in controlling student groups.[13] Case law is not well developed regarding reasonable assignments for paraprofessionals.

SUMMARY STATEMENT

The seeking of alternatives to in-class learning is an activity calculated to improve and enhance learning. Implementation of such plans should proceed with a recognition that increased risks may be inherent in the arrangements. The school districts, the private property owner, and the staff personnel may be affected by the possibilities discussed here. It is incumbent on each to reduce or eliminate the dangers to students which may be created thereby. Within the framework of these precautions, "full speed ahead." It is our contention that full awareness of the legal issues attending alternatives should facilitate rather than inhibit such procedures.

FOOTNOTES

1. Lee O. Garber and Reynolds C. Seitz: *The Yearbook of School Law—1971*. Danville, Illinois: The Interstate Printers and Publishers, Inc. 1971.
2. NEA Research Division: *Who Is Liable for Pupil Injuries?* Washington, D.C.: National Education Association, 1963, p. 17.
3. Edmund E. Reutter, Jr. and Robert R. Hamilton: *The Law of Public Education*, Minneola, New York: The Foundation Press, Inc., 1970, p. 276.
4. 47 AmJur (2d) sec. 156, 149.
5. NEA Research Division, *Who Is Liable?* pp. 57-58.
6. Clary v. McDonald, 200 N.E. (2d) 805.
7. 39 O Jur (2d) p. 576, 604.
8. Robert L. Drury, *Ohio School Guide.*, Cincinnati, Ohio: W. H. Anderson, 1966, sec. 6.37.

9. Ibid.

10. Butler v. District of Columbia, 417 f (2d), 1150.

11. Lee O. Garber, Robert L. Drury, and Rogert M. Shaw, *The Law and the Teacher in Ohio*. Danville, Illinois: The Interstate Printers and Publishers, Inc., 1966, p. 79.

12. *McKinney's Consolidated Laws of New York*. St. Paul, Minnesota: West Publishing Co., 1970, pp. 438-440.

13. William R. Hazard, *Education and the Law*. New York: The Free Press, 1971, p. 420.

17

New Learning Places for High School Students in the St. Louis Public Schools

DAVID J. MAHAN

> There is great concern today among the general public that our high schools are lowering their academic standards through programs such as work/learning and community service. What we are experiencing is a change of academic standards, not a lowering of them. The schools are becoming more process-oriented, rather than cognitive directed. I always remember the inscription beneath the bust of Mark Twain in the Hall of Fame; it reads: "Loyalty to petrified opinion never yet broke a chain or freed a human soul."
>
> Statement by Robert G. Chollar, President of the
> Charles F. Kettering Foundation and I/D/E/A.

The curriculum of the American high school has been a controversial topic in American education since the nineteenth century. Early struggles centered around the issue of courses of study being dominated by college entrance examinations. Later the question of adding vocational subjects became a matter of considerable debate, with many viewing such an addition as lowering academic standards and the value of a diploma. In the twentieth century the "Cardinal Principles Report," the Life Adjustment Commission, and post-Sputnik criticism have attempted to restructure the high school curriculum. Course or subject content was the chief topic of these controversies. The question of relevancy of courses for future entrance into college or business was usually the major focus of discussion.

Written especially for this book. Dr. Mahan is Assistant to the Superintendent, St. Louis Public Schools.

Relevance of high school curriculum continues to be a forceful issue in the American high school. Many of the aspects of this issue are quite familiar to the historian of American education, i.e., the subjects are not relevant to real life situations, skills acquired by most students do not help them get jobs, and courses of study are too heavily geared to college entrance requirements. These examples apply chiefly to course content and in this respect have precedence in earlier criticisms. In addition to content, present criticisms involve the process of education. Students, teachers and parents are expressing serious dissatisfaction with the traditional process of secondary instruction which consists of students attending class lectures or discussions led by an instructor for a set number of minutes each day. Although some progressivists and reconstructionists earlier called for a change in the process of secondary instruction, their voices were not heard. In recent years, however, a demand for change in process has increased to the extent that it is almost as much a part of curriculum change as is subject content.

Students are expressing their dissatisfaction with traditional courses and are asking for topics concentrating on present issues such as politics, religion, social conditions, and societal values. They also are demonstrating their discontent with sitting in classrooms and participating in learning situations which they view as passive experiences with little if any relevance or excitement. In their dissatisfaction and often frustration, they are asking for a voice in selecting the content to be studied in the classroom. Furthermore, they are requesting that high school credit be given for their participation in services, activities and experiences which occur outside of the classroom.

In response to these student demands for change, many high schools are initiating innovations in curriculum and the learning process. These changes are slow and at best are reaching only a minority of students. However, in some cases the changes are most significant in moving away from traditional programs. Philadelphia's Parkway Program, Chicago's Metro High School, and Portland's John Adams High School are some of the better known examples.

Students in the St. Louis public schools, like their peers across the nation, are expressing their dissatisfaction with the traditional high school program. The large numbers of students from low income homes intensify the problem of student dissatisfaction in St. Louis, since the traditional curriculum is even less meaningful for many of them. In response to a lack of interest in the traditional curriculum, the school system has initiated several innovations. Many of them concentrate on developing new courses or changing course content. In addition to new courses, the school system has several programs which restructure the learning process by taking it out of the classroom.

Moving the learning process out of the classroom is obviously a more significant change in the curriculum of a school system than adding new courses or changing content. The latter has occurred frequently in the past. The effort to extend instruction beyond the classroom is a recent development that involves a change in the learning process. This change has potential for expanding the learning of students by opening many avenues and opportunities that are not possible within the confines of the high school. In theory the total community with its numerous institutions can become the formal learning environment of the student. Furthermore, learning occurring through performing a task in a community institution or agency becomes a realistic experience which has immediate value. In this respect learning is a means to an end and not merely an end in itself. The often heard criterion of "relevancy" is achieved.

While the demand to change the high school curriculum has received much publicity, only a small percentage of students are enrolled in innovative programs which are taking the learning process out of the classroom. The St. Louis public schools are no exception to this pattern. However, these programs are major changes in the learning process, and they represent the beginnings of a trend toward which the school system is committed to move in the future. At the present time there are three major programs in the St. Louis schools that are taking learning out of the classroom and into the community. They are work study, service, and community involvement programs.

WORK STUDY PROGRAMS

In 1968 the St. Louis public schools initiated a work study program with Stix, Baer & Fuller, one of the large department stores located in the downtown area of the city. In this program, twenty students attended a class located in the store for a half day and then spent the other half day working in the store. They received three units of credit for the academic classes and one unit for work experiences. In addition the students were paid an hourly rate for their fifteen hours of work per week in the store.

This work study program differed from the traditional distributive education course which has existed in school systems for several years. First, the academic class was conducted away from the school in a work location. Second, the academic curriculum was revised so that learning occurred through real problems and tasks of retail merchandising. And third, there was extensive coordination of academic and work experiences by a teacher who was assigned to the students during both phases of the program. In afternoons when students were working in the store, their teacher made contacts with supervisors to review their individual progress.

Participants selected for this first work study program were high school juniors and seniors who were not interested in traditional high school courses. In no way was the program featured as one for low ability students. Instead it represented an alternative for those who were not challenged or excited by the traditional high school program.

The early responses of school staff, students, parents, and company officials were highly positive and school administrators made a commitment to expand the work study concept. In following years numerous companies and institutions have cooperated in initiating work study programs. Among these companies and institutions are: Boyd's Department Store, Bell Telephone, Blue Cross and Blue Shield, McGraw-Hill Publishing, Ralston Purina, Standard Oil, Sinclair Oil, St. Louis Post Dispatch, and several of the large banks and hospitals. Some students are also working in the school system in clerical and general office aide functions. This year approximately 700 students are participating in work study programs.

In expansion of work study programs, there has been some variation from the original plan of organization. Academic classes for some of the programs are held in the high school and students travel to a work location for their half-day, on-the-job assignment. This variation is a result both of space limitations and the number of students assigned to a specific business or institution being too small or large for establishment of a separate class. While this difference in location of academic class exists, all work study programs have the following characteristics: students participate in realistic work experiences, they earn a salary and receive one unit of credit for their on-the-job work, and they learn employable skills.

Any review of a new instructional activity must ask the question, "What do students think of it?" Often programs which are sound in theory and appeal to adults become dismal failures for students. In St. Louis two key criteria give evidence of the popularity of work study programs with students: attendance and dropout rate. Last year the attendance rate for work study students was approximately 93 percent and the dropout rate was approximately 6 percent. The attendance rate for students in programs where academic classes were held at the site of their work assignment was 97 percent and the dropout rate was 2 percent. The results compare with an 88 percent attendance rate and 12 percent dropout rate for all students in the school system. The performance of work study students is even more significant when it is remembered that these students were highly dropout prone and often had low attendance patterns prior to coming into work study programs.

Why does work study appeal to students? School staff feel the following factors are responsible for this appeal to students. First, the students are involved in realistic work assignments. Employers do not assign "busy work" to them. The types of institutions in the program are diverse and the specific job assignments with each institution are varied. Students know that they are responsible for certain tasks and their contribution is a part of the total operation of the business or institution. This type of responsibility does not exist in the regular classroom. Failure to meet individual responsibilities in the classroom may result in low grades for the student, but it does not affect the class as a whole or other members of his class. However, in a work assignment the student soon learns that failure to perform his responsibilities affects others both individually and collectively.

There are two very practical aspects which appeal to students. One is the off-campus setting of the work study location. Many students are attracted simply to learning in a nonschool site. A second appeal is that upon graduation their diploma is granted from their regular high school and is the same as that granted to students completing the traditional high school program. Many work study students enter postsecondary educational programs after graduation instead of taking full time employment.

Another vital factor in the success of work study programs is that students develop employable skills. They become consciously aware of their proficiency in these skills. One obvious result is an enhancement of the self-confidence of the students, especially for many who come from low income homes. Another result is that the skills enable the students to enter sectors of the business community which otherwise would be closed to them. They have excellent opportunities for full time employment after graduation with their work study business or institution.

Learning academic subjects within a context of a job assignment is a feature of those programs where teachers have been able to coordinate closely academic and job activities. Students see academic knowledge and skills as an immediate necessity required for proficiency in tasks which their employer assigns to them. Proficiency in completing assignments results in payment of modest salaries. Although modest, these salaries are a primary incentive for entrance and continuation in work study programs.

The individual attention that occurs in work study activities is of considerable value to many students. In the traditional high school program a student has four or five different teachers each day. It is impossible for a teacher to become as well acquainted with the abilities and needs of a student in this arrangement as in a situation where he has the student in class for a half day and then is able to monitor the student's progress for the remainder of the day in an on-the-job assignment. Work study students enjoy this increased individual attention and profit from it.

While the work study programs have the above appealing features, effective implementation and operation require competent professional instruction. The school system administration carefully selects teachers for work study classes. Key criteria include creativity, openness to change, flexibility in classroom organization, ability to develop new curriculum materials, and a high commitment to helping students succeed in a new program. These teachers work with much dedication to their tasks both in instructional and counseling duties.

These teachers have low student ratios and afternoons available for curriculum development, supervision of work assignments and conferences with job supervisors. Much of the effectiveness of the programs is due to the availability of small ratios and planning time. Thanks to a grant from the Danforth foundation, teachers were employed during the summer to develop curriculum materials which are directly related to work study programs. These materials consist of curriculum packages in which English, mathematics and social studies are taught in world-of-work topics, i.e.: consumer finance, checking and savings, understanding your payroll check, and social-psychological aspects of getting along with others.

The work study programs, like any innovation, have problems. One obstacle is getting an employer to take a risk on a student whose high school record of grades and attendance may be extremely low. Through the successful performance of numerous students in such a category, some employers become more willing to take risks. Another immediate problem is the very limited expansion of the programs due to economic conditions in the city. Most companies are not able to expand their enrollment and it is difficult to start programs with new companies. Work study is directly affected by economic conditions of the community.

CAREER OPPORTUNITY PROGRAM

A second program which extends learning out of the classroom is the Career Opportunities Program which is funded under a grant from the Education Professions Development Act. COP is a national project directed under the Office of Education to recruit and train individuals from low income areas for careers in education. The typical pattern of the project throughout the nation combines study in a college program and service as a paraprofessional in schools located in low income neighborhoods. Another aspect of emphasis is the use of a team approach in assignment of participants to schools.

The St. Louis public schools received a Career Opportunities Program grant in 1970-71. The purposes of the COP project in St. Louis follow national goals. Participants are assigned in teams to schools in low income areas. These teams are unique in that each one consists of three different groups of participants: veterans, mature women aspiring to become teachers, and high school seniors. The seniors attend high schools which qualify as low income schools under the federal guidelines of Title I of the Elementary and Secondary Education Act. Approximately 90 seniors are enrolled in the COP project.

COP is really a combination work study and service activity. Its instructional value applies both to the senior who is learning in activities located out of the classroom and also to elementary students who are receiving instructional services of the tutors. The schedule of the seniors is typical of a work study program. They spend a half day in their high school taking three academic subjects. During the remainder of the day, they serve as educational aides on a COP team. The students receive one high school credit and one college credit for their service as a COP aide. The college credit is held in escrow at Harris Teachers College, a four-year teachers college operated by the St. Louis Board of Education.

There are three criteria for recruitment and selection of students: enrollment in a high school located in a low income area, interest in a career in education, and potential for future completion of college. The third criterion does not require a high grade point average. A student who has a weak high school record but indicates potential if challenged by a program is eligible. The program takes risks with students.

Two or three seniors are assigned to each team. This year there are forty teams working in as many schools. In their assignments, the seniors have a challenging opportunity to learn in a context out of the typical classroom. The COP organization has two major conditions which enhance learning by the seniors. One is their direct and active involvement in planning and implementing learning activities for elementary children. The other is an ongoing program of supervision and inservice given to all the seniors.

One of the basic findings of studies on tutoring programs is that tutors profit more than those being tutored. This condition is most evident in the COP project in that seniors sharpen their academic skills. Even more significantly, they develop skills which relate to child behavior, group dynamics, communication, and the instructional process.

They are not assigned make-work or dull clerical tasks. Instead teachers and principals use these young people in an infinite variety of ways. Their activities include tutoring, teaching small groups, making curriculum materials, grading tests, producing and directing plays, supervising after-school activities, preparing bulletin boards, and making presentations to parent groups.

Effective operation of the above activities requires some instructional expertise on the part of the seniors. Development of this expertise is achieved through ongoing supervision and support by the school principal and teacher and also by a COP staff supervisor. The latter has frequent contact with the seniors, observes them performing their tasks, and counsels with them regarding problems or needs in either their high school or service activities. An ongoing program of group inservice activities also helps build instructional competencies in the seniors. The COP staff and resource consultants give workshops concentrating on a wide range of topics related to improving classroom instruction. Seniors participate along with other members of the COP teams in these sessions. By the end of the school year each senior experiences a range of educational tasks and a rather comprehensive amount of training in instructional techniques.

Special Inducements of COP Projects

The COP project has several features which appeal to students. First, there is a financial factor which is not to be denied. Each student receives a modest salary for the 15 hours served in a school each week. However, there are several nonfinancial benefits which attract students. One is the realistic aspect of their work. They know that their work is an integral part of the elementary educational program. They actually see children learn from their tutoring, drill and teaching activities. Another feature is the relevancy of their work experiences to their future goals. The COP seniors are interested in careers in education. Their training and work as aides is directly related to a college teacher education program and to service as teachers.

A special feature of the COP project is that seniors receive support and training to improve their competencies continuously. Through supervision and consultation they are aware of their individual growth and development. For example, the teaching of reading is one area in which they develop instructional skills. All of the seniors spend some time assisting the remedial reading specialists. In this assignment they develop some skills in a very specialized area of instruction. There is a relevancy to the skills and information they learn from teachers, supervisors, and consultants because it can be immediately used in carrying out their paraprofessional tasks.

The career ladder aspects of the program are a special appeal to most of the students and their parents. Upon graduation the students will enter a teacher education program at Harris Teachers College and will serve as COP aides while in college. The scholarship and stipend benefits represent an opportunity to go to college for most of these students, since they come from low income homes.

The project offers students an opportunity to become emotionally involved and committed in a service to others. Through the development of skills and successful completion of tasks, the students achieve self-confidence. Their sense of self-value and importance is enhanced. With self-confidence and a feeling of self-importance, they can become strongly involved in a project with the belief that they can make a real contribution.

Problems of COP Projects

While the COP project is one of our more encouraging activities, it obviously has some problems. One pertains to students who are academic risks. In some previous cases, students who were academic risks had to be enrolled in special college tutorial programs after graduation. Hopefully, these students can make sufficient progress to complete a teacher education program and thereby realize their aspirations. Frequent counseling of students is a necessity in the program.

Scheduling and transportation are other problems. Frequently it is difficult for students to schedule a block of time for the three academic courses needed for college entrance. The amount of time required for transportation from a high school to an elementary school in some cases limits the amount of time students have to spend in their paraprofessional assignment. Furthermore, it usually prevents them from being able to participate in after-school activities at their high school.

The school system is committed to expanding service projects in the future. One major problem is funding of student stipends or salaries. However, our experience indicates that if programs are sufficiently challenging and exciting, students will participate in them without salaries. Credit will be given for service activities. School administrators envision possible service programs which will go beyond the classroom into such institutions as hospitals, public health centers, welfare departments, and neighborhood centers.

CITIZENSHIP EDUCATION CLEARING HOUSE PROGRAM

Several community involvement programs in the St. Louis schools are presently extending learning beyond the classroom and into a variety of centers throughout the city. The catalyst for these programs is an organization entitled Citizenship Education Clearing House (CECH). CECH was initiated in 1967 under the Higher Education Coordinating Council for Metropolitan St. Louis. It has a director and an advisory board of distinguished citizens from numerous areas of the community. The purpose of CECH is to make high school social studies an experience in citizenship by getting students actively involved in solving community issues which are of interest to them. CECH programs have operated in both city and suburban schools of the St. Louis area. Funding has come from foundations, business, industry, and other sources.

The CECH program began with two classes in one high school. In 1971-72, there were eight high and six middle school classes participating in the program. While the classes are a part of the CECH program, each class has the freedom to initiate any project of its choice. The major role of the CECH staff is to provide inservice training for teachers, make resource persons available to classes, and disseminate information about the various projects.

Special Action Project Accomplished

Initiation of a project by a class begins with students selecting an area of special interest. This selection usually starts with students listing a number of local, state or national issues which they consider to be of major concern. From this list, an area is selected which can be a special project of the class and which can be carried out within the school year. Many of the projects have involved two areas of special concern to students in recent years: political elections including candidates and issues, and the ecology movement. Classes are active in elections of candidates for local, state and national offices. Students bring speakers into the schools to discuss issues. After selection of a candidate, they then work through political organizations performing various duties including passing out literature, telephoning voters, addressing envelopes, and distributing sample ballots at the polls. Students have actively supported local and state tax and bond issues including school tax and bond elections, a local bond issue for improved facilities for juvenile detention, and a state income tax election with emphasis on increasing state aid for education.

Ecology projects have concentrated chiefly on eliminating different types of pollution. One consisted of a campaign to collect nonreturnable glass. The glass was collected, crushed, and sold. Proceeds were used to help improve a community center. A class is presently attempting to establish this glass collection project on a permanent basis. Other projects include: volunteer service at hospitals and orphanages, rehabilitation of neighborhoods, voter registration campaigns, participating with the police department in a neighborhood survey of residents, and helping operate a community lunch program.

The CECH classes give students an opportunity to become actively involved in a project that is interesting to them. Learning activities occur both in and out of the classroom with a considerable amount of time being spent out of the classroom. There are several features of the project which appeal to students. One is certainly the opportunity for students to select the project and plan the activities. Numerous research studies in business and education have demonstrated the importance of involving participants in the selection and development process of an innovation. When such involvement occurs, participants tend to be more strongly committed to making a project succeed. In the CECH programs, when a project is selected, it is because a group of students want it. Planning and operation of it is their responsibility. Because the project is basically theirs, commitment to successful operation is high.

The program meets the frequently heard criterion of relevance. Projects involve a specific problem or issue of concern to students, and activities are directed toward resolution of some aspect of the problem or issue during the school year. Another feature is the emotional involvement of students in the projects.

Limitations of CECH Projects

The CECH projects have two major limitations. One is the small number of students involved. Only about 400 students are participating. The number who could be challenged by this type of learning experience is obviously much higher. Expansion in numbers is a major goal. A second limitation is the amount of time in the formal school day devoted to the projects. Some projects are of such a nature that students could profit from spending the entire or at least most of the school day on them. Flexibility in scheduling of student learning activities is a future goal.

COMMITMENT TO EXTENDING LEARNING
BEYOND THE CLASSROOM

The St. Louis public schools are committed to continuing and expanding the above programs. In addition we hope to initiate other activities which take learning beyond the classroom. One is the development of service programs to various community agencies and institutions. The focus would be on students receiving credit for service to the community in some type of aide capacity. Emphasis would be placed on students selecting a service activity of particular interest to them.

Another plan to extend learning will consist of the opening of an experimental high school which will operate on a "school without walls" basis. The school will open in September of 1972 with approximately 150 students selected from across the city. Emphasis will be placed on using resources in the city as much as possible. Students will have the opportunity for independent study. Instructional activities will be conducted both within and out of the school. Those learning activities held out of the school will include classes at various community institutions, independent study or research, and involvement in some type of community service or project. *Hopefully, the types of activities at the new "school without walls" will begin to occur on at least a limited scale in all St. Louis high schools. The administration is committed to expanding the number and type of learning experiences in the high schools so that students can select from several learning alternatives instead of being required to follow a traditional program.*

ADMINISTRATIVE AND OPERATION CONDITIONS FOR LEARNING IN NEW PLACES

The effectiveness of the above programs in offering students learning activities out of the classroom is a result of their unique aspects as briefly described. However, there are several administrative and operational conditions which also are major factors in the effectiveness of these learning activities. The following administrative and operational conditions are common to the programs described above and are applicable to other instructional activities that may be conducted out of the classroom.

Staff Selection

Highly competent teachers are in charge of the learning activities. Because of the innovative nature of the programs and the relatively small number of students involved, administrators have been very selective in recruitment of staff. The Hawthorne effect of the activities contributes to keeping already competent and enthusiastic teachers excited about the program.

Inservice Training

Inservice training for staff is a part of all the programs. Ongoing inservice sessions help teachers become aware of techniques and activities that are especially important to the operation of their specific learning activities. Along with inservice training, teachers have more time for planning. This planning includes both general program goals and activities and individual class programs. Involvement in planning general program goals and activities certainly has positive implications for commitment. Time for planning of daily activities is obviously important to the development of effective learning experiences.

Supervision of Students

Provision for supervision of students in activities away from the school is also a vital aspect of the programs. Staff assignments are structured so that there is sufficient time for this supervision. This arrangement enables teachers to coordinate classroom and nonclassroom experiences more effectively so that they reinforce each other.

Development of Materials

The development of special curriculum materials is another important condition for effective learning. Materials are especially crucial for work study programs. The preparation of these materials requires considerable time of teachers. This investment in time, however, results in learning being more immediately meaningful to students.

SUMMARY

Extending learning beyond the classroom is one response to criticisms of the instructional process in secondary schools. This innovation is widely expanding instructional experiences for students and is making learning an active rather than passive process. The St.

Louis school system has three major programs that are extending learning beyond classrooms. The work study, Career Opportunity Program, and Citizenship Education Clearing House projects were described. These programs appeal to students because of the following aspects: realistic academic and work assignments, development of responsibility, increase in self-confidence and self-importance, emotional involvement and commitment to an activity, development of special skills, increased coordination between academic and project tasks, orientation into a vocational or professional career, and the opportunity to exercise choice in selecting instructional activities. The effectiveness of the programs in the St. Louis schools is due to these program aspects and also to several key administrative and operational conditions. These conditions include highly competent staff, ongoing inservice training, adequate supervision of students in assignments out of the classroom, and special curriculum materials. The programs are, in a very real sense, pilot projects for the entire school system.

18

Alternatives for Now and for 2001

LEE R. McMURRIN

INTRODUCTION

The very survival of public school education is being challenged and threatened on every hand. The daily papers report problems that seem insurmountable. Those responsible for the management of school systems are painfully aware of the problems. Most school administrators are diligently seeking feasible solutions. During the past five years the implementation of solutions to pressing problems has accelerated due to the impact of the crises and the new sources of monies flowing out of Washington, D.C. But the new money is drying up and inflation is taking its toll on what the old money sources can accomplish. Unfortunately, most of the solutions to current problems have been short range rather than long range; extraneous rather than fundamental.

Planning is an essential function of management. If relief is to be found for a crisis-ridden school system, planning is necessary. By devoting more time and resources to the planning function, survival is possible and the restoration of public confidence will be accomplished over the ensuing years. Long range planning is a process of projecting and forecasting future events. Dealing with public education in the future tense is risky business. Nonetheless, it must be

Written especially for this book. Dr. McMurrin is Deputy Superintendent, Toledo Public Schools, Toledo, Ohio.

done. Through long range planning, uncertainties can be turned into possibilities. Long range planning permits those responsible for the education of the young to determine intelligently among many alternatives the future state of affairs.

It is suggested that long range planning be directly associated with persistent problems of the educational institutions. In this regard, long range planning is a step by step process that includes the determination of alternative solutions. The steps in this process are outlined as:

1. Make needs assessment.
2. Identify the problem.
3. *Determine the alternative solutions.*
4. Decide on implementation requirements.
5. Determine performance effectiveness design and criteria.

In planning for the future, all five steps are necessary with the option of recycling for revision and refinement. A brief description of each step follows:

1. *Needs Assessment.* The first step in the process of problem solving is to assess the needs as identified by a reference group. The reference group may include representatives of all those associated with a particular situation: students, teachers, principals, parents, taxpayers and citizens at large, or any combination. The need is defined as the discrepancy that exists between a standard and the present situation. The standard may be generally referred to as "what should be" and the present situation as "what is." With a back drop of philosophy, values, goals and general objectives of the organiza- tion, an assessment is made of the needs or the discrepancies between what is and what should be.

2. *Identification of Problems.* The problem is identified as a need that is rated as a priority based on organizational philosophy and goals. The problem identified for solution may include subproblems which relate directly to the general problem. The function of iden- tifying the problem is as specific as: (1) establishing requirements for resolution and (2) defining in some detail the desired outcomes. If a list of problems are identified in rank order according to urgency in the need for resolution, each should be processed one at a time with

the system requiring a recycling of each step. A recycling model is shown in Figure 1.

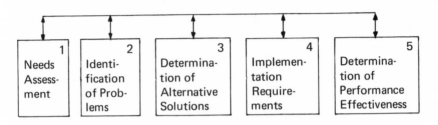

FIGURE 1

A Five-Step Recycling Model for Long Range Educational Planning

3. *Determination of Alternative Solutions.* After the problem has been identified, an analysis is made to determine the various solutions that satisfy the need. This analysis requires a consideration of objectives specific enough to estimate cost requirements for each of the possible solutions. A thorough examination of the alternative solutions should produce both advantages and disadvantages of each relative to producing the anticipated outcomes in a particular situation.

4. *Designation of Implementation Requirements.* Based on the analysis of possible solutions to an identified problem an appropriate solution is selected for implementation. This decision prepares the way for more specific planning directed toward the implementation of a selected solution of a particular situation. At this phase of the process more attention is given to specific ways of implementing the solution. The ways of reaching the solution are those items which are common to a program description with an attached budget. More specifically, some of the implementation requirements are suggested as: program objectives, procedures, training requirements, allocation, description and procurement of staff, scheduling of activities, and budgeting.

5. *Determination of Performance Effectiveness.* In planning the solution to a specifically identified problem one must be aware of the larger system. The larger system includes many programs with multiple effects on the performance of the product of the schools.

The fifth step in planning for the solution of a persistent problem is essential. Before the solution is applied to the problem situation, consideration is given to the design and criteria required to measure the effectiveness of the solution in terms of some overriding performance objectives of the organization. Planning at this step should provide for the measurement of performance objectives of the particular solution strategy and also provide for the measured effects of this performance level on the overall effectiveness of the institution.

If needed reforms are to occur in the educational system, consideration must be given to alternatives to the present classroom model of education. These alternatives to traditional classroom settings should emerge as educators plan for the resolution of problems, and school systems strive to adjust to the needs of an urban society. In the remainder of this discussion I will identify some basic assumptions and concepts which serve to guide our search for alternatives. This will be followed by a list of some alternatives currently operating in the Toledo public schools. Finally, I shall offer a description of a projected model of education for the year 2001.

BASIC ASSUMPTIONS AND CONCEPTS

There are some basic assumptions and concepts underlying the consideration of alternatives to in-class instruction. The basic assumptions are:

1. that formal education of the learner is deemed necessary by society which establishes educational institutions for this purpose,

2. that education takes place throughout life in various forms that are classified as formal, semi-formal and informal,

3. that technology continues to advance and these advances are eventually adopted by most members of a culture,

4. that education is essentially a product of the total environment and that only a portion of it is the result of formal education, and

5. that the rewards and satisfactions of urban living are enhanced through an environment that continues to stimulate learning for all the population.

For a moment let's consider that educational institutions are separate from the environment and that the learner is a free agent.

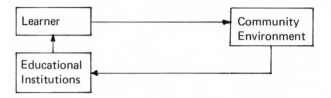

This diagram represents the concept that the educational institution in a formal manner develops the learner and returns the learner to the community which is a consumer of the skills and knowledge bestowed upon the learner. The community in turn provides the knowledge, skills and technology required of the institution. An expansion of this concept is realized by running the arrows in reverse.

This diagram represents the concept that the educational institutions produce knowledge that is consumed by the community, which through informal ways develops the learner who attends the educational institution and modifies his knowledge. In other words, there is interaction between the institution and the learner, the learner and the community and the community and the institution.

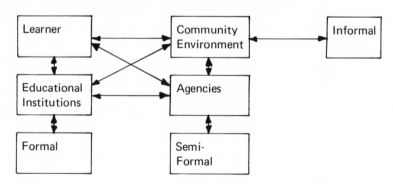

This diagram represents an interaction model of education that includes the learner, the community, agencies, and educational institutions. There are three types of educational inputs for the learner: formal, semi-formal, and informal. Formal educational experiences are provided by the educational institutions, semi-formal educational experiences are offered by the community social and service agencies, and informal educational experiences are a part of the unstructured educational environment represented by all other facets of community life.

SCHOOL COMMUNITY AGENCY COOPERATION

Public schools in large cities usually have a working relationship with several community agencies. In order to determine the extent of the cooperation of schools with various community agencies, two surveys were conducted in Toledo. The central office staff was requested to list the agencies that worked with the schools and to describe the programs and services rendered through a cooperative effort. In one capacity or another the school's central office personnel reported that they work with nearly all community agencies. These are the major programs:

1. The public school community coordinators attend meetings and observe programs sponsored by neighborhood councils and community centers in order to improve cooperation.

2. In the Community Lighted Schools program many public and private agencies use our facilities for meetings, classes and recreation.

3. The school sponsored Head Start program solicits the use of church facilities through the Toledo Council of Churches.

4. High school students in regular physical education classes receive swimming lessons from a nearby Y.M.C.A.

5. A new center for high school youth is opening, sponsored jointly by the Bureau of Vocational Rehabilitation and the Toledo Public Schools.

6. The STEP (Sheltered Training Experience Program) project is housed in the new facility for Goodwill Industries.

7. A special program for teaching vocational skills needed for employment in hotel services is centered in a downtown hotel.

8. The Chamber of Commerce is assisting in a job placement

program for all graduates of four city high schools with a high incidence of low income families.

9. Day care centers have been established with the resources of several agencies through the Community Planning Association.

10. Schools have assisted the Committee on Aging by developing educational programs for senior citizens.

11. A home repair program was initiated jointly by the Model Cities Agency and the Toledo Public Schools.

12. The Technical Society of Toledo sponsors the Science and Engineering Day activities for public and private school students and plans each year the Toledo Area Junior Science Research Symposium.

13. The Toledo Metropolitan Park Board hires a full time naturalist and provides park facilities for outdoor education and field trips planned for all 5th grade science classes.

14. Classes for Distributive Education take place in rooms furnished in downtown department stores so that the work experience portion of the program is in walking distance.

15. The Child Welfare Board assigns full time social workers at each of the four district offices for pupil personnel services (North, South, East, and West Centers).

16. The Toledo Metropolitan Area Drug Abuse Committee furnishes counselors, nurses, speakers, and information and training services to the schools.

17. The Y.W.C.A. is providing space in a downtown center for an educational program sponsored jointly by the Florence Crittendon Home and the Toledo Public Schools.

18. The Medical College is placing on-campus classes for emotionally disturbed children.

19. The Boys Club of Toledo has assisted in developing programs for the unteachable boys.

20. The Y.M.C.A. owned Camp Storer is contracted during the entire school year to provide facilities for a week-long trip to camp for elementary students with associated educational experiences in the out-of-doors.

In another effort to secure information on alternatives, surveys were mailed to 140 community service agencies in the Toledo Metropolitan Area. The executives of these agencies were asked to describe the classes for instruction and/or other services offered to school-age children, ages 5 through 18. The number of surveys returned was 79. Of these:

33 replied that no classes or services were offered to school-age children;

14 replied that classes for instruction were offered;

15 replied that school-related services were offered to school-age children; and

17 replied that classes for instruction were offered in cooperation with the Toledo Public Schools or a state agency.

One specific interest of this survey was to identify the type of classes offered for instruction by these agencies. These can be listed as follows:

Driver Education	Family Life Education
English as a Second Language	Remedial Reading
	Theatre
Folk Dancing	Nutrition
Civil Defense	Lipreading
First Aid	Health Education
Swimming and Life Saving	Job Training - Work Experience
Citizenship	
Sports and Athletics	Day Care Programs
Arts and Crafts	Nursery School
Typing	Pre-natal and Post-partum classes
Remedial Education	

Several school-related services are offered by the agencies. The respondents reported the following types of services:

Guidance counseling	Informational services
College counseling	Speakers
Career counseling	Birth control counseling
Job placement	Lectures
Educational tours	Bedside teaching
Financial counseling	Dial access tape library
Transportation	Suicide prevention counseling

Mental health services	Chest x-rays
On-the-job training	General health examinations
Family life counseling	Speech and hearing examinations
Psychological examinations	and therapy

As could be expected, the educational programs and services are offered to select populations. Basic instructional programs of the public schools are not offered by these agencies, namely: reading, math, science, social studies.

It was revealed in the survey that several projects are sponsored jointly by a social agency and the school system or another governmental agency. Among these were:

Concentrated Employment Program, Economic Opportunity Association.

Creative Arts, Economic Opportunity Association.

Tutorial Services, Drug Education Agency, Economic Opportunity Association.

Job training, Economic Opportunity Association.

Day Care and Head Start, Economic Opportunity Association.

Training for Mentally Retarded.

Migrant Education.

Residential Treatment and Educational Program for Adolescent Emotionally Disturbed Girls.

Practical Nurses Training Program.

Residential School, Ohio Youth Commission.

Residential School at Toledo Mental Health Center.

Preschool and Kindergarten Classes by the Toledo Society for Crippled Children.

The social and service agencies of Toledo provide a full array of instructional classes and other school related services. These learning experiences are given to individuals by appointment or by referral, based on demonstrated needs. Agencies in cooperation with the public schools design projects that satisfy the demand for servicing specific groups of children and youth. Many of these worthwhile activities for school-age children are alternatives to in-class education. These alternatives seem to have one or more of the following characteristics:

1. the learning experience is away from the school site,
2. the clients are serviced individually when needs are identified,
3. the service is offered by various classifications of personnel, not by formally trained classroom teachers,
4. the appointed time for instruction is individually scheduled,
5. the services and classes for instruction are either offered in neighborhood schools or churches, or in a centrally located office in the downtown area, and
6. the clients are serviced as long as they qualify by interest or by a need for service.

If the effort to cooperate with other agencies in educational programs and services grows and alternatives to classroom instruction increase, then the public schools are going to have to exert leadership in guiding and coordinating the activity. *In the future it will be the public schools or some other umbrella agency that will be responsible for the total educational program of the urban center.* Many of the alternatives to classroom instruction will be commonplace and institutionalized in the days to come. That which is thought to be nontraditional study today will become an accepted mode of learning in the future.

THE 2001 MODEL

Our large cities are in the midst of a social reform. In the crisis and conflict that surround the changes, schools are asked to participate in bringing about social justice, educate the underprivileged child, fit a generation for a new world of technical skills, and take racially different children and provide them wholesome and enriching educational and living experiences which lead to improved urban life. To accomplish this we must develop a new model for education.

Much research relates to the effects of poverty, discrimination, and other ills in our society which affect directly the child's ability to achieve. There are technological advancements providing the means to achieve the new educational model. These in turn require continuous use and further effort on the part of schools to educate the adult population for an ever-changing society.

In the new order of things, it is the future that must concern us. It is what we can do together as individuals of good will in our metropolitan areas that will make urban living more rewarding and satisfying.

A Brief Description of the Model

This educational model must move in a complete cycle of educational development, pointed toward realizing the full potential of America's children and youth. The emergent program is already supported by state and federal laws requiring an increasingly high standard of performance in keeping with our best knowledge and skill. The new model for improved education follows this sequence: (a) family life education program and work-study experience in a child care center for secondary youth; (b) hospital-sponsored clinics and educational seminars for expectant mothers; (c) well-baby clinics and child-development educational centers for all mothers and babies; (d) day care centers for young children, with educational programs coordinated for children and parent schedules; (e) pre-school education for all three- and four-year-olds, exempting only those who have an equivalent level of performance prescribed by the schools; (f) day care centers for children when they are not in school and when competent adult supervision is not available at home; (g) kindergarten-primary education for children ages five through nine in open space schools; (h) intermediate education for children ages 14 through 18 in study-work-play centers and expanded studies at a centrally located campus school; (i) job placement with continuous follow-up attention given to students graduated from secondary schools to guarantee their adjustment to the world of work through advanced training and with permanent assignment to the secondary school for guidance and counseling.

Family Life Education and Child Care

By common consent, the family is the principal institution for the formation of individual personality and the most cherished institution of our civilization.[1] The more we learn about child rearing, the more we are convinced that the family is very important. Clearly, parents in a changing world need as much assistance as they can get.

Secondary school youth in the future are going to be required to take family life education and have work experience in a child care center operated by the school system. Success with programs such as the "Teen Tutors," organized in one mid-Ohio city school district, supports the type of program proposed here. Students in family life classes put their new knowledge to work on a regular schedule at a child care center. The program should be designed to prepare boys and girls alike to do a better job rearing children. The child care center provides a living laboratory to test ideas and homemaking skills.

Prenatal Clinics

It is essential for the sake of a healthy child that the mother receive the best of medical and environmental care during pregnancy. Expectant mothers will be required to go on schedule to prenatal clinics operated in hospitals. These will offer not only medical care, but an educational program. Prenatal clinics will assist in: (a) proper nutrition, (b) mental health, (c) preparation for labor and delivery, (d) instruction in child care, (e) education in child growth and development, (f) counseling and referral service to other agencies, (g) continuation of formal educational studies if clients are still in high school.

Well-baby Clinics

We now know the importance of the first years of life. Nevertheless, it has been said that we are shamefully ignorant about what happens between the time the baby leaves the hospital and the time he shows up in a nursery school.[1] Infancy is probably the most exciting and fruitful period of human life to study. It is particularly important that mothers be given information as to what babies are able to learn and what experiences they should have during the first months of life. Mothers and babies will continue to get medical checkups which will identify physical problems. Early identification will be made of exceptional children so that immediate adjustments are made in the care of the child. Psychological and mental health problems experienced by the mother will be identified and appropriate services provided. A permanent record will be kept of the child's growth, development and responses to stimuli. Including fathers in some sessions at the well-baby clinics will bring them directly into learning experiences which they in turn should offer and expect from their children.

Day Care Centers for the Very Young

A day care center will be located convenient for the mother. If she must return to work, the day care center operated by the school system could be located within or close to the place of employment. Day care centers for the very young will be stationed in the neighborhood so that working mothers may use the service if desired, and so that the child could be placed in the center while the mother goes shopping, takes adult education classes, or is occupied by other duties. These centers will be small, well equipped and adequately staffed. Community volunteers and high school students will assist with routine services as well as providing special attention to the children. Records will be kept on the growth and development of each child, and close relations maintained with the parents and those providing supportive services.

Nursery School Education

Small nursery schools will be located in neighborhoods within walking distance for most of the children. The three- and four-year olds will come to school by appointment and, if possible, accompanied by a parent. The appointments will be worked out for the family by the day care center. Learning experiences will be programmed individually for each child. Activities at this school will be intense, with cognitive development as a focus. The school will have a rich learning environment with learning stations located throughout a spacious room. This will permit easy movement from one vital learning station to another. Parent education will be an important aspect of this program.

Kindergarten-Primary Education

Bloom concludes that the individual develops about 50 percent of his mature intelligence between conception and age four, another 30 percent from ages four to eight, and the remaining 20 percent from ages eight to seventeen.[2] Thus, the early environment is of crucial importance in laying the base for further development. The experiences children have had at home, at school, and in the community before they enter the kindergarten, have great impact upon the type of program which best meets their needs during the growing years from age five through ten. Obviously, some children come with a rich background of experience. Others, even with the best efforts of parents and community, need compensatory education. At this level, parents and school interaction should be continued so that parents may assist, supplement and reinforce the development of skills, knowledge and values.

The task of educators today is not simply that of bringing the lower-class child to the point where he is equal to his middle-class counterpart when he enters the primary grades. Rather it is one of unlocking cognitive and motivational potential of all children. To accomplish this, educational planners should change the structure of the educational enterprise as a whole.

The new early childhood education will include: (a) a sound foundation of learning experiences for all children; (b) a curriculum aimed at cognitive growth, concept formation, abstract reasoning values, and perceptual refinement; (c) teachers with an appreciation for different life styles, guiding the students to creative understanding and acceptance of individuals who are different; (d) an entire faculty with differentiated roles and staff specifications.

The new kindergarten-primary educational program for large urban centers can only be realized by drastic changes in our approach to learning experiences. The entire urban center can be viewed as a large learning laboratory for the young, completely eliminating the conventional concept of a classroom represented by a teacher standing in front of approximately 30 children. Classroom organization of this type will no longer exist.

Description of Kindergarten-Primary Model

The Tele-Computer Console. A tele-computer console, located in the home or apartment dwelling, will be programmed by the school for rerunning educational programs originated via television and computer. Homework has been a part of the educational scheme for years, but the school has never been able to monitor the actual learning experience. Technology makes it possible. The student's performance on a given task would be recorded in the computer and evaluated by the school. Educational programming would be such that none of the experiences offered via this console would stand alone but would be part of an overall scheme of learning.

The One-Story, Open-Space School. In the neighborhood will be a one-story school, completely open, without corridors, halls, and stairways. Each student will be individually programmed, and the school will be open year-round, with no opening or closing dates. Students are not required to be at the school all at one time. They will be treated on an individual basis. The layout of the school interior will be much like a department store. Each student will have something similar to a charge plate which he will use to record his experiences at several check points in the school.

Each program is to be worked out by a specialist through a counseling session with the student's parents. Private tutoring will be available, but most learning experiences will be so well developed and paced that technicians will give most of the assistance and supervision.

A child care center will be an auxiliary service, offered by the school and separate from the learning area. Students turned over to the school for custody during the day would receive care in the center, with provision made for rest, food, exercise, entertainment and social adjustment.

The school's manager and professional teaching staff will develop educational programs for each student. Child care workers and other paraprofessionals will be available for routine tasks and technical services.

There will be tele-computer outlets in the school for children who do not have them at home. Parents interested in the progress their children are making at school can receive a report at any moment over the computer outlet installed in their home or at school.

There will be no attempt to put the children in classifications in this school such as kindergarten, 1st, 2nd, 3rd, and 4th grade. Students may enter the school any time during the year when they become five years old, and leave the school and enter the intermediate school when they become ten years old.

In a school such as this, it would be difficult to give enough time in diagnosing and initially programming a new student's education if all students enrolled on the same day. By scheduling enrollments at various days throughout the year, the staff can give full attention to the few students enrolling. Also, since students in transient neighborhoods come and go almost weekly, the school would have to gear up for this type of operation. Arrangements of staff time for this purpose would make it a normal rather than a traumatic experience for students to enroll and withdraw from school.

Multi-Story Learning Center. A multi-story learning center will be centrally located in one of the more congested areas of the city, possibly near the downtown area. The layout of the floors will be similar to the open-space school in the neighborhood, with floors tied together by escalators and elevators. The various floors allow for classification of learning activities ranging from concrete to the abstract, or from quiet to noisy activities. In this building there will be permanent displays of scientific and historical significance. Although students will be programmed individually, here they will be required to form cooperative work teams for group projects. Here basic skills learned in the small neighborhood open-space school are applied to larger and more cooperative tasks. Students of diverse background and socioeconomic status will interact with a greater understanding and appreciation of differences. Fully air-conditioned, the center will be open year-round, each day of the week from 8 a.m. to 9 p.m., on a schedule similar to nearby stores and offices. Shuttle buses will come every 15 minutes into the center from neighborhoods. A child care section will have to be available for students who need rest, relaxation, food, and care. The center will have the same technology available to it as that of the open-space schools in the neighborhood.

Residential School and Campsite. On occasion, all children will go during the year to the residential school and campsite. The students' outdoor laboratory will be here. A full time staff will be at the residential school and campsite. They will be trained to offer unique experiences to multi-age and multi-ethnic groups of students living, learning and working together.

Provisions for Special and Exceptional Students. Every attempt will be made to include exceptional students in the full program for kindergarten-primary education, with individual attention from specialists. This group should not be isolated from students or the experiences they receive at any of the settings described above.

Provisions for Neglected Children. Children whose parents cannot provide good learning experience at home or cannot cooperate with the schools in following programs outlined for them will spend a disproportionate time at the residential school. Some children may become permanent citizens at this school, going home only on weekends and holidays. Resident students would have experiences similar to those of other students, since they would have tele-computer outlets in their dormitories and would be taken into the multi-story learning center for special learning activities. They would mix with other students. A full educational program would be planned for these students and every effort would be made to improve the quality of their home environment so that the child could return home.

Intermediate School Education

The education of the children ages 10 through 14 will be an extension of the design outlined above for the kindergarten-primary level. A tele-computer console will be programmed for advancing skills in reading and math. New subjects such as exploratory and introductory foreign language will be offered for continued practice and skill development.

The one-story open-space school in the neighborhood will provide the initial learning experiences in new subjects with facilities for more practice as necessary. Of particular value to intermediate age students will be the work stations for exploratory arts, crafts, electricity, graphics, typing, construction and manufacturing industries; and laboratories for exploratory sciences such as physics, chemistry, astronomy, biology, geology, and physiology.

For the intermediate student a recreation center will be open in the neighborhood from morning into the evening. Students will be scheduled in coordination with learning activities planned by the schools. This will be done in consultation with parents and will be made convenient to the household schedule of activities. In some respects the recreation center will serve some of the same purposes as the day care center provides for younger children.

The multi-story learning center is designed to accommodate those learning activities that are group-oriented. The new skills learned at the open-space school are applied to group projects and activities. It is here that students will participate in drama, band, orchestra, social studies research and community service projects, science experiments, seminars on current topics, and home, industry and business projects.

The residential school and campsite will be available to intermediate students as it is to the primary students. Students at the intermediate level will spend at least a week each year at the camp. The learning experiences will center around their academic programs with definite application to group living and to the out-of-doors.

Secondary Education for a Metropolitan Area

Secondary education in the future will be planned around the needs of rural, suburban, and city youth. Every attempt will be made to coordinate all the educational activities for high school youth in the metropolitan area. The changes now taking place in our society and the problems of youth growing up in metropolitan areas require a fundamental change in our secondary school programs. The new model for secondary education will be fashioned after these trends; all woven together into a new organization. This organization will incorporate some of these trends:

1. more flexibility and diversity in the educational program
2. greater career orientation and training
3. integration of the so-called academic and career subjects into individually planned programs of studies
4. more purposeful educational efforts toward both immediate and long range objectives
5. extensive use of the community as a learning laboratory
6. improved use of technology in the acquisition and transmission of new knowledge
7. frequent interaction between youth of different social, economic, ethnic and cultural backgrounds
8. progress measured primarily by performance criteria rather than time spent in class
9. extensive use of paraprofessionals for routine services and for technical assistance
10. time available for students to receive private lessons from master teachers
11. emphasis on development of professional staff in regular day schedule
12. participation of all students in work, study, and recreational activities during the entire year
13. more flexibility in the use of time and facilities
14. development of a life style of learning appropriate for the requirements of an urban society

The Secondary School Model

The program of studies will continue to be planned by counselors and curriculum specialists. However, it will be planned for each student. Facilities available to fulfill the requirements of the program are: (a) school system; (b) a community center for study, work and recreation; (c) a campus school centrally located, serving at least four community centers. In a small city, the campus would be in the center of the city. The four community centers would be placed in housing areas in four directions away from the center of the city. All facilities would be tied together by television and computer. In a large metropolitan area, several of these models would form pie-shaped districts, moving out from the central city. Each campus school area would include central city, fringe area, suburban, and rural areas. Each would eventually serve as a center for commercial, recreational, community and educational activities.

The Community Center. One thousand to two thousand pupils in a given attendance area would use the community center for study, work and recreation. A large instructional materials center would provide printed, audiovisual, and programmed learning materials, with individual study carrels assigned to each pupil, and rooms for small group discussion and private tutoring.

To follow up the individual laboratory experiences programmed for the students would be large rooms with work stations for the particular science, with the necessary storage and work areas to perform the research.

Each community center would have unique skill shops where students not only learn the particular skill, but eventually produce materials for the benefit of the entire educational enterprise. Several skill shops would be recommended by business and industry for each community center. Students could move from these experiences to a job, with the necessary entrance skills. In addition, the skill shop will serve to retrain adults in the community. Since students will be programmed in these shops individually and not as class groups, adults can be scheduled during the day or evening.

The community center would also provide for intramural and interscholastic athletics. Gymnasiums, swimming pools, tennis courts, bowling alleys, poolrooms would be here for use from early morning through late evening each day. School community newspapers would be published here. Food service would be available, with club activities for students and adults. One hundred or more tele-computer consoles would be available here for students who would not have them in their homes or apartments. Transportation and communication links between the community centers and the campus school would be on almost a continuous basis.

The Campus School. Located conveniently for the use of 4,000 to 8,000 high school students would be an attractive campus, landscaped with buildings designed to inspire the pursuit of learning and cultural activities. Since not all students would be using the campus at the same time, it would be designed to handle conveniently, without congestion or crowding, a maximum of 2,000 students. Architecturally, the campus would reflect the culture and goals of the community.

The campus school will: (a) provide for educational research and development for the area; (b) be for social interaction between young people from various home backgrounds and with adults with different life styles and resources to offer the students; (c) structure strategies for bringing about change leading to educational improvements; (d) provide for relevant teacher education which includes preservice for university students and in-service education for the teaching and administrative staff; (e) emphasize the importance of

FIGURE 2
Model School System for Metropolitan Area for Year 2001

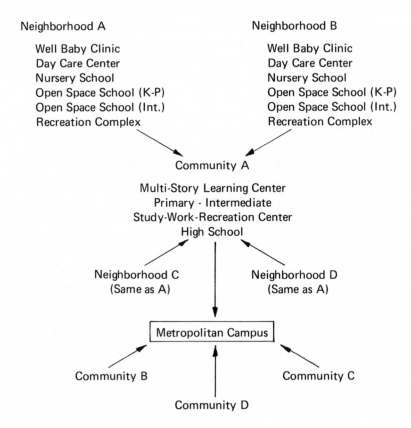

the arts and the humanities; (f) bring together diverse groups to engage in well planned and meaningful learning and human relations experiences.

The campus will provide for special study centers such as Toledo's present Russian-Chinese Studies Center, the Afro-American Curriculum Center, and the Mexican-American Curriculum Office. Office facilities will be given to community agencies. There would be a special building available for the performing arts, rooms for large group instruction and dramatic presentations as well as small rooms for seminars. The entire organization of the Model School System for 2001 is represented in Figures 2 and 3.

FIGURE 3

Model School System for Large Metropolitan Area for Year 2001

Campus A and Satellite Communities and Neighborhoods	Campus B and Satellite Communities and Neighborhoods
Campus C and Satellite Communities and Neighborhoods	Campus D and Satellite Communities and Neighborhoods

CONCLUSION

Many different responses can be made to the 2001 model of education. In many respects the model does not include the traditional modes of education. Coping with this magnitude of change over the next 30 years will be too much for some. To others, the model may appear to be a combination of several innovations taking place today. It is hoped that the model is not seen as a fixed object to arrive in the year 2001 but a description of various alternatives to present educational models which suggest a future pattern.

To project a model of education based on our analysis of present trends is to plan for the future. If these alternatives to present practices prove to serve the best interests of urban society, then we will take the change in stride and add our assistance to its adoption. If this glimpse into the future is viewed to be detrimental to the aims and goals of urban living, then we should attempt to alter the course of events by influencing others; so that this model or another resembling it does not occur.

If change is inevitable, then the intelligent course of action should rest with the weighing of alternative solutions to needs that are assessed to be important to our future. It is hoped that through long range planning those concerned and responsible for educational endeavors of the community can discover solutions to some very difficult problems facing our schools. Using the problem solving approach, alternative solutions which at present are unknown may be created.

FOOTNOTES

1. Maya Pines, *Revolution in Learning: The Years from Birth to Six,* (New York: Harper & Row, 1966).
2. Benjamin S. Bloom, *Stability and Change and Human Characteristics,* (New York: John Wiley and Sons, 1964).

19

The Kinds of Educational Programs We Need — Now

MARK R. SHEDD

You've given me quite a topic to tackle today: "The Kinds of Educational Programs We Need—Now." My first thought is, simply, "the kinds that work."

At first that might sound a little absurd, but, unfortunately, when you stop to think about it, it isn't absurd at all. The sad fact is that a great deal of what we have now *is not* working, and the breakdown is particularly acute in the urban sector. With this in mind I would submit that it certainly would behoove us as educators and curriculum developers to come up with something that does work.

In Philadelphia, we think we have come up with a few new wrinkles to educating the secondary school student; yet we're only making a small dent in a massive problem, mainly because for so very many years in the past no one really had the guts to ask the question you are asking today. And that question is, how are we going to prepare now so that six, eight, or 10 years from now we won't find ourselves with the same staggering problems, or, for that matter, problems of an infinitely greater magnitude than those that face us today?

We can no longer hide behind the old saw that says if the student doesn't learn it's the student's fault. We've got to fact up to the fact that *all* students are capable of learning at different levels and at

Mark R. Shedd, Superintendent of Schools, Philadelphia, Pennsylvania. Remarks for the Continuous Education Council, ASCD, October 29, 1971.

different speeds, and if they don't learn, then it's the system that's at fault; it's our fault, not the student's. We simply can no longer be content with educating the bright kids and letting the rest row their own boat up the river of joblessness and uselessness. We've done that for too long, now, and in case you think this is all rhetoric, let's take a look at a few of the facts.

In big cities across the country, one out of every three high school students drops out of school, and the ones that come to school attend only 70 per cent of the time. Worse yet, the average inner-city high school student reads two years or more behind national norms.

Absenteeism alone has a staggering impact on the ability of urban youngsters to learn. During the past school year, we had in Philadelphia approximately 18,000 high students—some 30 per cent of our enrollment—absent every day. That's an almost unfathomable 3,240,000 student days lost during the school year. In junior high school, there were another 10,000 youngsters (20 per cent) out of school each day, for a loss of another 1,800,000 student days. At the elementary and kindergarten level an additional 17,500 boys and girls (10 per cent missed school every day for a yearly loss of 3,150,000 pupil days).

Standardized test scores indicate that some 40 per cent of the children in our elementary schools, or 56,000 youngsters, read at such low levels they can be considered functionally illiterate. More than 6,000 of these children, who are totally disillusioned with the learning process because they can't read, simply drop out of our schools each year.

Yet, these problems certainly aren't confined to the big cities. Suburban areas, too, have their share. Dropout rates and absenteeism are rising at an alarming rate there, too. Student activism is closing school after school for days at a time. And in the area of high school drug abuse, nationwide statistics are staggering.

There are some 18 million students in the nation's public secondary schools, and somewhere between 16 per cent (President Nixon's estimate, which he labels "deliberately cautious") and 25 per cent to 35 per cent of them (the estimate range of most doctors, educators and drug abuse authorities) are experimenting with marijuana. This means that up to 6 million students are taking drugs illegally.

Some 12 per cent to 15 per cent (up to 2.7 million youngsters) are taking marijuana and other "soft" drugs on a regular basis.

Some 2 per cent to 3 per cent (or some 500,000 youngsters) are hooked hopelessly on hard drugs like heroin.

In Pennsylvania, a survey by the state health department showed that 11 per cent of the state's high school population, or 123,000 students, are frequent users of illicit drugs.

In New York city alone, there are more than 100,000 heroin addicts. Approximately 25,000 of them attend the city's public schools. In 1970, 900 persons, including 224 students, died from the use of heroin. In 1966, 30 New York students died from heroin.

In Philadelphia, drug-related deaths climbed to 186 in 1970, more than five times the number of local servicemen killed in Vietnam. In 1970, 805 drug cases came before juvenile court, compared with 17 in 1965 and 403 in 1969.

Nationwide, arrests of persons under 18 for narcotics violations grew an almost unbelievable 1,860 per cent from 1960 to 1968, according to the Federal Bureau of Narcotics.

Perhaps no one has more eloquently put his or her finger on the ineptitude of past efforts of education at the secondary level than Angela Kitzinger, of the California State Department of Education, who, addressing herself to drug abuse education, says:

> Having carried responsibility for drug abuse education for some 70 years, what have we accomplished? We have indeed exposed generations of high school students to thousands, perhaps millions, of assembly programs designed to scare out of them for all time any curiosity about, inclination toward or hankering about narcotics. We have written hundreds, probably thousands, of courses of student and curriculum guides.
>
> Yet, look at the state of affairs today—a generation of young people increasingly committed to drug abuse; a generation of adults who view alcohol, nicotine and over-the-counter drugs as necessities of life; a drug-oriented society. Insofar as we are accountable, wherein have we failed? And where do we go from here?

That statement can easily be applied to many other areas of high school education, and I'd like to address myself to Dr. Kitzinger's plea: "Where do we go from here?"

I think the first direction we can travel is to recognize that whether students are turning on with drugs, or turning off through absenteeism, or tuning out by dropping out, they all have one big thing in common: they are turning to alternatives to what they have now; the great majority of them are disenchanted, disillusioned, or disgusted with the kind of education they are getting in our high schools today. And that is where we have failed.

The worst part of it is that the kids have been trying their damndest to tell us this for years. Their music, for instance, is deep in this kind of lament, and the spokesmen for the young have been trying to penetrate our generally deaf ears.

Marshall McLuhan, who is as much a philosopher of youth as he is a philosopher of the media, had this to say several years ago:

> The young today live mythically and in depth. But they encounter instruction in situations organized by means of classified information—subjects are unrelated, they are visually conceived in terms of a blueprint. Many of our institutions suppress all the natural direct experience of youth.
>
> The student finds no means of involvement for himself and cannot discover how the educational scheme relates to his mythic world of electronically processed data and experience that his clear and direct responses report.
>
> The young today reject goals. They want roles—r-o-l-e-s. That is, total involvement. They do not want fragmented, specialized goals or jobs.
>
> The dropout represents a rejection of nineteenth-century technology as manifested in our educational establishments.

To this contention, McLuhan quickly adds:

> Today's television student is attuned to up to the minute 'adult news'—inflation, rioting, war, taxes, crime, bathing beauties—and is bewildered when he enters the nineteenth-century environment that still characterizes the educational establishment, where information is scarce but ordered and structured by fragmented, classified patterns, subjects and schedules. It is naturally an environment much like any factory setup with its inventories and assembly lines.

The Beatles, in one song that sold four or five million copies, gave us these laments of a youth:

I used to get mad at my school.
Teachers who taught me weren't cool
holding me down
turning me round
filling me up with their rules.

Simon and Garfunkel in another song that sold millions of copies also told us about the students' view of the generation gap—of the lack of communications between youth and adults, between teachers and students—when they sang:

> And in the naked light I saw
> ten thousand people, maybe more.
> People talking without speaking,
> people hearing without listening,
> people writing songs that voices never share
> and no one dare
> disturb the sound of silence.

And Bob Dylan, another spokesman for our youth, taunted us by singing: "Something is happening and you don't know what it is, do you Mr. Jones?"

I can't emphasize too strongly that you and I are the Mr. Joneses of Bob Dylan's world, and we have simply got to figure out what's happening—and what to do about it.

What McLuhan is saying is that most schools and school systems have become anachronistic. They are out of phase with the everyday realities of their students' lives. They do not illuminate the concerns of youngsters. They appear disconnected from the "real" world. They are irrelevant.

McLuhan is on the right track, I believe, whether or not one is in complete agreement with his criticism or his particular world view. He is on the right track because he is *trying to listen to what kids are saying* and trying to make some sense out of it in terms of today's world. For we can talk about many "realities"—social and otherwise —in big city school systems.

There is the reality of anachronistic buildings, and the reality of fiscally-starved systems, the reality of low test scores and high drop-out rates, the reality of segregation, the reality of teachers who lack the experiences to work with and feel comfortable with kids from slum backgrounds. All of these realities are operative to a greater or lesser extent in any urban school system, and they are important. There should be no mistake about that.

But I would maintain that all the money, the most exciting new facilities, integrated student bodies, teachers with *a world of training and classrooms with electrified environments and every shelf swim-*

ming in attribute games, paperback books and special science material won't really make the difference unless we can connect with the reality of the kids.

And if we are going to connect with that reality, we are going to have to give students the kinds of educational options that will take precedence over drugs and gangs and whatever else diverts today's youngsters away from academic pursuits.

But even if we can all agree that education must mean creating options, must mean focusing at least as much on process as on product, must mean enabling students to respond to stimuli in a flexible, varied and creative way, the question still remains, which stimuli?

And part of the answer to that question, I am convinced, is to be found in the ways schools connect to the society around them.

To begin with, any analysis of our urbanized, technologized, fragmented, specialized and rapidly changing world reinforces the importance of a curriculum that emphasizes process over and against content. We and our children are increasingly bombarded by a huge range of stimuli and the welter of new events, new situations and new knowledge.

I don't think I have to labor the obvious: This means a curriculum which emphasizes the skills of rational thinking and analysis, the emotional and intellectual ability to cope with a bewildering array of forces and influences and make sense out of them, the ability to control and shape environment rather than being helplessly manipulated by it, whether the forces of manipulation are defined as the mass media or socioeconomic forces.

Certainly the Coleman report's clear finding that a child's sense of his ability to control his own destiny supports this view of curriculum. Translated into pedagogical terms, this means, I am convinced, increasing emphasis on discovery techniques of learning, development of rich and varied school environments which permit children to explore and question and, most important, make mistakes without being condemned, graded and degraded for them.

It means a process of curriculum which involves students in goal-setting and encourages goal-directed behavior and guided independence. At the secondary school level, this means, for instance, that the most important thing we can do is involve students directly in the planning of curriculum, as well as in more traditional areas of student participation, such as the establishment of dress codes. And I might add, this is precisely what we are doing in a number of our large high schools in Philadelphia through establishment of joint student-teacher-parent planning bodies.

At the elementary school level, it means creating a classroom and adopting a mode of teaching which relies heavily on improvisation—individualizing instruction to let the inclinations, interests and experiences of each child guide his learning as much as possible.

If this seems to imply criticism of our standard school curricula, and I trust it does, I think it important to stress that the criticism is structural and environmental—not personal and individual. For the basic need I am discussing, and the kids are demanding, is a need to change the structure and environment of schools. This is inherent in what it means, today at least, to relate schools more closely to the realities of urban America, and to create new options for the citizens of urban America. And this relationship means more than simply simulating in the classroom the kinds of situations existing in the society at large.

In part, to back off process and emphasize content for a moment, it means schools which deal directly and honestly with the problems and issues of the day, which may call for less emphasis on the war of 1812 and more emphasis on the war on poverty. It may call for an emphasis on group process and group dynamics in schools, especially if we are to confront directly the interpersonal and intergroup problems which are at the root of so much racial tension in this country.

It certainly means, I believe, eliminating the institutional walls which so often alienate and divide schools from the life of their communities. Just as we are getting away from the idea of the self-contained classroom and building schools without walls to permit team teaching and more flexible diversified and individualized approach to instruction, so we should be getting away from the idea that instruction is contained by the structural walls of a school. The best place for learning for some kids may well be in a storefront; for all kids there is no doubt some instruction that best takes place in the ghettoes, or the art museums, or the city halls, or the industries of our city.

To create schools without walls, then, means both to take the classroom out into the real world and to bring the real world into the classroom. But it has another dimension as well, and that is to bring the values, the aspirations, the needs and concerns of community into the classroom. Ultimately, I believe, this means moving well beyond our traditional concepts of what community involvement has meant and opening the doors to the community as full participants in the procedures and decision making of schools.

Here again, the phrase "community participation" connotes a number of things to me. It implies, for instance, a much greater effort by the schools to shape vocational programs to the changing needs of business and industry. Most important, it means eliminating the hostility gap between low-income communities and their middle-class oriented schools. I don't think there is any doubt that an alienated or apathetic community thwarts the basic purpose of education. It sets up an environment that thwarts the spirit of adventure, discovery and pride that must accompany learning.

Again, a new process is important—a process that may take the form of neighborhood curriculum committees or of neighborhood boards. And a new attitude is important as well—an attitude that supplants the condescension of "culturally-deprived" with the equality of appreciation for "other-cultured." Value judgments, as we all know, can be murderous in school if it is the child's whole existence which is being judged.

I believe the schools have a lot to gain, in the long run, by breaking down the walls between classroom and community, between professional and layman, although I realize the process is threatening to some and never painless. But I think the community, particularly but not exclusively the ghetto community, has a lot to gain as well. To live in a ghetto is, by definition, to be cut off from the sources of power and the exercise of power. Schools can start to give the community a chance to determine its own destiny, while simply reaffirming the basic tradition of lay control of education policy. This means decentralization—budgetary, curricular and otherwise.

I have tried so far to give some sense of what I mean by testing curriculum against the reality of the kids, of redefining and programming education more in terms of that reality, and of connecting schools to the society around them.

Perhaps the most important aspect of all is a curriculum which is based on the recognition of the school as a social organism. Curriculum to me does not mean simply certain kinds of content, x skills in y subjects in z years. It does not even mean simply a much closer integration of teacher training and curriculum content which is inherent in the notion of curriculum as process. That is, the content can't be separated from the way its taught, despite the prevalent practice in our universities of separating methods and content courses.

Rather, curriculum means the total school experience. It means the atmosphere in the hallways and the quality of relationships between people in the school—between student and student, student and teacher, teacher and teacher, teacher and principal.

Part of this is a matter of curriculum philosophy—the extreme need for a balance between the affective and cognitive domains. Part of it is a question, again, of the influence of the student and the influence of community in a school. A big part of it is the whole question of expectations: what the school communicates to students and community about themselves, what the teachers communicate to each other about teaching, on both the verbal and the nonverbal level, and through the whole system of behavior and rewards encouraged in any school. Occasionally, we have all entered schools where the silence is deadening, the order stifling, where regimentation is mistaken for discipline and spontaneity is interpreted as impudence, where the teachers cow before the principal and the students cow before the teacher. When this happens, I would argue, this is the curriculum of the school: this is the real instruction and the lessons found in lesson plans are all but irrelevant.

Now, obviously, I'm not telling you something you haven't heard before. Silberman said it most eloquently and pointedly in *Crisis in the Classroom,* And many others similarly have attacked this kind of education sterility. What I'm saying is that instead of merely attacking it, and agreeing that it's no good, we've simply got to do something about it and do it quickly.

One of the first things we can do is to junk what I like to call the three tyrannies of education: time, space, and the system. Perhaps nothing works more at odds with student enthusiasm in secondary schools than the traditional lock-step of the bell schedule, where the bell rings every forty seven and one-half minutes, dictating a move here or there, come Hell or high water, regardless of whether a class has finally gotten its teeth into something that's really interesting. "Forget it," the bell says. "Your time is up. Move on."

And space. So many desks in an egg crate classroom. So many egg crate classrooms in an egg crate school. So many egg crate schools in an egg crate school system. That's tradition. Yet, open space, with plenty of room to move about, to be free to learn about different things in different classrooms at different paces. That's education.

Then, perhaps the most trying, the most frustrating of all problems facing the school administrator, particularly the big city superintendent, . . . is the system, the bureaucracy . . . where it takes forever for fresh ideas to filter up from the classroom and for positive action to filter back from the top.

Finally, when you wrap all three in the shroud of impending financial disaster that eats constantly at the very foundation of public education in America today, you have a pretty good idea of what's wrong with our schools.

No wonder you asked me to talk about education of the future. Things simply can't do anything but get better.

Seriously, there *are* ways to rejuvenate today's secondary education, and if we can still manage to keep just one breakneck step ahead of the spectre of bankruptcy, we just might be able to accomplish the task.

Certainly, the term "relevance" has been all but ground into the dust by now, and most of us have instituted programs in ecology, black studies, consumer fraud, drug abuse, and the like, in an effort to establish a link with the reality of kids, a curriculum of concerns. And this is a major step in the right direction. But my contention is that we've just begun to dent the tough crust of tradition, to get underneath it, to chip it away and to get at the real roots of a better educational thrust.

We've got to get more into computers and gaming, into TV cassettes and other innovative media approaches to making education infinitely more interesting—even entertaining. If we don't do it, the performance contractors will be clamoring for the chance.

We've got to substitute new thought process, like affective education, for the old sit-down-shut-up-and-memorize-the-facts school of learning. We've got to develop alternatives for what we have today, whether they be new and vastly sophisticated science curriculums designed to turn out a new generation of Einsteins, or simply better vocational education, career development and work-study programs that will enable our graduates to walk out of high school right into a good job.

But I warn you right now that whatever we come up with, if the students aren't part of the process, it won't be worth a damn.

Kids today are influenced like never before by the society around them. There are people being maimed and killed on their TV sets every night, both in Vietnam and on the street corners of America by policemen and private detectives and gangsters and who-knows-how-many-other TV-land good guys and bad guys packing guns.

There are civil rights riots and college campus riots on the tube right in front of their eyes. They can get drugs just about anywhere. Some of their parents are swinging. Dad launches into all kinds of admonitions about the evils of marijuana while he thinks nothing of getting pleasantly inebriated on martinis.

The breakdown of what has long been a rigid value system in this country is occurring right before their eyes, in living color. So they've established their own value system, their own revolt against what they consider the duplicity of the adult generation. And they want a piece of the action in any changes affecting them from here on in, particularly when it comes to education.

I contend we can and should give them a piece of the action. It's either that or repression, and the last person who tried repression this side of the iron curtain—Adolf Hitler—didn't fare too well.

One way we can give them a piece of the action is through programs like Affective Education, education built around the concerns and emotions of kids instead of what we adults think their concerns and emotions are; an education that emphasizes process rather than rote facts.

We have more than 9,000 students in the program now in Philadelphia. They use a variety of affective learning techniques, such as fantasy, improvisation, synectics, role-playing, group dynamics and games, right in the classroom. Students are openly encouraged to express themselves and their concerns.

Goals of the program are to help students develop more positive attitudes toward learning, toward themselves, their teachers and their peers by gaining a greater conscious control over themselves, their interpersonal relationships and their environment.

Extensive evaluation last year, involving affective education students and a control group, shows the program is working. For instance:

Students in affective classes viewed their classroom climate as dramatically different and more interesting than did students in control classes.

Students in affective groups demonstrated more positive attitudes toward their teachers.

Affective students were absent from class half as often as control students and received considerably fewer discipline referrals.

They also differed dramatically from control students in what they felt they learned during the year.

This, I would submit, is the kind of curriculum of concerns, the kind of education that deals with the reality of kids, that we will see in the high schools of the future, and there's no reason we can't, as my assigned topic would suggest, begin to do it *now*.

Another new concept we're bound to see much more of in the schools of tomorrow is the whole area of schools without walls, where the city is the classroom, and kids learn both the basics and almost anything else they want to learn.

Here again in Philadelphia we have considerable experience in this area with our Parkway Program, the country's first so-called "school without walls." Youngsters may learn photography at the museum of art, literature at the public library, journalism at the Philadelphia Inquirer, politics and government at city hall, business at the Insurance company of North America or Smith, Kline & French, or perhaps car repair at the corner garage and botany in Fairmount Park.

They pick their own courses, help select their own teachers and generally make education fun. It's really no wonder, then, that in the last lottery to expand the program we had some 10,000 applicants for 125 places.

Evaluation here, as you might guess, closely parallels the Affective Education program, and entrance has become so sought after that for some reason or other, all the old taboos of suburban parents sending their youngsters to a city school are somehow forgotten when it comes to Parkway.

As a matter of fact, suburban parents and educators have just this year established two Parkway-type programs of their own, and invited some 70 or 80 of our youngsters to come on out and join in.

Now, realistically, I'm not about to stand here and say that with a few Parkway Program bandages and a couple of shots of affective education you're going to cure all the ills that face secondary education today. That would be absurd. Even if we could wave some kind of magic wand that would transform all our high schools into Parkway setups with small classes and unique facilities, and then wave it again to thoroughly train 3,000 teachers in affective techniques, you'd still have your problems of discipline, absenteeism, racism, and gangs. You'd still have thousands of kids caught up in the whole vicious circle of urban poverty and despair.

What I am saying is that if we begin today to listen to our students and to begin with them, to put together Parkway type experiences and to plan to build affective techniques into our schools of the future, maybe, just maybe, your children and mine won't be sitting in this very room 20 or 30 years from now trying to figure out what in blazes to do about the sorry mess in the high schools of their day.

I hope, I strongly hope, that they won't have to ask themselves the same soul-searching questions we're asking ourselves here today.

20

The Parkway Program

PHILADELPHIA PUBLIC SCHOOLS

A SCHOOL WITHOUT WALLS

On February 17, 1969, 143 Philadelphia High School students took to the streets, without leaving school. They were the first students of the Parkway Program, a new kind of high school which challenged many traditional concepts of secondary education: There were no grades, no dress codes, few "rules." There was not even a school building—instead, students were encouraged to find their classrooms, their curriculum and in some cases their teachers from among the plentiful resources of their urban community. They were sent to learn where the action was.

The Program tested many long accepted principles in educational organization; however, Parkway students and teachers were not the first to test them. What set Parkway apart from many recent educational "experiments" were three important features: The Parkway Program was a public program, fully accredited and supported by the School District of Philadelphia; the students were not specially screened or hand-picked, but were chosen by random lottery from applicants representing all eight Philadelphia school districts; and the Program was committed to operate at a cost which would be equal to or less than the amount required to run a traditional school for a comparable number of students.

From a brochure on the Parkway Program, School District of Philadelphia.

The question underlying the Program's foundation was simple: could the resources of the urban community, concentrated as they were within a relatively small geographical area, be used to educational advantage for a broad cross-section of secondary school students? Few doubted that they could be, however, methods of *how* they might be utilized so that both the students and the city would benefit mutually were yet to be established. The Program was left with the task of trying to integrate school children with the life of the community, a life which, under normal conditions, they were not expected to enter until leaving school behind them —for although schools are supposed to prepare students for a life in the community, most schools so isolate students from the community that a functional understanding of how it works is impossible. Few urban educators now deny that large numbers of students are graduating from our urban secondary schools unprepared for any kind of useful role in society. Since society suffers as much as the students from the failures of the educational system, it did not seem unreasonable to ask the community to assume some responsibility for the education of its children.

However, if community institutions—cultural institutions, business institutions, scientific institutions—were to accept students, take students into their organizations, it was clear that the students themselves would have to learn to operate differently than they did in their former school situations. The structure of the Parkway Program is designed, then, not only to expose students to the community but to meet the demands of the community. Neither the educational system nor the community can do the job alone: what is necessary is a structure in which the two can interact, in which the educator and the community professional can combine their abilities to provide students with the most profitable educational experience.

If such cooperation is to be achieved, it is obvious that the educational institution and the community institution have to stop operating by different rules: the student cannot be expected to go from a passive, unresponsible role in the classroom to an active, effective one in the city. The structure of the classroom must change: rather than encouraging the student to accept, it has to teach him to challenge; instead of teaching him that success comes with inaction and dependence, it has to show him that action and independence bring results. Teachers have to teach differently—teach skills which work in life as well as on paper, because in a "school without walls" the students need to *use* the skills they picked up this morning the same afternoon.

The objective of the Parkway Program, then, was no less than to put the school in step with the pace of the community, so that students could operate in both. The organization of the Program is not unlike that of a successful business, a business in which individuals, independently and in groups, must work effectively and responsibly toward real solutions to real problems. The structure of the Program is as much the work of the students as of the educational administration, for one of the first problems presented to students was "How do you make a school which teaches students what they need and want to know?" The students continue to take an active role in the planning and administration of their school, for it is their goals which must determine the Program's future directions. Parkway does not aim to be a "school of the future"—but it is not a school of the past. What Parkway hopes to be is a school for *now,* and a school which will be able to keep up with "now" as the years go by.

ORGANIZATION AND ADMINISTRATION

The Parkway Program is organized into several "units" or "Communities," each of which is limited to 200 students. Each unit operates independently of the others, has its own headquarters, its own staff and its own curriculum. While each unit conforms to a common structural organization, each unit will interpret that organization according to the needs of its immediate population. The principle is simple: condense a large number of people in a small area and you necessarily sacrifice your capacity to treat each member of the group as an individual. Each individual's effectiveness within the group is reduced each time the size of the group is increased. So, if one wishes to maintain an organization in which flexibility, and effective individual action are possible, it is necessary to keep the group relatively small.

Therefore, as the Parkway Program expands, it does not increase the size of existing units, but forms new ones. Few new students at Parkway, then, walk into a pre-existing organization. Instead, a new student finds that he and 199 other new students, in addition to a given number of staff—some of whom may also be new—face before anything else the job of setting up an organization and making it work. They are not bound to do things as former units have done them: it is entirely possible on the other hand, that they will find a better way, which older units might later adopt. Day to day administrative functions are performed within units by staff and students under the guidance of a volunteer "head teacher."

All Parkway unit operations are coordinated by a small central staff working with the Director of the Program. This staff is primarily concerned with planning and development, as well as maintaining communications among units. As of September 1971, Parkway had 800 students in four units.

STUDENT SELECTION

The Parkway Program is a public high school, and as such, is open to any Philadelphia student in grades 9-12 who volunteers for it, regardless of his academic or behavioral background. If more students apply than places are available, Parkway students are chosen by lottery. An equal number of places are allocated to each of the eight geographically determined school districts in Philadelphia so that a cross-cultural, heterogeneous representation is insured within the Program's student body. To further expand the scope of the Program's internal population, a limited number of places, also filled by lottery, are made available to applicants from suburban and parochial systems.

STAFF

Like the students, staff members must volunteer for the Parkway Program. The Program maintains a student-teacher ratio of approximately 16 to 1, and for every teacher a "university intern" (undergraduate or graduate students representing both local and out of state universities) is added to the staff. Teachers are interviewed and hired by committees representing the Parkway organization, the school district, community professionals, parents, and students. Parkway teachers must meet the usual requirements for certification, and the majority of Parkway teachers formerly taught in traditional schools.

The Parkway staff, teachers and interns, are responsible for the basic Parkway curriculum, for student guidance, and for recruiting additional instructional help and materials from within the community. The Parkway teacher's day, then, is likely to be divided between classroom teaching, student counseling, and administrative work with the faculty member himself determining the proportions according to his own interest and skills.

FACILITIES

One of the most outstanding aspects of the Parkway Program is that it has no school building. Although central headquarters are provided for each Parkway Program unit where teachers have office space and students have lockers, all classes operate in community facilities. It can accurately be stated that the first obligation of a Parkway teacher is to find a place in which to teach his class: the finding of space is an activity shared by all members of the Program, including students, and is considered an educational activity in itself, requiring a thorough investigation of the city and its spatial resources. The city offers an incredible variety of learning labs: art students study at the Art Museum, biology students meet at the zoo; business and vocational courses meet at on-the-job sites such as journalism at a newspaper, or mechanics at a garage. Academic classes are likely to be found meeting anywhere, with churches, business conference rooms, vacant offices, and public lobbies among those facilities most commonly in use.

The search for facilities occupies a good part of each semester, and may become almost a full-time occupation for those members of the Program who are best at it. Old Parkway students seldom pass an empty building without noting the address and passing it on to someone who will try to find out who owns it, and whether the Program can "borrow" it. The Program pays for none of its facilities, but instead looks for "wasted space," space which is maintained 24 hours a day, but which is in use perhaps less than five or six of those hours. Students then, in going from class to class, will travel around the city (normally on foot), and may visit as many as five or six different institutions in the course of a day.

FUNDING

The operational and instructional costs of the Parkway Program are roughly equal to those of traditional schools in Philadelphia on a per/student basis. The Program was established on a Ford Foundation planning grant, however after less than a year of operation, most of the Program's operational expenses were assumed by the School District of Philadelphia. The District will continue to support the operating costs of the Program, but additional funding from private sources may be sought to develop organizational models which will make further expansion of the Program possible, and to devise an evaluation model which will determine Program's long-term effect.

As the Parkway Program expands, it is anticipated that it can be operated at a per/student cost which is less than that required by a traditional school building: the bigger it grows, the less expensive it becomes. The saving lies in the fact that the Program does not require the School District to provide or maintain expensive school buildings, equipment and grounds. As students are added to the Program, the Program expands its exploration into the resources of the city—both physical and human. New areas of the community are opened so that, instead of being concentrated in one area, Parkway students are spread out to make the greatest possible use of the city's industrial, cultural, and scientific organizations. No part of the community is void of resources which can be turned to educational value: even a semi-rural or rural neighborhood offers possibilities. The expansion of the Program, then, is limited only by size of the total community—a community which, at present, has been only barely penetrated.

CURRICULUM AND INSTRUCTION

The Parkway student finds, at the beginning of each semester, between one and two hundred courses of study available to him. Studies are classified according to subject areas in which student must meet requirements for graduation; however, a wide choice of alternatives is offered in each area, and each student may choose his own way of approaching the subject. In English he may study Shakespeare, Television Production, or Basic Reading. A study of municipal government can be substituted for a study of the Civil War for American History credit. "Math" may mean Algebra, Accounting, Computer Programming, or Retail Merchandising. Science can be Biology, or work at a local hospital. The choice in each case is the student's, but it can be made only after a thorough examination of the student's needs, interests and goals. It is the faculty's job to see that each student makes this self-analysis.

The Parkway curriculum can be broken into five basic areas, each described briefly below. These five areas can be further divided as follows: Faculty Offerings and Institutional Offerings are concerned primarily with the instruction of the student; Tutorial, Town Meeting, and Management Groups involve the student in the operation of the Program itself in an educational way. While each student puts together his own program from activities available, choosing his own ways of learning, each student will in some way be involved with all of the following activities:

Faculty Offerings

This group includes all of those courses taught by the Parkway staff, including interns, and it represents the basic Parkway curriculum. While all major subjects are covered—English composition, geometry, typing, languages, and so on, many staff members take the opportunity to teach in areas where they have a special interest—17th century poets, for example, or the history of civil disobedience, the ecology of the city, medieval art, advanced music theory. It is because the program permits its teachers to teach in their own areas of interest and specialty that the catalogue of faculty offerings more resembles a college catalogue than the usual high school course list. Curricular flexibility of this kind also enables each faculty member to work up to his greatest potential, with the benfits going to the teacher, the student and the Program alike.

Institutional Offerings

Faculty offerings comprise roughly half of the courses of study available to the Parkway student. The other half is made up of courses taught by individuals and institutions in the community within specialized areas. These individuals and institutions are recruited by Parkway students and teachers as interests in a given area are recognized: student interest in medically related professions led to the establishment of a series of courses in local hospitals—cooperation from the hospitals was not hard to solicit in the light of the shortage of trained para-medical personnel. Auto Mechanics is taught in a garage by the garage's employees. Art students study at the art museum and at local art colleges under the guidance of these institutions' staff members. Journalism students study with reporters at a newspaper; an architect teaches architecture; a series of community mothers teach home economics; a local jeweler teaches her specialized skills; a large industry teaches business management. Given the variety of resources which together make up an urban center, no student should find the guidance in a preferred subject impossible to locate. If the course isn't available, the student and staff set to work to make it available at the earliest opportunity. Parkway students have studied leathercraft, veterinary medicine, Swahili, and child psychology with the best specialists the city can offer. If a student interested in cemetery management should join the Program, there is little doubt that a person would shortly be found to help him.

Community professionals are not paid, and are generally motivated to assume responsibility for the education of students out of an interest in the future of their own fields. Few professions have been untouched by the shortage of adequately trained personnel—many have seized gladly the opportunity to interest students in chemistry, insurance, nursing, and so on as early as possible. The advantage to the student of "trying on" a number of professions while still in high school is enormous. A student who has been "turned off" by the system for years, may find his interest in academic subjects rekindled when he begins to study, say, architecture, and has the chance to finally see to what use those academic skills may be put.

Tutorial

The Tutorial group consists of two faculty members and roughly 16 students, selected randomly. All students and teachers are committed to this group, meeting four hours weekly.

The functions of the Tutorial are several, and central to the successful operation of the Program. Listed briefly, the Tutorial is a basic skills unit in which all students are provided with essential background in English and Mathematics; a guidance unit, in that the Tutorial leader is responsible for helping students choose courses of study intelligently and for seeing that the student is enrolled in courses which will help him meet his goals; an evaluation unit, in which the objectives and progress of the Parkway Program itself is regularly discussed; and a human relations, or support unit, for while a student may be engaged in a constantly changing course of study according to his own interests, the Tutorial remains a constant in the sea of variables—a place where he is expected to learn to work effectively with a group which he did *not* choose, a group which is likely to contain many people very different from him in background. Learning to function under these conditions is not easy, but it is perhaps the most important thing a student should learn.

Activities in Tutorial sessions are determined by the group, and may vary widely. The eight or nine Tutorial groups within one unit may all, at the same time, be doing completely different things: One group may be concentrating on math skills, while another is planning the establishment of a lunch program. Still another might be planning a trip to a local movie, with an eye toward discussing it later. A fourth might have elected to study the question of the value of college as opposed to alternative plans such as Peace Corps, Army, or a job. The important thing is for the group to define and attack a problem, the solution of which will benefit all members of the group, and ultimately, perhaps other members of the Program as well.

Management Groups

Management Groups are student organizations which help run the Parkway Program. The procedure is simple: a specific problem or question is identified, and a Management Group is organized to solve or answer it. The purpose of the Management Group is both to involve students in the administration of the Program in a genuinely serviceable way and to provide them with an opportunity to develop real leadership and management skills. Past Management Groups have undertaken to work in the areas of Public Relations, finding space for classes, determining ways of improving communications within and between units, discovering "who *really* has the power at Parkway." The groups do not always succeed in solving the problem they have undertaken, but failures to solve a problem may be as educational as success, if the student can identify the reasons for the failure, and restructure the problem accordingly.

Town Meeting

Each week, a student will usually attend town meeting, a gathering of the full student body and staff of his unit to discuss, fight about, and perhaps solve problems facing the community. A town meeting may be chaired by a teacher, an intern or a student. An agenda is compiled and the items, which may range from how to get a water cooler to a discussion of whether teachers should have veto power over students, are discussed. Town meeting is the House and the Senate of the Parkway organization, and it alternately provides lessons in group organization and group frustration. It also insures that not a week goes by without each member of the Parkway community finding out what is on everyone else's mind.

From these activities—Tutorial, Town Meeting, Management Groups, courses in the classroom and in the community—the Parkway student makes his schedule. With that much to do, it is little surprise that most Parkway students commit themselves to a longer than average school day, often starting at nine and ending after five. There is unlimited opportunity to vary the schedule and few students get the chance to fall into a tedious routine. As one student put it, "It's better than regular school, but it's tougher. Because you're on your own. No one is going to tell you what to do and how to do it—you have to decide for yourself. And if you make the decisions, you take the responsibility. That's just the way it is."

EVALUATION

Evaluation at the Parkway Program is an ongoing process in which the student must take at least as great a part as the teacher. In many respects, evaluation is itself the central course of study at the Parkway Program: students must constantly evaluate their goals, needs, and objectives in order to choose courses; they must daily evaluate the effect of those courses in light of their needs and interests. At Parkway, evaluation is a living part of daily activity, not a postmortem which takes place after the damage has been done.

A formal evaluation takes place at the end of each semester— three times a year. At that time, students and faculty take time to assess their progress, each other's progress, the Program's progress. No "grades" or "marks" are assigned. Each student's record is composed of documents written jointly by the teacher and the student in each course the student takes (including tutorial and work/study programs). The evaluation form will include: The teacher's description of the course and the teacher's evaluation of the work of the student; the student's evaluation of the course, and the student's evaluation of his own progress in it; and the student's evaluation of the teacher, with suggestions for improvement. Reading lists, portfolios of significant work and test scores such as college boards may be added. Three times a year, the whole packet is xeroxed and sent home instead of a report card by tutorial leaders.

The formal evaluation may take as long as two weeks, however it is considered a part of the curriculum without which the other parts would be useless. Soon some scholar (or perhaps a management group) might like to review the history of the Program, and compare the changes which have taken place with the changes suggested in the evaluation forms. He will find a high degree of correlation. Based on evaluations, courses of study have been abolished or initiated, teaching methods have changed, structural changes in the curriculum have come about. The evaluation is not only for the benefit of the student. It is also for the benefit of the organization in which the student operates, for no student can be expect to learn or grow in an institution which is not willing to grow with him.

"A STATE OF MIND"

Making inquiries about the Parkway Program can be a frustrating business. Nearly every question one might have about our operations, methods, and procedures is likely to meet with the same unrewarding response: "It depends." No description of the Program can pretend to be inclusive, or even completely accurate, for Parkway is a Program based not on rules, but on exceptions. It is a Program in which learning is defined not as a subject, a teacher, a classroom, but as a process—a process which may take place anywhere, in many forms. Even a question as simple as "how do you teach algebra" is likely to meet with a barrage of answers—a different one from each math teacher on the staff. A Parkway student put it concisely: "Parkway, you see, isn't a place. It's a state of mind."

In a way, then, the most outstanding features of the Parkway Program—the lack of a building, the use of community resources, the small informal classes—are not really what Parkway is about. What Parkway is about is an *attitude* toward learning, an attitude which suggests that learning is an enjoyable, profitable experience —not something which one stoically endures. In order to serve this attitude, and to encourage it, the Parkway Program draws on the spectacular resources of the Philadelphia community. However, to say that without those resources better education is not possible is a denial of acccepted educational principles. Even in a traditional class, within a school building, with a traditional curriculum, it is possible to structure the educational experience so that the student feels he has a stake in it. But it must first be admitted that each student has a *right* to make decisions about his own education, and that unless the student is permitted to make those decisions, his education can never be as useful to him as it might be.

"A State of Mind": Until learning is recognized as exactly that, and not a programmed encounter with pre-set ideas and materials, the educational system will continue to slide backward, instead of moving forward. By setting the boundaries of students' education, educators do students a great disservice, for if the student is permitted to set his own boundaries, he will likely end up going much farther and much deeper than his teacher would have prescribed. One Parkway teacher explained the effect of a self-determined curriculum this way: "You take two students studying physics, and you want to know which is studying physics because he *has* to, and which is studying it because he *wants* to. In lab, they may both look like they are doing the same thing. You could, of course, ask the students which is which. But my way would be to wait until the end of the semester and see which one knows the most about physics. The kids who *wanted* to study it will come out ahead every time."

Without the community influence, without the help of the specialists, without the access to cultural and business centers, would there be a Parkway? According to most Parkway students, there would be. "Parkway means teachers caring about you, and listening to you, and helping you learn what you want to learn," one student said. "That doesn't have anything to do with the place or the subject. In my old school the teachers were good and the subjects were OK—but the truth was, nobody gave a damn."

Unless the student has the support of the educational institution, unless he feels that it is working with him and not against him, unless he feels that his interests and needs and goals will be taken into account, no wealth of resources will help that student learn. If the student *is* assured of all these things, however, he will learn almost anywhere. He can't help it. For learning, almost like breathing, is a natural thing. We need only to encourage it and show the student how to channel it.

Educators are perhaps fortunate that they have to work with raw material which is ultimately capable of taking over and processing itself—if they let it. If we put a student on the right track, and lend him our support, he will solve most of his own problems—and maybe some of ours as well. We can start to look forward to a time when schools are graduating effective, capable, happy individuals. If, however, it continues to be the case that the best a student can hope for is to be processed by a machine—even a good machine—we can only continue to rely on those few who have, against all odds, still somehow managed to learn something in spite of their education.

21

The Imperatives in Urban Education

HARVEY B. SCRIBNER

There has been a good deal of discussion about the crisis in urban education. The structure of the urban schools has been found loaded with "social dynamite."[1] The environment of the schools has been portrayed as inhumane and joyless.[2] The basic programs of the schools have been indicted for lack of relevance; and compensatory programs, which were supposed to perform educational rescues for the disadvantaged, have been found tragically wanting.

All this is part of the crisis. So, too, are the scandalous rates of student failure, the often crippling systems (and levels) of school finance, and the dwindling public confidence in the very utility of the schools. Unfortunately, the vast majority of these indictments are based on fact, not fantasy. And, unfortunately, discussion of the crisis has so far greatly outstripped the nation's will to resolve it.

The Urban Education Task Force Report (the so-called Riles Report, named for the chairman of the Task Force, Wilson Riles) documents both the condition and the situation of the nation's urban public schools. It is not a pleasant report. Its data and its analyses tell us what the outraged city parent, the turned-off city student, and the perceptive—and often frustrated—school professional have known all along: namely, that the schools in the heart of the nation's biggest

Text of an address by Dr. Harvey B. Scribner, Chancellor of the New York City public schools, at the Thirtieth Annual Superintendents Work Conference, Teachers College, Columbia University, July 16, 1971.

cities are simply failing to serve the educational needs of a terribly large proportion of their students. The report tells us, too, that the public school systems of the largest cities are, more often than not, in genuine institutional peril.

The remaining years of the 1970s, I would predict, will be pivotal years for the public school systems of this country, especially those in the cities. The schools in the large cities are presently balanced on a knife-edge, and I am honestly not convinced in which direction they ultimately will tip.

There is, it seems to me, a chance that the pressures on the big-city school systems will produce a healthy burst of institutional renewal —a period in which the urban schools will become not only more effective institutions, but also more responsive and more humane. There is an equal chance, however, that these same pressures will conspire to produce more defensiveness than creativity—and that the city schools, if they survive at all, will grow more susceptible to the powerful special interests, more inequitable in the distribution of educational opportunity, and increasingly more repressive in their policies. Should this occur, we will likely witness the development of competing systems of schooling which may or may not reflect the democratic principles on which the nation's public schools at least theoretically rest.

In the course of the last ten years, we have witnessed an abrupt transition in this nation from a period of relative certainty and relative confidence to a time of uncertainty and doubt. The great dream of the early 1960s, as Peter Schrag has perceptively said, has come to an end. "We thought we had solutions to everything," Schrag wrote in reflecting on the Sixties: "poverty, racism, injustice, ignorance; it was supposed to be only a matter of time, of money, of proper programs, of massive assaults. . . . But it is now clear that the confidence is gone, that many of the things we *knew* no longer seem sure or even probable."[3]

In the Sixties, indeed, we who managed the public schools of America operated on the implicit assumption that we professionals possessed the remedies for the educational ills of the nation: all we required was the money to apply them. The growth curve was up, and so was the spending power of the schools. The federal government intervened on our side. Public support for education, in city and suburb alike, for both the schools and for the universities, achieved unparalleled heights. And yet we look back now and find little evidence that the schools are fundamentally different in character than they were before the great reform effort began. "The atmosphere has changed," President Fischer of Teachers College has said: "Students' hair is longer, their clothing scruffier, and their language less inhibited. The teachers ... are more outspoken, better organized, and less compliant. . . . But the institutional character of the schools—their purposes, forms and functions—look . . . much as they did in 1960."⁴

My message this morning is a simple one. It is that the *program approach* to school reform—so popular in the decade just passed—is obsolete. It is no longer enough to speak of education reform *solely* in terms of the new math and the new physics; *solely* in the context of more books for the library and new equipment for the language laboratory; *solely* in terms of special programs for special groups of students; *solely* on the premise that a new school building equals better education; *solely* in the belief that more money would solve everything; exclusively on the assumption that the basic structure of American schooling is essentially sound, and that what is needed at most is some fresh plaster and new paint. It won't wash. We have traveled that route before and changed little that is truly basic in the nature of schooling.

The President has just signed a school aid bill worth 5.5 billion dollars to the nation's school systems. And I would wager a month's pay that large portions of that sorely needed money, unless something drastic happens very soon to the tendencies of the schools, will be poured down the same narrow funnels which have proved so unhelpful to so many students in the past. We'll use the same basic mixes: teachers will teach and kids will listen; programs will be packaged with new names and old content. And we'll come back in one year or two years asking for more money because many of the schools are still a disaster area, failing to comprehend that *our* limited professional imagination—yours and mine—is a significant contributor to the disaster.

All the shortcomings of the federally-supported school programs are not attributable to the nature of the legislation or the quality of the Government's guidelines. Some are, to be sure. But other shortcomings of these programs are directly attributable to the traditional instincts of school managers—the instinct to protect the patterns of the status quo, the instinct to shy from high risk, the instinct to speak of *our* schools and to keep parents—especially the parents of the poor—at arm's length when it comes to the design, operation and evaluation of educational programs.

In the cities of this country and increasingly elsewhere, the *program approach* to school reform will no longer suffice. It will, in fact, guarantee a deepening crisis by allowing the basic systems of schooling to go unaltered while cosmetics are applied.

What is demanded today is a *structural approach* to school reform —the kind of reform which is inherently more radical because it strikes at the foundations of the schools, and not at their trappings. In the cities, and probably elsewhere, we will not be contemplating meaningful school reform in this decade unless we focus on the systems and the policies of the schools, their attitudes and assumptions, the connections between the schools and the rest of the world, the style of teaching and the style of learning, the way education is measured, and both the content of individual courses and the pattern of courses that schooling presently comprises.

In urban schooling in particular, I view the following five goals as essential elements of structural reform in this decade:

First, to drastically reshape educational programs on the basis of a new definition of what education is.

Second, to devise new patterns of internal school organization and governance, particularly at the secondary level.

Third, to develop new strategies of teacher education based on the genuine collaboration of schools and colleges.

Fourth, to decentralize the big-city school systems.

Fifth, to develop workable systems of school accountability.

School reform in the urban centers of this country requires the development of what John Hersey would call "new forms."*

First, the schools of urban America need to rethink what constitutes education and how one becomes educated, and reprogram themselves accordingly. This is not to contend that all programs must be discarded for the sake of change. It is to suggest that the schools,

---

*From Hersey's *Letter to the Alumni*

both elementary and secondary, generally provide far too little choice to the students and parents who are their consumers and their owners.

At the elementary level, the schools need to identify those specific (though broadly defined) provisions which are essential to learning, and then construct learning environments around such provisions. I mean *simple* provisions: children learn in different ways and at different rates; children have different interests and aspirations; all children need a sense of well-being, confidence and personal security; all children need to succeed at something once in a while, and so on.

What do we call these environments? Open classrooms? British infant schools? Montessori programs? Traditional classrooms? I don't care what the label is—provided the classroom meets the basic criteria: Is it conducive to learning and human growth? And does it foster the individual student's self-development of such presumably desirable attributes as being responsible and exercising sound judgment?

The only thing "wrong" with traditional classrooms in elementary schools is that there are too few alternatives to them. The traditional classroom—the one dominated by the teacher with 30 desks in five rows—is useful for some youngsters and acceptable to many parents. But there are other styles of teaching, also; and there are many youngsters who would likely learn more and learn better in other kinds of classrooms. Given the diversity of students in this country, especially in the cities, it is incumbent on the schools to provide a variety of styles of classroom environment at the elementary level, and let parents, with counsel and advice from the school staff, pick and choose among them.

Similarly, more educational options should be the goal of urban secondary schools. Given the learning resources of the city-at-large, given the wide diversity of students in the urban high school, and given the widespread lack and high cost of school space in the city, there is every reason for the urban high school to develop a wide assortment—in both content and style—of educational programs.

The urban high school, for example, should do far more than is generally done in granting academic credit for work experience, for travel, for independent study, for personal reading and research, for community service, for tutoring other students—in brief, for skills and knowledge acquired *outside* the classroom. In addition, the urban high school should develop a range of educational programs which deliberately set many of its students free of the high school building and allow them to utilize the museums, libraries, businesses and municipal agencies as part of their formal educational experience. In short, the more the urban high school comes to view itself as a broker in citywide educational experiences (as opposed to a building with a captive student body), the more real, and more useful, the high school education will become.

Second, the schools of the cities need to develop new forms of internal school governance and organization. Two basic principles apply. First, the school that expects to foster respect for the democratic process must clearly reflect democracy in its own affairs. Second, most urban schools are simply too large; their size alone serves to counteract any effort that is made to make them warm, informal, personal, humane places.

With respect to the principle of democracy, I would hope, for example, that the primary constituencies of the urban high school—students and staff—would begin to develop the capability of governing their own affairs as a democratic community. Let them—students and staff—work out their own systems of legislating regulatory policies, and their own systems of discipline and review. This process itself would represent a first-rate educational experience, far more rewarding than many courses in government or civics or politics. And we might thus begin, also, to lower the level of tension which prevails in most big-city high schools.

In the name of democratic principles, I would also hope that an increasing number of urban school authorities would solicit and weigh the advice of parents in the selection of school principals. It is their children whose future is at stake, their money that pays the bills: they deserve a guaranteed and genuine advisory role in the choice of school principals, both elementary and secondary.

I also believe—though it has not been universally popular in this city to say so—that high school students deserve a similar advisory role in the selection of high school principals. This is not to advocate that students *select* their principals, but, rather, that they participate as *advisors* in the selection process. If they can vote for the President at the age of 18, they surely can offer some sound advice at least as to the kind of principal a particular high school requires.

With respect to the matter of school size, it is clear that tension, impersonality, rigidity and large size usually go hand in hand. Thus, for example, each time the urban school system constructs another school for four or five thousand students, as many cities continue to do, it is more than likely asking for difficulty at some time in the future. Several possible solutions exist. One is to reorganize the large existing school into a collection of smaller units, or mini-schools. Another is the more extensive use of leased space as an alternative to the construction of new school buildings. The leasing of relatively smaller units of space in lofts, storefronts, office buildings, housing units and apartment buildings would accomplish two objectives. It would assist the effort to organize smaller groups of students, and contribute to the creation of linkages between school and community.

Third, the schools of the cities, and elsewhere, need to develop new forms of teacher education. School reform, in my judgment, is linked to reform of the teacher training programs: we change both or neither. To reform the schools but not the teacher training programs would be to create schools which cannot be properly staffed. To reform the teacher training programs but not the schools would be to train teachers for schools that do not exist.

In seeking to construct new forms of teacher education, I would suggest several guidelines. First, teacher education programs should be planned jointly, and perhaps run jointly, by the schools and the colleges. Second, the overall strategy should encompass both pre-service and in-service education. Third, the center of gravity of teacher education should be shifted from the college campus to the school classroom—with prospective teachers learning to teach in the natural setting of actual classrooms populated by the regular run of youngsters. Fourth, the competence of teachers-in-training should be judged on a performance basis, and not on the basis of accumulated academic credit. Fifth, college faculty who train teachers should teach regularly in the same kinds of school classrooms in which their students will ultimately work. And, finally, theory and clinical practice should be blended, rather than separated between formal courses on the campus and clinical experience in the schools.

Fourth point: the city schools should decentralize their policy making. Call it community control; call it decentralization (as is done in New York City); call it whatever you choose: but carve up the centralized power. Until this is done—until the urban parent achieves some sense of potential influence over the schools which he pays for and to which he sends his children, little can be done to renew the spirit of the schools or to raise the level of their educational quality.

Decentralization of the urban school systems will not yield instant benefits in student achievement. And the politics of the operation are guaranteed to produce citywide pain, and instances of localized trauma. In addition, as Maurice Berube has said, there will remain the always unfinished tasks of generating new financial support and new kinds of educational programs. But as Berube has said, "without the necessary structure [of community control] . . . more money and more imaginative programs will have little effect."[5]

The name of the game in urban education, in other words, should be maximum public involvement. And involvement of parents and communities in school policy making is virtually impossible in the cities, I would submit, until centralized power is transferred to a network of relatively autonomous, locally-elected community school boards.

Finally, the schools of America must develop new forms of school accountability. That is to say, the schools must devise some instrument, some system, some means which the public can use to measure the effectiveness of the schools, and thus hold the schools accountable for how they perform. This will require the setting down of specific performance objectives for both students and staff. It will necessitate that actual performance be measured against such goals. And it will demand—if students are to benefit—that the schools be reshaped as weaknesses are pinpointed.

The concept of accountability is based on the notion that since the public schools are owned and financed by the public, the public should be provided the opportunity and the capability to assess the effectiveness of its schools. The public should have the means to assess whole schools, whole programs, entire systems of educational management. The system, in turn, should be able to evaluate and train its staff on the basis of specific performance criteria; by this, I mean characteristics of teacher behavior which are observable, which can be validated, and which are reasonably attainable. Accountability, in short, should be the instrument which the public can use to establish institutional goals and measure institutional competence, and which the schools can use to evaluate staff. It is a rare school system today which can honestly say it possesses such a capability.

Frank Jennings said recently that the educational systems of this country, at all levels, "succeed to the extent that they do through an enormous waste in souls." He added that the single, most telling indictment of mass education is that *educators* have tolerated the system in its present form "long after its smothering wastefulness has been discovered for what it is."[6]

That, indeed, is the overriding imperative in urban education, and all education: to recognize the wastefulness, and to do something about ending it.

This is not the exclusive province of us professionals. But we have more than a minor share of the responsibility.

My friend Dean Corrigan of the University of Vermont has said that "because of our past evasion of responsibilities, our unwillingness to change schools and colleges, it is now five minutes to midnight." What he calls the "normal necessary adjustment" can no longer pass for reform. Until we begin to cut deeper into the system, until we begin to deal with the question of school purpose, until we begin to challenge the assumptions and traditions of the schools, we who would be school reformers will be dealing with little of real significance.

FOOTNOTES

1. The phrase is James Bryant Conant's.

2. Among other contemporary writings, see especially Charles Silberman's *Crisis in the Classroom* (New York: Random House, 1970).

3. Peter Schrag, "End of the Impossible Dream," *Saturday Review*, September 19, 1970.

4. John Fischer, "Who Needs Schools?", *Saturday Review*, September 19, 1970.

5. Maurice R. Berube, "Community Control: Key to Educational Achievement," *Social Policy*, July/August 1970.

6. Frank G. Jennings, "The Mission of Education," *Teachers College Record*, September 1970.

22

Toward the 21st Century

NEW YORK PUBLIC SCHOOLS

INTRODUCTION—MEETING THE FUTURE

"High school is irrelevant to my life!" "Why should we be forced into that rigid ivory tower? The street is where it's at." "High schools do not meet the needs of . . ."

Students, newspapers, films, boards of education and countless professional critics have been repeating these generalizations.

The 92 high schools of New York City have developed, revised and continued to examine their programs in order to meet the changing needs of the hundreds of thousands of students in our cosmopolitan city. However, the accelerated rate of change in society, school population and technology in recent years is such that we have recognized the need to step up the pace of curricular innovation and boldly move into new models for secondary education. This report, therefore, is not only a summary of the fluid changes that have been continuously taking place but is also a recognition of the need to redesign the high schools.

Excerpts from "Toward the 21st Century," recommendations for the New York City High Schools by the Task Force on School Redesign of the Office of High Schools and the Chancellor's Center for Planning.

PROPOSALS FOR IMMEDIATE ACTION

New Ways of Learning and Development

Organizational Changes to Permit Free Learning

a. Flexible scheduling and varied time blocks can be explored to provide a wide variety of learning schedules. Students might not have to be in school five days a week. Some schools, for instance, have placed students as assistants in hospitals and other community institutions one day a week and have modified the regular school program to accommodate these boys and girls. More flexible scheduling might allow extended concentrations as needed for deeper study.

b. It might be possible to excuse certain youngsters for an independent semester in which an approved program of community service, research carried on in museums, libraries, etc., might be substituted for a semester of schooling under a teacher's direction.

c. Every high school in the city should have a special relationship with at least one college or university, involving an interchange of students, classes, space and staff.

d. A Center modeled on the Board of Cooperative Education Services (BOCES) could be established in each borough, open from 8 a.m. to 10 p.m. with students able to leave their home high schools for career training.

e. Each high school might offer one or two areas of specialized curriculum such as international studies, urban affairs, ecology, human relations, etc., with increased opportunity for youngsters to transfer in the last two years of high school to these specialized centers.

The Community As School

1. New York City pioneered in Cooperative Education 60 years ago. The Cooperative Education program is growing rapidly in a variety of flexible directions, with more than 8,000 now employed. Work-study internships with pay are opening up in new areas through the use of job developers in each borough. A new ophthal-

mic dispensary category is an example of expanded areas of employment with related in-school basics. Students are moving in and out of school buildings in a variety of time arrangements such as alternate weeks, alternate two weeks (the hospital cooperatives), alternate six weeks (the practical nurses), alternate half days. The community colleges are beginning to work closely with opportunities to continue in career areas opened to students in their high school cooperative course.

The opportunities to expand cooperative education are as varied as the creativity of each school's administration and coordinator, working with the central Cooperative Education Bureau. At present, for example, two new ideas are being tried:

   a. To have excellent science students out of schools alternate weeks working in laboratories, while studying every needed subject, some through independent study and some through work with science teachers on Saturdays.

   b. To form satellite schools, on-the-job sites with classroom teachers assigned there to teach the basics and related skills.

2. The concept that much of a student's learning can and should take place outside the school in business, industry, cultural institutions and municipal agencies is already being planned in the "City As School" program proposed for the high schools of Brooklyn.

3. Each borough and its schools could immediately begin to explore opportunities and ways of moving students out into the community, essentially developing their own city-as-school program. Lessons are taught and individual progress made in a wide variety of community agencies, supervised by an in-school coordinator.

4. There could be considerable expansion of the existing partnership with the Economic Development Corporation and with the Urban Coalition. Schools are developing individual relationships with corporations in the city. The flexibility in crediting experiences is a function of the creativity of individual school collaborative planning groups.

5. More urban studies courses could be developed, courses which involve students in studying the problems out where the problems are. Such courses as the four-year syllabus in urban studies at Mother Butler High School in the Bronx can be programmed for most students.

6. There could be a much greater use of the freedom to bring all kinds of community people and experts of various kinds into the high school at the request of the principal. Teachers and students are free to suggest a wide variety of discussion leaders, whose personal closeness to the world of culture, industry, service makes lessons much more meaningful. The teachers and students should be more conscious of this freedom and make regular creative use of it.

7. The flexible scheduling in the subschools suggested under "Humanization and Involvement" makes possible great freedom of movement out of a school building with no rearrangement of other classes necessary.

Service and Responsibility

1. Build into the curriculum credited opportunities to take direct positive social action toward changing "the system" through such accredited programs as:

   a. An expansion of Junior Volunteers (a kind of junior Vista) for service in municipal and community agencies.

   b. An out-of-school service responsibility in an agency such as a mental health unit of a city hospital or a day care center can be combined with seminar discussions held in school with class-mates and a teacher-coordinator.

   c. An internship in city government conducted in a similar fashion, comparing observations made in the Department of Corrections, the Housing and Rehabilitation Office, the Department of Sanitation, etc. One school gives this course for able seniors who plan to major in government in college.

   d. An interchange with a neighboring intermediate school for expanding individual tutoring of youngsters.

2. Increase the consciousness of the student government toward projects such a voter registration, adopting a village and coordinating with community councils in clean up, renovation and other ecological projects. The work of Students for Environmental Action is being coordinated with in-school groups in many high schools.

3. Encourage pride in one's minority culture and interest in other

cultures by offerings of both types with curricula written by students and teachers.

4. Strengthen the unit in American Studies on Civil Disobedience to encourage the study of the implications of accepting responsibility and of recognizing consequences of a chosen action.

5. Student courts have been tried with little success. Make this a project for the high school consultative council to discuss ways in which students can be inspired to assume responsibility for one another. Increase the use of buddies—e.g., Junior-Freshman, Senior-Sophomore.

6. Encourage student groups to take their productions to such community agencies as Senior Citizens, Veterans Homes, etc. One school combined the advantage of puppet-making for non-English-speaking students with the thrill of service in demonstrating the puppet skits in local children's wards.

. . .

Mastering the Future

Introduction to Careers

a. There must be regular provision for career conferences, in which people from the business and professional world are available in the school in terms of consultation on the economic trends and kinds of skills being called for in the midst of change. There are constantly developing new careers about which educators know very little.

b. Schools can initiate a pattern of weekend and possibly summer visitations to broad types of industries or services to get some feeling for what is done and the human qualities necessary to perform these offices.

c. Programs such as Correlated Curriculum have been helpful by coordinating instruction in English, mathematics, science and broad career areas such as health careers, industrial careers and commercial careers, to introduce young people to occupational areas and to show the relationship of many types of learning to career success. In the Cooperative Education program described in "The

Community as School" section, students are exposed to opportunities to which their entry level jobs will lead, and see the relationship of learning to future vocations.

d. Students need more opportunity to become acquainted with a range of careers and skills. It should be possible, perhaps during the ninth grade and again in the 12th, to devote part of each week to visitation of the many institutions and agencies which service a community. Youngsters might be afforded a kind of curriculum which allows them to attend school four days a week and to be assigned to an industry, business, professional activity or community service one or more days a week throughout the four years of schooling so there could be an exposure to the range of career directions.

e. There can be assigned to each school people with a specific responsibility of acting as job developers, working with business, industry, community groups, etc., in encouraging movement out of school to a job and/or back to school as children grow and attempt to sample different types of valuable experiences. Crediting systems can be worked out to allow business exploration class credit. Examples include Occupational Food Service, Occupational Child Care and Occupational Clothing, given under the jurisdiction of the Office of Home Economics.

f. Reconsideration should be given to the necessity for having students attend school continuously until their 21st birthday. It might be more helpful for certain individuals to choose to withdraw from school for periods of anywhere from a half year to a year to try vocational learning. This is feasible, however, only if the doors to returning are open. Then the school and the world of work could be considered as joint partners in a combined effort to give a youngster direction and to provide him with whatever skills or knowledge will be helpful in his making wise choices and being equipped to pursue them.

g. Programs of recognition of the dignity and desirability of career areas other than the "white collar" should be promoted. Data about earnings and satisfactions in various blue collar occupations should be available to all students. Speakers should include many representatives from such areas. School awards should include recognition of achievement in vocational areas. Schools and, indeed, our nation must gradually return to a recognition of the dignity (already clear in salary levels) of "labor."

h. There is the whole range of occupational skills to which students should be exposed *without* having to make a specific career choice while in high school.

A few of the careers that are liable to expand rather than become obsolete are:

> Health services
> Community service
> Construction trades
> Teaching
> Electronics
> Aircraft
> Computer science
> Civil service
> Retail sales
> Banking
> Industrial management
> Secretarial and commercial

Students need to be able to sample and become acquainted with all of these possible careers and with the particular skills needed for each. The new single diploma permits more freedom in sampling, and increased guidance is needed in this direction.

i. More special job-oriented subschools could be created, such as the Correlated Curriculum and Pre-Tech programs, with interdisciplinary teams of teachers, the primary aim of the subschools being to explore and sample the whole range of work opportunities. All students, especially the so-called college bound, should be able to opt into or out of such a subschool for a term or a year as they choose.

j. There could be job-placement and follow-up for all students who drop out and for all students who graduate but do not go on to college. This would mean an expansion of the Auxiliary Service Centers, already doing just that for many dropouts.

k. There could be a special program set up to enable students to pass the civil service exams. Many schools give such courses but do not involve the rest of the student body. Short brush-up courses and acquaintance with the nature of the many civil service jobs should be available. Many are fascinating careers which students would not consider unless so directed.

.   .   .

LONG RANGE PROPOSALS: MODELS FOR THE FUTURE

The City-As-School Model

The Parkway Program in Philadelphia is developing into several communities, each of 180 students, 10 teachers, and a director. In each such school, students attend tutorials and town meetings at the site (a section of an office building) and pursue studies in actual examples from industry, technology, business, art, theatre, of the skill or discipline of concern. They learn "physics with a physicist, auto repairs with a mechanic." The small size of the student body is a key feature. Effort is made to open spots for students from each district by an organized selection of volunteers. Effort is also made to select from the volunteers, students of all ability levels.

In Chicago, the Metropolitan Studies School is another example of the same approach. In New York, the City-As-School program has been proposed, using 10 Brooklyn high schools (100 students in each) and Brooklyn cultural centers.

The Public Education Association has worked with industry to build this approach in Manhattan. The Park East Pilot High School Project already underway sees the Yorkville area as a source of many art and culture sources.

The model envisioned would thus consist of many small organizations combining the creativity of community awareness with the business sense of large organizations and the advantages of collaborative student-teacher planning.

A School of Muncipal Affairs, Civil Services and Urban Planning

In this model a school would be organized closely around the life and government of our city. The school would center curricular offerings around the problems and programs of New York. Through courses, visits, involvement of municipal officials, appropriate service with municipal agencies, etc., students would attempt to learn about and deal with such matters as housing and slums, transportation, water supply, pollution, marketing, city planning, budgets, protective services such as those provided by the police, fire, and sanitation departments, health needs, schooling, welfare, recreation, etc. Teams might be established to assist particular communities in meeting such problems as improving their community services. Hopefully, graduates might ultimately move into positions of community leadership and municipal government.

. . .

The Collaborative Model

A further extension of the "open" and "do-it-yourself" models would be the collaborative school, similar to an experiment already under way in East Harlem—the Park East Pilot Program in connection with the planning of Manhattan's new Park East High School.

Under this "collaborative" model, small units (again, as small perhaps as 150 students plus teachers) would organize themselves on a voluntary basis. The students and teachers would select a location (the Park East Pilot School is currently located in a church basement), collaboratively design and fix up their home base space, collaboratively design the curriculum both inside the school and the programs that would take place outside the school.

An Auxiliary Services Model

Within the ordinary school population there is a range of youngsters with special problems that require personalized attention. For students with severe academic handicaps, for the emotionally disturbed, for students with violent or criminal tendencies, for drug abusers and similar youngsters, a quite different, more individualized and supportive type of learning assistance is required. Such a school model would, in a sense, not be an institution at all but a network of services and auxiliary facilities that, taken as a whole, would add up to a complete but different kind of educational program. At least one such Auxiliary Services Center can be established in each borough. Such Auxiliary Services models have already been introduced.

The first step in introducing a youngster to this network of auxiliary services calls for a careful screening of students who have been referred by schools or who have sought out this additional help themselves. Once a student is admitted to the program there is a variety of different services available to every individual— intensive guidance, counselling and psychiatric services, tutoring as necessary, placement and opportunity for high school equivalency as desired by the student. Colleges and universities can help staff these networks with trained student teachers, regular college students and academic staff. Parents can be involved as tutors and in other helpful capacity. Special equipment and facilities might also be offered by institutions of higher education.

The point of this Auxiliary Services model would be to bring all of the resources of the city to the assistance of troubled young people.

A Moveable School

An unusual but possible model for the future would be a school that could move around the city, not on land but on water. A floating school (built as a complete ship or barge) is economically feasible and could be used as either a complete school to relieve overcrowding or as a resource center for special purposes available in different parts of the city at different times of the year. All of the boroughs have unused water and dock space. This would be one way of making this tax free space productive. The school could be designed as any one of the other models proposed.

23

The City as Classroom

STEPHEN K. BAILEY

The late Robert Benchley began one of his many delightful spooferies with the arresting words, "Now, I don't want to be an alarmist. . . . " This opening gambit was followed by a few dots and a couple dashes, and Benchley continued, "Aww! What the heck! Sure I want to be an alarmist!"

I should, I think, like to be an alarmist, but alas I have the wrong audience. Secondary school principals in this day and age are not likely to be alarmed by anything said by an over-30 college professor. And outside of California, the title "Regent" brings no terror whatsoever to anyone.

The fact is that you people are alarmed daily by expert alarmers. Actually, you have become so inured to alarms that a sudden flurry of peace and quiet would probably be psychologically unnerving. I am reminded of the lighthouse keeper on a fog-shrouded reef off the Grand Banks who for 30 years listened to an automatic cannon which went off every three minutes to warn away craft that could not see the light through the fog. Thirty years! Boom! Every three minutes! One early morning when the lighthouse keeper was asleep, something went wrong with the cannon trigger-mechanism and sud-

From "The City as Classroom," *Bulletin of the National Association of Secondary School Principals*, Vol. 55, No. 351, January 1971, pp. 163-172. Stephen K. Bailey is chairman of the Policy Institute, Syracuse University Research Corporation.

denly it failed to go off. The lighthouse keeper bounded out of bed screaming: "My God! What was that!"

There is a lot of dogma around these days that says that only urban principals have any troubles, and that only suburban principals are smart. I do not intend to beat a dogma with a stigma, but I can only tell you that some rural high schools are manned by principals who, in their ability to respond to crises, would put many of our urban and suburban school administrators to shame. Like the time the hulking farm boy burst into the rural principal's office and said: "Principal, in my right hand I got a 10 inch bread knife. In my left hand I got an $18 bill that some city slicker passed off on me and that my pappy says is counterfeit. Now that knife in my right hand tells me that you are going to give me change for that $18 bill in my left hand." The principal retorted, "You're damn right, young man. Do you want 2 nines or 3 sixes?"

CITIES LONG-TIME EDUCATORS

There is a touch of irony in the notion that "the city as classroom" is a novel idea. Cities have been classrooms for longer than schools have been. Beginning with the training of scribes and artisans in ancient Thebes and Babylon, through the marketplace teaching of Socrates, through the guild apprenticeships of the Hanseatic League, through the spacial disjunctiveness of the medieval universities, up to the present era, a vast dimension of the educational development of the human race has taken place inside cities but outside of formal schoolrooms.

Alas, today, as we all know, our great cities are classrooms for a lot we wish our kids would not learn: how to pop drugs; how to be a successful bully or extortionist; how to pick pockets and shoplift without being caught; how to break windows, bend parking meters, strew toilet paper, and paint obscenities on public buildings; how to con others into sympathy; how to hate and injure and terrorize; how to beat raps. Social injustice in the cities is a fantastic teacher. Sir Thomas More, in his biting 16th century satire, *Utopia,* pointed to the fact that crime in England was alarmingly common, but that in a grotesquely unequal society, crime was the only means of livelihood open to a great number of persons. In as terrible a voice as his pen can conjure, More fairly shouts at the England of his day, "What other things do you do than make thieves and then punish them?"

Can anyone deny that our own cities are, in part, classrooms for making thieves and then punishing them?"

But our cities do more than make thieves. They set and symbolize the value preference of the overwhelming majority of our people. The city manufactures the cultural wasteland that is universally disseminated on film, tape, and microwaves; the city prints the pornography and the scandal sheets; it rips the ears with rivets, pneumatic drills, horns and subways; it spews poisons into the air and pollution into our waters. Its overcrowding dehumanizes our souls, and destroys our sympathy.

"CLASSROOMS IN HELL"

"Hell," wrote George Bernanos, "is not to love any more." Many of our cities are classrooms in Hell, and across the faces of teeming millions burdened by the hurried meaninglessness of the daily grind are etched the words that Dante read as he and Virgil crossed into the Inferno, "Abandon hope, all ye who enter here!"

It is the city as classroom that gives reinforcement to so many of the dismal aphorisms of this century: "You can't beat city hall!" "Never give a sucker an even break!" "It's all politics." "Don't get involved!" "Aww, so what?" "Get it while you can!" "I'm for me!" "Up the establishment!" "Off the pigs!"

It has always been one of the self-centered follies of educators to believe that the school as classroom is an effective antidote to the city as classroom. Now that the city has entered the school in terrifyingly new and disruptive ways, perhaps we can begin to appreciate how limited in truth our past efforts have actually been. We are not even as successful as ancient monasteries; we cannot even keep the evil world at bay. Actually part of our failure has been our attempt to do just that.

What are nice guys like us doing in a world like this? Why does not someone pass a law or something? It is a sign of our growing maturity that we have come to realize the tragic depth of our condition—that laws are not enough, that legislation leaves many problems simply untouched. I say this not because new laws are not needed. (I happen to agree with Lord Macauley that "reformers are compelled to legislate fast because bigots will not legislate early.") I say it because at the root of our troubles are psychological difficulties that mark a bitter, if transient, point in our fitful evolution as a species. We have not escaped the bonds of ego, tribe, and possessions. In consequence, we clutter and threaten our world with the hostilities of status and possession—and this in face of the reality that the universalization of technology and the very bustle of numbers on this globe place a premium upon mutuality, self-transcendence, and reason if the species is in fact to survive.

Our task is not to fashion a new syllabus or a new curriculum. Our task is to fashion new kinds of human beings. And here, wonderfully and perversely, we cannot succeed unless we learn to use all of the educative resources that are to be found in our cities. We cannot succeed unless we find ways to use our cities as classrooms.

In view of what I have previously said about the city as classroom, one might wonder what possible nutrients the city has for transforming human nature in any positive sense. The answer is that the nutrients are legion, for up to this point I have given you a one-sided view only.

THE CITY A RICH RESOURCE CENTER

If the city makes thieves and destroys human values, it also makes saints and reinvigorates human values. The city makes citizens out of strangers. The city is the focal point for the creation and reproduction and display of almost everything that is beautiful and ennobling and memorable in our civilization. It is in the great cities that theaters and symphonies and museums and libraries are located. In and around cities are the centers of the vast enterprises of commerce and industry, of medicine and social service, of transportation and communications that hold such enormous promise for the future of the human race. Cities are the foci of modern guilds and labor unions whose apprenticeships are such an important part of our total educative system. In the cities, professional and aesthetic talent of exquisite quality abounds. Cities are pluralistic; cities offer options. According to E. B. White, "The urban inhabitant is in the happy position of being able to choose his spectacle and so conserve his soul."

If cities turn out the "kitsch" of soap operas and crime series for TV, they also support Sesame Street and Jacques Cousteau. If the slums manufacture violence, they also create a myriad of quiet heroes (and some not so quiet) who see beyond the years "thine alabaster cities gleam undimmed by human tears." If most lives are lived, as Thoreau contended, in quiet desperation, the city creates models of heroism, and reminds all of us of the words of Thoreau's Concord neighbor, Ralph Waldo Emerson: "Great men, great nations, are not boasters or buffoons, but perceivers of the terror of life, and have manned themselves to face it."

WORKING EXAMPLES OF CITY AS CLASSROOM

How, in fact, can the city be used as a classroom?

Others will give you chapter and verse of some ways that the vast educative resources of the city have been and are being tapped by imaginative school systems. I shall mention only a few highlights and for-instances:

The exciting work of the Quincy Vocational Technical School in Quincy, Mass., in turning to the area's industries to discover the special skills necessary to fill the local job needs. "Project Able," as it is known, is revolutionizing the school's curriculum and its teaching emphases;

"Project Score," also in Quincy, where teachers supervise kids after school hours in a variety of service and community research assignments;

"Project EPIC" in the Cranston, R.I., public schools where 12th grade social studies students work with community leaders and informed citizens in investigating specific community, national, and international problems—using the combined resources of the school and the community;

The Philadelphia Parkway School Project, about which you will hear much at this convention. It may not be universalizable in the sense of doing away completely with walled schools, but its basic theme of using the city as fully as possible as an educative resource is most certainly universalizable. Parkway addresses itself to one of the central educational dilemmas of our times. In the words of James Coleman, "Modern society is information-rich and action-poor for the young";

The direction pointed last summer by Jerry Bruner in collaboration with a conference sponsored by the Office of Child Development of HEW: opening up on a national scale opportunities for adolescents to take responsible roles in caring for young children. The Education Development Center of Cambridge, Mass., proposes to carry out this idea, utilizing day-care centers and offering professional training in child care for secondary school students;

The Germantown, Pa., Area School Project involving students and community representatives in regular cooperative ventures ranging from curriculum-building in the humanities, arts, and social sciences to direct community service through established agencies. Over 100 community people, agencies, and institutions have been effectively utilized by the schools. High school course credit is given for at least some of these programs;

The recent exciting prospectus of the Berkeley, Cal., Unified School District for creating competing options for public school students of all ages, based on the pluralism in the community. Parents and community representatives would be involved with the schools in various programs in and out of the regular school buildings;

The community experiments of the John Adams High School in Portland, Ore., as a part of the National ES '70 consortium of high schools interested in improving vocational education;

"Project Unique" in Rochester, N.Y., which among other things has conducted an experimental class (known as Sibley's Satellite School) on the fourth floor of a downtown department store—this as a way of bringing educational innovation to the attention of the citizens at large;

The Wave Hill Environmental Studies Center's project in Harlem and south Bronx in which children are encouraged to explore city streets and report back on particular physical features. Thus such mysteries as moss growing in the crannies of decaying walls can serve as an introduction to classroom lessons in biology; and

The Educational Talent Pool Reserve scenario developed by ECCO (the Educational and Cultural Center of Onondaga Country) in my home town of Syracuse. ECCO is one of the 16 regional educational planning centers set up by the State Education Department in New York. The Talent Pool Reserve would be a list of human resources in the area (housewives, engineers, artists, accountants, inventors—you name it) who would make a life-long commitment, offering adjunct educational contributions to the schools and colleges of the region.

I have only scratched the surface. New ways to tap the educative resources of cities are mushrooming daily. They extend from bringing exciting citizens and programs into the schools as adjunct "instructors" to work-study and in-service training programs that involve moving the youngsters out of traditional schools entirely. I do not have an exhaustive catalog of these uses of cities as classrooms. Perhaps NASSP could perform a useful clearing-house function for you—for all of us. I commend this notion to your leadership.

NEED TO OVERRIDE TRADITION

But as exciting as all of this is and can be, it represents today only a drop in the bucket. All too many of our urban and suburban schools are tradition-bound, custodial, crisis-ridden, and cynical. One principal in my city tried to reassure a baffled substitute teacher in an urban school last month by saying, "Look, if you have kept any semblance of order for half the time, you're a huge success." But it may be the very notion of order that is at fault. Even when achieved, it may be wrong. As my colleague Ralph Hambrick has put it, "A classroom of 30 children all the same age, sitting neatly in rows, with hands folded, so quiet that one 'can hear a pin drop' may be the real chaos in the schools." Kids—and especially troubled kids—are hyperthyroid. Getting them out of the formal classroom may be the only way to command their attention. What many of them are screaming at us is what Alfred North Whitehead wrote in quiet prose, "Without adventure," Whitehead suggested, "civilization is in full decay." One of the ways to get adventure back into education is to expose kids directly to the charterless frontiers of urban pathology and to the wondrous options of urban creativity and life styles.

Cities are ecological laboratories. They are places where the sheer numbers of interacting people provide a marvelous observatory for human behavior and for behavioral consequences. Cities provide the delights of privacy as well as that terrifying companion of privacy: loneliness. Cities teem with conflicts; and with the political, governmental, and economic means for resolving conflicts peacefully. Cities are masses of unsolved problems—a sufficient number of problems to keep the lives of untold generations seeking solutions filled with adventure.

And cities, to repeat an earlier theme, are vast educative resources in their myriad occupational, professional, and aesthetic manifestations.

It may be heresy, but I believe firmly that state educational departments, including my own, must take a whole new look at the idea of compulsory attendance—at least as presently interpreted. As adults, we make claims on our society for almost endless options—to take care of differences in talent, aspiration, and energy. And yet we insist on locking youngsters into developmental straightjackets. Why should some classes not take place in industrial settings under the joint sponsorship of industry and labor? Why should restless kids, age 14 or 15, not have the chance to drop out of traditional schools at will, and without stigma, and to drop into nontraditional classrooms in city museums, libraries, performing arts centers, and auto-repair garages? Why should not some of the three R's be taught at home through cable TV, or at a work site through tutorials of specially organized classes?

Until we face up to these needs and possibilities, we will continue to have vast amounts of unrest in our schools. It is true that reforms of the kind suggested would mean that existing insurance laws, educational regulations, and labor laws would have to be re-examined and modified. But why not? Most of these laws were put on the books in a totally different era. They are hardly sacrosanct in a world of exploding educational technologies like cable television, home video cassettes, and mobile science laboratories that enormously extend the range of locations where education can take place.

We are in trouble. Fortunately we now recognize that we are. No lid is going to be placed on the bubbling caldron we observe. Not even alliterative Vice-Presidents have that power. Restless, rootless youngsters need something to live by, something to capture their imagination, something to absorb their energies, something to give them a sense of adventure and meaning. And they desperately need models, people models, who give a damn about them and who by example demonstrate that civilized behavior can be exciting and joyful. There are an insufficient number of these models in our schools. Only the larger community can supply them in sufficient quantity and intimacy.

SCHOOL BUILDINGS STILL NECESSARY

There is always a danger that in conjuring an exciting future, one will be massively unfair to the past and present. Even if it were desirable (which it is not) suddenly to empty our schools and turn all youngsters loose in the asphalt jungle, the logistics of such an operation would be quite impossible, for as far ahead as I can see, most formal education will have to take place inside school buildings. Most children will have to be taught by certified teachers, not by shop foremen or industrial engineers. The consequence of this reality is that we must apply our best minds to bringing the best of the city into the classroom at the same time that we exploit the classroom potential of the city itself.

The model of the city—at least, the city at its best—has a lot to offer the schools, for the city permits enormous options. It allows talents to be developed and successes to be achieved in a variety of ways. It praises the ballet dancer, whether or not she can do calculus. The city is patient about differing learning speeds. The city allows a number of ways for its citizens to participate in the making of decisions that affect them. The city's labor market is the ultimate validating instrument of educational achievement. To do a particular job, the city says, "You've got to know something, or know how to do something." The city provides many reinforcing ways of learning simple realities.

These are some of the lessons the city has for the schools. If we take these seriously, we can begin to make our formal classrooms into exciting and productive educational enterprises. As Saul Touster has written with great eloquence, the traditional "delivery" model of teaching must give way to a "field-of-force" model—his useful imagery for minimizing the classroom lecture and maximizing meaningful and diverse educative exposures and experiences, in and out of the classroom.

There are many great teachers hidden in the homes and places of employment of our great cities. These must be sought out and used with increasing frequency and effectiveness. But most of our teachers are, and will continue to be, inside the schools. It is their capacity to take lessons from the city, as well as their capacity to use the city for educational purposes, that will determine the future of the collective enterprise in which we are engaged. All many of them need is your leadership and your inspiration.

Sixty years ago, H. G. Wells wrote an obscure novel called *The New Machiavelli*. In it the main character says at one point, "If humanity cannot develop an education far beyond anything that is now provided, if it cannot collectively invent devices and solve problems on a much richer, broader scale than it does at the present time, it cannot hope to achieve any very much finer order or any more general happiness than it now enjoys."

This says it all. I leave you with only one piece of gratuitous advice. When you return to your respective homes and offices and find the same crunch, the same in-basket, the same crises, the same weariness, take a moment, look out the window at your surrounding city and say out loud, "I was once told that only professionals like me could and should run schools. It isn't true now, if it ever was."

And then, mentally, I want you to see yourself standing in a circle—an open circle—formed by the linkage of hands of supervisors, teachers, para-professionals, students, maintenance men, legislators, businessmen, artists, police, bus drivers, parents, older brothers and sisters, TV managers, in short, all your civic neighbors—and you are saying to them very simply, but earnestly, "We need each other."

24

Educational Reform and the Principal

LUVERN L. CUNNINGHAM

INTRODUCTION[1]

We live in an age in which most forms of authority, control, and leadership are challenged. The assault on "establishments" has always been a popular sport, but seldom have so many systems of authority attracted so much mistrust simultaneously.

The judicial system has been shaken as badly as any. The trial of the Chicago Seven produced public uncertainty about justice, about jurists, and about the legal profession itself. The Kennedy Chappaquiddick incident, the hearings, and the eventual inquest elevated old anxieties (rightly or wrongly) about equality of rich and poor before the law. The search for Supreme Court justices has exposed additional judicial system frailties, embarrassing to the legal profession and to laymen alike.

The administration of public welfare teeters on the rim of collapse in many places. The prospects of violence are as prominent in this field as in most others. Organization of the recipients of welfare is occurring in most large cities. The invasions of administrative offices, city councils, and state legislatures by welfare mothers and fellow travelers has become routine. Father Groppi is a household name in

Luvern L. Cunningham, "Educational Reform and the Principal," *Bulletin of the National Association of Secondary School Principals*, Vol. 54, No. 349, November 1970, pp. 1-23.

Wisconsin. From the perspective of the establishment he is the new "oleomargarine" of Wisconsin political affairs.

The institutions which deliver health services in our society are targets of public disdain too. Up to now the confrontations between clients and the health services' bureaucracies have been less physical. Few hospitals or clinics have been bombed; seldom have doctors or nurses been locked in their offices during takeovers. Nevertheless, the health system is under severe scrutiny. Medicare and Medicaid are apparently saturated with administrative malfunction. Their vulnerability to abuse has approached the threshold of national disgrace.[2]

Religious institutions, too, are under attack. The internal disquiet within the Catholic Church has spilled out across the world. Injustices within the Episcopal fold, especially the defrocking of members of the cloth, were in the public press recently. The seeds of transformations are here and there within and without most religious bodies.

The "uptightness" about education is so well known that we need only pause to describe briefly the most recent evidence of its weaknesses. Keith Goldhammer recently completed a study of nearly 300 elementary principals.[3] As most of us could have predicted, he found good schools and bad schools; exceptionally capable principals and some that were unbelievably inept. He noted that several of the best leaders and schools were in unlikely places—rotten, stinking, ghettos. Predictably, a few of the saddest examples were in good suburbs or silk-stocking sections of cities.

An elementary principal in a border city wore a side arm each day to keep his mostly white pupils in line. At the opposite extreme, the head of a school in the toughest part of a large city leads a student body, community, and faculty in a common, successful assault on indescribably difficult educational problems. Each situation is a mirror reflection of the man at the helm.

The Bank of America, ROTC, and inner-city PTA's are the targets of anarchists, radicals, and reformers, as well as garden variety advocates of change. Violence, abuse, drugs, race become confused with justice, equity, and love. Good guys look like bad guys. Flower children, the counter culture, the Weathermen—temporary phenomena or the wave of the future? Is today's violence just another peak in America's turbulent history? Who knows? Richard Hofstadter refuses to predict our violence future. He argues that our domestic tempo depends upon external matters—how rapidly we can disengage from Vietnam, the world's response to our failure there, and our skill in avoiding similar entanglements in the future.[4]

And so it is with educational turbulence. Maybe it is cyclical; maybe today's disquiet will subside; maybe the traditional American values of achievement, success, hard work, and respect will surface once again.[5] Maybe not.

A BIT ABOUT REFORMING

Most of us [in the University Council on Educational Administration] are professor types, possessing modest specializations (organizational theory, political analysis, cost-benefit technology, administrative science) bound together by an affection for educational administration. We are not dedicated reformers. When we choose to apply our concepts, theories, models, or frameworks to phenomena of interest, we do so within reasonably antiseptic environments. And some of our better scholars lend us a hand from time to time. For example, James Anderson has described several forms of authority (Weberian) in his useful book on education's bureaucracy.[6] The first is "charismatic," the second "traditional," the third "rational-legal." Each of these makes sense to us; we are able to feel their presence from our experience in organizations. Obviously there *is* authority in charisma. (The film *Patton* provides a splendid contemporary example.) Similarly, the weight of tradition is powerful and compelling, as witness the perpetuation of rituals such as commencements and alumni mumbling through "Hail to Alma Mater." And "rational-legal" authority is chokingly apparent everywhere.

But what about the layman—the reformer out there who is not privy to our tools? He has never heard of James Anderson or Max Weber.

Pro-establishment or not, one can develop sympathies for reformers. Modern institutions (or organizations, if you prefer) are frightfully involved. Their complexities overwhelm insiders, let alone outsiders who would make them over. If one were a protagonist set upon changing an institution, where would he begin? Schools, although they are floundering institutions, are like angleworms. Despite being cut up they live on. Schools may be the Volkswagens of the institutional industry. They hold the market despite few changes in the basic model.

An operating bureaucracy is the arena where several authority systems interface. Those interfaces produce either harmony or tensions, functional or dysfunctional behaviors. In any event, they must be topics of interest for those bent upon reform. The systems within systems, layers upon layers, interfaces upon interfaces, are what drive reformers to despair. (The anarchists, on the other hand, may discover that what they hoped to achieve through the instrument of chaos is already here.)

WHY SCHOOLS?

Why do we have schools? We have them because persons who preceded us believed that the society (and the individuals who made it up) would be better served if learning were organized. They decided that things to be known were too numerous and too complex to be learned in random, haphazard fashion. They were stimulated by the need to satisfy rather basic needs—food, clothing, shelter, preservation. But beyond those loomed the prospect of conquering frontiers, inquiring into infinite unknowns, and testing the mettle of mind and body against perplexing problems.

Max Rafferty, whatever else one may say about him, has a flair for language. In critiquing A. S. Neill's *Summerhill* he summarily dispatches Neill (and his kind) and simultaneously defends the concept of schooling that we have developed in our society.

> Summerhill is old hat, you know. Not new. Not revolutionary. Not even shocking.
> It's hard to pinpoint the first educational quack. I suppose the line of frauds goes back well beyond Jean-Jacques Rousseau, but that heartless mountebank will serve as a starting point.
> Jean-Jacques was a real character. With an irresponsibility characteristic of his entire philosophy, he fathered several bastards and thoughtfully shunted them into foundling asylums for his more humdrum fellow-citizens to support. At various times he practiced voyeurism, exhibi-

tionism, and masturbation with equally feverish enthusiasm, preserving himself from any legal unpleasantness by pleading softening of the brain. He fought viciously, if verbally, with every normal intellect in Europe, and died insane.

Rousseau spawned a frenetic theory of education which after two centuries of spasmodic laboring brought forth a by-blow in the form of A. S. Neill's neolithic version of the hallowed halls of academe: Summerhill. According to the confused Frenchman, education was running, jumping, shouting, doing as one pleased. The first impulses of nature are always right. Keep the child's mind idle as long as you can. And suchlike rot.

This sort of guff is as old as the human race. The child is a Noble Savage, needing only to be let alone in order to insure his intellectual salvation. Don't inhibit him. Never cross him, lest he develop horrid neuroses later on in life. The cave children of the Stone Age grew up happier, better adjusted, and less frustrated than do ours today, simply because they were in a blissful state of nature. So just leave the kids alone. They'll educate themselves.

Twaddle.

Schooling is not a natural process at all. It's highly artificial. No boy in his right mind ever wanted to study multiplication tables and historical dates when he could be out hunting rabbits or climbing trees. In the days when hunting and climbing contributed to the survival of *homo sapiens,* there was some sense to letting the kids do what comes naturally, but when man's future began to hang upon the systematic mastery of orderly subject matter, the primordial, happy-go-lucky, *laissez-faire* kind of learning had to go. Today it's part and parcel of whatever lost innocence we may ever have possessed. Long gone. A quaint anachronism.[7]

We Americans became insatiable achievers. And schools were our instruments.

Now the achievement ethic is in ill repute among the young, and seriously questioned by a good many others. Why raise the standard of living further? Why venture into space? Why not live? Why not value self and others? Why not end war by refusing to make it? Why not? If the schools are the instruments of achievement and we no longer wish to achieve, then why have schools? A very tough question indeed.

The absence of harmony and the incidence of dysfunctional tensions cause establishment and nonestablishment types to argue that there must be a better way. The search for a "better way" and its implications for principals is the object of this exercise.

REFORM CONCEPTS: TOO LITTLE, TOO LATE

There are literally hundreds of new institutions either in their early months of life or on the drawing boards. Donald Robinson reports that there are two or three new "alternative" schools born every day.[8] Many are short-lived (average life 18 months), ill-planned, often conceived out of frustration.[9] They represent an "institutional counter culture," and in my judgment we should take them seriously. By themselves, however, they will not produce the educational reformation most of us are groping for. At best they may test new and old ideas in the short run, and some may continue as established institutions in a sharply reordered educational firmament of the future.

In this section I have chosen to deal with a sampling of concepts and institutional forms chosen from a collage of reforms. As I have indicated, I am pessimistic about their individual worth contrasted with what seems to be in order in the way of educational reform.

Apprenticeship

The first of these is apprenticeship as advocated by Howard Becker. In a paper titled "A School Is a Lousy Place to Learn Anything In," Becker argues the values of apprenticeship—for everyone in the society.[10] Despite extended passages detailing the weaknesses in our schools and his misgivings about schools, he does not quite join forces with the abolitionists.

So that we begin together in the exploration of Becker's ideas, here is his second paragraph:

> The myth schools produce tells us that in school people learn something they would not otherwise know. Teachers, who do know that thing, spend their full time teaching it to their pupils. The myth further explains that schools pass the cultural heritage of our society on to succeeding generations, both the general heritage we acquire in elementary and high school and the more differentiated aspects taught in colleges and graduate and professional schools. Finally, while educators readily admit the shortcomings of schools, they do not conceive that anything in the essence of a school might produce those shortcomings or that any other institutional form might perform the educational job more adequately.[11]

Becker goes on to challenge other prevailing mythologies. He notes that schools (all kinds of schools) do not achieve the results they set out to achieve. His evidence is sketchy but persuasive: Osler Peterson (1957) examined the quality of medical practice among general practitioners in North Carolina and discovered that there was no relation between the medical school that doctors graduated from and the quality of their practice, nor was there a relationship between quality of practice and their rank in medical school graduating classes. Hoffman, studying actors, discovered that almost none of the actors regarded as "good" by their peers ever attended a drama school. Philip Jacob (1957) reviewed hundreds of studies of the influence of college on student values and found little evidence of a liberalizing change. A more recent piece of work by Simon, Gagnon, and Carnes (1969) indicates that college experience has almost no influence on political attitudes. Finally Astin (1968) cast considerable doubt on the effect of college on students' intellectual development and learning. Bright students do just as well irrespective of the college they enter. The same is true for "dull" ones. The variation in academic ability on entrance entirely accounts for the difference in the Graduate Record Examination scores of graduates of different schools.

Seeking an explanation of this dismal record, Becker wonders if the organization of the school is the villain. Universal curricula, patterned movement, standardized evaluations, rigid authority structures, and obsolete reward systems are cited as likely causes.

The chief alternative to learning things in school is to learn them on the job, especially if on-the-job training is defined broadly. The person doing the learning is the apprentice. Becker does not limit the term to its normal usage in a unionized trade. Thus an apprentice would learn from people, where they are, from whatever they do. Becker reports comprehensively on ironworker and meatcutter apprenticeships. He notes their deficiencies as well as their virtues. One of the most severe limitations is that no one is required to teach; another is the harshness of the socialization process. The virtues include relevancy, individualization, and immediate and sustained performance evaluation.

Becker acknowledges that there are severe problems in schooling and in apprenticing. He concedes that we will always have schools because we will always find ourselves in the dilemma of preparing people for unknown futures. He concludes that "schools may be lousy places to learn anything in," but so are apprenticeships. The question which he leaves to the likes of us is: Can there be a more fundamental linking of these two educational forms?

Residential Schools

The residential school is hardly a new educational form. Private residential, high-prestige schools exist throughout the world. They are sometimes coeducational, sometimes special purpose. Those like Summerhill are residential, coeducational, and philosophically distinct.[12]

Summerhill has produced a cult. The celebrated A. S. Neill, Summerhill's founder and living patron saint, joins John Dewey, Jean Piaget, and Maria Montessori in the ability to provoke discipleship. Persons feel so deeply about Neill's educational philosophy and Summerhill's practices that many efforts to reproduce Summerhill will occur. The bitterness of Summerhill's critics likewise promises to enrich the debate. And in subtle ways it will affect the revolution.

John Holt is a convert to the Summerhill cult. He argues that the key words are "to begin." "We must therefore take Neill's thought, his writing, his work, and Summerhill itself, not as a final step, but as a first one."[13] Max Rafferty (quoted earlier on Summerhill) observes that ". . . Summerhill is a dirty joke. It degrades true learning to the status of a disorganized orgy. It turns a teacher into a sniggering projectionist of a stag movie. It transforms a school into a cross between a beer garden and a boiler factory. It is a caricature of education."[14] Bruno Bettelheim blends respect with cautious restraint in his appraisal of Summerhill. Bettelheim is a phenomenal educational theorist and practitioner himself, heading the most unique residential school in the world for severely disturbed children. Bettelheim reveals disappointment in the bunglings of his own disciples and predicts that Neill will experience the same fate. He sees Summerhill and Neill as inseparable. He believes that Summerhill's successes have never been recorded nor can they be. Neill's gifts are so subtle that they are not even known to himself, thus they cannot be shared. (The same could be said of Bettelheim.) Far from giving an unqualified endorsement, Bettelheim disagrees with Summerhill's emphasis on unrestrained heterosexual experience and complete freedom. Contrary to John Holt, he urges Neill's followers not to try "to set his philosophy into deadly practice."[15]

The discussion of Summerhill is offered as an example of a particular form of schooling. Controversial in the extreme, it will likely attract a host of imitators despite admonitions. As with Montessori there will be Neill schools in many places—and in my judgment rightly so, if we wish to take seriously our commitment to diversity in educational forms. Such schools would not be inimical to large-scale reforms reviewed later.

Quite a different semi-residential school has been designed by the System Development Corporation in Santa Monica. It differs sharply from Summerhill in philosophy and clientele. It is hard to label this school. Its planners call it an experimental school for urban poor. Its designers are for the most part noneducators. And as I read their description I found myself alternately pleased and astounded. Pleased at the blending of promising ideas in a single design—astounded that they were being advanced as new.

In brief, the school is to serve severely disadvantaged people; to include those traditionally enrolled in grades K-12 on one campus (the old Gary plan); to maximize community inputs into the learning enterprise; to utilize an ombudsman for grievance purposes; to remain open 15 hours per day; to give each student an individual room that is his for study or whatever; to secure new types of professionals with freshly defined responsibilities; and to employ every student enrolled as a member of the school work force.[16]

Efforts will be made to combine cognitive development with work skills. Since the student age range is about five through 18, the work assignments for which youngsters will be paid will be skillfully differentiated. The school is expected to coexist with conventional public schools and if successful be imitated on a large scale.

For me the most exciting feature of the proposal is its work-ethic. Molding an entire school around internal jobs is a difficult if not unachievable objective. Nevertheless, it is a bold notion and deserves a trial. The student-at-work feature is described as follows:

> Every student will have an opportunity to hold a job alongside his academic program. Some portion of each day, the student will work. The

jobs will be varied in type, skills required, hours worked, and wages received; within broad limits, all jobs will be open to all students, with placement a function of proficiency, maturity, past performance, and job availability. In brief, there will be a work culture as nearly optimal as possible and still reflecting the patterns that exist in the larger society. The work will be significant, the money will be real, the opportunities will be visible, and the prerequisites will be realistically related to academic progress.

Since this feature is unusual and might be misunderstood, three points of clarification need to be made. First, students will *not* be paid for "going to school"—i.e., for the business of progressing academically. They will be paid for work at school; the prime prerequisite for getting one of the jobs will be that they are going to school. In practice, this distinction will not be confused; the two are separate, though importantly related, activities.

Second, this will not be "make-work" for which the students get paid. It will be, in fact, the business of operating the school. School is a microcommunity; it mirrors most of the functions of society at large—transportation, food, building and maintenance, supply, clerical work, administration, training, equipment repair, purchasing, not to mention child care and teaching. These are jobs that must be done if the school is to operate; they are normally assigned to hired (classified) employees; in this case the employees will be students.

Third, the emphasis is on opportunity for employment, not on vocational training. If, for example, an academically talented student wants to work in equipment repair, he can; it is the fact of his employment that is of primary importance. If at the same time he will be learning a skill that will benefit him in later life, all the better; but he need not be making a career decision when he applies for "work at school"[17]

The SDC school is a drawing-board effort as yet. It has promise—nice conceptualization; expensive, new personnel; and an attractive philosophy. But it remains untested. And if tested, and it works, it will be but a pebble on the beach of needed educational reform.

Pennsylvania Advancement School

Established in 1967, the Pennsylvania Advancement School is now in its third year. It is located in Philadelphia, functioning with Title I and Title III support, plus school district and foundation funds. It is a nonprofit corporation guided by a distinguished board of directors.

The school is not a school—at least not in the traditional sense. It has students, teachers, psychologists, and a curriculum. But it does not exist primarily for the benefit of its enrollees. It exists as a model for change, a center for experimentation, a location for professional education of teachers, counselors, administrators, and paraprofessionals. The school enrolls underachieving seventh and eighth grade boys from Philadelphia public and parochial schools. The school is housed in an old factory building which has been extensively renovated to provide visual stimulation and flexible space utilization.

New approaches are devised to effect useful community inputs, to use purposefully the scarce resources of universities, to rotate interested professionals in public and parochial schools through appointments to the staff, and to follow up students who spend 14-week terms enrolled in the nonschool.

The school is a stimulus enterprise. Terribly useful in its own right for the fortunate few students that it affects directly, it is much more significant as an idea producer, tester, and sharer; more important as an unconventional burr under conventional saddles; valuable as threat and salvation simultaneously.

The summary report of its first two years produces passion and pathos.[18] Committed personnel, with exciting ideas, confront problems the magnitude of which remains unmeasured. It is similar to a hundred other efforts (many spawned by Title III), each joyful and anguish-ridden simultaneously.

Family Development Centers

Two years ago in Columbus a number of us were casting about frantically for ideas to assist the Columbus Public Schools in overcoming some of their ghetto-education problems. We were confronted with the universal urban data: dropouts, low achievement (especially in reading), deteriorating confidence in schools, and the clustering of aggravated deficiencies in certain families, to list a few.

We were impressed with the need to invent a new concept of institution—one that would permit simultaneous educational experience for the total age spectrum. Our admittedly crude formulation bears the name "Family Development Center." The attractiveness of the idea was enhanced by the availability of a superb facility in which to house the institution.

The objective is to create a powerful educational environment where adults and children can learn together; where public welfare, health, and educational resources can be concentrated efficiently; where employment skills, household skills, and artistic temperaments can be developed simultaneously; and where instruction can be supplied by families in which each member has teaching responsibilities.

The learners in the center would be families. Selected families of all races would be invited to move into housing facilities selected for that purpose. (In Columbus a soon-to-be-abandoned military base would be the site.) The families chosen should be representative of the broader society but among then would be unemployed families having parents with low educational levels and children who have learning problems. Faculty families would live there too.

The faculty of the center would be made up of professionals from a number of fields. The entire environment would be a learning laboratory. The members of the faculty families would be teachers and learners simultaneously. The curriculum would be extraordinarily rich, quite informally organized, and designed to meet cognitive, affective, and motor skill needs. The faculty would have at its fingertips the city, its libraries, its museums and art centers, its theaters, its universities, its employment potentials. Instruction would be individualized, with all types of teaching approaches being used.

For some purposes—art, music, physical education, and recreation —adults and children might learn together. For other purposes, classes and seminars would be formed. Classes would not be restricted even then to conventional age ranges. The classrooms could be anywhere—on the site or in the downtown area or in the suburbs— wherever learning purposes could best be served.

Learning families where the adults were unemployed would be among those chosen. Extensive efforts would be addressed to bringing the adults to the point of employability. During the early period of the family's enrollment at the center, family support would be on the basis of welfare payments. As soon as employable skills could be developed for adults, part-time employment would be sought. From this point forward the adults would work and learn simultaneously. Each family's curriculum would be individually planned and fitted into the program of studies created for the center.

Training for males in the trades could be achieved through the repair and remodeling of housing on the site for families. Skilled craftsmen and their families could be incorporated into the faculty for this learning purpose. Children of all ages could be involved too in assisting with painting, yard care, athletic field care, and the maintenance of other facilities.

Faculty families could be chosen on the basis of diversity of talents as well as willingness to participate in such an exciting venture. Faculty families should have teaching potential in the basic learning skills, the arts, music, homemaking, recreation, physical education, health education, social skills. Formal teaching certificational requirements in many cases would need to be abandoned for at least some family members.

Learner families would leave the center after adults and children were brought to social, educational, and employability levels satisfactory for effective and responsible citizenship.

The staff of the center would include social workers, medical and psychiatric specialists, and psychologists and their families. The center should also have a well-trained research staff. Social workers could assist with many of the welfare and employment problems; they could also help with family selection and relocation. The physical and medical health specialists would make their contribution in many important ways.

The minimal length of learner familiy tenure would be one year. Some families might need to stay longer than that period of time. Families could enter and leave at various points in the year. The staff of the center would help in locating housing, appropriate educational facilities, and employment for families when they left. Emphasis would be placed on locating black families in areas where open housing agreements exist.

To summarize, this institution would act simultaneously on several problems:

1. It would be directed at removing educational deficiencies of children and adults simultaneously.

2. It would focus public health, public welfare, and public education resources on common problems.

3. It would be racially, socially, and economically integrated.

4. It would, if successful, break the educational and poverty cycle and return adults immediately to independent earner and taxpaying status. Children would have improved chances for economic independence as adults.

5. The cost would be modest when compared with continued welfare, public health, and compensatory educational costs over at least two generations, if not many more.

6. The cohesiveness of families would be sustained and strengthened during a period of intensive development for all family members.[19]

The Commune as an Educational Enterprise

Communes are being created across the world. The "family" of Charles Manson is currently the most celebrated and hopefully the least imitated. But it, and apparently dozens more, are cropping up in the rural and desert regions of the Southwest. Like the experimental schools, most of them are doomed to short life. They are for many temporary way stations in and out of the hippie and/or counter culture.

These are not new phenomena. Therefore, some are likely to become permanent. And like Gypsy colonies, they will produce a fascinating culture where all aspects of life will go forward, including education. Communes, like the Amish and Mennonite religious groups, will raise new problems for educational authorities as they debate the pros and cons of forced school attendance. It is likely that superb education will go forward in some of them, especially where the adults are themselves well educated. In the now blurred future, it is possible for some communes to create a promising blend of cognitive, affective, and skill development combining the best in formal teaching, apprenticeship, and free exploration of a complex environment.

*　　*　　*

The experimental efforts described here are noble. As indicated earlier, they are examples selected from literally hundreds of high-expectation, blithe-spirit-sponsored attempts to revitalize sagging institutions. After a decade of emphasis on innovation, we have only inched up on some traditional problems, chiefly in the cognitive domain and mostly for middle-class children at that. Meanwhile a mass of other issues have surfaced, dwarfing those modest achievements.

Somehow we must locate large-scale reforms that reside somewhere between abolition of schools and where we are at the moment. The responsibility of principals in the short run is to participate in the debate and conceptualization of such matters. The responsibility for principals (and for professors, for that matter) in the long range is very much in doubt. In this section several policy domains are explored. Should the reforms discussed independently be achieved collectively, then there will have been a revolution.

POTENTIAL ARENAS FOR EDUCATIONAL POLICY REFORM

Compulsory Education

In a brief article in the *Phi Delta Kappan* last November, I suggested that compulsory education be abandoned, especially in ghetto communities.[20] It was interesting that among the many letters and comments about the *Kappan* article only one individual (a secondary school principal about to retire) questioned wistfully whether we should "really" abandon such a cherished principle, even though it isn't working. From another perspective, a conservative New Hampshire newspaper applauded the proposal with front-page editorial space.

Kids are violating attendance laws with abandon in many places and the existence of such laws simply forces an unnecessary repressive strain on the institution.[21] Suspension or expulsion is a hollow threat for thousands of students. They could care less. Forced attendance has been the cornerstone on which a series of control measures have been constructed historically. Many resources have been invested in their enforcement, actually reducing our capacity for more constructive changes.

Education, which emphasized cognitive growth, once was a cherished objective in America. It seems much less attractive in these times, at least to some. The tension among proponents of cognitive, affective, and skill objectives will not in my judgment be easily resolved. To expect one educational program or one institution to achieve each of these emphases may be unrealistic in the Age of Aquarius. To provide educational opportunities which maximize diversity, it may make sense to expand educative choices for students, allowing them to choose a program which emphasizes skill or affect or cognition. Such a notion might be linked to a national voucher system (described later) allowing students to select from a number of educational options those that seem most compatible with their life styles and aspirations.

Removing the compulsory requirement is a fantastic step. We fought two centuries to achieve it. We believe genuinely in the right for each child to an education. We are imbued with the sense that the state must protect against the intransigent parent or child who holds out against being educated. We find it incredible that the environment external to the school may be more educative than that internal to the school. Nevertheless, those seem to be the realities and the compulsory attendance policy is bound to be carefully scrutinized as a consequence.

The removal of this expectation (linked with the adoption of a voucher system, community control, and the discontinuance of credentialing) may breathe new vitality into the society and transform institutions. Students, given the option to choose their own educational form, will have to make hard choices pretty much on their own.[22] Schools if there are such, will have to be qualitatively distinguished to attract clientele. Professional accountability will be a genuine, grass-roots reality. The system, if it could be so labeled, would be self-adjusting. That is, there would be motivation on the part of the client and the institution to achieve the most harmonious accommodation of expectations and satisfactions.

The Voucher System

Milton Friedman advanced the concept of marketplace education in the early 1960s.

> Governments could require a minimum level of schooling financed by giving parents vouchers redeemable for a specified maximum sum per child per year if spent on "approved" educational services. Parents would then be free to spend this sum and any additional sum they themselves provided on purchasing educational services from an "approved" institution of their own choice. The educational services could be rendered by private enter-

prises operated for profit, or by non-profit institutions. The role of the government would be limited to insuring that the schools met certain minimum standards, such as the inclusion of a minimum common content in their programs, much as it now inspects restaurants to insure that they maintain minimum sanitary standards.[23]

Erickson,[24] Jencks,[25] and Sizer[26] have stepped up the tempo of its review within the establishment. The Office of Economic Opportunity has completed a limited feasibility study of voucher systems under the directorship of Christopher Jencks at Harvard. Parents in as many as four communities will be provided vouchers equivalent in value to what would be expended for the education of their children in public schools. They can then make a free choice of educational institution and present the vouchers in payment for educational services. The public or private school will be able to convert the vouchers into dollars for operating expenses.

Early hostility to the concept may ebb, although several major education groups have already gone on record in opposition. Like most ideas subjected to intensive examination, strengths and weaknesses are being exposed. The voucher system scores high on expanding options, stimulating diversity, and denationalizing the educational system. It produces problems in exercising quality control over the educational services available and in protecting against a new, potentially even more severe, set of discriminations against poor people. How will poorly educated parents know enough to spend their vouchers well?

As Erickson has pointed out, a voucher system that provides the same resources (voucher values) to the poor as to the rich would be inherently discriminatory.[27] Erickson argues for larger allocations to poor families, and the Jencks plan for OEO implementation includes this feature. Friedman's original advocacy did not allow for this distinction, although he recognized that some needy families might require more support than others.[28] He refers to essentially public school-private school options too, which seems unnecessarily restrictive given today's need for diversity. Vouchers could be exchanged for a vast range of educational service such as tutorials, museum and library services, nursery schools, literacy classes, private lessons, apprenticeships, dialogues, concerts, lectures, cable television, sensitivity sessions, encounters and counseling services.

Community Control

The national stir about extended citizen participation and community control may be only a way station along the route to a sharply
reformed governance structure.[29] Should compulsory education be
abandoned and the voucher system adopted, then the public school
system as we have known it would no longer be an essentially monopolistic enterprise. It would be a competitor right along with other
public and private agencies delivering educational services. The function of the board of education would have to be expanded to include
the general supervision of all institutions and individuals that
would qualify as places where vouchers could be expended.[30]
Community control boards would become institutional and individual licensing bureaus rather than policy planners for a single set of
public institutions. Responsibility for the determination of educational standards and educational service quality levels would reside
with the boards. They would adjudicate grievances and specify
methods for assuring wise voucher expenditure decisions on the part
of parents unable to make those choices adequately.

The role and function of state educational government would be
affected too. If today's local districts or new community control
districts within large cities were delegated responsibility for licensure
and quality maintenance, many of the current state-level services and
functions could be abandoned. State boards would serve as a super
appeal board in the redress of local grievances. State departments
could collect and disburse all public monies for education, collect
data on performance levels of alternative forms of schooling, and
continue to operate custodial institutions.

The persons serving on community education boards would find
themselves subjected to new sets of pressures. At the same time,
however, they should be able to guide the community to achieving a
rich new set of educational potentials. The accountability monkey
would be directly on those who provide educational services—public
schools, private schools, tutors, private teachers, other agencies quali-
fying for voucher acceptances.

The public investment in facilities, maintenance, and supporting
services may need to be examined in terms of equity vis-a-vis the
entrepreneurial dispenser of educational wares. In time, public

schools, in the traditional sense, may give way. Those continued would be special schools for educating the physically handicapped and mentally retarded children. Other public buildings could be sold to profit and/or nonprofit corporations. In some cases current administrators and faculties may choose to incorporate, and through voucher support, operate the school and be responsible for maintenance, improvements, insurance, and bond retirement. Over a period of years, a decade or so, the majority of a community's youngsters could be attending schools that enjoy considerable autonomy at the school level and reside within a community-controlled governing structure that possesses amazing freedom and control simultaneously.

Credentialing and Tenure

The pressures are severe these days to assess once again the credibility of licensure. Similar distrust in tenure persists at the college and university level as well as within the lower schools. The long fight to achieve tenure legislation in many states seems anachronistic in the face of mounting concerns about its dysfunctional features now.

Should the first three changes I've described (compulsory education, voucher, community control) come about, surely the licensure and tenure practices we have now would crumble. Positioning accountability so forcefully on local communities would require reappraisal of who should teach, counsel, or administer. The escalating distrust of authority, the devaluing of expertise, the substitution of affective goals for cognitive achievement, each imposes new demands on professional performance. It seems unwarranted to expect that all currently credentialed persons can transform themselves affectively or cognitively to meet new performance criteria. Therefore the security of tenure and protection of licensing must be reappraised.[31]

If the diversification of education is achieved through the voucher system, then it stands to reason that large numbers of new teachers will be activated and legitimized by community control boards. On first inspection it may appear that the welfare of large numbers of professionals will be threatened. But given the time lag between now and the implementation of such large-scale changes, today's professionals would either move out of education into other positions, update themselves to pass muster in the new schools, set themselves up as tutors, or convert to emergent roles that are now on the drawing boards.

Public retirement systems will need to be expanded too to serve a number of new clients. Attention to policies of obsolescence will become a high-order priority for those who govern such systems. The human problems associated with sharp policy reform will necessarily impose new burdens on our retirement structures. Substantial reformulations of early retirement or short-term retirement options will be required.

Community Experience

Paul Goodman makes an eloquent case for de-institutionalizing education, turning the learner into the community, and treating each youngster as a person capable of making sensible educational choices. He accepts the need for some form of schooling as unavoidable, even attractive under conditions of freedom. "The school should be located near home so the children can escape from it to home, and from home to it."[32] Furthermore, the school should be administered entirely by its own children, teachers, and parents.[33] Goodman is Dewey-like, sympathetic to A. S. Neill, but still independently creative. His capacity to visualize the educational potential of living itself is rare indeed. His sense of exploiting the educative resources of the environment supersedes that of most advocates of the community school or community education. He is Rousseauian but with a more advanced vision of how the educative process can go forward, balancing formal inputs from institutions with more naturalistic inputs from the environment.

For another purpose recently I was speculating about public services that students could render in an effort to halt decay in the physical environment (the ecology pitch). Students enrolled in traditional schools could pick up roadside trash, paint public buildings, repair streets, wash and repair public vehicles, haul away abandoned automobiles, investigate water pollution, trim hedges in parks, plant flowers, arrange art exhibits, edit agency reports, staff public day-care centers, work in emergency rooms at county hospitals, and counsel the elderly in public nursing homes. One could spin off a thousand tasks, each achievable, which collectively would lead to upgrading the physical and maybe even the social environment. And they would be educative.[34]

Such advantages could be achieved through conventional schooling if we were to build in a break in the continuity of educational experience. A semester or year-long period for modestly organized and loosely supervised community experience makes a lot of sense. It need not come at the same time for every student but at some time for all. The advantages are fairly apparent: (1) confrontation with the real world; (2) early assumption of citizen responsibility; (3) apprenticeships in public service occupations; (4) refinement of practical skills; (5) accumulation of new knowledge, and (6) performance appraisal in noncognitive arenas.

A policy of this order would not be expensive and could in fact be coupled with a shortening of the 12-year lower school educational requirement to 10 or 11 years or be seen as a noncredit substitute for one or more years of formal work. In time it may even become a college entrance requirement.

*   *   *

This discussion of several policy options has ignored a number of equally provocative possibilities. Discontinuing secondary education is one that has been advanced. Reallocating existing resources, with heavy investment in the preschool years and declining investment in later years, is another. Introducing a formal, publicly supported education period (probably one year) for everyone 30 years of age or older is still another.

The anxiety of professionals is elevated by the need for reform but even more so by the explosive, frustration-saturated environment within which reformers must proceed. Is it possible to change anything? Especially an institution with so many types and layers of authority?

What do the needs for reform, the domains for change, and the anguishes of reformers mean for principals? In the opening section I indicated that I was pessimistic about the prospects for piecemeal, incremental changes. School systems may be chewed up by forces over which they have no control long before this approach can be effective. At the least, today's principals can hold the line and anticipate the apocalypse. At best they can participate in the formulation of large-scale reforms. Principals, in the final analysis, know more about educating than any other group in the society.

John Barth was quoted in *The New York Times* recently as saying that if he were face to face with his student assassin he would be bored. Like Barth, many of us are bored—by protest, by violence, even by nonviolence.

We're sick of hackneyed phrases—empty of meaning, drained of emotion. We're sick of frauds, charlatans, pseudoes, liberals, conservatives, whites, blacks, and reds. Advocates of change have become Pavlovian; they have lost their finesse. Adversaries and establishment types are drowning in the slime of their own rhetoric. Causes are empty; defenses are hollow. Respect, love, quality have vanished.

But these are wasted yearnings. The issues are before us. There is no escape with dignity. The problems extend beyond the personal or professional capacities of principals or professors. Solutions, if they can be found, however, will be more socially satisfying if professionals are prominent partners in the achievement of reforms. It is pathetic to observe newcomers to the educational fraternity reinventing the wheel—especially when we are not confident that we need a wheel anymore. The vast reservoir of experience and education possessed by the nation's building-level leaders should not be cast aside promiscuously. Rather, it should be one among many prominent resources invested in shaping the institutions of the future.

FOOTNOTES

1. I have taken liberty with the title of this paper. (The program indicates the topic to be "Alternative Ways of Organizing Schools with Implications for the Principalship.") This paper, rather than an example of academic elan, has some of the earmarks of a confessional. I have wrestled with the topic, words, assumptions, deadlines —and ended with frustration. The product too perfectly mirrors the

vacillation, uncertainty, searchingness that seems to mark academician and practitioner alike in these times. So active are the winds of change in education it seems ill-advised to separate concerns for the principalship from the broader set of educationally significant events. Thus these comments relate with greater frequency to larger problems, more remotely to the immediate implications for the principalship. To the extent that this violates the purposes of this seminar, I apologize.

2. See the January 1970 issue of *Fortune* for a review of the medical profession and its problems.

3. Keith Goldhammer, et al. *Issues and Problems in Elementary School Administration;* Final Report, Project No. 8-0428, February 1970.

4. Richard Hofstadter. "The Future of American Violence." *Harper's,* April 1970, p. 52.

5. This paper reflects some ambivalence on this matter. Its basic thrust, however, is based on the assumption that institutional transformation within education is just beginning.

6. James G. Anderson, *Bureaucracy in Education,* Baltimore: The Johns Hopkins Press, 1968, pp. 1-5.

7. Max Rafferty in Harold H. Hart, ed., *Summerhill: For and Against.* New York: Hart Publishing Company, Inc., 1970, pp. 11-12.

8. Donald W. Robinson. " 'Alternative Schools': Challenge to Traditional Education?" *Phi Delta Kappan,* March 1970, pp. 374-75.

9. Ibid.

10. Howard Becker. "A School Is A Lousy Place to Learn Anything In." Unpublished paper, Autumn 1969. Prepared at The Center for Advanced Study in the Behavioral Sciences, Stanford, California.

11. Ibid., p. 1.

12. A. S. Neill. *Summerhill: A Radical Approach to Child Rearing.* New York: Hart Publishing Company, Inc., 1960.

13. John Holt in Harold H. Hart, ed., *Summerhill: For and Against,* p. 97.

14. Rafferty, *Summerhill: For and Against.* Ibid., p. 24.

15. Bettelheim, *Summerhill: For and Against.* Ibid., pp. 99-118.

16. *An Experimental School for the Urban Poor: Preliminary Design Formulation.* Santa Monica, California: System Development Corporation. January 1970.

17. Ibid., pp. 7-8.

18. *The Pennsylvania Advancement School.* Report on the First Two Years. Issued by The Pennsylvania Advancement School, Fifth and Luzerne Streets, Philadelphia, Pennsylvania, 19140 in July 1969.

19. Much of this description is taken from *A Report to the Columbus Board of Education.* Columbus Ohio: The Ohio State University Advisory Commission on Problems Facing the Columbus Public Schools, June 1968, pp. 98-104.

20. Luvern L. Cunningham. "Hey, Man, You Our Principal?" *Phi Delta Kappan,* November 1969, p. 128.

21. Last April, California newspapers reported large numbers of students staying away from schools where teacher strikes were in effect (San Francisco and Los Angeles), and administrators were trying to keep the system running. The *San Francisco Examiner* (April 20) carried an account of elementary, junior, and senior high school students who were truant in order to take part in or observe protests in Berkeley during mid-April.

22. There may be need for educational advisers, much in the pattern of legal services for the poor, to assist ghetto children and their parents in the wise use of options.

23. Milton Friedman. *Capitalism and Freedom.* Chicago: The University of Chicago Press, 1962, p. 89.

24. Donald A. Erickson. "Private Schools and Educational Reform." *Compact,* February 1970, pp. 4-5. For additional appraisals of the voucher concept, read Robert M. Krughoff. "Private Schools for The Public." *Education and Urban Society,* November 1969, pp. 54-79. See also Christopher Jencks, Robert Havighurst, and A. S. Clayton in the September 1970, *Phi Delta Kappan.*

25. The project that Christopher Jencks heads is described in the *Saturday Review* (January 24, 1970, p. 65).

26. Theodore R. Sizer, "The Case for a Free Market." *Saturday Review,* January 11, 1969, pp. 34-42, 93. Also Theodore R. Sizer and Phillip Whitten. "A Proposal for a Poor Children's Bill of Rights." *Psychology Today,* August 1968, pp. 59-63.

27. Erickson, "Private Schools," p. 4.

28. Friedman, *Capitalism,* p. 87.

29. For a review of the problems and issues in community control, see Luvern L. Cunningham. *Thoughts on Governing Schools.* Columbus: Charles E. Merrill Publishing Company, 1970.

30. Donald A. Erickson. "The Public-Private Consortium: An Open Market Model for Educational Reform." Paper delivered to the 1969 UCEA Career Development Seminar, Alternative Models for Organizing Education in Metropolitan Areas, held at the State University of New York at Buffalo, November 1969.

31. For a fascinating review of educational reforms, including comments on licensure, read Paul Goodman. "No Processing Whatever." Beatrice and Ronald Gross, eds. *Radical School Reform*. New York: Simon and Schuster, 1969; pp. 98-106.

32. Ibid., p. 101.

33. Ibid.

34. A much more elaborate conception of noninstitutional educative potential is contained in Marshall McLuhan and George Leonard. "Learning in the Global Village." *Radical School Reform. Ibid.;* pp. 106-15.

25

Options

HERBERT KOHL

A storefront school is just one of many alternative educational institutions. There are many others—inside and outside the public school systems. In the city where I work, for example—Berkeley, California—there are six alternative schools within the public school system and at least another half dozen outside of it. These schools range from kindergarten through high school, and have anywhere from a dozen to 300 students.

Within the Berkeley Unified School District there are two minischools on the site of two different elementary schools. Each of these minischools has approximately 180 students and six teachers. One of the minischools is based on the English Infant Schools; the other is oriented towards Third World (black, Chicano, Asian and native American) studies.

At Jefferson Elementary the whole school is divided into three sections—one traditional, another bilingual and involving people in the Chicano community, a third open and stressing individualized learning. Parents and teachers have a choice as to which part of the school they will participate in.

On the secondary school level there is one open junior high school called The Odyssey. The school is located in the basement of the Lawrence Hall of Science, a museum. It has 100 students. The stu-

Herbert Kohl, "Options," *Grade Teacher Magazine*, Vol. 88, February 1971, pp. 50-52, 59.

dents have considerable freedom to set their own programs and time schedules. The physical plant of the school is being designed and built by the students in collaboration with the Farallones Institute, a design group consisting of young architects and planners from the University of California at Berkeley. In addition to designing spaces within the school, the students have built a small town of tree houses and geodesic domes on a nearby hillside.

On the premises of Berkeley High School is another minischool called the Community High School. It has some 300 students. Community High is divided into "tribes" consisting of about 80 students and two teachers each (as well as some student-teachers assigned to each tribe). The tribes work on common themes that center on the interests of the people involved. For example, one tribe focuses its studies on ecological issues. Another is involved in contemporary art while a third is concerned with contemporary politics and psychology—the students call that particular tribe "Ferns and Bombs." Students and teachers choose their tribe according to their interests.

The sixth alternative within the Berkeley public schools is Other Ways of which I am part. Other Ways is a nonprofit corporation that contracts with the Berkeley public schools to work with 75 students from the seventh to the 12th grades. The corporation is also involved in teacher training and publishes curriculum materials. But the school is its prime activity.

The director of Other Ways (this year, Arnold Perkins; last year, me) is an employee of the school district with principal status. The rest of the staff works for the corporation.

Other Ways attempts to use the resources of the Berkeley community—we send our students to learn where people are actually working. We have students learning to cook in restaurants, to fix cars in auto repair shops, to pot at potters' studios, to make clothes at a tailor's, to make sandals at a shop where sandals are sold.

Our students use the computers of the university in Berkeley. They attend a local junior college for classes we can't offer, take karate and aikido at a local studio where self-defense techniques are taught.

We put one entire staff salary into paying community people to teach our students. We want the students to be able to move throughout the community and relate to adults in working and learning situations.

MATCHING THINGS UP

We do have classes, however. At the beginning of the year the staff announces what it wants to teach, and the students announce what they want to learn or teach themselves. Then we match things up. If there are no takers for a class, we drop it. If students want to learn things the staff can't teach, we go out and find people who can teach them. Some of the classes we are undertaking at present are:

Wilderness Survival. This class consists of a few study sessions a week involving learning about edible plants, trapping animals, purifying water, building shelters, etc. One day a week the class goes into the woods and practices survival techniques.

Urban Survival. If wilderness survival is about how to survive in the woods, urban survival is about how to survive in the jungle of the city. This class studies public institutions, getting and keeping jobs, finding places to live, developing psychological stability in urban settings, food-buying cooperatives, rent strikes, neighborhood politics, etc.

The Unconscious and Decision Making. This is a class on dreams and other unconscious processes. It deals with how problems are solved in real situations—problems like who to marry and what to do with oneself. It also deals with the sources in the unconscious of mathematical, scientific, and artistic creation. One of the purposes of this class, which I teach, is to help each individual explore the way in which he or she actually makes or avoids decisions.

Human Behavior. This is a rap class specifically devoted to considering day-to-day problems the students face in their lives. It considers racism, sex, violence, parents, friends, drugs, all in an open ended free swinging way in which the main participants and teachers become the students themselves.

Among other classes we offer are: guerrilla theater; abstract mathematical concepts and the mathematician as a creator; science and looking; systems, the scientist, and the person; black economics; speed reading; boat building and navigation; media; photography; the community and the individual.

At present there is an attempt in Berkeley for all of the experimental programs to come together, share resources and develop alliances so they can support rather than compete with each other. We would like all students and teachers to have the opportunity of choosing the environment they would like to teach and learn in. Right now, however, we still represent a small minority of teachers and students within the Berkeley public schools.

Outside the Berkeley public school system there are a group of interesting free schools. Eventually we hope that the system will be flexible enough to bring these alternative schools under the umbrella of public education without destroying their uniqueness.

One interesting nonpublic school is the People's Community School. It meets in People's Park Annex and in homes throughout the community. It also has the use of a storefront for afternoon programs. The school has approximately 30 students from four to 12 years of age. The students learn what they care to and are exposed to a variety of environments and experiences. There is real value in holding classes in people's homes whenever possible. The environments are more comfortable than the standard public classroom and there is less of a sense that youngsters are expected to be quiet, obedient and passive. I hold classes at my home whenever possible.

In addition to the People's Community School there is an open nursery and primary school called Muju Quibo that meets in one of Berkeley's churches. There are also a number of schools that have developed on communes around Berkeley. There is the Canyon School in Canyon, California, where teachers and students are commune members and everyone knows everyone else on a personal level. The school is open and friendly; more like an extended family than in the usual school. The youngsters are generally very busy on one project or another and everyone in the community is considered a potential teacher.

IN SCHOOL AT HOME

In Berkeley there are several alternative high schools. One, the Floating Opera Company School has fewer than 20 students, meets in people's homes and uses the resources of the community (the parks, museums, bookstores, libraries, shops) as its facilities.

Another school (with which Other Ways shares classes and facilities) is Bay High School. The school meets in a Lutheran church building and has 50 students. The staff of the school is oriented towards electronics, science and construction, as well as politics and the social sciences. In order to survive financially the school set up a workshop that produces high quality speaker systems for rock groups (they made the entire sound system for the group Santana). The students and teachers both learn in the shop and work there to support the school. I suspect that schools that develop independent economic bases, as Bay High has done, will become increasingly prevalent.

Bay High, by the way, has several offset presses which are available to other open schools in Berkeley. They also have a room that has been turned over to the Berkeley Educational Switchboard—a telephone answering service tended by four young people who make available information about educational and legal services for the young in Berkeley. If anyone has any questions about the schools all they need do is phone the Switchboard. All of the information collected and stored at the Switchboard is available on request.

Doug Hall, one of the teachers at Bay High, is also developing another idea for alternative schools. He and a group of artists and artisans are about to rent a large factory and turn it into a series of studios, shops, and offices. The building will serve as a working place for the people involved and as a school for apprentices as well. Students at this school will learn where the work is taking place.

There is no need to keep the public and the nonpublic innovators in schooling separate. We are all doing similar work, work in which we as individuals are most comfortable and feel able to survive. At present there is a need for all of us who want to change the schooling of our young people to share knowledge, experience, and whatever little power we have. We have to learn from each other and accept that there are—and ought to be—many options for schooling available to young people. There is no such thing as "the" free or "the" open school. There are as many varieties of freedom and openness as there are people living reasonably free and open lives.

26

Cleveland Urban Learning Community

PROMOTIONAL CIRCULAR

The Cleveland Urban Learning Community is an experimental High School located in downtown Cleveland. It is a school which is trying to make High School education relevant for its 80 students. Rather than learning subject matter in isolation within a classroom the CULC student sees this "subject matter" at work by learning from people who earn their living by using chemistry at the Glidden Durkee labs or English language skills at a newspaper press room. Other relevant learning experiences in which CULC students are involved include:

working with John Murrel at Fuller, Smith and Ross Ad Agency to earn art credit

studying the probation system with Joe Janesz to earn government credit

teaching retarded children at Harper School for psychology credit

working with a Cleveland author to obtain English literature credit

learning from a TV technician at Higbee's to obtain a television production credit

working with a housewife on budgeting and running a home to obtain math credit

---

Written by the Cleveland Urban Learning Community, Cleveland, Ohio.

going to Encore Manufacturing Company to learn the skills of being a secretary

working with an architectural firm to obtain credit in artistic design

What do these individuals do when working with a CULC student? First of all the student is there to learn from the experience and skills of the resource people. The student is not employed by the individual or organization involved. The resource person volunteers to give some of his time during the day to explain and to help a student "learn." The learnings of CULC students at a resource are supplemented by seminars at the CULC center where resource experiences are outlined and shared with other students and a staff person. Time spent with a resource person varies from a one-time visit to a long term twice-a-week meeting between student and resource person at an organization or company.

Presently the CULC is recruiting resource people who are interested in being involved in the education of today's youth. We feel that our students benefit highly from a relevant educational setting. We also feel that our resources benefit from having contact with youth in the city.

27

The Whole Town Is Their High School

TOM KAIB

"Oh, by the way, anyone who is going to graduate next year can't be a candidate for next year's board," Larry Rosenfeld told his fellow students.

"Any other requirements?" asked Maria DeFranco.

"Yeah. You got to be a straight A student and be on the varsity."

They roared. These 42 kids rocked the red room with their laughter. One girl almost choked. Larry had caught her on an inhale.

Straight A. Varsity. No way. That's what it's not all about here. This is the Cleveland Urban Learning Community (CULC)—an experimental high school without walls, without teachers as you know them. The city is the classroom; every person in the city is a possible learning resource.

The students pick and design their own courses, depending on what they want to study. Like motorcycle mechanics, the undertaking business, black history and, oh yes, English, chemistry, drama, creative writing.

At this meeting of students in the red room, the table was strewn with newspapers, ashtrays, magazines, coats and Cleveland Public Library book bags. They were deciding how to nominate candidates for the executive board.

Tom Kaib, "The Whole Town Is Their High School," the Cleveland *Plain Dealer* magazine, *Sunday*, March 28, 1971.

There was long hair, mustaches, even a beard or two. They wore Levi's and old Army shirts, boots, leather jackets.

"Some of the old biddies in the building see the long hair and think hippies and dope," said Tom Davis Jr., a public relations man with offices there. "But these are good kids; they don't bother anybody."

Davis knows where it's at. He writes a night-life-column for *The Plain Dealer.*

CULC's headquarters is on the fifth floor of the Commerce Building on E. 4th Street between Prospect and Euclid, hard by Otto Moser's saloon.

From HQ the students shoot out on foot, by bus and by car to their learning resources—Cleveland State and Case Western Reserve Universities, City Hall for government, County Jail, the courts, a free drug clinic, CEI for computer training, Glidden-Durkee for chemistry.

At CULC headquarters are the staff and several rooms where seminars are held to bring together all the knowledge they've picked up outside. And to learn from each other.

"I saw kids opening to each other, expanding," said the Rev. Thomas Shea, S.J., of an interracial group he started. He is the founder and executive director of CULC. But around here he is not Father Shea, just Tom. "Some students probably don't even know the last names of some staff persons," he said.

He's still a priest, lives at St. Ignatius High School where he used to teach and says mass daily. So does the Rev. John Kysela, S.J., another staff member. Around here he is John.

But the real boss at CULC, president of its governing executive board, is Larry Rosenfeld, 18, a student. The board has four students and four adults—parents and resource people outside of the CULC staff. Father Shea and another staff member are ex-officio members. They can't vote.

When we called Father Shea about doing this story, he said fine, but he'd have to check with the publicity chairman. This is Brian Lowey, a student who transferred from St. Ignatius because "It was either fit this mold or get out. So I got out.

"I wanted to plan my own knowledge. I want to be a teacher and here I can just put together all the courses that will make me a better teacher and take them. And I think it's really great."

He and Mark Herskovitz, chairman of the recruiting committee, introduced us to CULC and gave the OK for the story.

"It was a personal thing with me," said Mark. He dropped out of Cleveland Heights High School last fall and worked for two months until CULC opened Nov. 2.

"Heights is trying to do a lot of good things and there are a lot of nice people there but I just couldn't take it after the summer pilot program here. Sitting in classrooms. I just couldn't take it.

"My grades were really rotten. I was going through a tremendous personal change and I wasn't doing any work in school. My parents are happy I'm doing something here because I wasn't doing anything there. We'll just have to see what I do here.

"It's just pass/fail. But if you want to be evaluated competitively for school, you can ask a staff person to do it."

"They are not teachers," said Mark. "A teacher is like, you know, like a person who gets up in front of a classroom and imparts his knowledge. Mainly the staff people here try to get you out into the community. They're like coordinators and you can talk to them about what you are getting out of the subject and what you want to get and how to get it. Things like that. And they do teach, sometimes, too. Like they've helped me a lot with my science."

Mark plans to study science in college. "Case Western Reserve has already set up a special program for CULC students, helping us with entrance. And there are colleges that are almost like CULC."

CULC's accreditation comes from St. Ignatius High School which issues credits and diplomas.

The committee he heads, recruiting, exists because CULC tries to be a microcosm of Cleveland.

"Part of our philosophy is that a mixture of students coming from different backgrounds can learn from each other in their reactions, different or same, to learning," explained Father Shea.

"Our policy was that we would have a geographic, racial, sexual representation of the city of Cleveland on a population basis. And they took the 18 public school districts of Cleveland, the students themselves, and set up a quota system."

But despite more than 100 applicants, the balance is hard to achieve. Too many boys, not enough girls. Too many from the suburbs, not enough from the city.

The quota system was devised during a seven-week summer program last year. Father Shea, besides teaching at Ignatius, was a trustee in the Cleveland Council on World Affairs and worked with the junior council for eight years. This brought him into contact with students from all over the city. And teachers. When he and Father Kysela got the idea for the summer program, there was no dearth of interested students.

"And we learned some things about what our staff should be like," Father Shea said. "We had 15 applicants. John and I interviewed them. Then we had a full day workshop with all 15. We had CULC experiences, parents of students, role playing. We watched how they reacted to CULC situations. We also had two observers. Then we put our notes together and presented our judgments to the executive board."

Where did the staff come from?

"Two came from the Urban League, Lavenia Ferguson and Mike Nance, one through a teacher dropout center in Amherst. Damon (Cranz) had taught in Twinsburg for four years so he knew this area. He came from an experimental school in New York. Allyson (Handley) just happened to meet someone who told her about our school." (Allyson, a Canadian, came to Cleveland where her husband is working on his Ph.D. at CWRU. She heard about CULC from another Ph.D. candidate there.)

Joan Zimm, a part-timer, is a physics teacher at Cuyahoga Community College. The secretary, Efigenia Centeno, came from the Ohio Bureau of Employment Services. After she arrived, CULC found she had been to college. Now she teaches a modern dance course.

So they have one teacher dropout and several student dropouts from other schools at CULC.

That's certainly not what it's all about either.

"We have two identifiable dropouts," said Father Shea, "and neither was in school before. But I don't know that they had ever been in. So I don't know what dropout means. I honestly don't. So what are you dropping from?"

What he means is someone like Maria DeFranco. She said:

"I used to go to Beachwood High School and all through the last couple of years, mostly the 11th and 10th grades, it was just like floating through it, you know? I was getting good grades and doing exactly what they wanted me to do. But I wasn't doing anything for me. It wasn't fulfilling enough for me.

"I was carrying on this big sham, that this really was fulfilling. And, like, I didn't run away from it. I was really happy there. There was no work and I had friends there. We would joke around and I'd cram for the tests to get a good grade on them.

"Then I heard about CULC from a teacher there. I'd been talking to her about it all. About education and what I thought it should be. She knew Tom Shea so she told me about Tom and I joined the summer program." Maria was a gym leader at Beachwood and plans to study art. "They had a really fantastic art course there."

Was it a shock leaving a regular high school and coming to CULC?

"It was at first because I wasn't used to having to make it on my own. You know. And then once I got acclimated to it, to the idea that I had to do it on my own, then it went OK."

Maria doesn't miss Beachwood particularly. "I felt that I got out of Beachwood what I could by the 11th grade."

She still sees her friends there "once in awhile" and her boyfriend is away at school.

"I have no regrets. My parents, like my dad, when I was going to Beachwood, we had nothing in common. Like, he wasn't interested in what went on in my English class or what I did today in gym class. But once CULC started we had a whole new ground to talk on and to communicate on. Like, if he started saying something and mentioned the name of some street in the city, like I knew what he was talking about."

Her father is a sewer contractor and owner of the Buckeye House Restaurant.

"And there were just so many things that we had in common. And he really likes this idea because he feels it's going to prepare me for the future and make me closer to knowing what I want."

What Maria wants is to study art. She has applied to the Philadelphia College of Art and the Cleveland Institute of Art.

She's taking the courses she needs for a high school degree and college entrance. But she's learning more.

She has bottomless dark eyes and long hair. Usually she wears blue jeans and a short-sleeved sweatshirt. But she's studying sociology.

"One day I went around to different foster homes in the area. For kids who had gotten out of juvenile homes. With a foster care specialist. She was with the OYC (Ohio Youth Commission).

"You had to wear a skirt and smile a lot. Except it wasn't so good to smile so much and wear a skirt. Because they thought at first I was another girl from one of the institutions, you know? But if they knew I was just a little student . . .

"It was a tricky situation. With a lot of the girls I couldn't relate no matter what I was dressed like or what I looked like. I felt really hard, you know. Black intercity girls and it would have been hard for me to relate to them any way."

But Maria does relate at CULC. She shares several courses with DeeDee Perry and Veronica Davis, two pretty black girls.

Clifton Baker is another nondropout kind of dropout. He's been to 10 different schools in his 18 years, eight because his family moved, two by choice—Lutheran East, where he had an interracial scholarship, and CULC, where he could study electronics.

"I miss Lutheran East very much. If they would have had an electronics course I never would have left. I can survive well in the system, after two years there.

"Up until the sixth grade, I got really poor grades, Cs, Ds and this type of thing. But at the point of seventh grade, I was put into a transition class, which people think of as a class for dumb students and this type of thing. But really, the work that we did was equal to the students in the regular stream as far as what we had to do and the knowledge we got out of it.

"But the difference was we had a teacher and a teacher's aide in the room and the teacher's aide could help us and we got double help.

"At seventh-grade level I got a basic system together and learned how to cope with the system. And I made the honor roll."

You ask Clifton (not Cliff) about a "staff person." "I'm not objectional to the regular school system. And terms. I don't get mixed up with things like the clothes and the way people talk. It doesn't mean anything to me."

Clifton is probably the sharpest dresser at CULC. While many, including Father Shea, smoke, Clifton does not.

He's this kind of man. "I have another year in school but will be through all my credits for state graduation this year. I could graduate if I wanted to but I'm going to stay another year and go to summer school at Glenville."

Clifton has just finished writing and shooting a videotape in Higbee's television studio. It is a training film on how to develop a roll of film. Next, he hopes to hook up with a recording studio. He sees his future in communications and wants to get a first class FCC engineer's license.

The running around town?

"It has its good and bad aspects. It's twice as much work getting around. An hour at CSU costs another hour of travel. I'm working harder now, with no teacher. Quite a bit harder.

"In a regular school system you sit there and the teacher pours out a certain amount of information and you take your book home and reinforce it by reading over certain areas. That's about all it is.

"Here, you're your own teacher. Like in my history class, I have no teacher at all. It is basically an independent study type thing. I've got 14 books stacked up on my kitchen table now and I'm writing up a report on the Revolutionary War and the results and where the black man was in each period of American history.

"And actually, I'm taking a double course history class because I've got to have the basic knowledge of American history. So I have to do them both. And since I don't have a teacher pointing out information, I have to read everything and find out just about everything.

"With math here, I have two hours of seminar time with the teacher. That's twice a week. So I have to spend four hours independently studying, in order to keep the level right, because I'm very concerned with being able to compete with the best. You know, of being on an equal level with those in a regular school system. Because, I never know, this school may fail this year and I may have to go back."

This year, CULC is supported by grants from the Clemens W. Lundoff and Hilda T. Lundoff Fund, the George W. Chisholm Fund through the Cleveland Foundation, the George Gund Foundation and the Martha Holden Jennings Foundation. Parents and other private sources have contributed for other expenses.

CULC probably saved the life of a big, gangling kid named Tom Litto.

"I went to St. Patrick's and then West High and I hated it. If it wasn't for CULC I'd probably be on the corner with the rest of the guys, looking for a job."

Tom is 16. His dad is a painter and a cousin gave him a motorcycle in a basket. One of his CULC courses is working two days a week at West Side Sports Cycle on Lorain Avenue to learn how to make a motorcycle out of the parts in that basket.

He has a little trouble reading. His reading course, designed by him, is to absorb and understand the state manual and pass the written exam to earn his learner's permit and then his driver's license. Now that's what a 16-year-old calls incentive.

A couple of days a week Tom helps tutor retarded children at a school in his neighborhood.

And his mother, Mrs. Lois Litto, teaches a CULC course called math in the home, which concerns itself with budgeting and keeping a checkbook in balance, things like that. One time her students picked a given occupation and its salary, worked out a food budget, actually went shopping and prepared the meal.

Larry Rosenfeld is the hairiest kid in CULC. He's also the boss, but there isn't much correlation. He was on the student council at Shaker Heights High School and class president a couple of times.

He doesn't miss anything from Shaker. "Not really. I can't think of anything that I miss. Except maybe one thing. I'm not sure about the way I can learn physics or chemistry here. You know, the survey type of thing. I miss that a little bit."

Physics is Larry's thing, but he plans to study liberal arts in college.

His father is teaching American history at Heights High School after 20 years as a lawyer. "You know, he'd taken 20 years of law."

Larry helps teach at the Montessori School at St. Patrick's on the near West Side.

The worst thing about Shaker High?

"I don't know. There were just so many bad things. Sitting in class, not being able to talk and move around. Rules."

On another day in the basement of Old Stone Church on Public Square, Ed Joseph has called it a day. "How can we work here? The ladies are clearing the tables for lunch, this guy is running around taking pictures. I don't even know who he is."

"Plain Dealer. Doing a story on CULC."

"Hey, that's fine. Tell it like it is. We got no place to work. Just get started and the silverware starts to rattle. We get a legitimate theater and they want $600. What're we supposed to do?"

A couple of ladies in white were asking us to pull our coats off of a table. "C'mon, we got to feed the people."

CULC was not "the people." Ed and the students were dipping into a plastic bucket of chocolate chip cookies Aggie Balek had made for a semi-free CULC lunch—25 cents a plate. But a holiday had nixed that so she would try again in two days.

The holiday was on Monday. No school, no CULC. The lunch was supposed to be on Tuesday. It came on Thursday. Aggie did the beans and franks and brought them in.

Eating is tough, finance-wise, on CULC students, second to transportation.

"I usually get a bowl of soup and a Coke at the Stand 'n' Snack—58 cents," said Tom Litto.

"Not that thing," we said as Jerry Mays grabbed the Yellow Pages to pose for a picture on the street. "Get something that looks like a school book."

"That's one of our basic texts," said Father Shea. "Finding resource people."

That's part of what it's all about.

28

Observations on One Alternative: Metro High

NATHANIEL BLACKMAN

I am convinced that many of our experiences at Metro are unique and relating them will have little value elsewhere. However, your editor has persuaded me that there are commonalities in the process of attempting to administer alternatives to in-class teaching.

The most pervasive obstacle is, in retrospect, the most logical source of opposition: the system that is, as it is. With malice toward none and with a hope that some readers can devise a superior strategy to minimize this condition, I must, if I am to be helpful to other innovators, repeat: The existing school system has built in obstacles to frustrate attempted alternatives. There is nothing personal about this. It is just that practices and policies have been accumulated to serve the system as it is. We really have no right to be surprised when these same practices serve to oppose programs seeking to alter the system. An alternative is, in essence, a threat to the system and regardless of the good hearts of all concerned, the routine practices of the system will regularly be applied to blunt or even kill an alternative.

That, fellow would-be innovators, should be your major concern—finding a way to keep your alternative alive and thriving despite the anonymous, ubiquitous system. The "better" organized the system, the more difficult your task. I cannot emphasize this too strongly.

Written especially for this book. Nathaniel Blackman is principal of the Chicago Public High School for Metropolitan Studies.

Your system is, like mine, probably staffed with great people but unless you evolve a plan for dealing with this phenomenon they will find it their reluctant duty to do you in. An old Pogo cartoon has a special relevance to this point. The punch line has Pogo saying something like: "I have met the enemy and he is us." Those who would attempt to administer alternatives really should know this.

POTENTIAL PROBLEMS

These reflections will be presented under two headings: groups of problems which are associated with alternatives and some suggestions which, I believe can be introduced into your high school tomorrow, whether you intend to design alternatives or not.

Nitty-Gritty Administrative Problems. Here the administrator is faced with the problem of being creative and innovative, but at the same time not to fail. If there is any element of experimentation involved in designing and implementing an alternative, it seems to me that there must be some tolerance for occasional failures. Obviously, this does not relieve the administrator from the responsibility of using all of his ingenuity and persuasion in advance to keep such failures to the inevitable minimum. In the same vein the administrator has a mandate to be different, but he is, in essence, told to be different by following the same old procedures. This is particularly true in relation to routine procedures such as ordering supplies, turning in reports, ordering equipment.

Another instance of this built-in brake for alternatives is the entire range of Standard Operating Procedures designed for pupil personnel practices. Recently at Metro we had to refuse faculty requests for overnight field trips because such trips are against Board policy. This is the same type of problem encountered by requests to visit other programs or to exchange students with other institutions.

Another aspect of this same phenomenon is what I shall call the "time-lag" problem. It may be well for a traditional high school to carry on a program with limited supplies and equipment because of delay caused by obtaining signatures and processing requisitions. Sometimes this may be as much as six months or even a year. However, alternatives really do not permit the luxury of this kind of time lag. Somehow, there has to be a short circuit to permit a better response to developing conditions.

Risk-Taking. This element runs through much of what has been said above. As administrator of an alternative, I am prepared to take certain risks—risks which could affect my career. However, to secure the necessary cooperation from other administrators and employees throughout the system, it is as if they must be willing to take some risks of their own. Obviously, I have no right to request this of them. Therefore, it seems that someone must design a strategy which permits me and my faculty to accept these risks and at the same time to have the freedom to secure the cooperation of others unwilling or unable to take risks.

Words and Actions. Everyone knows that it is, at the moment, fashionable to favor experimentation. Consequently, those of you who design alternatives will find no end of verbal testimonials on your behalf. The problem is to translate these kinds of verbal commitments on the part of boards of education or superintendents into concrete resources such as approval of programs, release of the budget, changes in procedures and the like. Perhaps, one needs to negotiate these kinds of things in advance of attempting the full scale implementation of alternatives.

Knowledge of Results. Our teachers are often concerned at the lack of appropriate standards by which to evaluate their programs. In effect, they really have nothing in the city to use for a direct comparison. Students, too, wonder whether they are learning all that they should. Parents, especially, frequently worry whether our alternative approaches are providing the essentials of the traditional curriculum.

Somewhat related to this is a teacher concern because of the lack of visible support from higher echelons. That is to say, even though we have selected a faculty willing to endanger their careers by doing something different, they still need the gratification of knowing that what they are doing is considered important by people in charge. They have a natural concern that the absence of important superiors in and around their work place can indicate the lack of approval of the alternative approach.

Training Programs. It is difficult to persuade institutions of higher education to alter their procedures in any way to dove-tail with our concerns. There are really no training programs to prepare me as an administrator, or my faculty as teachers, to design and implement alternatives to in-class teaching. Moreover, the same colleges influence greatly the programs of high schools and in this way serve as another potential block to implementing alternatives.

THINGS TO SHARE

The foregoing was predominantly negative. We can, however, already suggest and advocate some elements of our program for immediate integration into other schools. A few of the practices which we have utilized are already of sufficient merit that they can be shared in this manner.

Student Involvement. Our faculty has found it possible and necessary to recognize students as young adults with the capability of assuming some responsibility for the determination of their particular educational objectives. Some involvement of students in curriculum development and internal governance of the school is most helpful.

Community Resources. Obviously, a program such as Metro makes daily use of community resources in regard to the teaching program. There are other business and cultural institutions which would welcome an opportunity to be involved with schools anywhere, but they have not yet been approached. When such institutions are approached, they must be given sufficient information and guidance to direct their efforts. A general plea to: "help us" is really not very useful.

Student Teaching. The diverse backgrounds of our students provide a resource for the school program. Some students can accept teaching responsibilities for one or another element of a lesson. For example, our students started a course on drugs because they said that they know more about drugs than adults.

Mini-Courses. We found it helpful to break down the school year into segments of nine to ten weeks. This prevents the long-run dismal experience of failure and allows a student to become involved in varied areas of learning.

Informality. This will probably not be everyone's cup of tea.

However, our faculty and our students have found that it facilitates learning if they remove barriers to communication brought about by formal terms of address and separate student-faculty facilities throughout the building. The faculty does not see this as a threat, but as a facilitator of a good learning climate.

CONCLUSION

If I can look back on these reflections, I find that an essential element is missing. The concerned administrator could well read this article and ask: "If alternatives are all that difficult, why bother?" The answer to that is, happily, not difficult. It follows.

I, for one, bother with alternatives because of beautiful people. Beautiful students who constantly surprise me with their achievements. A beautiful faculty which amazes me by their capabilities to work long hours at well-nigh impossible tasks. And even some beautiful bureaucrats who look the other way and cut pieces of red tape from time to time.

Above all, I bother with alternatives because they provide a chance of making a difference in the education of kids. Some of the things we do here at Metro will not only be tolerated, they may eventually be applauded and even accepted by the larger school system. When this happens, we will have extended the options for kids and in this way made a difference which to me justifies the very real sacrifices associated with administering an alternative.

29

Parents as Partners

VITO PERRONE

Our effort at the New School, University of North Dakota, is directed toward opening up the schools to alternatives, to different community-school-university relationships, to an affirmation in practice of what teachers and schools have long assented to intellectually: namely, that learning is a personal matter and varies for different children, proceeds at many different rates, takes place in a variety of environments (sometimes even in school), and demands a commitment on the part of teachers to take children seriously.

As an outgrowth of the foregoing, our program has attempted to stimulate serious discussion about the potential of individuals other than professional educators in meeting the diverse needs of children, now and in the future. In this context, we have given emphasis to the role of parents as major educational contributors in the classrooms. Parent participation has become a central characteristic of the New School's effort not only at the public school level but at the University itself. Though I do not believe that the New School experience in North Dakota, which is of course my point of reference, fits the many complexities of the urban scene, it may establish a basis for some serious thought about the possible contributions of parents to the schools.

Dr. Vito Perrone is Dean of the New School of Behavioral Studies at the University of North Dakota, Grand Forks, North Dakota. These comments are based on a talk he presented at the seminar on "How to Restore Parent Confidence in Public Education," conducted by the Center for Urban Education in Los Angeles, California, January 25-26, 1971.

INVOLVING PARENTS IN EDUCATION

In fostering alternative educational approaches in the schools, the New School staff has found that parents and their children are our principal supporters. In the process, they have become, at least in many of the communities in which we've been working, active participants on the educational scene. Indifference about what goes on inside school classrooms is rapidly being replaced by serious interest. The increased interest and direct involvement have raised the level of educational discussions and at times have had the effect of increasing the tempo of criticism about what goes on inside the school. Some of the school people in the state are not particularly pleased about that, believing that we have encouraged problems that didn't exist previously. It is true that in the 30 school districts of our state, we *have* raised many questions that were not under discussion before. At the same time, I believe the questions are legitimate and, in the long run, will prove very helpful in improving the quality of education that exists for children.

Change is always difficult, even where it is looked upon as desirable. Sometimes superficial things act as an impediment. For example, many of our young teacher-interns who are attempting to introduce more open classrooms share the values and dress of what has been termed the "youth culture." Their life styles are often at variance with that which has been standard among teachers. School administrators and boards of education have not found this easy to cope with. Because of this, we have encouraged the interns to engage parents quickly. Our experience has been that because parents are particularly interested in their own child—and not the "school system" as an institution—they have fewer difficulties with issues of life style. And we have discovered that parents appreciate the openness of the teacher-interns and the positive encouragement they have received to become involved in the life of the classroom.

What does it mean to be involved in education? I can think of one particular man who may serve as a good example. The North Dakota Farm Bureau carried out a rather extensive investigation of our program last year. And on their investigating committee was a man who pointed out to me that he and his wife had served on the school board in a small community in the western part of the state for some

35 years. He invited me to visit his community to see a school that was named after him. We discussed his involvement in education during the many years he has been on the board. He, of course, felt that he had been very active. I, in turn, asked him several questions that related to the school: for example, what specifically was going on in the school, how many of the teachers did he know, what did he know about the teachers, how many hours had he spent in 35 years actually sitting through classroom instructional activity? It wasn't long before he finally said, "Dammit, I haven't been involved seriously in school at all. I've heard about it. The various superintendents told me a great deal, but I've never really sat through a whole day. I was seldom in the building when school was in session."

We have encouraged parents to sit through entire days in schools in order to get a better "feel" for what is happening to their children. The reaction of those who have done so is interesting. Many sense the dull routine that goes on in school, the long periods of sitting and waiting, the repetition, the boredom. We have found that such experiences are excellent vehicles to get parents involved because they stimulate serious questions about schools.

In order to move beyond that point, we have conducted a large number of parents' workshops, primarily to assist parents in becoming more conversant with the materials that are used in schools and the ways in which teachers organize learning experiences for children. We have found it desirable to have parents and teachers work alongside each other in the workshops. Not only have teachers and parents come to know each other better, but parents discover that many teachers, like themselves, "struggle" with materials and their use. And parents find, on occasion, that they are considerably more able than many of the teachers. Reducing the gap between teachers and parents is a healthy development. Parents feel more comfortable about participation when that is the case, knowing that their contribution will be respected.

PARENTS COUNCILS

One outgrowth of our 1970 summer workshop for parents was the New School Parents Council, made up of representative mothers and fathers of children who are in our cooperating schools. These parents meet with our faculty and preservice students one day each month, participating in discussions that relate to their aspirations for their children and organizing to increase the level of parent participation in their home communities. They also engage in classroom observations and discussions about classrooms. As already noted, one of the prime vehicles for parent education in the home communities has been workshops which bring parents and teachers together for a variety of purposes, from developing science materials to constructing cardboard furniture. The workshops, which have also focused upon reading, science, mathematics and creative arts, have assisted large numbers of parents to become more active in bringing a parent perspective to the school. And this is subsequently reflected in the purpose, materials and styles of the school.

Through the Council, parents have set up workshops in their home communities where they are actually training other parents to get more deeply involved in the life of the school. It is a major organizational effort. But what has surprised us is that, even with minimal effort, suddenly the thing is just blossoming in the state. Parents have organized workshops in areas of reading, in the language arts, in cardboard carpentry, in many science areas. An example from a science workshop might be interesting. While they were on campus, Parents Council members happened to participate with several of our graduate students in a workshop in elementary science study (ESS) materials. Several parents commented that they didn't see these materials in their children's schools and asked about the cost.

The individual conducting the workshop informed them that most of the materials could be easily and inexpensively constructed and that most of what they were working with at the moment had been constructed by college students. Some kits, costing approximately $12 commercially, were constructed by students at a cost of from 25 to 50 cents. That must have made an impression because the parents from one community organized a workshop designed to construct science materials for the school. They made a number of ESS-type kits for every classroom in one elementary school for less than $50. The fellowship that was developed was positive. But possibly more important, parents gained insights into the process and orientation of elementary school science and an increased sense of their potential to contribute positively to the school.

The statement that follows was developed for distribution at a recent parent meeting. It addresses some basic issues that the New School and its Parent Council are concerned about.

One of our growing concerns about public education is the isolation of the school from the community. As school systems have increased in size and scope, as commercial materials have become the basis for curriculum, and as teaching staffs have become more professionalized, the direct involvement of lay members of the community has declined. This decline has been costly. Schools are not as effective as they could be in meeting the varied needs of children.

The teacher in the classroom is limited by her experience. The larger her experience is, the better. But regardless of the scale, the lives of children in classrooms could be further enriched by the use of other human resources that exist in every school community. There are many community people with varied interests, talents, and vocations who could make numerous contributions to children—and teachers— in the school setting. Our hope is that school systems will become more open to increased, direct, parental participation.

The question is often asked: what kinds of contributions can parents make to the school classroom? Without attempting to be all inclusive, we offer the following activities as representative of what parents are capable of handling and exemplifying what large numbers of parents in North Dakota schools are participating in:

a. Reading to children.
b. Listening to children read.
c. Assisting children in such activities as sewing, cooking, knitting, auto mechanics, woodworking, art, music, dance, etc.
d. Presenting slides and films of trips to interesting places.
e. Taking small groups of children on field trips associated with the children's interests.
f. Assuming responsibility for interest centers in science, art, writing, etc.
g. Sharing unique cultural backgrounds with children, such as religious holidays, dances, and food.
h. Sharing hobbies.
i. Preparing instructional materials.

Such activities bring children in contact with more adults. Not only is this a personally enriching experience for the children, it also provides increased opportunities for individualization. Another outcome is an increased opportunity for parents to relate the home to the school and the school more directly to the home. Schools often lack this dimension.

Parental participation also has the potential of increasing public understanding of education. It can help reduce the problems of providing instruction for large classes and increases the possibility of children working closer to their potential rather than just getting along.

Our experience shows that parents want to be involved but often don't know where to begin. We have found, too, that many parents feel schools by and large have not encouraged them, that they have in fact discouraged participation, unwittingly or otherwise. The most successful programs have developed where administrative and teacher support was clearly evident. Success was achieved not by sending notes home suggesting that "parents feel free to visit," but by organizing for active participation and by making parents feel they can contribute. It is important that teachers make personal contacts with parents—informal coffees have been helpful—to talk about ways to become involved. Home visits early in the year or gatherings in a home also have been helpful. Occasional Workshop meetings in homes would be beneficial. Some teachers have sent checklists to parents with positive suggestions and have then developed a mechanism for them to make a beginning in the classroom. Real commitment by the administration might include regular time-outs for parents and teachers to plan and organize.

Parental participation programs have been more successful in classrooms where individualized and personalized instruction is being fostered. A classroom in which the teacher is the central figure and where children do most things at the same time and in the same way is one where parents find difficulty joining in. Such classrooms are fading out, so this limitation may not be as serious as it has been. The role of the teacher is changing from that of the central figure to a coordinator of educational experiences for children. It is still her room and her responsibility to see that the children get quality schooling, but many people can share in the accomplishment of the task.

We are aware that some teachers and administrators view parental involvement, especially if it is pursued too seriously, to be an interference. And some find that it calls into question the professional competence of the school itself. We look upon increased parental participation as a positive effort to develop a closer partnership with the school and not as a challenge to the school. We understand that there may be some problems; the outcome, however, should be enriching to the lives of children.

LISTENING CENTERS

Another parent involvement was with Listening Centers, in which several children can listen on earphones to an audiotape or a record. Such Centers are particularly useful in classrooms which stress individualized instruction. While it is desirable to have a Listening Center in each classroom, many schools have one for every four to six classrooms because of the costs involved. One of our staff members demonstrated the use of Listening Centers to parents, also comment-ing in passing that the price for the typical commercial variety is approximately $120 while those being used in the demonstration were made locally for $22. (Instructions for making Listening Cen-ters were included in a New School newsletter and made available to parents and schools.) Two members of our faculty have organized University Electronics which produces Listening Centers for schools in North Dakota at a cost of $22 to $28 each, depending on the size. As a result, schools are equipping entire buildings for about the cost of one comparable commercial unit.

This, like the previous example of science materials, is opening another dimension of education to parents. While I would not care to suggest that all commercial materials found in schools are unneces-sary or that they are overpriced, it is clear that in many instances alternatives do exist.

We have particularly stressed the use of "homemade" materials. Schools are being cluttered up with so much commercial equipment that most parents are frightened when they see it all. Many parents whom we tried to get seriously engaged in education have raised this question: "What do I have to contribute at home after seeing what's at school?" Part of our answer has been to work hard at equipping schools with materials that are very common in the community. Several of our interns have developed science units around materials that parents have in the home, things they often throw away. Use of common materials has the effect of linking the home and school environment.

TALKING OVER ISSUES

Previously, I said something about parents' concerns about their children in school. I should expand on that in light of our experi-ence. We have attempted to discuss with parents the ways in which they relate to their children and what they view as important.

We have asked, for example: "Are there differences in intelligence among your own children. Are there differences in interests? Are there differences in feelings? Are there differences in behavior?" Most parents recognize that their children differ in many ways and are able to describe the differences. We have asked them also in what way they act on those differences, if at all. For example, "Do you ever separate your brighter children from your duller ones, placing them on different sides of the table?" Most parents, of course, reject that. "And what about the school? How should it act on the differences of children? What about the tracking and labeling in schools? How do children react to being 'bluebirds' and 'buzzards'? What effect does it have on children?" Parents have little difficulty reacting to such questions. To our questions on control, parents have commented that they do not hover over their children at home, feeling no need to watch them all the time! The relationship of this kind of discussion to the school is obvious.

In a number of elementary schools there is such concern about safety that hammers and saws, wood, bottles, matches etc., are forbidden. How have parents reacted? In one science workshop with parents, a faculty member was shaking a compound in a glass container. In the process, he said: "The principal of the school won't permit such containers in the classroom because someone might get cut. What do you think? Do you look upon it as dangerous?" The parents' response was: "You ought to see what the children do at home!" We have found parents typically less concerned about bottles, hammers and saws in the classroom than most of the school administrators with whom we deal.

What about the relationship between learning and playing? I have not met very many parents (and I speak also as a father of six) who have a problem with the issue of learning vs. playing. Parents generally see a very direct relationship between learning and playing as they observe their own children. Yet a great number of parents have come back from a school day and have quoted the teacher as saying, "Stop playing; we have to get back to work." The notion of working and playing, learning and playing, is one that I think the school people have gotten caught up with in a negative way; we've not found the parents to have a serious problem with that.

When we discuss goals and evaluation with parents, they have tended to look upon individuality as something that ought to be encouraged in the school; they are supportive of the goal of independence. They are concerned—even though they might not use the language this way—about learning how to learn, about the kinds of commitments their children are making, and the ways in which they carry out these commitments; they are concerned about their youngsters' ability to take responsibility, which deals with the area of evaluation as well.

School administrators in many parts of North Dakota—and this is true nationally as well—have been quite pleased about parent-teacher conferences as mechanisms for evaluation and communication. As a matter of faith, they also believed that parents were pleased. The parent-teacher conference was the topic of discussion at several meetings with parents. Summarized in paraphrased form, their responses were: No, we don't find them very helpful; we don't know what questions to ask the teacher; we don't know the teacher very well. We sense the teacher is uncomfortable and we are uncomfortable. Furthermore, we always sense that there's somebody waiting at the door to get in after us; hence, we do not overstay our allotted ten minutes' time. Conferences tend to be too short. Parents, I think, surprised many administrators in our state with regard to the parent-teacher conference. They talked about it as being very artificial. They were troubled about the fact that the teacher would often say, as was quoted in one instance: "Well, Mrs. T., you know, your youngster is just an average child." And Mrs. T's comment was: "I almost hit him. Because I couldn't care less about that. You know, that isn't even an important issue. I *know* what my child is." She had concerns that I believe were considerably more valid, but somehow were not the concerns generally expressed by the professionals.

Educators have often been concerned about being too "progressive" for parents in their communities. My experience suggests that parents are generally willing to risk a good deal more than the professionals, whether they reside in North Dakota communities or in the urban centers outside. We have found, too, that parents do want to be more deeply involved in education and are willing to get involved if there is something meaningful for them to do. The one thing that you will find in many of the schools where there are New School interns is the presence of parents. There are parents in the classrooms reading to children, listening to children read, sharing hobbies—sewing, knitting, cooking, etc. Parents also are taking children out of the school for a variety of "field-trip" experiences.

CREATING OPEN CLASSROOMS

Our thrust at the school level is toward an open classroom. Many of the professionals are concerned about whether children in open classrooms are learning anything. The children tend to be good ambassadors. Parents are aware that their children are enormously excited, and that's good; the children are anxious to get to school, and that's good. Parents have also commented that their children are reading more than ever. That, too, is positive.

I want to comment briefly on one particular school staffed by seven New School interns, five of whom are men. The school serves an Indian reservation community; most of the children attending the school are bused long distances. In the two years that we've been engaged in that school, average daily attendance has gone up significantly, especially in grades 5 and 6. You can't walk into the building without being overwhelmed by the number of parents who are there in that building. There are few schools serving Indian children in the state where one sees more parents. And fewer still that can demonstrate better student attendance. (Academic achievement, too, has shown significant gains over the past two years.)

SOME CONCLUSIONS

We have succeeded in involving parents to the extent where they ask many crucial questions: What in the world is the curriculum about? Is it really about "covering materials"? Is the school's major concern moving children from grade 1 to grade 2 to grade 3 to grade 4? We've gotten parents to consider—and without them, we wouldn't have moved in this direction—vertical groupings of seven-, eight- and nine-year old children. Alternative evaluation systems have also gone into effect. In many schools the traditional report card has been set aside in favor of evaluation systems that bring the child, the parent and the teacher together. In such a setting self-evaluation is promoted. The child can begin to discuss where he has been, his new interests, areas where he is experiencing difficulty. It is from this base that curriculum can be built, and it provides the parent and the teacher with a starting point to be more helpful to the child.

Do parents ever ask "regressive" questions? Yes! Do parents ever make life in the classroom difficult for teachers? Again yes! I recently spent several hours with one of our young teacher-interns discussing a problem he was having. The young man had developed a very exciting program in a small rural community about 40 miles from Grand Forks, North Dakota. His conflict arose when a parent came to him and said, "The year is halfway through. I assume, therefore, that my youngster should be halfway through his fifth grade math book." This parent, who was an engineer and farmer, had developed a test for his youngster that related to a chapter that was about halfway through the book; his son didn't do particularly well on the test. The father told the young intern that he wasn't satisfied with his youngster's mathematics skills; that he had taken him through the multiplication tables through 16 and the son had not come back with all the correct answers. The intern's response was, "I don't know what 16 times 16 is, but I could work it out. In fact, I'm not sure I know very many of the tables beyond 10." Well, the father was quite upset. He has since gone about trying to organize a group of parents to confront the school board with his concern about what the children are learning. To date, he's only gotten four parents to agree to go to a school board meeting with him. The other parents (some 20 sets) are quite satisfied and, in fact, very pleased with what's happening with their children. The concerned parent, however, has been vociferous enough to cause several of the supportive parents to ask their children questions about mathematics and other curriculum areas.

Needless to say, our young intern is somewhat anxious about that. Encouraging parents to become involved in the life of the classroom does carry risks. The risks, however, are small when compared with the possibilities. (In the circumstance just noted, the young intern did not lose his own support of an open environment.)

In some schools, children are going to move from an informal classroom school to a very traditional setting. This is one of the main concerns of parents. They have been quoted as saying: "I like what my child is about, I like the way his interests are developing, but I'm not so sure I'm going to like it next year. What's going to happen when he gets into that very traditional setting?" Children are pretty adaptable; they usually sense what it is that a teacher is about and what it is that a teacher expects. They are pretty good at managing to do what that system demands that they do. What is more, we've also found that children are pretty good at pushing the next teacher.

I recall one instance with a particular teacher in a community in the western part of the state. She was hitting us hard—writing letters to the editor and commenting negatively to almost everyone she talked with. She was just so afraid of what was going to happen when she got the kids who had come through those other two grades. They would be wild, unmanageable, and so forth. I heard from her recently, and she wanted to apologize for the previous two years. She made the comment that she had spent the first month and a half with this group of children trying to control them, and that she'd never had an experience like that. She spent all her time keeping them in their seats, for example. Finally, it dawned on her that these children were really excited about learning, and, in fact, they were pushing her beyond the point where she could cope with them in a learning sense. And she was asking for help.

I am increasingly convinced that much of the devastating criticism leveled at schools can be attributed to their lack of accessibility. Parents are wondering what their children are doing in school. That they wonder says something. Children's schooling does not carry over into the home, and there is a strong sense among many parents that children's interests at home are not starting points for what goes on at school. (By and large, they are correct.) One of the basic beliefs upon which school officials act is that they organize schools and develop programs "according to the wishes of parents in their community." My experience suggests that most school officials have little knowledge about parental interests in education. Parents are not dealt with seriously. They have few opportunities to engage in intense educational discussions. They have long been kept out of the schools and on the defensive (just as schools are now on the defensive for their obvious failures). These conclusions are based upon rather full discussions with several thousand parents in communities throughout the United States. The insights I have gained into education from these discussions surpass greatly what I learned in my professional training. I am more certain than ever that parents have much to contribute to the schools by assisting teachers in establishing goals, contributing directly to the instructional program, and evaluating educational outcomes.

Epilogue

A Perspective on Alternatives

NEED FOR CHANGE

If it is not implicit in what has gone before let me make it explicit: This is not an apology for the present educational institution. We believe that it is at present unable to help secure answers to new social problems. We also accept this as a valid task for public schools. Clearly, a massive reformulation of the institution of education is now needed. These alternatives are not offered as a kind of emergency scotch tape tinkering with the system to keep it going. They are offered as examples, possibilities, ideas and suggestions of ways of going about the renewal of the educational system. Implicit in presentation of an array of diverse efforts is our assumption that what is needed now is not so much *an* answer, but rather the trial of a great variety of alternative arrangements.

We have not belabored the deficiencies of the existing institution. This is an easy game which leads nowhere except to the ego gratification of the critic and to the addition of yet more obstacles to whatever success the out-of-time schools are able to eke out. For example, do taxpayers need additional philosophical justification to justify their nonsupport of schools while waiting for the courts and the federal government to come to the rescue? I think not, nor can I agree with the critics who maintain that the youngsters will be better off with no school than with the makeshift structures available. Nevertheless, we assume that none of our readers are complacent with the status quo in education.

VOUCHERS AND PERFORMANCE CONTRACTING

No attention has been given to vouchers and performance contracting in these pages, although some writers did allude to these
developments. Our main reason for omitting them is the lack of real
alternatives involved. The procedures used need not differ from the
usual classroom instruction. Sometimes special materials are supplied
and different personnel are involved, but the procedures are little
changed. True, the practice of immediate material reinforcement of
learning (M & M's, premium stamps) is unusual, but it is integrated
into the regular classroom routine.

Vouchers, for the present, do not necessarily imply alternatives to
in-class teaching. They probably make available alternative choices of
schools, not alternative ways of learning. At any rate, we shall soon
have thorough reports of the effects of the voucher plans.

FREE SCHOOLS

Much of what was said above applies to the variety of "free
schools" which arise under various sponsorship. Some of these are
truly beautiful places which endure on a small scale so long as a
small, dedicated group of gifted adults devotes body and soul to the
effort with great personal sacrifice. Experience gives us little reason
to hope that we can institutionalize this approach. Even the dedicated reformers eventually become exhausted and since they seem
essential, their withdrawal blunts or stops the thrust of the free
school.

Further, many types of free schools, aside from the way teachers
and pupils are attracted and the governing arrangements, cannot be
distinguished from other schools by their methods. The classroom
procedures may be similar or identical in all ways with other schools.
Even the curriculum may be unchanged. Again, as with vouchers, we
are dealing with alternative choices of schools rather than alternative
ways of learning.

Our attitude toward vouchers, performance contracting and free
schools may be applied to alternatives as well. If presented as a kind
of "solution" to the problems of education, they must be rejected

out-of hand. The problems are too complex and too much is involved to bring it all right by hiring a commercial learning laboratory or increasing freedom of choice of schools. In our frantic search for solutions, it is tempting to place our hopes on hard-headed expertise and the profit motive (performance contracts) and the control of supply and demand (vouchers, free schools) in a free economy.

Our bias: It is not so simple. And so it is with alternatives. Hopefully, we have not presented them as a kind of solution so much as suggestions of improvements. For one thing, we do believe there will not be a solution but multiple solutions. Further, those solutions are of an order of importance and complexity far beyond the scope of this effort.

SUPERVISING ALTERNATIVES

If alternatives are to become anything more than a one-time happy accident, it is clear that some notice must be taken by the appropriate administrators. For many reasons, it is not really good practice to "get out of the way and let the creative teacher do his thing." For one thing the teacher and the learners, no matter how fiercely independent they may appear to be, need the administrator's interest and approval. Too many innovative activities are isolated from institutional view and live and die unnoticed. And that, for the educational system, no matter how helpful to the small group of participants, is failure. For one thing, it detracts from the importance (remember Hawthorne) to participants and makes it impossible for the results to influence the larger system.

Consider also that, for the present and for some time to come, alternatives are a new phenomenon for the larger social system—the community. Someone needs to run interference to see that the police do not detain seemingly truant pupils out of school during school hours. The bus drivers of public transportation need to be prepared in advance to extend the student rate to children boarding their vehicles at places where the drivers know full well there are no schools (city hall, museums, factories, social centers, shopping centers). The business community needs to be reassured that the schools are not abdicating their latent function of keeping children out of the way of customers and businessmen.

And, most importantly, parents need to be involved, informed, and persuaded. They need to know when children will keep irregular hours and, most difficult to explain, they need to accept the substitution of actual experience for the familiar textbook centered homework assignment. *Administrators must not underestimate this problem.* We are prone to be rather cavalier in our attitude toward parents with regard to innovation. Recall the gratuitous insult to parents when "new math" was introduced. Parents could no longer understand, let alone help children with their homework. And this was homework in the old, familiar sense of sit down, look at the book and do the problems. Parents were exposed to a possible loss of face with their new math children. A serious threat to the home-school partnership was created by this unilateral "improvement."

And who will help teachers to select and evaluate alternatives? Left to chance any alternative can become merely the substitution of one orthodoxy for another. This is not really adding to the options at all. There is a very real danger that alternatives will be selected by teacher interest and convenience. For example, I happen to have a good friend who is a building contractor and he will let my pupils observe the entire process of estimating the cost of a structure. Or maybe my nephew is a dentist who will let certain of my pupils in on the mysteries of his craft. Serendipity is not to be denied, but it cannot become the organizing element for alternatives. The important point to remember in this regard is that we are not substituting goals, but means. True, many of our goals need to be reexamined but that is not the function of alternatives.

So, here, we come to an important issue in the supervision of alternatives. Teachers identifying or creating alternatives will do so in order to find superior or at least as effective means of attaining the objectives of the curriculum. Hence, evaluation becomes important in both selection and retention of alternatives. Alternatives are selected by establishing their potential relevance to objectives. They are evaluated according to the extent to which they enable pupils to master the objectives. If all sorts of other happy findings are attached to alternatives, so much the better, but our reason for going to the alternative in the first place is relevance and potential effectiveness for certain objectives. Not because I have a friend and a nephew.

So, alternatives need tender loving care. They need to be carefully sought out and to be protected from their undiscriminating friends as well as their reactionary enemies. Without administrator support they cannot thrive. Without sympathetic exposure to the entire system, they cannot spread. Without careful public relations, parents will not permit their children to participate. Without administrative coordination and management the efforts of the most creative teachers will be plagued by never ending trivial annoyances interspersed with colossal disasters. And without evaluation we have no grounds to deal with any of the concerns noted.

From time to time I meet administrators who resist evaluation. When faced with my simplistic argument: "Well doesn't it help if we know in advance what we are trying to do?" they reply that some of their gifted teachers can't say exactly what it is they are trying to do, they just do it, and quite well too. I can't argue with this, but I do raise the question of how many teachers are of this gifted artist type and how many are mere mortals.

The emphasis on relevance to stated objectives does not preclude particularized and individualized programs. It just means that alternatives should be planned and evaluated for some agreed upon purpose. Neither does it preclude the creation of alternatives to accomplish new objectives. It does place the administrator in the position of constantly evaluating the comparative efficacy of whatever instructional means are employed—traditional or novel.

A TREND TOWARD ALTERNATIVES

We have seen in the programs described in these pages clear evidence of the beginning of a trend toward increased use of out-of-class learning activities and out-of-class learning places. The growth of this trend is occurring at the same time as other agencies begin to assume more responsibilities for educational programs. Clearly, there will soon be a need for some kind of coordinating agent to focus these varied efforts. As it is now, programs of different agencies often compete and duplicate some areas while others go neglected. Perhaps we are ready for an organized system of education which will not be limited to the system of schools. Perhaps then the superintendent of schools would be the chief administrator, but more likely there will evolve a superintendent of education with responsibilities for coordinating all of the educational efforts, wherever located.

This discussion may seem somewhat premature, but, if alternative ways of learning flourish, they, too, will require more coordination. The various "gentlemen's agreements" which now permit clients of one educational institution to use the resources of another cannot survive the inevitable increase in the need for such sharing.

It seems that in order for a community to receive greater service from its educational resources, some planning and pooling of resources is needed. Moreover, it also seems as though conditions are becoming more favorable for such interagency cooperation.

With few exceptions, the alternatives considered are the results of dynamic leadership, often of a small group. If the alternatives (or, of course, other appropriate alternatives) are to become available on a broad scale, administrative leadership and planning will be essential. Much needs to be done merely to "enable" teachers to consider alternatives. Some of this enabling activity will be political, some managerial, but much will be psychological. A climate must be created to encourage creativity and evaluation. If the "system" does not value these things, they have small chance of surviving on a small scale and almost no chance of widespread utilization.

Aside from enabling others to act, administrators might wish to institute an inventory of resources available in the school community. Then, some way of relating the educational needs of teachers and pupils to the resources needs to be attempted. The least an administrator should do is to let teachers know he will not oppose the use of alternative ways of learning. Hopefully, many will go beyond that to offer much needed help in securing alternatives and evaluating their effectiveness.

There is an alternative to finding out about other ways of meeting educational objectives. It is to continue with the present way of offering education in classrooms. Administrators are asked to examine the assumptions underlying such a decision. I don't think they will find it a feasible alternative.

SELECTED READINGS

"Alternatives to the System in Education." *Saturday Review,* June 20, 1970, p. 76.

"Anyplace Can Be A Classroom." *American Education,* December 1969, pp. 15-19.

Bane, Mary Jo. "Essay Reviews." *Harvard Educational Review,* 41 February 1971, pp. 79-87.

Bennett, D. B. "Environmental Education: A Regional Approach; Yarmouth Intermediate School Environment Center." *National Association of Secondary School Principals Bulletin,* 54 October 1970, pp. 56-60.

Block, M. H. "Community College in the City." *Educational Technology,* 10 October 1970, pp. 52-53.

Brownell, S. M. "Desirable Characteristics of Decentralized School Systems." *Phi Delta Kappan,* 52 January 1971, pp. 286-88.

Chase, W. W. "Design for Regenerating a City; Human Resource Center." *American Education,* 6 March 1970, pp. 8-13.

Coles, R. "Those Places They Call Schools." *Harvard Educational Review,* 39 Fall 1969, pp. 46-57.

Commission on Non-Traditional Study. *New Dimensions for The Learner: A First Look at The Prospects for Non-Traditional Study.* New York: Commission on Non-Traditional Study, 1971, paper, p. 15.

Cuban, Larry. "Teacher and Community." *Harvard Educational Review,* 39 Spring 1969, pp. 253-73.

Cummings, M. A. "World of Work." *Instructor,* 80 March 1971, p. 36, *passim.*

Davis, Richard H. "Alternatives to Compensatory Education." Mimeographed. Address to School of Education, University of Wisconsin; Milwaukee, n.d., 1971, p. 9.

Dixon, Nathaniel. "Wider Windows for Elementary Schools." *Childhood Education,* 47 February 1971, pp. 250-53.

Dixon, Paul. "Playing Games with Reality." *Smithsonian,* 2 January 1972, pp. 43-45.

Douglas, L. "Community School Philosophy and the Inner-City School: A Challenge for Citizens and Educators." *Urban Education,* 5 January 1971, pp. 328-35.

Draves, David D. "Expand Freedom of Choice in Schools." *School Management*, 15 September 1971, pp. 10-11.

Dyer, J. P. "Modernizing Social Studies Instruction." *Social Studies*, 62 January, 1971, p. 23, *passim*.

"EFL Proposes No More Walls of Ivy: College In The City An Alternative." *College and University Business*, 2 Summer 1970, p. 64, *passim*.

"Education Without Schools?" *Notre Dame Journal of Education*, 1 Spring 1970, entire issue.

Educational Policy Research Center. *Alternative Futures and Educational Policy*. Menlo Park, California: Stanford Research Institute, 1970.

Eurich, Alvin, *et al. High School 1980*. New York: Pitman, 1970.

Evaluation of Phase I of The Reorganization and Rescheduling Plan at Brookline High School. Chestnut Hill, Massachusetts: Center for Field Research and School Services, 1970.

Fantini, Mario D. "Education Agenda for the 1970's and Beyond: Public Schools of Choice." *Social Policy*, 1 November and December 1970, pp. 24-31.

Featherstone, Joseph. *Schools Where Children Learn*. New York: Liveright, 1971.

Greenberg, J. C. and Roush, R. E. "Visit to The School Without Walls. Two Impressions; Parkway Program in Philadelphia." *Phi Delta Kappan*, 51 May 1970, pp. 480-84.

Griffiths, Daniel E. "Proposals for Education in This Decade." *New York University Education Quarterly*, 11 Fall 1970, pp. 2-9.

Grimm, David P. "Antipollution Show Gets on The Road." *Smithsonian*, 2 January 1972, pp. 24-29.

Grossman, Edward. "A Rough Cure for Adolescence." *Harper's Magazine*, May 1967, p. 69, *passim*.

Hansen, Soren and Jesper, Jensen. *The Little Red Schoolbook*. London: Stagel, 1971.

Hapgood, M. "Open Classroom: Protect it From its Friends." *Saturday Review*, May 18, 1971, pp. 66-69.

Helvey, T. C. "Educational Facilities in the Urban Environment." *Educational Technology*, 10 September 1970, pp. 33-35.

Herman, Barry E. "Community School: New Thrust in Education." *Educational Leadership*, 28 January 1971, pp. 419-23.

"Hilltop Center." *Grade Teacher,* 88 February 1971, pp. 41-42.

Honn, F. R. "What's Happening?" *Journal of Secondary Education,* 45 October 1970, pp. 285-87.

Howe, Harold. *Picking Up the Options.* Washington, D.C.: Department of Elementary School Principals, National Education Association, 1968.

Hubbell, John G. "You'll Never Be Afraid To Try." *Readers Digest,* March 1969, pp. 1-6.

I/D/E/A Reporter, Fall 1971, entire issue.

Illich, Ivan. *Deschooling Society.* New York: Harper & Row, 1971.

————. "The Alternative to Schooling." *Saturday Review,* June 19, 1971, p. 44, *passim.*

Jackson, R. B. "Student Community Halls: A New Relevance for High Schools." *Journal of Secondary Education,* 45 April 1970, pp. 163-66.

Kaplan, Ralph. "The Knowledge Industry." *The Center Forum,* March 1, 1969, pp. 20-21.

Kimbrell, G. and Pilgeram, M. "Work Experience Education: An Answer to the Question, Who Am I?" *Journal of Secondary Education,* 45 May 1970, pp. 205-8.

Lauter, Victor. "The Gown Goes to Town." *Junior College Journal,* 40 November 1969, p. 35, *passim.*

Leeper, Robert R. *Curricular Concerns in a Revolutionary Era.* Washington, D.C.: Association for Supervision and Curriculum Development, 1971.

Leith, Malcolm. "Morgan Community Nature Center." *Grade Teacher,* 88 February 1971, pp. 43-45.

Levine, Daniel U., ed. *Models for Integrated Education.* Worthington, Ohio: Charles A. Jones Publishing Co., 1971.

———— and Havighurst, Robert J., eds. *Farewell to Schools.* Worthington, Ohio: Charles A. Jones Publishing Co., 1971.

Levine, R. H. "They Made a Better School." *American Education,* 5 November 1969, pp. 8-10.

Malone, J. E. "School the Community Built." *National Association Secondary School Principals Bulletin,* 54 October 1970, pp. 39-49.

Mason, Ralph E. and Haines, Peter G. *Cooperative Occupational Education and Work Experience in The Curriculum.* Danville, Illinois: Interstate, 1965.

Meeker, Robert J. and Weiler, Daniel M. *A New School for the Cities.* Santa Monica, California: Systems Development Corporation, 1970.

Miller, Paul A. "In Anticipation of the Learning Community." *Adult Leadership,* 17 January 1969, p. 306, *passim.*

Mills, W. P. "Projects for Real." *Times Educational Supplement,* October 23, 1970, p. 27, *passim.*

Moss, Ruth. "Students Go Out and See For Themselves How a Community Works." *Chicago Tribune,* January 2, 1972.

National Committee for Support of the Public Schools. *How to Change the System.* Washington, D.C.: National Committee for Support of the Public Schools, 1970.

Olsen, E. G. "Pattern for Progress." *California Teachers' Association Journal,* October 1969, pp. 12-14.

Outward Bound. Reston, Virginia: Outward Bound, Inc., n.d., Program Booklet, p. 27.

Parsons, Tim. "The Community School Movement." *Community Issues,* 2 December 1970, entire issue.

Pettigrew, T. F. "Metropolitan Educational Park." *Science Teacher,* December 1969, pp. 23-26.

Project Wingspread: Final Report. Chicago: Board of Education, 1971.

Rasberry, Salli and Greenway, Robert. *Rasberry Exercises.* Freestone, California: Freestone Publishing Co., 1970.

Reimer, Everett. *School Is Dead: Alternatives in Education.* Garden City, New York: Doubleday & Co., Inc., 1971.

————. *An Essay on Alternatives in Education.* Cuernavaca, Mexico: Centro Intercultural de Documentacion, 1970.

Resnik, Henry S. "High School With No Walls: It's a Happening in Philadelphia." *Think Magazine,* 35 November and December, 1969, pp. 33-36.

Rippey, R. M. "Research in The Community: Woodlawn Experimental School Project." *School Review,* 79 November 1970, pp. 133-40.

Rogers, V.R. "Open Education." *Instructor,* 81 August 1971, p. 74, *passim.*

Saxe, Richard W. *Schools Don't Change.* New York: Philosophical Library, 1967.

————. "The Wonderful One-Horse Self-Contained Classroom." *Educational Forum,* 35 May 1971, pp. 536-37.

"A School Without Walls: A City for a Classroom." *Nations Schools,* 84 September 1969, pp. 51-54.

Schultz, F. M. "Community As a Pedogogical Enterprise and the Functions of Schooling Within it in the Philosophy of John Dewey." *Educational Theory,* 21 Summer 1971, pp. 320-37.

Scully, Malcolm G. "Skepticism Greets Carnegie Proposals at Trustee Conference." *The Chronicle of Higher Education,* October 18, 1971, p. 5.

Shipley, S. S., and Cole, E. and Crecca, E. "Away We Go." *Instructor,* 81 October 1971, p. 36, *passim.*

Sigmon, Robert L. "Learning Through Service: Making Education Contemporary." *Appalachia,* 4 November-December 1970, pp. 13-15.

Think, 36 September and October, 1970, entire issue.

Totten, W. F. "Community Education: Best Hope for Society." *School and Society,* 98 November 1970, pp. 410-13.

————. "Community Schools Alter Role of Business Officials." *Nations Schools,* 86 September 1970, p. 22, *passim.*

Walsh, John. "The Open University: Breakthrough for Britain." *Science,* November 12, 1971, pp. 675-78.

Williams, R. J., and Rodgers, N. G. "Classroom in the Out-of Doors." *National Association of Secondary School Principals Bulletin,* 54 March 1970, pp. 42-47.

Wray, J. E. "Alternative Systems of Education: Milwaukee's Federation of Independent Community Schools." *Integrated Education,* 8 November 1970, pp. 39-44.